Bloom's Classic Critical Views

SAMUEL TAYLOR
COLERIDGE

Bloom's Classic Critical Views

Alfred, Lord Tennyson
Benjamin Franklin
The Brontës
Charles Dickens
Edgar Allan Poe
Geoffrey Chaucer
George Eliot
George Gordon, Lord Byron
Henry David Thoreau
Herman Melville
Jane Austen
John Donne and the Metaphysical Poets
John Milton
Jonathan Swift
Mark Twain
Mary Shelley
Nathaniel Hawthorne
Oscar Wilde
Percy Shelley
Ralph Waldo Emerson
Robert Browning
Samuel Taylor Coleridge
Stephen Crane
Walt Whitman
William Blake
William Shakespeare
William Wordsworth

Bloom's Classic Critical Views

SAMUEL TAYLOR COLERIDGE

Edited and with an Introduction by
Harold Bloom
Sterling Professor of the Humanities
Yale University

BLOOM'S LITERARY CRITICISM
An imprint of Infobase Publishing

Bloom's Classic Critical Views: Samuel Taylor Coleridge

Copyright © 2009 Infobase Publishing

Introduction © 2009 by Harold Bloom

Bloom's Literary Criticism
An imprint of Infobase Publishing
132 West 31st Street
New York NY 10001

Library of Congress Cataloging-in-Publication Data
Samuel Taylor Coleridge / edited and with an introduction by Harold Bloom; Janyce Marson, volume editor.
   p. cm. — (Bloom's classic critical views)
   Includes bibliographical references and index.
   ISBN 978-1-60413-428-5 (acid-free paper)
   1. Coleridge, Samuel Taylor, 1772–1834—Criticism and interpretation. I. Bloom, Harold. II. Marson, Janyce. III. Title. IV. Series.
   PR4484.S26 2009
   821'.7—dc22

                       2009012453

Volume editor: Janyce Marson
Series design by Erika K. Arroyo
Cover designed by Takeshi Takahashi
Printed in the United States of America
IBT IBT 10 9 8 7 6 5 4 3 2 1

Contents

WORKS

Contents

Series Introduction

Bloom's Classic Critical Views is a new series presenting a selection of the most important older literary criticism on the greatest authors commonly read in high school and college classes today. Unlike the Bloom's Modern Critical Views series, which for more than 20 years has provided the best contemporary criticism on great authors, Bloom's Classic Critical Views attempts to present the authors in the context of their time and to provide criticism that has proved over the years to be the most valuable to readers and writers. Selections range from contemporary reviews in popular magazines, which demonstrate how a work was received in its own era, to profound essays by some of the strongest critics in the British and American tradition, including Henry James, G.K. Chesterton, Matthew Arnold, and many more.

Some of the critical essays and extracts presented here have appeared previously in other titles edited by Harold Bloom, such as the New Moulton's Library of Literary Criticism. Other selections appear here for the first time in any book by this publisher. All were selected under Harold Bloom's guidance.

In addition, each volume in this series contains a series of essays by a contemporary expert, who comments on the most important critical selections, putting them in context and suggesting how they might be used by a student writer to influence his or her own writing. This series is intended above all for students, to help them think more deeply and write more powerfully about great writers and their works.

Introduction by Harold Bloom

Coleridge was a great, fragmentary poet and the major theoretician of the English romantic imagination. As a person he was volatile, dependent, addictive: a brilliant ruin. As a conversationalist he surpassed his era, except for Lord Byron. As a poet he could not achieve epic, in any of the romantic period's longer masterpieces: William Blake's *The Four Zoas*, *Milton*, and *Jerusalem*; William Wordsworth's *The Prelude*; Byron's *Don Juan*; Shelley's *Prometheus Unbound* and the unfinished masterwork, *The Triumph of Life*; Keats's two *Hyperion* fragments. And yet he achieved perfection in *The Rime of the Ancient Mariner* and the fragments *Christabel* and "Kubla Khan." Add "Dejection: An Ode," and you have four indispensable major poems, with "Frost at Midnight" perhaps adding a fifth.

Coleridge could and should have accomplished much more as a poet. He deferred to the greater psychic strength of his best friend Wordsworth, but that is only part of his inhibiting anxiety. Increasingly a moral critic, he began to censor his own visions, and so yielded to the drabness of things as they are. The poet Swinburne, a remarkable literary critic, saw Coleridge most clearly: "Coleridge was the reverse of Antaeus, the contact of earth took all strength out of him." There is a more positive aspect to that truth: Coleridge made contact with sea, fire, and air, and from that he kindled a poetic art unlike any other, except Shakespeare's. The cosmos of natural magic in *A Midsummer Night's Dream* and *The Tempest* revives in Coleridge's handful of extraordinary poems.

As a literary critic, metaphysical thinker, and lay theologian, Coleridge's powers were extraordinary but never fully shaped into an incontrovertible form. *Biographia Literaria* and *Aids to Reflection* are disjointed works, brilliant and surpassingly valuable only in scattered places. I find them less satisfactory than the massive *Notebooks*, splendidly edited by Kathleen Coburn. Essentially Coleridge was an aphorist, most illuminating in single sentences and lucid paragraphs.

In his criticism, Coleridge is best on Wordsworth and on certain aspects of Shakespeare. Wordsworth prompted Coleridge to the marvelous realization that the function of romantic poetry is to manifest the power of the poet's mind over "a universe of death," Milton's phrase for the Chaos and Old Night through which Satan heroically voyages on his way to the New World of Eden in *Paradise Lost*.

Coleridge's formulation seems to me crucial for understanding modern poetry from Wordsworth down to the present moment. In Walt Whitman's *Song of Myself*, T.S. Eliot's *The Waste Land*, Wallace Stevens's *The Auroras of Autumn*, and Hart Crane's *The Bridge*, the central anguish always resolves into the question: where does the poet stand in relation to the four-in-one of Night, Death, the Mother, and the Sea?

Whether critics rebel against Coleridge—Walter Pater and Northrop Frye—or seek to build on him—I.A. Richards and Kenneth Burke—he remains indispensable to their enterprise. As poet-critic, Coleridge always will be read and employed, because of what Shelley termed "the exceeding lustre and the pure / Intense irradiation of a mind."

BIOGRAPHY

Samuel Taylor Coleridge
(1772–1834)

Samuel Taylor Coleridge was born October 21, 1772, in Ottery St. Mary, Devonshire, where his father was vicar. In 1782, after his father's early death, he was admitted to the Christ's Hospital school, where his circle included Leigh Hunt and Charles Lamb. In 1791, Coleridge went on to Jesus College at Cambridge to prepare for the ministry but left school in 1793 to enlist in the 15th Light Dragoons. In 1794, he obtained a discharge and returned to Cambridge, but before the year was over he found himself more interested in radical politics than in religion and left school permanently without taking a degree.

Coleridge's first published poems, a series of sonnets to famous radicals including William Godwin and Joseph Priestley, appeared in the *Morning Chronicle* in 1794–95. He then published a verse drama, *The Fall of Robespierre* (1794), written in collaboration with his friend Robert Southey. He and Southey jointly conceived a philosophical scheme they named Pantisocracy and planned to establish a commune on the Susquehanna River in the United States. Coleridge married Sara Fricker in 1795, and in 1796 their first son, Hartley, was born. *Poems on Various Subjects,* which included "Monody on the Death of Chatterton" and "The Eolian Harp," appeared in 1796, and between March and May of that year Coleridge also published his own liberal periodical, *The Watchman*. Between 1797 and 1798, he composed a series of poems addressed to Wordsworth and his sister, Dorothy, with whom he had formed a close friendship since their initial meeting in 1797. During this period he also wrote "Kubla Khan: A Vision in a Dream" and *The Rime of the Ancient Mariner* and started three other ballads, including *Christabel*.

In response to the French invasion of Switzerland, in 1798 Coleridge published "France: An Ode," which marked the beginning of his disillusionment with the course of the French revolutionary movement. Shortly after, while traveling in Germany, Wordsworth and Coleridge anonymously published *Lyrical Ballads* (1798), a selection of their work that included four poems by Coleridge. In 1799, Coleridge entered the University of Göttingen, where he studied the works of Kant, Schelling, and Schiller. After returning to London later that year, he published a translation of Schiller's *Wallenstein*. It was also shortly after returning from Germany that Coleridge first met Sara Hutchinson, Wordsworth's future sister-in-law, with whom he fell in love, an episode reflected in his poems "Love" (1799), "To Asra" (1801), and "Love's Sanctuary" (c. 1801). Coleridge's unhappiness was compounded by an increasing addiction to opium, and it was in a mood of near despair that he composed "Dejection: An Ode" in 1802.

In 1804, he traveled alone in an attempt to recover his spirits and health and served for two years as secretary to the governor of wartime Malta. Afterward, he journeyed through Sicily and Italy. Coleridge returned to England in 1806 and, after separating from his wife, began living with the Wordsworths and Sara Hutchinson in Colerton, Leicestershire. In 1809–10, Coleridge, with the help of Sara Hutchinson, edited and published *The Friend*, a political, philosophical, and literary journal, of which twenty-six issues appeared. By the time the journal ceased publication, Coleridge had become estranged from both Sara Hutchinson and the Wordsworths, and for the next several years, after leaving for London in 1811, he experienced bouts of depression, a condition again worsened by his continuing addiction to opium. During this time, he continued to lecture publicly, and in 1813 he published *Remorse*, a revision of an earlier play, and *Osorio*, performed that year at the Drury Lane Theatre.

Between 1810 and 1816, Coleridge lived intermittently with John Morgan and his family, who did much to sustain him through his illness and depression. During this period, he began seeking treatment for his opium addiction. In 1816 he began living at Highgate, the family home of the physician James Gillman, where he was to remain until his death. Under Gillman's care, Coleridge's health began to improve, and he started publishing more frequently. *Christabel and Other Poems*, including "Kubla Khan" and "The Pains of Sleep," appeared in 1816 and was followed in 1817 by *Biographia Literaria*, his major critical work; *Sibylline Leaves*, the first edition of his revised collected poems (later expanded in 1828 and 1834); and *Zapolya*, a long dramatic poem based on Shakespeare's *The Winter's Tale*. These works brought Coleridge a whole new generation of admirers. His remaining prose works, which reflect his increasingly orthodox Christianity, include his two lay sermons (1816, 1817), the *Aids to Reflection* (1825), and a pamphlet, *The Constitution of Church and State* (1828). After Coleridge's death on July 25, 1834, his *Literary Remains*, edited by Henry Nelson Coleridge (4 vols., 1836–38), and *Confessions of an Enquiring Spirit* (1840) were published. Other posthumously published volumes include his *Notebooks* (3 vols., 1956–73) and *Letters* (6 vols., 1956–71).

PERSONAL

Samuel Taylor Coleridge (1797)

In a 1797 letter to Thomas Poole, the young owner of a local tannery known for his democratic opinions, Coleridge talks about the sibling rivalry with his brother Francis. Apparently, Coleridge was favored by his parents, who paid him more attention and gave little gifts to the young Samuel. As a consequence of this favoritism, Coleridge recollects being mistreated by their nurse, Molly, an old family retainer. The result of this domestic rivalry was that it put Coleridge in bad temper, which was then obvious to school-mates who would in turn torment him. As a retreat from this vicious cycle of rejection, Coleridge turned to reading, in which he took great pleasure. With fondness, the poet remembers visiting his aunt's shop at Crediton where he read such tales as Tom Hickathrift, Jack the Giant Killer, and all manner of adventure stories when only six years old. Coleridge was, by all accounts, a precocious child. He read widely with great interest, exhibiting true intellect and great imagination. At the same time, his bookish nature left him indolent, for he did not engage in sports, preferring to spend his time daydreaming. Both genius and laziness would follow the poet into old age, causing most critics to admire his imagination while regretting that he could have done so much more had he been able to organize his insight and understanding into finished works.

From October 1775 to October 1778.—These three years I continued at the reading-school—because I was too little to be trusted among my Father's School-boys—. After breakfast I had a halfpenny given me, with which I bought three cakes at the Baker's close by the school of my old mistress—& these were my dinner on every day except Saturday & Sunday—when I used to dine at home, and in a beef & pudding dinner.—I am remarkably fond of

Beans & Bacon—and this fondness I attribute to my father's having given me a penny for having eat a large quantity of beans, one Saturday—for the other boys did not like them, and as it was an economic food, my father thought, that my attachment & penchant for it ought to be encouraged. My Father was very fond of me, and I was my mother's darling—in consequence, I was very miserable. For Molly, who had nursed my Brother Francis, and was immoderately fond of him, hated me because my mother took more notice of me than of Frank—and Frank hated me, because my mother gave me now & then a bit of cake, when he had none—quite forgetting that for one bit of cake which I had & he had not, he had twenty sops in the pan & pieces of bread & butter with sugar on them from Molly, from whom I received only thumps & ill names.—So I became fretful, & timorous, & a tell-tale—& the School-boys drove me from play, & were always tormenting me—& hence I took no pleasure in boyish sports—but read incessantly. My Father's Sister kept an every-thing Shop at Crediton—and there I read thro' all the gilt-cover little books that could be had at that time, & likewise all the uncovered tales of Tom Hickathrift, Jack the Giant-killer, &c &c &c &c—and I used to lie by the wall, and mope—and my spirits used to come upon me suddenly, & in a flood—& then I was accustomed to run up and down the church-yard, and act over all I had been reading on the docks, the nettles, and the rank-grass.— At six years old I remember to have read Belisarius, Robinson Crusoe, & Philip Quarle—and then I found the *Arabian Nights'* entertainments—one tale of which (the tale of a man who was compelled to seek for a pure virgin) made so deep an impression on me (I had read it in the evening while my mother was mending stockings) that I was haunted by spectres, whenever I was in the dark—and I distinctly remember the anxious & fearful eagerness, with which I used to watch the window, in which the books lay—& whenever the Sun lay upon them, I would seize it, carry it by the wall, & bask, & read—. My Father found out the effect, which these books had produced—and burnt them.—So I became a dreamer—and acquired an indisposition to all bodily activity—and I was fretful, and inordinately passionate, and as I could not play at any thing, and was slothful, I was despised & hated by the boys; and because I could read & spell, & had, I may truly say, a memory & understanding forced into almost an unnatural ripeness, I was flattered & wondered at by all the old women—& so I became very vain, and despised most of the boys, that were at all near my own age—and before I was eight years old, I was a character—sensibility, imagination, vanity, sloth, & feelings of deep & bitter contempt for almost all who traversed the orbit of my understanding, were even then prominent & manifest. From October 1778 to 1779.—That which I began to be from 3 to 6, I continued from 6 to 9.—In this year I was admitted into the grammer school, and soon outstripped all of my age.—I had a dangerous putrid fever this year—My Brother George lay ill of the same fever in the next room. My poor Brother Francis, I remember, stole up in spite of orders to the contrary, & sate by my bedside, & read Pope's Homer to me—Frank had a violent love of beating me—but whenever that was superseded by any humour or circumstance, he was always very fond of me—& used to regard me with a strange mixture of admiration & contempt—strange it was not—: for he hated books, and loved climbing, fighting, playing, & robbing orchards, to distraction.—My mother relates a story of me, which I repeat here—because it must be regarded as my first piece of wit.—During my fever I asked why Lady Northcote (our neighbour) did not come & see me.—My mother said, She was afraid of catching the fever—I was piqued & answered—Ah—Mamma! the four Angels round my bed an't afraid of catching it.—I suppose, you know the old prayer—

Matthew! Mark! Luke! & John!
God bless the bed which I lie on.
Four Angels round me spread,
Two at my foot & two at my head—

This prayer I said nightly—& most firmly believed the truth of it.— Frequently have I, half-awake & half-asleep, my body diseased & fevered by my imagination, seen armies of ugly Things bursting in upon me, & these four angels keeping them off.

—Samuel Taylor Coleridge, letter to
Thomas Poole, October 9, 1797

Dorothy Wordsworth (1801)

Dorothy Wordsworth, the poet's sister, always bore great affection for Samuel Coleridge. Her journal entry of November 10, 1801, was written at a time when Coleridge had become tired of married life and had returned to London after a fifteen-month interval at Greta Hall, in the lake country in Keswick, Cumberland. Though Coleridge had hoped to enjoy a promising domestic life there—along with an appreciative landlord, William Jackson, who had great respect for his esteemed tenant—the situation at Greta Hall began to unravel. Coleridge unwittingly managed to get Jackson entangled in financial problems due to the poet's mismanagement. He had also grown accustomed to depending on the Wordsworths and longed to return to their company, though Greta Hall was about fifteen miles away from where his friends resided. Added to Coleridge's woes were his opium addiction, which no longer served as a source of poetic inspiration, as well as the knowledge that Wordsworth was busy working on *The Prelude*, while he was despairing, static, and unproductive.

———*~/\/\/~* ———*~/\/\/~* ———*~/\/\/~*

Poor C. left us, and we came home together. We left Keswick at 2 o'clock and did not arrive at G(rasmere) till 9 o'clock. . . . C. had a sweet day for his ride. Every sight and every sound reminded me of him—dear, dear fellow, of his many walks to us by day and by night, of all dear things. I was melancholy, and could not talk, but at last I eased my heart by weeping—nervous blubbering, says William. It is not so. O! how many, many reasons have I to be anxious for him.

—Dorothy Wordsworth, *Journal*,
November 10, 1801

WILLIAM WORDSWORTH (1805)

With such a theme,
Coleridge! with this my argument, of thee
Shall I be silent? O capacious Soul!
Placed on this earth to love and understand,
And from thy presence shed the light of love,
Shall I be mute, ere thou be spoken of?
Thy kindred influence to my heart of hearts
Did also find its way.

—William Wordsworth, *The Prelude*,
1805, book 14, pp. 275–282

GEORGE GORDON, LORD BYRON (1811)

Coleridge has been lecturing against Campbell, Rogers was present, & from him I derive the information, we are going to make a party to hear this Manichean of Poesy.

—George Gordon, Lord Byron, letter to
William Harness, December 8, 1811

JOHN GIBSON LOCKHART (1819)

John Gibson Lockhart (1794–1854), a Scottish writer and editor, is best known for his definitive biography of Sir Walter Scott. In 1817, Lockhart joined the staff of *Blackwood's Edinburgh Magazine*, originally conceived to provide competition to the Whig-supporting *Edinburgh Review*. Despite the magazine's conservative sympathies, it published the works of the radical Percy Bysshe Shelley as well as those of Samuel Taylor Coleridge. In the following excerpt, Lockhart comments on Coleridge's unattractive facial features, noting though the profound look in his eyes that so many others, including Wordsworth, had commented on.

Coleridge has a grand head, but very ill balanced, and the features of the face are coarse—although, to be sure, nothing can surpass the depth of meaning in his eyes, and the unutterable dreamy luxury in his lips.

> —John Gibson Lockhart, *Peter's Letters to*
> *His Kinsfolk,* 1819, letter 54

WILLIAM HAZLITT "MY FIRST ACQUAINTANCE WITH POETS" (1823)

Hazlitt pays homage to Coleridge, depicting him as a prophet and comparing him to St. John, as he preached on war, church, and state. Hazlitt praises Coleridge's ability to render his sermon poetically, reveling in Coleridge's aptitude for combining poetry with philosophy, uniting truth with a pleasing manner of speaking, which instilled in Hazlitt a reason to believe in the future.

It was in January, 1798, that I rose one morning before day-light, to walk ten miles in the mud, and went to hear this celebrated person preach. Never, the longest day I have to live, shall I have such another walk as this cold, raw, comfortless one, in the winter of the year 1798.—Il y a des impressions que ni le terns ni les circonstances peuvent effacer. Dusse-je vivre des siecles entiers, le doux terns de ma jeunesse ne peut renaitre pour moi, ni s'effacer jamais dans ma memoire. When I got there, the organ was playing the 100th psalm, and, when it was done, Mr. Coleridge rose and gave out his text, "And he went up into the mountain to pray, himself, alone." As he gave out this text, his voice "rose like a steam of rich distilled perfumes," and when he came to the two last words, which he pronounced loud, deep, and distinct, it seemed to me, who was then young, as if the sounds had echoed from the bottom of the human heart, and as if that prayer might have floated in solemn silence through the universe. The idea of St. John came into my mind, "of one crying in the wilderness, who had his loins girt about, and whose food was locusts and wild honey." The preacher then launched into his subject, like an eagle dallying with the wind. The sermon was upon peace and war; upon church and state—not their alliance, but their separation—on the spirit of the world and the spirit of Christianity, not as the same, but as opposed to one another. He talked of those who had "inscribed the cross of Christ on banners dripping with human gore." He made a poetical and pastoral excursion,—and to shew the fatal effects of war, drew a striking contrast between the simple shepherd boy, driving his team afield, or sitting under the hawthorn, piping to his flock, "as though he should never be old," and the same poor country-lad, crimped, kidnapped, brought into town, made drunk at an alehouse, turned into a wretched drummer-boy, with his hair sticking on end with powder and pomatum, a long cue at his back, and tricked out in the loathsome finery of the profession of blood.

Such were the notes our once-lov'd poet sung.

And for myself, I could not have been more delighted if I had heard the music of the spheres. Poetry and Philosophy had met together, Truth and Genius had embraced, under the eye and with the sanction of Religion. This was even beyond my hopes. I returned home well satisfied. The sun that was still labouring pale and wan through the sky, obscured by thick mists, seemed an emblem of the good cause; and the cold dank drops of dew that hung half melted on the beard of the thistle, had something genial and refreshing in them; for there was a spirit of hope and youth in all nature, that turned everything into good. The face of nature had not then the brand of Jus DIVINUM on it:

Like to that sanguine flower inscrib'd with woe.

—William Hazlitt, "My First Acquaintance
with Poets," *Liberal,* April 1823

Samuel Taylor Coleridge (1833)

Stop, Christian passer-by!—Stop, child of God,
And read with gentle breast. Beneath this sod
A poet lies, or that which once seem'd he.
O, lift one thought in prayer for S. T. C;
That he who many a year with toil of breath
Found death in life, may here find life in death!
Mercy for praise—to be forgiven for fame
He ask'd, and hoped, through Christ. Do thou the same!

—Samuel Taylor Coleridge, "Epitaph," 1833

Sara Coleridge (1834)

Sara Coleridge attests to the great affection she and Mrs. Plummer shared for her beloved father who, despite the burden of ill health, persevered in his work and produced nothing that was less than brilliant and divinely inspired. Sara also speaks of Joseph Henry Green (1791–1863), a young surgeon Coleridge met in 1818 while delivering a course of lectures at the Philosophical Society on Fleet Street. Green was in attendance at the first of these lectures, which covered everything from biblical history to classical and romantic art. It is here that Green first met Coleridge. As professor of anatomy at the Royal College of Surgeons, Green was interested in establishing a philosophical and ethical basis for the practice of medicine. As Coleridge's literary executor, Green was also destined from the start to play an important role in Coleridge's life, acting as a father to the poet in his final days. During the final phase of his life at Highgate, Coleridge is said to have repeated his formula for the Trinity to Green, though with great difficulty as he slowly drifted into a coma. Green was apparently deeply affected by Coleridge's death. As the sole executor, he was instructed to sell Coleridge's effects, which comprised books and manuscripts, and invest the proceeds on behalf of Mrs. Coleridge.

Sara also recalls the great affection Mrs. Gillman bore for the poet and the salutary effects his presence had on the Gillman household, with "his forgiving nature, his heavenly-mindedness, his care not to give offense unless duty called on him to tell home truth; his sweet and cheerful temper, and so many moral qualities of more or less value, and all adorned by his Christian principles." Sara draws strength in her portrait of her father, a man loved and revered. She takes joy in the fact that he will continue to be read and admired by posterity, whether or not they wholly agree with his theories. Like so many other critics and commentators on Coleridge's prose writings and philosophical speculations, Sara perceives that her father's most precious gift will be in teaching others a new method of critical thinking. Sara concludes her letter to Mrs. Plummer by taking exception to De Quincey's hurtful commentary in an article for *Tait's Magazine*, though she protests that as a good Christian, she will not respond in kind. De Quincey, an opium addict like Coleridge, apparently always spoke with candor when voicing his personal observations, including his reports of Coleridge's public lectures. Coleridge apparently did not organize his lectures beforehand and was thus forced to speak extemporaneously. Moreover, Coleridge sometimes simply failed to show up or, when he came late, used his illness as an excuse. De Quincey would take note of the crowd's growing impatience, observing that, either because of anger or uncertainty, the public would eventually cease to attend.

—⟨v/v/v⟩— —⟨v/v/v⟩— —⟨v/v/v⟩—

My dearest L, your affectionate and interesting letter gave me great pleasure, and gratified my feelings in regard to my dear father, whose memory still occupies the chief place in my thoughts. Your appreciation of his character and genius, my dear friend, would endear you to me were there no other ties between us. In his death we mourn not only the removal of one closely united to us by nature and intimacy, but the extinction of a light which made earth more spiritual, and heaven in some sort more visible to our apprehension. You know how long and severely he suffered in his health; yet, to the last, he appeared to have such high intellectual gratifications that we felt little impulse to pray for his immediate release; and though his infirmities had been grievously increasing of late years, the life and vigor of his mind were so great that they hardly led those around him to think of his dissolution.

His frail house of clay was so illumined that its decaying condition was the less perceptible. His departure, after all, seemed to come suddenly upon us. We were first informed of his danger on Sunday, the 20th of July, and on Friday, the 25th, he was taken from us. For several days after fatal symptoms appeared, his pains were very great; they were chiefly in the region of the bowels, but were at last subdued by means of laudanum, administered in different ways; and for the last thirty-six hours of his existence he did not suffer severely. When he knew that his time was come, he said that he hoped by the manner of his death to testify the sincerity of his faith; and hoped that all who had heard of his name would know that he died in that of the English Church. Henry saw him for the last time on Sunday, and conveyed his blessing to my mother and myself; but we made no attempt to see him, and my brothers were not sent for, because the medical men apprehended that the agitation of such interviews would be more than he ought to encounter. Not many hours before his death he was raised in his bed and wrote a precious faintly scrawled scrap, which we shall ever preserve, recommending his faithful nurse, Harriet, to the care of his family. Mr. Green, who had so long been the partner of his literary labors, was with him at the last, and to him, on the last evening of his life, he repeated a certain part of his religious philosophy, which he was especially anxious to have accurately recorded. He articulated with the utmost difficulty, but his mind was clear and powerful, and so continued till he fell into a state of coma, which lasted till he ceased to breathe, about six o'clock in the morning. His body was opened, according to his own earnest request—the causes of his death were sufficiently manifest in the state of the vital parts; but that internal pain from which he suffered more or less during his whole life was not to be explained, or only by that which medical men call nervous sympathy. A few out of his many deeply attached and revering friends attended his remains to the grave, together with my husband and Edward; and that body which did him such "grievous wrong" was laid in its final resting-place in Highgate church-yard. His executor, Mr. Green, after the ceremony, read aloud his will, and was greatly overcome in performing his task. It is, indeed, a most affecting document. What little he had to bequeath (a policy of assurance worth about £2560) is my mother's for life, of course, and will come to her children equally after her time. Mr. Green has the sole power over my father's literary remains, and the philosophical part he will himself prepare for publication; some theological treatises he has placed in the hands of Mr. Julius Hare, of Cambridge, and his curate, Mr. Sterling (both men of great ability). Henry will arrange literary and critical pieces—notes on the margins of books, or any miscellaneous productions of that kind that may be met with among his MSS., and probably some letters will appear if they can be collected. I fear there will be some difficulty in this; but I have understood that many written by him at different times exhibit his peculiar power of thought and expression, and ought not to be lost to the world if they could be recovered. No man has been more deeply beloved than my dear father; the servants at the Grove wept for him as for a father, and Mr. and Mrs. Gillman speak of their loss as the heaviest trial that has ever befallen them, though they have had their full share of sorrow and suffering. Mrs. Gillman's notes, written since his death, are precious testimonies to me of his worth and attaching qualities. In one of them she speaks of "the influence of his beautiful nature on our domestics, so often set down by friends or neighbors to my good management, his forgiving nature, his heavenly-mindedness, his care not to give offense unless duty called on him to tell home truth; his sweet and cheerful temper, and so many moral qualities of more or less value, and all adorned by his Christian principles. His was indeed Christianity. To do good was his anxious desire, his constant prayer—and all with such *real* humility—never any kind of worldly accommodating the truth to any one—yet not harsh or severe—never pretending to faults or failings he had not, nor denying those he thought he had. But, as he himself said of a dear friend's death, 'it is recovery and *not death*. Blessed are they that sleep in the Lord—his life is hidden in Christ. In his Redeemer's life it is hidden, and in His glory will it be disclosed. Physiologists hold that it is during sleep chiefly that we grow; what may we not hope of such a sleep in such a Bosom?'" Much more have I had from her, and formerly heard from her lips, all in the same strain; and during my poor dear father's last sufferings she sent a note to his room, expressing with fervency the blessings that he had conferred upon her and hers, and what a happiness and a benefit his residence under her roof had been to all his fellow-inmates.

The letters which I have seen of many of his friends respecting his lamented departure have been most ardent; but these testimonies from those who had him daily, hourly, in their sight, and the deep love and reverence expressed by Mr. Green, who knew him so intimately, are especially dear to my heart. My dear Henry, too, was deeply sensible of his good as well as his great qualities; it was not for his genius only that he reverenced him, and it has been one of many blessings attendant on my marriage, that by it we were both drawn into closer communion with that gifted spirit than could otherwise have been the case. There was every thing in the circumstances of his death to soothe our grief, and valuable testimonies (such as I have mentioned, with many, many others) from valued persons have mingled their sweetness in the cup.

We feel happy, too, in the conviction that his writings will be widely influential for good purposes. All his views may not be adopted, and the effect of his posthumous works must be impaired by their fragmentary condition; but I think there is reason to believe that what he has left behind him will introduce a new and more improving mode of thinking, and teach men to consider some subjects on principles more accordant to reason, and to place them on a surer and wider basis than has been done hitherto. It is not to be expected that speculations which demand so much effort of mind and such continuous attention to be fully understood, can ever be *immediately* popular—the written works of master spirits are not perused by the bulk of society whose feelings they tincture, and whose belief they contribute to form and modify—it is through intervening channels that "sublime truths, and the maxims of a pure morality" are diffused among persons of various age, station, and capacity, so that they become "the hereditary property of poverty and childhood, of the workshop and the hovel." Heraud, in his brilliant oration on the death of my father, delivered at the Russell Institution, observes that religion and philosophy were first reconciled—first brought into permanent and indissoluble union—in the divine works of Coleridge; and I believe the opinion expressed by this gentleman, that my father's metaphysical theology will prove a benefit to the world, is shared by many persons of refined and searching intellect both in this country and in America, where he has some enthusiastic admirers; and it is confidently predicted by numbers that this will be more and more felt and acknowledged in course of time. My dear L, I will not apologize to you for this filial strain; I write unreservedly to you, knowing that you are alive to my father's merits as a philosopher and a poet, and believing that you will be pleased to find that he who was misunderstood and misrepresented by many, and grossly calumniated by some, was and is held in high honor as to moral as well as intellectual qualities by good and intelligent persons. "Hereafter," says a writer in *Blackwood*, "it will be made appear that he who was so admirable a poet was also one of the most amiable of men." The periodicals have been putting out a great many attempts at accounts of his life—meagre enough for the most part, and all more or less incorrect as to facts. We have been very much hurt with our former friend, Mr. De Quincey, the opium-eater, as he chooses to be styled, for publishing so many personal details respecting my parents in *Tait's Magazine*. As Henry says, "the little finger of retaliation would bruise his head;" but I would not have so good a Christian as my father defended by any measure so unchristianlike as retaliation, nor would I have those belonging to me condescend to bandy personalities. This, however, was never intended by my spouse; but I believe he has some intention of reckoning with the scandal-monger for the honor of those near and dear to us. Some of our other friends will be as much offended with this paper of his as we are. He has characterized my father's genius and peculiar mode of discourse with great eloquence and discrimination. He speaks of him as possessing "the most spacious intellect, the subtlest and most comprehensive" (in his judgment) that ever existed among men. Whatever may be decided by the world in general upon this point, it is one which, from learning and ability, he is well qualified to discuss. I can not believe that he had any enmity to my father, indeed he often speaks of his kindness of heart; but "the dismal degradation of pecuniary embarrassments," as he himself expresses it, has induced him to supply the depraved craving of the public for personality, which his talents would have enabled him in some measure to correct.

—Sara Coleridge, letter to
Mrs. Plummer, October 1834

CHARLES LAMB
"THE DEATH OF COLERIDGE" (1834)

Charles Lamb's essay pays tribute to his childhood friend for whom at first he cannot grieve, stating that he long felt Coleridge hovering between this world and the next, that the poet always "had a hunger for eternity." Following this initial lack of emotion, Lamb reminisces about the years he spent with Coleridge at Christ's Hospital, where they were part of the esteemed group, the Deputy Grecians. Lamb especially eulogizes Coleridge as a gifted conversationalist, one who could discourse all night and so captivate his listeners that none dared interrupt him. He recalls how Coleridge could explain the most complex arguments in a way that was perfectly understandable. For Lamb, Coleridge's spirit infuses his own day-to-day living, entering his thoughts at any given moment.

Founded in 1152 by royal charter of Edward VI, Christ's Hospital was born of the earlier dissolution of the monasteries and founded with the aim of helping the poor and destitute of London. It provided a free education to a large number of children. When young Samuel entered its doors in 1782, Christ's Hospital was a conservative institution, funded mainly by philanthropists, with minimal facilities and food and strict enforcement of church attendance. It was composed of three main schools based on a student's abilities and career expectations. Young Samuel was sent to the Grammar School, reserved for the brightest pupils who were destined for a legal career, the military, or the Church. Among this select group was a further division of the highest honor, known as the Deputy Grecians. From this esteemed group, which eventually included Coleridge, three or four students would be prepared for either Cambridge or Oxford. Though a charity school, Christ's Hospital fostered a number of writers and scholars from the ranks of the Grecians, among them Charles Lamb, Leigh Hunt, George Dyer, and Thomas Middleton, the classical scholar who became Coleridge's friend and protector. For his part, Coleridge was an insatiable reader and obtained his books from a public lending library in nearby King Street.

When I heard of the death of Coleridge, it was without grief. It seemed to me that he long had been on the confines of the next world,—that he had a hunger for eternity. I grieved then that I could not grieve. But since, I feel how great a part he was of me. His great and dear spirit haunts me. I cannot think a thought, I cannot make a criticism on men or books, without an ineffectual turning and reference to him. He was the proof and touchstone of all my cogitations. He was a Grecian (or in the first form) at Christ's Hospital, where I was Deputy Grecian; and the same subordination and deference to him I have preserved through a life-long acquaintance. Great in his writings, he was greatest in his conversation. In him was disproved that old maxim, that we should allow every one his share of talk. He would talk from morn to dewy eve, nor cease till far midnight, yet who ever would interrupt him,—who would obstruct that continuous flow of converse, fetched from Helicon or Zion? He had the tact of making the unintelligible seem plain. Many who read the abstruser parts of his *Friend* would complain that his works did not answer to his spoken wisdom. They were identical. But he had a tone in oral delivery, which seemed to convey sense to those who were otherwise imperfect recipients. He was my fifty years old friend without a dissension. Never saw I his likeness, nor probably the world can see again. I seem to love the house he died at more passionately than when he lived. I love the faithful

Gilmans more than while they exercised their virtues towards him living. What was his mansion is consecrated to me a chapel.

—Charles Lamb, "The Death of Coleridge," 1834,
Works, ed. E.V. Lucas, 1903, vol. 1, pp. 351–352

Thomas De Quincey
"Samuel Taylor Coleridge" (1834–35)

De Quincey provides an unflattering portrait of Coleridge's character, pronouncing him the agent of his own destruction vis-à-vis his opium addiction, though acknowledging his enormous poetic skills. De Quincey relates that he offered to liberate Coleridge from all financial anxieties for a year or two through the offices of Joseph Cottle of Bristol. De Quincey laments the fact that, though he took pains to shield Coleridge from the details of this charitable gesture, the poet did find out through some carelessness on the part of Cottle. Above all other considerations, though, De Quincey is aggrieved that Coleridge lost the battle with his own addiction, succumbing to serious physical consequences.

The fine saying of Addison is familiar to most readers—that Babylon in ruins is not so affecting a spectacle, or so solemn, as a human mind overthrown by lunacy. How much more awful, then, when a mind so regal as that of Coleridge is overthrown, or threatened with overthrow, not by a visitation of Providence, but by the treachery of its own will, and by the conspiracy, as it were, of himself against himself! Was it possible that this ruin had been caused or hurried forward by the dismal degradations of pecuniary difficulties? That was worth inquiring. I will here mention briefly that I did inquire two days after; and, in consequence of what I heard, I contrived that a particular service should be rendered to Mr. Coleridge, a week after, through the hands of Mr. Cottle of Bristol, which might have the effect of liberating his mind from anxiety for a year or two, and thus rendering his great powers disposable to their natural uses. That service was accepted by Coleridge. To save him any feelings of distress, all names were concealed; but, in a letter written by him about fifteen years after that time, I found that he had become aware of all the circumstances, perhaps through some indiscretion of Mr. Cottle's. A more important question I never ascertained, viz. whether this service had the effect of seriously lightening his mind. For some succeeding years, he did certainly appear to me released from that load of despondency which oppressed him on my first introduction. Grave, indeed, he continued to be, and at times absorbed in gloom; nor did I ever see him in a state of perfectly natural cheerfulness. But, as he strove in vain, for many years, to wean himself from his captivity to opium, a healthy state of spirits could not be much expected. Perhaps, indeed, where the liver and other organs had, for so large a period in life, been subject to a continual morbid stimulation, it might be impossible for the system ever to recover a natural action. Torpor, I suppose, must result from continued artificial excitement; and, perhaps, upon a scale of corresponding duration. Life, in such a case, may not offer a field of sufficient extent for unthreading the fatal links that have been wound about the machinery of health, and have crippled its natural play.

—Thomas De Quincey, "Samuel Taylor
Coleridge," 1834–35, <i>Collected Writings,</i>
ed. David Masson, vol. 2, pp. 163–164

Caroline Fox (1836)

William Cooper tells us that he used often to see S. T. Coleridge till within a month of his death, and was an ardent admirer of his prominent blue eyes, reverend hair, and rapt expression. He has met Charles Lamb at his house. On one occasion Coleridge was holding forth on the effects produced by his preaching, and appealed to Lamb, "You have heard me preach, I think?" "I have never heard you do anything else," was the urbane reply.

—Caroline Fox, <i>Journal</i>, December 18,
1836, <i>Memories of Old Friends,</i>
ed. Horace W. Pym, 1882, p. 14

Joseph Cottle (1837)

In the following excerpt, Joseph Cottle discusses the extent of Coleridge's laudanum habit, comparing him to George Psalmanazar (c. 1679–1763), whose real name is not known. A man with a strong drug addiction of his own, Psalmanazar was an English literary imposter with an apparently impressive ability to learn languages. Posing as a Japanese convert to Christianity, he presented himself as a Formosan and went so far as to publish <i>An Historical and Geographical Description of Formosa</i> (1704), which invented a fictitious language that in turn was used to teach students at Oxford. Psalmanazar eventually admitted to the duplicity in 1706, after his work was called into question.

In discussing the losing battle with so potent a narcotic as laudanum, Cottle speaks of the unwarranted faith Coleridge placed in his doctor's skills with respect to helping him get past his opium addiction; though Coleridge, at the same time that he purported to be withdrawing, was in fact consuming enormous amounts of the drug and thus perpetrating a grand deception, most tragically on himself more so than his friends. Coleridge owed much to his friend Josiah Wade of Bristol, a successful tradesman who went to great efforts to heal the poet and offered both his hospitality and financial support to the ailing writer. Wade had even enlisted the help of a Dr. Daniel, the surgeon Cottle refers to, but it was a daunting and ultimately unsuccessful endeavor. Cottle concludes with an entertaining anecdote about the efforts Coleridge would go to in circumventing his doctor's order to abstain from taking opium. Coleridge apparently sent a companion on a bogus errand in order that he might enter an apothecary shop and make the forbidden purchase.

It is here necessary to state, in order that the reader may possess a clear knowledge of Mr. Coleridge's case in the year 1814, that I received information, from an undoubted source, informing me, Mr. C. had been long, very long, in the habit of taking, from two quarts of laudanum a week, to a pint a day; and on one occasion he had been known to take, in the twenty-four hours, a whole quart of laudanum! This exceeds the quantity which Psalmanazar ever took, or any of the race of opium consumers on record. The serious expenditure of money, resulting from this habit, was the least evil, though very great, and which must have absorbed all the produce of Mr. C.'s lectures, and all the liberalities of his friends. It is painful to record such circumstances as the following, but the picture would be incomplete without it.

Mr. Coleridge, in a late letter, (with something, it is feared, if not of duplicity, of self-deception) extols the skill of his surgeon, in having gradually lessened his consumption of laudanum, it was understood, to twenty drops a day. With this diminution, the habit was considered as subdued, and at which result, no one appeared to rejoice more than Mr. Coleridge himself. The reader will be surprised to learn, that, notwithstanding this flattering exterior, Mr. C, while apparently submitting to the directions of his medical adviser, was secretly indulging in his usual overwhelming quantities of opium! Heedless of his health, and every honourable consideration, (to which, on other occasions, Mr. C. was as much alive as most men) he contrived to obtain, surreptitiously, the "fatal drug," and thus to baffle the hopes of his warmest friends!

This was a conduct not peculiar to Mr. C. but every thorough opium eater, in his craving for the forbidden poison, would break through any impediment, rather than submit to so urgent a privation; especially, as it is often the only antidote to the stings of the internal monitor. It is this subjection of the will to the passion, which invests opium with such terrific qualities.

Mr. Coleridge had resided, at this time, for several months, with his kind friend, Mr. Josiah Wade, of Bristol, who, in his solicitude for Mr. C.'s benefit, had procured for him, as long as it was necessary, the professional assistance, stated above. The surgeon, on taking leave, after the cure had been effected, well knowing the expedients to which opium patients would often recur, to obtain their proscribed draughts; at least, till the habit of temperance was fully established, cautioned Mr. W. to prevent Mr. Coleridge, by all possible means, from obtaining that by stealth, from which he was openly debarred. It reflects great credit on Mr. Wade's humanity, that, to prevent all access to opium, and thus, if possible, to rescue his friend from destruction, he engaged a respectable old decayed tradesman, constantly to attend Mr. C. and, to make that which was sure, doubly certain, placed him even in his bedroom; and this man always accompanied him, whenever he went out. To such surveillance Mr. Coleridge cheerfully acceded, in order to show the promptitude with which he seconded the efforts of his friends. It has been stated, that every precaution was unavailing. By some unknown means and dexterous contrivances, Mr. C. still obtained his usual lulling potions! (which he afterward confessed.)

As an example, amongst many others of a similar nature, one ingenious expedient, to which he resorted, to cheat the doctor, he thus disclosed to a friend, (from whom I received it.) He said, in passing along the quay, where the ships were moored, he noticed, by a side glance, a druggist's shop, probably an old resort, and standing near the door, he looked toward the ships, and, pointing to one, at some distance, he said to his attendant, "I think that's an American." "Oh, no, that I am sure it is not," said the man. "I think it is," replied Mr. C. "I wish you would step over and ask, and bring me the particulars." The man accordingly went; when, as soon as his back was turned, Mr. C. stepped into the shop, had his portly bottle filled with laudanum, (which he always carried in his pocket) and then expeditiously placed himself in the spot where he was left. The man now returned with the particulars, beginning, "I told you, Sir, it was not an American, but I have learned all about her." "As I am mistaken, never mind the rest," said Mr. C. and walked on.

—Joseph Cottle, *Early Recollections,*
Chiefly Relating to the Late Samuel Taylor
Coleridge, 1837, vol. 2, pp. 169–172

THOMAS HOOD (1845)

Thomas Hood (1784–1859) was an essayist, journalist, and co-founder of the radical weekly periodical *The Examiner*. Hood met Coleridge at Charles and Mary Lambs' cottage in Colebrook on two separate occasions. The Lamb's country home was reported to be strewn with books in various states of disrepair. Bernard Barton, a Quaker poet as well as a friend and visitor of the Lambs at Colebrook, described their vast library: "I could but think how many long walks must have been taken to bring them home, for there were but few that did not bear the mark of having been bought at many a bookstall—brown, dark-looking books, distinguished by those white tickets which told how much their owner had given for each."

For his part, Hood provides an amusing account of an unfinished portrait Coleridge had in his possession. Coleridge apparently used this painting as proof of his popularity and would furnish it whenever there was a new review or public notice of his work. With benign intentions toward the poet, Hood provides a comical rendering of the poet's habit: "What a model, methought, as I watched and admired the 'Old Man eloquent,' for a Christian bishop! But he was, perhaps, scarcely orthodox enough to be trusted with a mitre. At least, some of his voluntaries would have frightened a common everyday congregation from their propriety." Hood goes on to note the rapid and widely varying subject matters on which Coleridge chose to discourse, including the manufacturing of sugar in Jamaica, all the while mesmerizing his company like his ancient mariner.

Amongst other notable men who came to Colebrooke Cottage, I had twice the good fortune of meeting with S. T. Coleridge. The first time he came from Highgate with Mrs. Gilman, to dine with "Charles and Mary." What a contrast to Lamb was the full-bodied Poet, with his waving white hair, and his face round, ruddy, and unfurrowed as a holy Friar's! Apropos to which face he gave us a humorous description of an unfinished portrait, that served him for a sort of barometer, to indicate the state of his popularity. So sure as his name made any temporary stir, out came the canvas on the easel, and a request from the artist for another sitting: down sank the Original in the public notice, and back went the copy into a corner, till some fresh publication or accident again brought forward the Poet; and then forth came the picture for a few more touches. I sincerely hope it has been finished! What a benign, smiling face it was! What a comfortable, respectable figure! What a model, methought, as I watched and admired the "Old Man eloquent," for a Christian bishop! But he was, perhaps, scarcely orthodox enough to be trusted with a mitre. At least, some of his voluntaries would have frightened a common everyday congregation from their propriety. Amongst other matters of discourse, he came to speak of the strange notions some literal-minded persons form of the joys of Heaven; joys they associated with mere temporal things, in which, for his own part, finding no delight in this world, he could find no bliss hereafter, without a change in his nature, tantamount to the loss of his personal identity. For instance, he said, there are persons who place the whole angelical beatitude in the possession of a pair of wings to flap about with, like "a sort of celestial poultry." After dinner he got up, and began pacing to and fro, with his hands behind his back, talking and walking, as Lamb laughingly hinted, as if qualifying for an itinerant preacher; now fetching a simile from Loddiges' garden, at Hackney; and then flying off for an illustration to the sugar-making in Jamaica. With his fine, flowing voice, it was glorious music, of the "never-ending, still-beginning" kind; and you did not wish it to end. It was rare flying, as in the Nassau Balloon; you knew not whither, nor did you care. Like his own bright-eyed Marinere, he had a spell in his voice that would not let you go. To attempt to describe my own feeling afterward, I had been carried, spiralling, up to heaven by a whirlwind intertwisted with sunbeams, giddy and dazzled, but not displeased, and had then been rained down again with a shower of mundane stocks and stones that battered out of me all recollection of what I had heard, and what I had seen!

—Thomas Hood, *Literary Reminiscences*,
c. 1845, no. 4

LEIGH HUNT (1850)

In the following excerpt from Leigh Hunt's *Autobiography*, the critic portrays Coleridge as a man who retained a childlike or boyish demeanor, even into old age. Musing on Coleridge's earliest days, when he first exhibited the dreamy and solitary nature that he would display the rest of his life, Hunt disagrees with Hazlitt's impression that the poet had an unearthly quality about him, "all head and wings," stating that he found the poet to be firmly rooted on solid ground, albeit with an ability to "conjure his etherealities about him in the twinkling of an eye." As to Hazlitt's negative opinion, Hunt attributes it to his resentment toward Coleridge for having given up his enthusiasm and support for political reform support during the early 1790s. Hunt, on the other hand, though disappointed with Coleridge, maintains that the poet was constitutionally unfit for such activities and should never have gotten involved in politics in the first place. "But Coleridge had less right to begin his zeal in favour of liberty than he had to leave it off. He should have bethought himself, first, whether he had the courage not to get fat."

Hunt takes exception to Hazlitt's hostile attitude toward Coleridge, a theme he returns to in subsequent discussions. Notably, Hunt likewise excuses Coleridge's lack of responsibility for his sensuality, which, Hunt argues, was something imposed on him over which he had little control and, moreover, absolutely prevented him from becoming a man of the world. "It was a mighty intellect put upon a sensual body; and the reason why he did little more with it than talk and dream was, that it is agreeable to such a body to do little else." Hunt sees Coleridge as the embodiment of an innate contradiction, for while his physical presence was substantial, his way of being in the world was metaphysical. Added to this strange amalgam of opposing character traits was the fact that he was addicted to opium, which, Hunt hastens to add, might have resolved this conflict in a man of lesser intellect such as Dryden. With respect to Coleridge's philosophical investigations and abstruse arguments, Hunt asserts that it was reasonable for such an extraordinary and powerful intellect to test the limits of knowledge. In his concluding commentary on Coleridge's final days at Highgate, Hunt praises the poet for the undefeated and youthful vitality of his verses. "Of all 'the Muse's mysteries'," Hunt writes, "he was as great a high priest as Spenser; and Spenser himself might have gone to Highgate to hear him talk, and thank him for his *Ancient Mariner*."

Coleridge was as little fitted for action as Lamb, but on a different account. His person was of a good height, but as sluggish and solid as the other's was light and fragile. He had, perhaps, suffered it to look old before its time, for want of exercise. His hair was white at fifty; and as he generally dressed in black, and had a very tranquil demeanour, his appearance was gentlemanly, and for several years before his death was reverend. Nevertheless, there was something invincibly young in the look of his face. It was round and fresh-coloured, with agreeable features, and an open, indolent, good-natured mouth. This boy-like expression was very becoming in one who dreamed and speculated as he did when he was really a boy, and who passed his life apart from the rest of the world, with a book, and his flowers. His forehead was prodigious—a great piece of placid marble; and his fine eyes, in which all the activity of his mind seemed to concentrate, moved under it with a sprightly ease, as if it was pastime to them to carry all that thought.

And it was pastime. Hazlitt said that Coleridge's genius appeared to him like a spirit, all head and wings, eternally floating about in etherealities. He gave me a different impression. I fancied him a good-natured wizard, very fond of earth, and conscious of reposing with weight enough in his easy chair, but able to conjure his etherealities about him in the twinkling of an eye. He could also change them by thousands, and dismiss them as easily when his dinner came. It was a mighty intellect put upon a sensual body; and the reason why he did little more with it than talk and dream was, that it is agreeable to such a body to do little else. I do not mean that Coleridge was a sensualist in an ill sense. He was capable of too many innocent pleasures to take any pleasure in the way that a man of the world would take it. The idlest things he did would have had a warrant. But if all the senses, in their time, did not find lodging in that humane plenitude of his, never believe that they did in Thomson or in Boccaccio. Two affirmatives in him made a negative. He was very metaphysical and very corporeal; so in mooting everything, he said (so to speak) nothing. His brains pleaded all sorts of questions before him, and he heard them with too much impartiality (his spleen not giving him any trouble), that he thought he might as well sit in his easy chair and hear them for ever, without coming to a conclusion. It has been said (indeed, he said himself) that he took opium to deaden the sharpness of his cogitations. I will venture to affirm, that if he ever took anything to deaden a sensation within him, it was for no greater or more marvellous reason than other people take it; which is, because they do not take enough exercise, and so plague their heads with their livers. Opium, perhaps, might have settled an uneasiness of this sort in Coleridge, as it did in a much less man with a much greater body—the Shadwell of Dryden. He would then resume his natural ease, and sit, and be happy, till the want of exercise must be again supplied. The vanity of criticism, like all other vanities, except that of dress (which, so far, has an involuntary philosophy in it), is always forgetting that we are half made up of body. Hazlitt was angry with Coleridge for not being as zealous in behalf of progress as he used to be when young. I was sorry for it, too; and if other men as well as Hazlitt had not kept me in heart, should have feared that the world was destined to be for ever lost, for want either of perseverance or calmness. But Coleridge had less right to begin his zeal in favour of liberty than he had to leave it off. He should have bethought himself, first, whether he had the courage not to get fat.

As to the charge against him, of eternally probing the depths of his own mind, and trying what he could make of them beyond the ordinary pale of logic and philosophy, surely there was no harm in a man taking this new sort of experiment upon him, whatever little chance there may have been of his doing anything with it. Coleridge, after all, was but one man, though an extraordinary man: his faculties inclined him to the task, and were suitable to it; and it is impossible to say what new worlds may be laid open, some day or other, by this apparently hopeless process. The fault of Coleridge, like that of all thinkers indisposed to action, was, that he was too content with things as they were,—at least, too fond of thinking that old corruptions were full of good things, if the world did but understand them. Now, here was the dilemma; for it required an understanding like his own to refine upon and turn them to good as he might do; and what the world requires is not metaphysical refinement, but a hearty use of good sense. Coleridge, indeed, could refine his meaning so as to accommodate it with good-nature to every one that came across him; and, doubtless, he found more agreement of intention among people of different opinions, than they themselves were aware of; which it was good to let them see. But when not enchained by his harmony, they fell asunder again, or went and committed the greatest absurdities for want of the subtle connecting tie; as was seen in the books of Mr. Irving, who, eloquent in one page, and reasoning in a manner that a child ought to be ashamed of in the next, thought to avail himself, in times like these, of the old menacing tones of damnation, without being considered a quack or an idiot, purely because Coleridge had shown him, last Friday, that damnation was not what its preachers took it for. With the same subtlety and good-nature of interpretation, Coleridge would persuade a deist that he was a Christian, and an atheist that he believed in God: all which would be very good, if the world could get on by it, and not remain stationary; but, meanwhile, millions are wretched with having too little to eat, and thousands with having too much; and these subtleties are like people talking in their sleep, when they should be up and helping.

However, if the world is to remain always as it is, give me to all eternity new talk of Coleridge, and new essays of Charles Lamb. They will reconcile it beyond all others: and that is much.

Coleridge was fat, and began to lament, in very delightful verses, that he was getting infirm. There was no old age in his verses. I heard him one day, under the Grove at Highgate, repeat one of his melodious lamentations, as he walked up and down, his voice undulating in a stream of music, and his regrets of youth sparkling with visions ever young. At the same time, he did me the honour to show me that he did not think so ill of all modern liberalism as some might suppose, denouncing the pretensions of the money-getting in a style which I should hardly venture upon and never could equal; and asking with a triumphant eloquence what chastity itself were worth, if it were a casket, not to keep love in, but hate, and strife, and worldliness? On the same occasion, he built up a metaphor out of a flower, in a style surpassing the famous passage in Milton; deducing it from its root in religious mystery, and carrying it up into the bright, consummate flower, "the bridal chamber of reproductiveness". Of all "the Muse's mysteries", he was as great a high priest as Spenser; and Spenser himself might have gone to Highgate to hear him talk, and thank him for his *Ancient Mariner*. His voice did not always sound very sincere; but perhaps the humble and deprecating tone of it, on those occasions, was out of consideration for the infirmities of his hearers, rather than produced by his own. He recited his *Kubla Khan* one morning to Lord Byron, in his lordship's house in Piccadilly, when I happened to be in another room. I remember the other's coming away from him, highly struck with his poem, and saying how wonderfully he talked. This was the impression of everybody who heard him.

It is no secret that Coleridge lived in the Grove at Highgate with a friendly family, who had sense and kindness enough to know that they did themselves honour by looking after the comfort of such a man. His room looked upon a delicious prospect of wood and meadow, with coloured gardens under the window, like an embroidery to the mantle. I thought, when I first saw it, that he had taken up his dwelling-place like an abbot. Here he cultivated his flowers, and had a set of birds for his pensioners, who came to breakfast with him. He might have been seen taking his daily stroll up and down, with his black coat and white locks, and a book in his hand; and was a great acquaintance of the little children. His main occupation, I believe, was reading. He loved to read old folios, and to make old voyages with Purchas and Marco Polo; the seas being in good visionary condition, and the vessel well stocked with botargoes.

—Leigh Hunt, *Autobiography*, 1850, chapter 16

Thomas Carlyle (1851)

In Thomas Carlyle's erudite analysis of Coleridge, he asserts that he desires to be generous to the poet, though he cannot support Coleridge's impossible agenda of applying a form of "logical alchymy" in order to delve into a realm of knowledge reserved for God alone. Carlyle accuses Coleridge of a benign self-deception by believing he could venture beyond the borders of permissible knowledge and thereby explain it. Carlyle is sympathetic yet critical of Coleridge, believing the poet to be genuinely blind to the tragic fact of his misapprehension, namely, that he has discovered a new foundation for faith. From Carlyle's perspective, Coleridge's misconception of his intellectual powers is indicative of a character flaw and thus renders him a tragic figure. "[T]ruly a ray of empyrean light;—but imbedded in such weak laxity of character, in such indolences and esuriences as had made strange work with it." For Carlyle, Coleridge was plagued by heart-rending burdens that he had not the strength to bear.

Let me not be unjust to this memorable man. Surely there was here, in his pious, ever-labouring, subtle mind, a precious truth, or prefigurement of truth; and yet a fatal delusion withal. Prefigurement that, in spite of beaver sciences and temporary spiritual hebetude and cecity, man and his Universe were eternally divine; and that no past nobleness, or revelation of the divine, could or would ever be lost to him. Most true, surely, and worthy of all acceptance. Good also to do what you can with old Churches and practical Symbols of the Noble: nay, quit not the burnt ruins of them while you find there is still gold to be dug there. But, on the whole, do not think you can, by logical alchymy, distil astral spirits from them; or if you could, that said astral spirits, or defunct logical phantasms, could serve you in anything. What the light of your mind, which is the direct inspiration of the Almighty, pronounces incredible,—that, in God's name, leave uncredited; at your peril do not try believing that. No subtlest hocus-pocus of 'reason' versus 'understanding' will avail for that feat;—and it is terribly perilous to try it in these provinces!

The truth is, I now see, Coleridge's talk and speculation was the emblem of himself: in it, as in him, a ray of heavenly inspiration struggled, in a tragically ineffectual degree, with the weakness of flesh and blood. He says once, he 'had skirted the howling deserts of Infidelity'; this was evident enough: but he had not had the courage, in defiance of pain and terror, to press resolutely across said deserts to the new firm lands of Faith beyond; he preferred to create logical fatamorganas for himself on this hither side, and laboriously solace himself with these.

To the man himself Nature had given, in high measure, the seeds of a noble endowment; and to unfold it had been forbidden him. A subtle lynx-eyed intellect, tremulous pious sensibility to all good and all beautiful; truly a ray of empyrean light;—but imbedded in such weak laxity of character, in such indolences and esuriences as had made strange work with it. Once more, the tragic story of a high endowment with an insufficient will. An eye to discern the divineness of the Heaven's splendours and lightnings, the insatiable wish to revel in their godlike radiances and brilliances; but no heart to front the scathing terrors of them, which is the first condition of your conquering an abiding place there. The courage necessary for him, above all things, had been denied this man. His life, with such ray of the empyrean in it, was great and terrible to him; and he had not valiantly grappled with it, he had fled from it; sought refuge in vague daydreams, hollow compromises, in opium, in theosophic metaphysics. Harsh pain, danger, necessity, slavish harnessed toil, were of all things abhorrent to him. And so the empyrean element, lying smothered under the terrene, and yet inextinguishable there, made sad writhings. For pain, danger, difficulty, steady slaving toil, and other highly disagreeable behests of destiny, shall in no wise be shirked by any brightest mortal that will approve himself loyal to his mission in this world; nay, precisely the higher he is, the deeper will be the disagreeableness, and the detestability to flesh and blood, of the tasks laid on him; and the heavier too, and more tragic, his penalties, if he neglect them.

—Thomas Carlyle, *Life of John Sterling*,
1851, part 1, chapter 8

GENERAL

George Gordon, Lord Byron (1809)

Shall gentle Coleridge pass unnoticed here,
To turgid ode and tumid stanza dear?
Though themes of innocence amuse him best,
Yet still obscurity's a welcome guest.
If Inspiration should her aid refuse
To him who takes a pixy for a muse,
Yet none in lofty numbers can surpass
The bard who soars to elegise an ass.
So well the subject suits his noble mind,
He brays the laureat of the long-ear'd kind.

> —George Gordon, Lord Byron, *English Bards,
> and Scotch Reviewers,* 1809, ll. 255–264

John Wilson "Observations on Coleridge's *Biographia Literaria*" (1817)

Writing for the conservative *Blackwood's Edinburgh Magazine*, John Wilson, a major contributor to the publication, excoriates the *Biographia Literaria*, the reference itself being placed in parentheses, for being a disorganized mess. Though he is not sure whether to attribute this atrocious piece to ignorance or laziness, Wilson is merciless in his attack. He finds the *Biographia* to be lacking in any cohesive theme or purpose, a work that moves erratically from one subject to the next, illuminating nothing. As to the personages Coleridge refers to, Wilson says they are beyond recognition: "[H]e so treats the most ordinary common-places as to give them the air of mysteries, till we no longer know the faces of our old acquaintances beneath their cowl and hood, but witness plain flesh and blood matters of fact miraculously converted into a troop of phantoms." Wilson also accuses Coleridge of having a misguided and absurd impression that the public appreciates him to the extent he believes it does and argues that he indulges in narcissistic delusion in comparing himself to Shakespeare, Spenser, and Milton in literary matters and other luminaries in philosophy and politics: "[H]e breaks out into laudatory exclamations concerning himself; no sound is so sweet to him as that of his own voice: the ground is hallowed on which his footsteps tread; and there seems to him something more than human in his very shadow." Nevertheless, for all his reservations, Wilson recognizes Coleridge as a genius, though it is born of his imagination rather than any real intellectual power. Thus the poet's portraits of nature are surreal and dreamlike but lacking in substance. When Wilson finally consigns Coleridge to oblivion, however, outraged that he has been so extensively reviewed, the reader is convinced that the essay serves as a vehicle for venting his uncontrollable jealousy toward an acknowledged genius. Wilson concludes his exposé with a veiled wish that Coleridge never existed.

***

Considered merely in a literary point of view, (Biographia Literaria) is most execrable. He rambles from one subject to another in the most wayward and capricious manner; either from indolence, or ignorance, or weakness, he has never in one single instance finished a discussion; and while he darkens what was dark before into tenfold obscurity, he so treats the most ordinary common-places as to give them the air of mysteries, till we no longer know the faces of our old acquaintances beneath their cowl and hood, but witness plain flesh and blood matters of fact miraculously converted into a troop of phantoms. That he is a man of genius is certain; but he is not a man of a strong intellect nor of powerful talents. He has a great deal of fancy and imagination, but little or no real feeling, and certainly no judgment. He cannot form to himself any harmonious landscape such as it exists in nature, but beautified by the serene light of the imagination. He cannot conceive simple and majestic groupes of human figures and characters acting on the theatre of real existence. But his pictures of nature are fine only as imaging the dreaminess, and obscurity, and confusion of distempered sleep; while all his agents pass before our eyes like shadows, and only impress and affect us with a phantasmagorial splendour.

It is impossible to read many pages of this work without thinking that Mr Coleridge conceives himself to be a far greater man than the Public is likely to admit; and we wish to waken him from what seems to us a most ludicrous delusion. He seems to believe that every tongue is wagging in his praise,—that every ear is open to imbibe the oracular breathings of his inspiration. Even when he would fain convince us that his soul is wholly occupied with some other illustrious character, he breaks out into laudatory exclamations concerning himself; no sound is so sweet to him as that of his own voice: the ground is hallowed on which his footsteps tread; and there seems to him something more than human in his very shadow. He will read no books that other people read; his scorn is as misplaced and extravagant as his admiration; opinions that seem to tally with his own wild ravings are holy and inspired; and, unless agreeable to his creed, the wisdom of ages is folly; and wits, whom the world worship, dwarfed when they approach his venerable side. His admiration of nature or of man,—we had almost said his religious feelings towards his God,—are all narrowed, weakened, and corrupted and poisoned by inveterate and diseased egotism; and instead of his mind reflecting the beauty and glory of nature, he seems to consider the mighty universe itself as nothing better than a mirror, in which, with a grinning and idiot self-complacency, he may contemplate the Physiognomy of Samuel Taylor Coleridge. Though he has yet done nothing in any one department of human knowledge, yet he speaks of his theories, and plans, and views, and discoveries, as if he had produced some memorable revolution in Science. He at all times connects his own name in Poetry with Shakspeare, and Spenser, and Milton; in politics with Burke, and Fox, and Pitt; in metaphysics with Locke, and Hartley, and Berkeley, and Kant;—feeling himself not only to be the worthy compeer of those illustrious Spirits, but to unite, in his own mighty intellect, all the glorious powers and faculties by which they were separately distinguished, as if his soul were endowed with all human power, and was the depository of the aggregate, or rather the essence, of all human knowledge. So deplorable a delusion as this has only been equalled by that of Joanna Southcote, who mistook a complaint in the bowels for the divine afflatus; and believed herself about to give birth to the regenerator of the world, when sick unto death of an incurable and loathsome disease.

The truth is, that Mr Coleridge is but an obscure name in English literature. In London he is well known in literary society, and justly admired for his extraordinary loquacity: he has his own little circle of devoted worshippers, and he mistakes their foolish babbling for the voice of the world. His name, too, has been often foisted into Reviews, and accordingly is known to many who never saw any of his works. In Scotland few know or care any thing about him; and perhaps no man who has spoken and written so much, and occasionally with so much genius and ability, ever made so little impression on the public mind. Few people know how to spell or pronounce his name; and were he to drop from the clouds among any given number of well informed and intelligent men north of the Tweed, he would find it impossible to make any intelligible communication respecting himself; for of him and his writings there would prevail only a perplexing dream, or the most untroubled ignorance. We cannot see in what the state of literature would have been different, had he been cut off in childhood, or had he never been born; for, except a few wild and fanciful ballads, he has produced nothing worthy remembrance. Yet, insignificant as he assuredly is, he cannot put pen to paper without a feeling that millions of eyes are fixed upon him; and he scatters his *Sibylline Leaves* around him, with as majestical an air as if a crowd of enthusiastic admirers were rushing forward to grasp the divine promulgations, instead of their being, as in fact they are, coldly received by the accidental passenger, like a lying lottery puff or a quack advertisement.

—John Wilson, "Observations on Coleridge's
Biographia Literaria," *Blackwood's Edinburgh
Magazine*, October 1817, pp. 5–6

WILLIAM HAZLITT (1818)

With respect to Coleridge's poetic production, Hazlitt has little positive to note, with the exception of *The Ancient Mariner*, which he finds remarkable and exemplary of Coleridge's extraordinary powers. Hazlitt does not believe that Coleridge has any dramatic talent, save for one isolated passage in part two of *Christabel*, where Hazlitt admires the description of the exchange between Sir Leoline and Sir Roland. Though he admits of Coleridge's true genius, he finds nothing in all his written works that is representative of Coleridge's brilliant mind. However, he remembers Coleridge as a dazzling conversationalist whose eloquence was nothing short of mesmerizing, with a "voice [that] rolled on the ear like the pealing organ." In this last regard, Hazlitt mourns the passing of a remarkable man and quotes consolatory lines from Wordsworth's *Ode: Intimations of Immortality*.

It remains that I should say a few words of Mr. Coleridge; and there is no one who has a better right to say what he thinks of him than I have. 'Is there here any dear friend of Caesar? To him I say, that Brutus's love to Caesar was no less than his.' But no matter.—His *Ancient Mariner* is his most remarkable performance, and the only one that I could point out to any one as giving an adequate idea of his great natural powers. It is high German, however, and in it he seems to 'conceive of poetry but as a drunken dream, reckless, careless, and heedless, of past, present, and to come.' His tragedies (for he has written two) are not answerable to it; they are, except a few poetical passages, drawling sentiment and metaphysical jargon. He has no genuine dramatic talent. There is one fine passage in his *Christabel*, that which contains the description of the quarrel between Sir Leoline and Sir Roland de Vaux of Tryermaine, who had been friends in youth.

> Alas! they had been friends in youth,
> But whispering tongues can poison truth;
> And constancy lives in realms above;
> And life is thorny; and youth is vain;
> And to be wroth with one we love,
> Doth work like madness in the brain:
> And thus it chanc'd as I divine,
> With Roland and Sir Leoline.
> Each spake words of high disdain
> And insult to his heart's best brother,
> And parted ne'er to meet again!
> But neither ever found another
> To free the hollow heart from paining—
> They stood aloof, the scars remaining,
> Like cliffs which had been rent asunder:
> A dreary sea now flows between,
> But neither heat, nor frost, nor thunder,
> Shall wholly do away I ween
> The marks of that which once hath been.
>
> Sir Leoline a moment's space
> Stood gazing on the damsel's face;
> And the youthful lord of Tryermaine
> Came back upon his heart again.

It might seem insidious if I were to praise his ode entitled 'Fire, Famine, and Slaughter,' as an effusion of high poetical enthusiasm, and strong political feeling. His Sonnet to Schiller conveys a fine compliment to the author of the Robbers, and an equally fine idea of the state of youthful enthusiasm in which he composed it. . . . His *Conciones ad Populum, Watchman*, &c. are dreary trash. Of his *Friend*, I have spoken the truth elsewhere. But I may say of him here, that he is the only person I ever knew who answered to the idea of a man of genius. He is the only person from whom I ever learnt any thing. There is only one thing he could learn from me in return, but that he has not. He was the first poet I ever knew. His genius at that time had angelic wings, and fed on manna. He talked on for ever; and you wished him to talk on for ever. His thoughts did not seem to come with labour and effort; but as if borne on the gusts of genius, and as if the wings of his imagination lifted him from off his feet. His voice rolled on the ear like the pealing organ, and its sound alone was the music of thought. His mind was clothed with wings; and raised on them, he lifted philosophy to heaven. In his descriptions, you then saw the progress of human happiness and liberty in bright and never-ending succession, like the steps of Jacob's ladder, with airy shapes ascending and descending, and with the voice of God at the top of the ladder. And shall I, who heard him then, listen to him now? Not I! That spell is broke; that time is gone for ever; that voice is heard no more: but still the recollection comes rushing by with thoughts of long-past years, and rings in my ears with never-dying sound.

> What though the radiance which was once so bright,
> Be now for ever taken from my sight,
> Though nothing can bring back the hour
> Of splendour in the grass, of glory in the flow'r;
> I do not grieve, but rather find
> Strength in what remains behind;
> In the primal sympathy,
> Which having been, must ever be;
> In the soothing thoughts that spring
> Out of human suffering;
> In years that bring the philosophic mind!

—William Hazlitt, *Lectures on the English Poets*, 1818

GEORGE GORDON, LORD BYRON
"DEDICATION" (1819)

And Coleridge, too, has lately taken wing,
But like a hawk encumber'd with his hood,—
Explaining metaphysics to the nation—
I wish he would explain his Explanation.

—George Gordon, Lord Byron,
"Dedication" to *Don Juan*, 1819

PERCY BYSSHE SHELLEY (1819)

In the following excerpt from *Peter Bell the Third*, Percy Bysshe Shelley satirizes Coleridge in a poem with almost the exact name as one written by William Wordsworth. While Wordsworth's *Peter Bell* tells the story of an immoral and superstitious itinerant potter who undergoes a transformation after encountering an ass that remained faithful to its deceased owner, here Shelley chooses to mock Coleridge for his friendship with the Wordsworths, "the Devil's petits-soupers," and for wasting his vast talents, "All things he seemed to understand," by falling prey to opium. Shelley's attitude toward Coleridge is one of great sadness for the stature Coleridge might have achieved, rather than the blatant attack on Wordsworth's creative skills that he makes elsewhere in Peter Bell the Third. For Shelley, a man who had boundless powers to illuminate the world with his brilliance is instead shrouded forever in a dreamy mist. Shelley's poem was not published until 1839, when Mary Shelley added it to the second edition of her deceased husband's *Poetical Works*. Apparently, Mary was uncomfortable with the fact that the poem made fun of Wordsworth and went so far as to include a favorable comment on the work: "Much of it is beautifully written—.... it has so much of himself in it, that it cannot fail to interest greatly...."

Among the guests who often stayed
Till the Devil's petits-soupers,
A man there came, fair as a maid,
And Peter noted what he said,
Standing behind his master's chair.
He was a mighty poet—and
A subtle-souled psychologist;
All things he seemed to understand,
Of old or new—of sea or land—
But his own mind—which was a mist.
This was a man who might have turned
Hell into Heaven—and so in gladness
A Heaven unto himself have earned;
But he in shadows undiscerned
Trusted,—and damned himself to madness.
He spoke of poetry, and how
'Divine it was—a light—a love—
A spirit which like wind doth blow

As it listeth, to and fro;
A dew rained down from God above;
'A power which comes and goes like dream,
And which none can ever trace—
Heaven's light on earth—
Truth's brightest beam.'
And when he ceased there lay the gleam
Of those words upon his face.

> —Percy Bysshe Shelley, *Peter Bell the Third*,
> 1819, part 5, stanzas 1–5

PERCY BYSSHE SHELLEY (1820)

You will see Coleridge—he who sits obscure
In the exceeding lustre and the pure
Intense irradiation of a mind,
Which, with its own internal lightning blind,
Flags wearily through darkness and despair—
A cloud-encircled meteor of the air,
A hooded eagle among blinking owls.—

> —Percy Bysshe Shelley, letter to
> Maria Gisborne, 1820, ll. 202–208

JOHN STERLING "COLERIDGE" (1839)

John Sterling (1806–1844), a little-known British poet, presents us with a lovingly crafted description of Coleridge as a gentle soul whose poetic powers never faltered, even when he grew old. Especially endearing to Sterling was Coleridge's noble spirit, which strove to spread his wisdom to anyone who would listen despite his deteriorating health: "Words like the Seraph's when in Paradise / He vainly strove to make his hearers wise." For Sterling, Coleridge had gained immortality by virtue of his tremendous visionary powers with "[t]hought beyond the stature given to man."

Like some full tree that bends with fruit and leaves,
While gentle wind a quivering descant weaves,
He met the gaze; with sibyl eyes, and brow
By age snow-clad, yet bright with summer's glow;
His cheek was youthful, and his features played

Like lights and shadows in a flowery glade.
Around him flowed with many a varied fall.
And depth of voice 'mid smiles most musical,
Words like the Seraph's when in Paradise
He vainly strove to make his hearers wise.
In sore disease I saw him laid,—a shrine
Half-ruined, and all tottering, still divine.
'Mid broken arch and shattered cloister hung
The ivy's green, and wreaths of blossom clung;
Through mingling vine and bay the sunshine fell,
Or winds and moonbeams sported round the cell;
But o'er the altar burnt that heavenly flame,
Whose life no damps of earth availed to tame.
And there have I swift hours a watcher been,
Heard mystic spells, and sights prophetic seen,
Till all beyond appeared a vast Inane,
Yet all with deeper life revived again;
And Nature woke in Wisdom's light, and grew
Instinct with lore that else she never knew,
Expanding spirits filled her countless forms,
And Truth beamed calmly through chaotic storms,
Till shapes, hues, symbols, felt the wizard's rod,
And while they sank in silence there was God.
O! Heart that like a fount with freshness ran,
O! Thought beyond the stature given to man,
Although thy page had blots on many a line,
Yet Faith remedial made the tale divine
With all the poet's fusing, kindling blaze,
And sage's skill to thread each tangled maze,
Thy fair expressive image meets the view,
Bearing the sunlike torch, and subtle clew;
Yet more than these for thee the Christian's crown
By Faith and Peace outvalued all renown.
This wearing, enter yon supernal dome,
And reach at last thy calm ideal home!
Enough for us to follow from afar,
And joyous track thy clear emerging Star.

—John Sterling, "Coleridge,"
Poems, 1839, pp. 153–155

ELIZABETH BARRETT BROWNING (1844)

And visionary Coleridge,who
Did sweep his thoughts as angels do
Their wings with cadence up the Blue.

—Elizabeth Barrett Browning,
A Vision of Poets, 1844, ll. 415–417

LEIGH HUNT (1844)

In this excerpt taken from Leigh Hunt's *Imagination and Fancy*, the author portrays Coleridge as a mixture of contraries, argumentative on intellectual subjects, yet afraid or anxious to bring his theories to conclusion, and thus mired in the discursive process. While Hunt concedes that Coleridge was a brilliant conversationalist and original thinker, the poet is portrayed as lacking the fortitude to bring his vast prose writings to conclusion. Rather, Coleridge's theological speculations were open-ended enough to adapt themselves to either Indian ("Brahmin") or Muslim ("Mussulman") philosophies. However, in considering Coleridge's poetic output, Hunt is of a different opinion, full of praise for the poet's unparalleled talents: "If you could see it in a phial," he notes, "like a distillation of roses (taking it, I mean, at its best), it would be found without a speck." At the same time, Hunt laments the fact that Coleridge, who was so generous in his praise of others, did not receive the same appreciation from his contemporaries, most notably from Hazlitt, whose hostility toward what he perceived to be the poet's abandonment of revolutionary causes allowed his anger to manifest itself in criticizing the otherwise exquisite *Christabel*, which in its minute and artistic depiction of treachery surpasses Shakespeare's Regan and Goneril and the accomplished *Ancient Mariner*. Hunt continues to extol Coleridge's poetic virtues, comparing him to Spenser; but above all poetic considerations, Hunt is most impressed with Coleridge's musicality, an emanation of his inner spirit and powerful imagination, to which "Waller's music is but a court-flourish in comparison." Hunt concludes his essay with regrets that he did not spend more time with Coleridge at Highgate, for Hunt, too, did not fully appreciate the poet while he was still alive.

⸺⸺⸺ ⸺⸺⸺ ⸺⸺⸺

Coleridge lived in the most extraordinary and agitated period of modern history; and to a certain extent he was so mixed up with its controversies, that he was at one time taken for nothing but an apostate republican, and at another for a dreaming theosophist. The truth is, that both his politics and theosophy were at the mercy of a discursive genius, intellectually bold but educationally timid, which, anxious, or rather willing, to bring conviction and speculation together, mooting all points as it went, and throwing the subtlest glancing lights on many, ended in satisfying nobody, and concluding nothing. Charles Lamb said of him, that he had "the art of making the unintelligible appear intelligible." He was the finest dreamer, the most eloquent talker, and the most original thinker of his day; but for want of complexional energy, did nothing with all the vast prose part of his mind but help the Germans to give a subtler tone to criticism, and sow a few valuable seeds of thought in minds worthy to receive them. Nine-tenths of his theology would apply equally well to their own creeds in the mouths of a Brahmin or a Mussulman.

His poetry is another matter. It is so beautiful, and was so quietly content with its beauty, making no call on the critics, and receiving hardly any notice, that people are but now beginning to awake to a full sense of its merits. Of pure poetry, strictly so called, that is to say, consisting of nothing but its essential self, without conventional and perishing helps, he was the greatest master of his time. If you could see it in a phial, like a distillation of roses (taking it, I mean, at its best), it would be found without a speck. The poet is happy with so good a gift, and the reader is "happy in his happiness." Yet so little, sometimes, are a man's contemporaries and personal acquaintances able or disposed to estimate him properly, that while Coleridge, unlike Shakspeare, lavished praises on his poetic friends, he had all the merit of the generosity to himself; and even Hazlitt, owing perhaps to causes of political alienation, could see nothing to admire in the exquisite poem of Christabel, but the description of the quarrel between the friends! After speaking, too, of the *Ancient Mariner* as the only one of his poems that he could point out to any one as giving an adequate idea of his great natural powers, he adds, "It is high German, however, and in it he seems to conceive of poetry but as a drunken dream, reckless, careless, and heedless of past, present, and to come." This is said of a poem, with which fault has been found for the exceeding conscientiousness of its moral! O, ye critics, the best of ye, what havoc does personal difference play with your judgments! It was not Mr. Hazlitt's only or most unwarrantable censure, or one which friendship found hardest to forgive. But peace, and honour too, be with his memory! If he was a splenetic and sometimes jealous man, he was a disinterested politician and an admirable critic: and lucky were those whose natures gave them the right and the power to pardon him.

Coleridge, though a born poet, was in his style and general musical feeling the disciple partly of Spenser, and partly of the fine old English ballad-writers in the collection of Bishop Percy. But if he could not improve on them in some things, how he did in others, especially in the art of being thoroughly musical!

Of all our writers of the briefer narrative poetry, Coleridge is the finest since Chaucer; and assuredly he is the sweetest of all our poets. Waller's music is but a court-flourish in comparison; and though Beaumont and Fletcher, Collins, Gray, Keats, Shelley, and others, have several as sweet passages, and Spenser is in a certain sense musical throughout, yet no man has written whole poems, of equal length, so perfect in the sentiment of music, so varied with it, and yet leaving on the ear so unbroken and single an effect. . . .

We see how such a poet obtains his music. Such forms of melody can proceed only from the most beautiful inner spirit of sympathy and imagination. He sympathizes, in his universality, with antipathy itself. If Regan or Goneril had been a young and handsome witch of the times of chivalry, and attuned her violence to craft, or betrayed it in venomous looks, she could not have beaten the soft-voiced, appalling spells, or sudden, snake-eyed glances of the lady Geraldine,—looks which the innocent Christabel, in her fascination, feels compelled to "imitate."

> A snake's small eye blinks dull and shy,
> And the lady's eyes they shrank in her head,
> Each shrank up to a serpent's eye;
> And with somewhat of malice and more of dread,
> At Christabel she look'd askance.
> The maid devoid of guile and sin
> I know not how, in fearful wise,
> So deeply had she drunken in
> That look, those shrunken serpent eyes,
> That all her features were resign'd
> To this sole image in her mind,
> And passively did imitate
> That look of dull and treacherous hate.

This is as exquisite in its knowledge of the fascinating tendencies of fear as it is in its description. And what can surpass a line quoted already in the Essay (but I must quote it again!) for very perfection of grace and sentiment?—the line in the passage where Christabel is going to bed, before she is aware that her visitor is a witch.

> Quoth Christabel,—So let it be!
> And as the lady bade, did she.
> Her gentle limbs did she undress,
> And lay down in her loveliness.

Oh! it is too late now; and habit and self-love blinded me at the time, and I did not know (much as I admired him) how great a poet lived in that grove at Highgate; or I would have cultivated its walks more, as I might have done, and endeavoured to return him, with my gratitude, a small portion of the delight his verses have given me.

I must add, that I do not think Coleridge's earlier poems at all equal to the rest. Many, indeed, I do not care to read a second time; but there are some ten or a dozen, of which I never tire, and which will one day make a small and precious volume to put in the pockets of all enthusiasts in poetry, and endure with the language. Five of these are The Ancient Mariner, Christabel, Kubla Khan, "Genevieve," and "Youth and Age." Some, that more personally relate to the poet, will be added for the love of him, not omitting the Visit of the Gods, from Schiller, and the famous passage on the Heathen Mythology, also from Schiller. A short life, a portrait, and some other engravings perhaps, will complete the book, after the good old fashion of Cooke's and Bell's editions of the Poets; and then, like the contents of the Jew of Malta's casket, there will be

Infinite riches in a little room.

—Leigh Hunt, *Imagination and Fancy,* 1844

MARGARET FULLER
"MODERN BRITISH POETS" (1846)

Margaret Fuller was a journalist, critic, and women's rights activist associated with the American transcendentalist movement. Her essay at first paints an unflattering portrait of Coleridge, declaring that his poetry has left insufficient material by which to render an opinion of his talents, while his dramas were complete catastrophes and his metaphysical inquiries were at best ill advised. However, Fuller pays passing tribute to Coleridge's smaller poems, commending him for his ability to depict a single attitude of mind: "Give Coleridge a canvas, and he will paint a single mood as if his colors were made of the mind's own atoms." Fuller's critique notwithstanding, she admits to having a great respect for Coleridge, while predicting that posterity's estimation cannot yet be measured as his legacy will be to inspire others without changing a thing. In regard to *Christabel* and *The Ancient Mariner*, Fuller finds both poems to be irrational and, as a person of common sense, she cannot judge them. "It is for his suggestive power that I thank him," she concedes.

Of Coleridge I shall say little. Few minds are capable of fathoming his by their own sympathies, and he has left us no adequate manifestation of himself as a poet by which to judge him. As for his dramas, I consider them complete failures, and more like visions than dramas. For a metaphysical mind like his to attempt that walk was scarcely more judicious than it would be for a blind man to essay painting the bay of Naples. Many of his smaller pieces are perfect in their way, indeed no writer could excel him in depicting a single mood of mind, as dejection for instance. . . . Give Coleridge a canvas, and he will paint a single mood as if his colors were made of the mind's own atoms. Here he is very unlike Southey. There is nothing of the spectator about Coleridge; he is all life; not impassioned, not vehement, but searching, intellectual life, which seems "listening through the frame" to its own pulses.

I have little more to say at present except to express a great, though not fanatical veneration for Coleridge, and a conviction that the benefits conferred by him on this and future ages are as yet incalculable. Every mind will praise him for what it can best receive from him. He can suggest to an infinite degree; he can inform, but he cannot reform and renovate. To the unprepared he is nothing, to the prepared, everything. Of him may be said what he said of Nature,

We receive but what we give, In kind though not in measure.

I was once requested by a very sensible and excellent personage to explain what is meant by *Christabel* and *The Ancient Mariner*. I declined the task. I had not then seen Coleridge's answer to a question of similar tenor from Mrs. Barbauld, or I should have referred to that as an expression not altogether unintelligible of the discrepancy which must ever exist between those minds which are commonly styled rational (as the received definition of common sense is insensibility to uncommon sense) and that of Coleridge. As to myself, if I understand nothing beyond the execution of those "singularly wild and original poems," I could not tell my gratitude for the degree of refinement which taste has received from them. To those who cannot understand the voice of Nature or poetry unless it speak in apothegms and tag each story with a moral, I have nothing to say. My own greatest obligation to Coleridge I have already mentioned. It is for his suggestive power that I thank him.

—Margaret Fuller, "Modern British Poets,"
Papers on Literature and Art, 1846

GEORGE MEREDITH (1851)

A brook glancing under green leaves, self-delighting, exulting
And full of a gurgling melody ever renewed—
Renewed thro' all changes of Heaven, unceasing in sunlight,
Unceasing in moonlight, but hushed in the beams of the holier orb.

—George Meredith,
"The Poetry of Coleridge," 1851

RALPH WALDO EMERSON "LITERATURE" (1856)

Ralph Waldo Emerson, the American critic and philosopher, traveled to England to meet several romantic poets, paying a visit to Coleridge on August 5, 1833. Here, Emerson expresses unbridled praise for the poet, declaring that Coleridge actually rescued English literature from the accusation that the English could no longer recognize true brilliance in one of their countrymen. It is with sorrow that Emerson reflects on the way in which the unfortunate facts in Coleridge's life and his inability to bring to fruition his philosophical writings will color the memory of one so richly deserving admiration: "It is the surest sign of national decay," Emerson laments, "when the Bramins can no longer read or understand the Braminical philosophy."

Coleridge, a catholic mind, with a hunger for ideas; with eyes looking before and after to the highest bards and sages, and who wrote and spoke the only high criticism in his time, is one of those who saved England from the reproach of no longer possessing the capacity to appreciate what rarest wit the island has yielded. Yet the misfortune of his life, his vast attempts but most inadequate performings, failing to accomplish any one masterpiece,— seems to mark the closing of an era. Even in him, the traditional Englishman was too strong for the philosopher, and he fell into accommodations; and as Burke had striven to idealize the English State, so Coleridge 'narrowed his mind' in the attempt to reconcile the Gothic rule and dogma of the Anglican Church, with eternal ideas. But for Coleridge, and a lurking taciturn minority uttering itself in occasional criticism, oftener in private discourse, one would say that in Germany and in America is the best mind in England rightly respected. It is the surest sign of national decay, when the Bramins can no longer read or understand the Braminical philosophy.

—Ralph Waldo Emerson, "Literature,"
English Traits, 1856

Matthew Arnold "Joubert" (1864)

Though Matthew Arnold finds much to fault in Coleridge's way of life and finds little merit in his writings, either poetic or critical, he nevertheless argues that Coleridge bequeathed an inestimable legacy to his country in having inspired others to think with the same passion and boundless energy that he applied to his own work: "Coleridge's great usefulness lay in .... the spectacle of this effort of his, a stimulus to all minds capable of profiting by it, in the generation which grew up around him."

In all his production how much is there to dissatisfy us! How many reserves must be made in praising either his poetry, or his criticism, or his philosophy! How little either of his poetry, or of his criticism, or of his philosophy, can we expect permanently to stand! But that which will stand of Coleridge is this: the stimulus of his continual effort,—not a moral effort, for he had no morals,—but of his continual instinctive effort, crowned often with rich success, to get at and to lay bare the real truth of his matter in hand, whether that matter were literary, or philosophical, or political, or religious; and this in a country where at that moment such an effort was almost unknown; where the most powerful minds threw themselves upon poetry, which conveys truth, indeed, but conveys it indirectly; and where ordinary minds were so habituated to do without thinking altogether, to regard considerations of established routine and practical convenience as paramount, that any attempt to introduce within the domain of these the disturbing element of thought, they were prompt to resent as an outrage. Coleridge's great usefulness lay in his supplying in England, for many years and under critical circumstances, by the spectacle of this effort of his, a stimulus to all minds capable of profiting by it, in the generation which grew up around him. His action will still be felt as long as the need for it continues. When, with the cessation of the need, the action too has ceased, Coleridge's memory, in spite of the dis-esteem—nay, repugnance—which his character may and must inspire, will yet for ever remain invested with that interest and gratitude which invests the memory of founders.

—Matthew Arnold, "Joubert,"
1864, *Essays in Criticism*, 1865

Dante Gabriel Rossetti
"Samuel Taylor Coleridge" (1880–81)

His Soul fared forth (as from the deep home-grove
The father-songster plies the hour-long quest,)

To feed his soul-brood hungering in the nest;
But his warm Heart, the mother-bird, above
Their callow fledgling progeny still hove
With tented roof of wings and fostering breast
Till the Soul fed the soul-brood. Richly blest
From Heaven their growth, whose food was Human Love.
Yet ah! Like desert pools that show the stars
Once in long leagues,—even such the scarce-snatched hours
Which deepening pain left to his lordliest powers:—
Heaven lost through spider-trammelled prison-bars.
Six years, from sixty saved! Yet kindling skies
Own them, a beacon to our centuries.

—Dante Gabriel Rossetti, "Samuel Taylor
Coleridge," *Five English Poets*, 1880–81

W.P. Ker "Samuel Taylor Coleridge" (1896)

W.P. Ker discusses an aspect of Coleridge's critical judgment that has received little attention—his penchant for long and complex arguments—stating that Coleridge clearly subscribed to his own advice that when one is engaged in a line of reasoning, the process by which it proceeds must be judged on whether it flows and not how long it takes. "If it cannot be said of all his arguments in the *Friend*, or in *Aids to Reflection*, that they 'evolve,' it is still almost always to be found that the movement of the discourse is in the form of large and continuous reasoning." This ability to hold the audience's attention to follow along as he attempted to prove his point is what Ker believes made his lectures so popular. This same magnetic quality can be found in Coleridge's prose writings as well. By almost all accounts, Coleridge was appreciated for his brilliant conversation, eloquent manner of speaking, and powerfully imaginative verse, while his prose works were often thought monotonous and lacking in cohesion and structure. Ker, however, contends that some of his prose works, most notably the *Biographia Literaria*, do in fact exhibit a balancing of the poetic with the metaphysical, especially in his theory of poetry. According to Ker, this same evidence of his ability to merge the poetic with the philosophical may also be found in his *Lay Sermons*. In regard to the 1828 version of *The Ancient Mariner*, Ker observes that the marginal gloss to the poem shows a more lighthearted application of the prose argument that, rather than a rambling, convoluted explanation, moves in a more staccato fashion, an argument done with an eye to aesthetics. "[I]t was minute work, piecemeal, following the lines of a composition already finished, giving no room for anything like his usual copious paragraphs of edification, compelling him to write for the mere beauty of writing." In conclusion, Ker has great respect and admiration for Coleridge's work on morals, for he was always careful to remain faithful to his critical agenda never to employ the rhetorical devices of his poetry or let anything stand in the way of his argument.

One of the most constant opinions in Coleridge's mind, one that is little short of the chief place among his critical judgments, is that which distinguishes between the continuous energy of genius and the cautious progress of less noble faculties, bit by bit, in small successive efforts. His own discourse, whatever its faults, has always something of the character that he himself admired in others. When the argument is least assured, and when the progress of the speculation is most impeded, there is still always in Coleridge's style the life and the living movement of one accustomed to long trains of thought; there is never any of the hard brilliance of the styles that are made out of separate finished pieces of thought and expression. The "criterion of genius," given in the Table Talk of 6th August 1832, is one to which Coleridge himself might have submitted the style of his own prose:—

> You will find this a good gauge or criterion of genius—whether it progresses and evolves, or only spins upon itself.

This (which leads to a striking comparison of Dryden and Pope, Charles Lamb and Hazlitt) is the repetition of an idea that governs very much of Coleridge's criticism of literature. If it cannot be said of all his arguments in the *Friend*, or in Aids to Reflection, that they "evolve," it is still almost always to be found that the movement of the discourse is in the form of large and continuous reasoning; and it is this apparent spontaneity that gives distinction to his writing, even when it is least effectual. No English prose is nearer to that of Goethe in its power of carrying the reader along, with or without his consent, till he is left wondering what it is that has got hold of him. The spell that drew so many people, of all orders of intellectual constitution, to listen to Coleridge talking, may still be found in his philosophical and critical writings; and, in spite of the scorner, it is still possible to "sit under" the eloquence of his sermons, merely because it is true eloquence, and not a battery of separate notes and epigrams.

The commonly accepted descriptions of Coleridge's manner in conversation are not altogether borne out by his recorded *Table Talk*. There is too much wit and too much sound sense, as well as too much interest in sublunar things, to agree well with the common account of Coleridge's "transcendental" monologues. That Coleridge in any way lost himself in metaphysics, will be almost incredible to any one who follows the journal of his daily conversation, on things in general and things in particular.

The monotony of some portions of his speculative books is in strong contrast to the quickness of most of his talk, as that is reported. There are, however, some of his prose writings, and especially the greater part of *Biographia Literaria*, in which there is a balance or a compromise between the metaphysical and the imaginative sides in his composition, and in which his metaphysics are condensed out of their nebulous state, into some of the most effective criticism of poetry to be found anywhere in English. Coleridge's philosophy has been shown, by philosophical scholars, to be futile in its adaptation of German systems for the benefit of English novices. It is not thorough or systematic enough for idealist philosophers; and for all other schools it is simply a weariness. But if his more ambitious attempts have failed, there can be no question, on the other hand, either of the wide influence of his philosophic spirit, as an encouragement to hopefulness and intellectual daring, or of the success of his work, when it was applied to subjects more palpable than those of metaphysical enquiry. His long-continued exposition of Reason and Understanding may have been unsatisfactory as philosophical literature, or profitable merely as an example of philosophical aspirations, by which many younger men were stirred to speculations of their own. But when the antithesis of Reason and Understanding appears in the pages of *Biographia Literaria* as the opposition of Imagination and Fancy, there is no need to look far for any justification or excuse. It may be necessary to remember Coleridge's immediate influence upon the minds of his contemporaries, in order to appreciate the *Aids to Reflection*; but the strength and beauty of his critical essays on poetry are enough to put out of account all external and accidental considerations. They stand on their own merits. There had been nothing like them in English, except Wordsworth's essays appended to the *Lyrical Ballads* of 1800 and 1815; and Coleridge had the advantage of Wordsworth both in greater freedom of view, and in greater accuracy of discrimination. In the play of his mind in *Biographia Literaria*, between the general philosophy of the poetic art, and the critical judgment of particulars in his answer to Wordsworth's theory of diction, there is no fluctuation of strength or skill; the philosophy of Imagination and Fancy is just as lively as the refutation of his friend's paradoxical rhetoric. In dealing with poetry, the energy of his speculation is not wasted, nor is its effect the merely formal, though glorious influence exerted on younger and better-disciplined minds, by the solemnity of his tone, apart from the weight of his doctrine. In his criticism of poetry, the matter and form of his writings are equivalent. Here, in place of the reiterated assaults on the citadel of metaphysics, the weary relapses, and perpetual new beginnings, there is a victorious and conquering progress, with prizes gained at every step in the march.

There is another field to which Coleridge escaped at times from the bewilderment of metaphysics, and in his own words was enabled "to pluck the flower, and reap the harvest from the cultivated surface, instead of delving in the unwholesome quicksilver mines of metaphysic depths." His lay sermons and other essays on politics and political science, are, like his aesthetic criticism, under the control of his common philosophical ideas; and here, also, the principles of "Reason" against "Understanding," are found to be anything but sterile.

Coleridge in his political philosophy appears as the successor of Burke, and the forerunner of Carlyle. To the difficulties of his own time he applied the instruments that Burke had left behind him; Burke's hatred of abstract dogmas and formulas, Burke's sense of the complexity of life, and of the need for insight into the particular circumstances of each individual problem. The second Lay Sermon ("Blessed are ye that sow beside all waters!"), anticipates more of Past and Present than ever seems to have been fully acknowledged by the author of the latter book. There is no weakness or faltering, no inconsequence or irrelevance, in this political essay, one of the best designed and most complete of all the works of Coleridge in prose. In scorn of the demagogue and his machinery, Coleridge resembles Burke and Carlyle; and hardly in these will there be found anything more fervent than Coleridge's recitation and appropriation of the words of the prophet: "the vile person shall no more be called liberal, nor the churl said to be bountiful." He is with Carlyle, or before him, in his comprehension of "the existing distresses and discontents," and his appeal to "the higher and middle classes" in 1817 is to the same effect, and helped by much the same arguments, as the appeal of Past and Present, or of the essay on "Chartism."

In Coleridge's prose there are many interludes of different kinds, and of all degrees of value. Of these the account of his interview with Klopstock, in Satyrane's Letters (Biographia Literaria), is one of the most singular, through the contrast of its short phrases and its ironical reserve, with the voluble expression of the author's more habitual didactic moods.

It is seldom that the prose of Coleridge is decorated in any adventitious way. There are many illustrations, but rarely any that look as if they had been stuck on for effect. The argument in its course discovers its own illustrations: "the wheels take fire from the rapidity of their motion," to borrow a phrase that Coleridge himself had applied to his own youthful oratory (Letter to Sir George and Lady Beaumont, 1st October 1803), before he used it in his splendid acknowledgment of the genius of Dryden. There is evidence, however, that when he chose he could play lightly with the weapons of prose argument. The marginal gloss to the *Ancient Mariner* (1828) is one of his finest compositions, in an unfamiliar mood; a translation or transposition of his poem, for a purely artistic end, such as had never come within the view of the *Watchman*, or any other of the serious monitors of Church and State. The exercise was wholly different from that to which he was accustomed. It was not the evolution of an argument; it was minute work, piecemeal, following the lines of a composition already finished, giving no room for anything like his usual copious paragraphs of edification, compelling him to write for the mere beauty of writing.

> In his loneliness and fixedness he yearneth towards the journeying Moon, and the stars that still sojourn, yet still move onward; and everywhere the blue sky belongs to them, and is their appointed rest, and their native country and their own natural homes, which they enter unannounced, as lords that are certainly expected, and yet there is a silent joy at their arrival.

Nowhere else in the works of Coleridge is the element of prose thus disengaged from matter. It is significant of Coleridge's spirit, that in his moral treatises he never relied on anything like the charm of this prose, to gain applause or acceptance for his doctrines. Whether he fought well or slackly, he was always a combatant in his prose essays, and never a vendor of merely ornamental rhetoric. He never allowed himself to be tempted by any attraction inconsistent with his purpose; his digressions were always prompted by something in the matter, never by the vanities of language; he used no rhetorical display except what was immediately intended to support his ethical strategy. It is this consistency that distinguishes his style, even in its most intricate and florid passages, from all the varieties of ostentatious literature.

—W.P. Ker, "Samuel Taylor Coleridge,"
English Prose, ed. Henry Craik,
1896, vol. 5, pp. 76–80

Francis Thompson "Academy Portraits: XIII. S.T. Coleridge" (1897)

In the excerpt below, Francis Thompson begins with a rather disparaging assessment of Coleridge's literary career. Though he praises the poet as a child prodigy at Christ's Hospital, he quickly moves on to Coleridge's journalistic failures and weakness for opium, while censuring his poetry for being plaintive and effeminate. Nevertheless, after disparaging his poetic works, Thompson launches into a discussion of Coleridge's influence on the following generations of poets and concedes that subsequent generations have managed to be inspired by him without adopting his faults of style, a "manner" of writing that is devoid of any identifiable style: "It is that he has incited the very sprouting in them of the laurel-bough, has been to them a fostering sun of song. Such a primary influence he was to Rossetti—Rossetti, whose model was far more Keats than Coleridge." However, Thompson's notion of influence on Coleridge's literary successors is an elusive theory and proves to be a difficult thesis for him to defend. To support his argument, Thompson introduces the English poet and critic Coventry Patmore (1823–1896), who similarly commented on the intangible qualities in Coleridge's works, as one can only speak of its effects without being able to identify any characteristic technique.

Further along in his attempt to understand how poets have been historically received by critics, Thompson takes issue with the fact that Coleridge has been labeled "affected," a term that he feels has been used in a wholesale manner and applied to many great poets from Wordsworth to Tennyson and Browning. Thompson maintains that it is the universal application of the term that has rendered it meaningless. "If this old shoe were not thrown at the wedding of every poet with the Muse," he writes, "what would become of our ancient English customs?" Thompson contends that this tradition of equivocation on the part of critics with respect to their treatment of living poets has finally resolved itself in posthumous adulation of Coleridge. Thompson believes that for three decades following Coleridge's death, critics felt free to unburden themselves of their negative feelings toward him, only to have come full circle to an unqualified appreciation of his poetry. *"The Ancient Mariner, Christabel, Kubla Khan, 'Genevieve'* are recognised as perfectly unique masterpieces of triumphant utterance, and triumphant imagination of a certain kind. They bring down magic to the earth." In his concluding remarks on *The Ancient Mariner, Christabel*, and "Kubla Khan," Thompson finds that *The Ancient Mariner* is a far more complete, thoroughly enchanting poem, while the other two works remain mere fragments. For Thompson, Coleridge's star burned out quickly in his youth, followed by a life of wasted poetic powers hastened by his opium addiction.

=·/v/·=   =·/v/·=   =·/v/·=

Coleridge is (with the exception of Pope) perhaps the only poet who was a genius to his schoolfellows—and, more wonderful still, to his schoolmaster. At Christ's Hospital his Greek and philosophy were things sensational to all. How he afterwards left Oxford and enlisted, how he made an indifferent trooper and was bought out, how he came in contact with Southey and later with Wordsworth; of the Pantisocratic scheme and its failure; of the *Lyrical Ballads* and their failure, Macaulay's schoolboy would think it trite to speak. Those were the golden days of the *Ancient Mariner* and *Christabel*; the days when even women like Dorothy Wordsworth sat entranced while the young man eloquent poured out talk the report of which is immortal. Of that Coleridge one could wish a Sargent or Watts to have left us a portrait, which would have settled, for one thing, whether his eyes were brown, as one observer says, or gray as others declare—though it is by a curious error that even De Quincey attaches to him the famous line of Wordsworth about the "noticeable man with large gray eyes." Then came ill-health and opium. Laudanum by the wineglassful and half-pint at a time soon reduced him to the journalist lecturer and philosopher who projected all things, executed nothing; only the eloquent tongue left. So he perished—the mightiest intellect of his day; and great was the fall thereof. There remain of him his poems, and a quantity of letters painful to read. They show him wordy, full of weak lamentation, deplorably feminine and strengthless.

No other poet, perhaps, except Spenser, has been an initial influence, a generative influence, on so many poets. Having with that mild Elizabethan much affinity, it is natural that he also should be "a poets' poet" in the rarer sense—the sense of fecundating other poets. As with Spenser, it is not that other poets have made him their model, have reproduced essentials of his style (accidents no great poet will consciously perpetuate). The progeny are sufficiently unlike the parent. It is that he has incited the very sprouting in them of the laurel-bough, has been to them a fostering sun of song. Such a primary influence he was to Rossetti—Rossetti, whose model was far more Keats than Coleridge. Such he was to Coventry Patmore, in whose work one might trace many masters rather than Coleridge. "I did not try to imitate his style," said that great singer who has but just passed from us.

I can hardly explain how he influenced me: he was rather an ideal of perfect style than a model to imitate; but in some indescribable way he did influence my development more than any other poet. No poet, indeed, has been senseless enough to imitate the inimitable. One might as well try to paint air as to catch a style so void of all manner that it is visible, like air, only in its results. All other poets have not only a style, but a manner; not only style, but features of style. The style of Coleridge is bare of manner, without feature, not "distinguishable in member, joint, and limb"; it is, in the Roman sense of *merum*, mere style; style unalloyed and integral. Imitation has no foothold; it would tread on glass. Therefore poets, diverse beyond other men in their appreciation of poets, have agreed with a single mind in their estimate of this poet; no artist could refrain his homage to the miracle of such utterance. To the critic has been left the peculiar and purblind shame of finding eccentricity in this speech unflawed. It seems beyond belief; yet we could point to an edition of Coleridge, published during his lifetime, and preceded by a would-be friendly memoir, which justifies our saying: "Be thou as chaste as ice, as pure as snow, thou shalt not escape calumny." The admiring critic complains of Mr. Coleridge's affectations and wilful fantasticalness of style; and he dares to cite as example that wonderfully perfect union of language and metre:

The night is chill, the forest bare;
Is it the wind that moaneth bleak?
There is not wind enough in the air
To move away the ringlet curl
From the lovely lady's cheek—
There is not wind enough to twirl
The one red leaf, the last of its clan,
That dances as often as dance it can,
Hanging so light, and hanging so high,
On the topmost twig that looks up at the sky.

Critics, wrapped in "cock-sureness," to warn, not to discourage you; poets, branded with affectation, to give you heart, not recklessness; we recall the fact that this lovely passage was once thought affected and fantastic. There is not one great poet who has escaped the charge of obscurity, fantasticalness, or affectation of utterance. It was hurled, at the outset of their careers, against Coleridge, Wordsworth, Shelley, Keats, Tennyson, Browning. Wordsworth wrote simple diction, and his simplicity was termed affected; Shelley gorgeous diction, and his gorgeousness was affected; Keats rich diction, and his richness was affected; Tennyson cunning diction, and his cunning was affected; Browning rugged diction, and his ruggedness was affected. Why Coleridge was called affected passes the wit of man, except it be that he did not write like Pope or the elegant Mr. Rogers—or, indeed, that all critical tradition would be outraged if a mere recent poet were not labelled with the epithet made and provided for him by wise critical precedent. If this old shoe were not thrown at the wedding of every poet with the Muse, what would become of our ancient English customs?

But critic and poet, lion and lamb, have now lain down together in their judgment of Coleridge; and abundance of the most excellent appreciation has left no new word about him possible. The critic, it is to be supposed, feels much the same delicacy in praising a live poet as in eulogising a man to his face: when the poet goes out of the room, so to speak, and the door of the tomb closes behind him, the too sensitive critic breathes freely, and finds vent for his suppressed admiration. For the last thirty years criticism has unburdened its suppressed feelings about Coleridge, which it considerately spared him while he was alive; and his position is clear, unquestioned; his reputation beyond the power of wax or wane. Alone of modern poets, his fame sits above the power of fluctuation. Wordsworth has fluctuated; Tennyson stands not exactly as he did; there is reaction in some quarters against the worship of Shelley; though all are agreed Keats is a great poet, not all are agreed as to his place. But around Coleridge the clamour of partisans is silent: none attacks, none has need to defend. *The Ancient Mariner, Christabel, Kubla Khan*, "Genevieve" are recognised as perfectly unique masterpieces of triumphant utterance, and triumphant imagination of a certain kind. They bring down magic to the earth. Shelley has followed it to the skies; but not all can companion him in that rarefied ether and breathe. Coleridge brings it in to us, floods us round with it, makes it native and apprehensible as the air of our own earth. To do so he seeks no remote splendours of language, uses no brazier of fuming imagery. He waves his wand, and the miracle is accomplished before our eyes in the open light of day; he takes words which have had the life used out of them by the common cry of poets, puts them into relation, and they rise up like his own dead mariners, wonderful with a supernatural animation. The poems take the reason prisoner, and the spell is renewed as often as they are read. The only question on which critics differ is the respective places of the two longer poems. *The Ancient Mariner* has the advantage of completion, and its necromancy is performed, so to speak, more in the sight of the reader, with a more absolutely simple diction, and a simpler metre. The apparatus—if we may use such a degrading image—is less. *Christabel* is not only a fragment, but incapable of being anything else. Not even Coleridge, we do believe, could have maintained through the intricacies of plot and in denouement the expectations aroused by the opening. The second part, as has been said, declines its level in portions. Yet, in opposition to the general opinion, we think that a more subtle magic is effected in the first part than in the *Ancient Mariner*—marvellous though that be. *The Ancient Mariner* passes in a region of the supernatural; *Christabel* brings the supernatural into the regions of everyday. Nor can we see, as some critics have seen, any flaw in the success with which this is done. Yet, perhaps, there are a few—chiefly poetic—readers to whom the most unique and enthralling achievement of all is *Kubla Khan*. The words, the music—one and indivisible—come through the gates of dream as never has poem come before or since. This, we believe, might have been completed, so far as a dream is ever completed; that is to say, there might have been more of it. Obviously, the thing has no plot, difficult sustainedly to execute. It is pure lyrism; and the tapestry of shifting vision might unroll indefinitely to the point at which the dream melted. For, unlike many, we have no difficulty in believing Coleridge's account of how the poem arose. We should feel it difficult to believe any other origin. We could no more see a shower without postulating a cloud than we could doubt this poem to have been rained out of dream. If there were a day of judgment against the preventers of poetry, heavy would be the account of that unnamed visitor who interrupted Coleridge in the transcription of his dream-music, and lost to the world for ever the remainder of *Kubla Khan*. In the other world, we trust, this wretched individual will be condemned eternally to go out of ear-shot when the angels prelude on their harps; together with all those who by choice enter concert-rooms during the divinest passage of a symphony.

The minor poems of this great poet are minor indeed. "Youth and Age," "Frost at Midnight," passages of "The Nightingale," and one or two more which might be named, in spite of a real measure of quiet beauty, could never support a great reputation. The "Ode to Dejection" has unquestionably fine passages, but hardly aims at sustained power. The Odes "To France" and "The Departing Year" are terrible bombast, though here again occur fine lines. The fingers of one hand number the poems on which Coleridge's fame is adamantinely based; and they were all written in about two years of his youth. The portrait which accompanies this notice shows the Coleridge of those younger days, with the poet not yet burned out in him; when we are told his face had beauty in the eyes of many women. It is of the later Coleridge that we possess the most luminous descriptions. A slack, shambling man, flabby in face and form and character, redeemed by noble brow and dim yet luminous eyes; womanly and unstayed of nature, torrentuous of golden talk, the poet submerged and feebly struggling in opium-darkened oceans of German philosophy, amid which he finally foundered, striving to the last to fish up gigantic projects from the bottom of a daily half-pint of laudanum. And over that wreck, most piteous and terrible in all our literary history, shines, and will shine for ever, the five-pointed star of his glorious youth; those poor five resplendent poems, for which he paid the devil's price of a desolated life and unthinkably blasted powers. Other poets may have done greater things; none a thing more perfect and un-companioned. Other poets belong to this class or that; he to the class of Samuel Taylor Coleridge.

—Francis Thompson, "Academy Portraits:
XIII. S.T. Coleridge," *Academy*,
Feb. 6, 1897, pp. 179–180

George Brandes
"Naturalistic Romanticism" (1905)

George Brandes holds the opinion that Coleridge intended to treat the fantastic and marvelous in a natural manner, an approach agreed on by Wordsworth and Coleridge before they began the *Lyrical Ballads* and a commitment to which Coleridge remained faithful. In the course of making his argument that Coleridge was predisposed toward this project of rendering the supernatural more real, Brandes provides a brief biographical sketch focused on those unsuccessful moments in his evolving literary career when Coleridge attempted to communicate with literal-minded people. All of these attempts were to no avail until that pivotal year of 1797, when he first made Wordsworth's acquaintance and thus launched his own poetical career, writing his most imaginative and impressive works, *The Ancient Mariner* and *Christabel*, both of which heralded a new epoch in English poetry.

Brandes contends that *Christabel* deserves to be thought of as a poem genuinely "permeated with the Romantic spirit," with its modern cadences and bold new theme, employing a meter that would influence Sir Walter Scott and Byron. Such English critics as Francis Jeffrey, the influential editor of the *Edinburgh Review*, should have been appreciative for what Coleridge contributed to the national literature, but they assailed the work instead of according it the respect it deserved. Most impressive for Brandes is Coleridge's unique handling of the demonic spirit, the peculiar power with which the wicked fairy is presented, as something never done before. Turning his attention to *The Ancient Mariner*, Brandes provides commentary on a German poem, *Der Camao*, which appears to be an imitation of Coleridge's poem. *Der Camao* concerns a revered bird that people of the Middle Ages kept in their homes as a way of insuring a wife's fidelity, for should the obligation be violated, the bird would die from the dishonor done its master. With his allusion, Brandes is referring to the hospitality theme in *The Ancient Mariner*, an issue important in the Middle Ages. Hospitality was considered a moral obligation, and any violations were taken seriously. Hospitality is an important concept encompassing ethical, political, and religious duties inherited from classical and medieval notions. Inasmuch as it partakes of a medieval literary tradition and contains an obvious Christian theme of guilt and expiation, the issue of hospitality arguably has relevance to Coleridge's work. As a core principal of the monastic tradition, the tenets of hospitality were considered crucial to the formation of Christian character both within the religious community and in society in general. Moreover, hospitality was considered part of Christian charity and an important way of fulfilling one's obligations to perform good works. In *The Rime of the Ancient Mariner*, the cruel treatment of the albatross is a clear violation of Christian charity and moral obligations and, thus, the true meaning of hospitality is therefore subverted.

Der Camao is also similar to *The Ancient Mariner* in that it, too, is founded on superstition. Brandes finds *Der Camao* to be the superior of the two poems with respect to its central poetic idea, which serves as an actual critique on Coleridge's ballad. Brandes also makes sure to acknowledge the importance of German intellectual tradition and literature in shaping Coleridge's development. Nevertheless, Brandes declares that *The Ancient Mariner* stands far above similar poems of the German romantic period for it remains firmly planted in the natural world: "The fresh breeze, the seething foam, the horrible fog, and the hot, copper-coloured evening sky with its blood-red sun—all these elements are nature's own; and the misery of the men tossing helplessly on the ocean, . . . —all these elements are realities, represented with English realistic force."

Brandes concludes that Coleridge's poetry is embedded in the natural world in a different way from the other English romantic poets. "It neither expresses strong, personally experienced emotions," Brandes contends, "nor reproduces what the author has observed in the surrounding world." Rather, to the author of the excerpt, Coleridge's work is just as in tune with the natural as a pastoral poem, capturing the beautiful melodies and colors of the external world. Brandes, like all other critics, laments that Coleridge was indolent by nature and wasted his powers through his opium addiction. This failure left him a mere observer of society in his last years, while the next generation of romantic poets was developing its own work independently.

⫷⫸⫷⫸⫷⫸

We have for a moment lost sight of Coleridge. When Wordsworth and he divided the new kinds of poetry between them, there fell to his share, as the reader will remember, a task which was the exact opposite of Wordsworth's, namely, the treating of supernatural subjects in a natural manner. He fulfilled it in his contributions to the volume published under the title of *Lyrical Ballads*, and indeed in the greater proportion of the little collection of poems which entitles him to rank high among English poets.

Samuel Taylor Coleridge was a country boy, the son of a Devonshire clergyman. He was born in October 1772. From 1782 to 1790 he was at school in London. It was during those school-days, spent at Christ's Hospital, that his friendship with another English Romanticist, his warm admirer,

Charles Lamb, was formed. From 1791 to 1793 he studied at Cambridge. He had neither means nor prospects, and in a fit of despair, occasioned either by his debts or by an unhappy love affair, he suddenly enlisted in the 15th Regiment of Light Dragoons, under the name of Silas Titus Cumberback.[1] It certainly does not seem to have been ambition (as in the case of Johannes Ewald a few years earlier) which prompted him to try his fortune as a soldier, but simply want of any other means of subsistence. He was only four months a dragoon. On the stable wall underneath his saddle, he one day scribbled the Latin lament:—

"Eheu quam infortuni miserrimum est fuisse felicem!"

This was discovered by his captain, who inquired into the position of affairs, and arranged with Coleridge's family for his return to Cambridge. On this followed the short period during which the young poet was an anti-orthodox democrat. As such he could expect no advancement in the University. His and Southey's glorification of Robespierre (the first act of *The Fall of Robespierre* was written by Coleridge, the second and third are Southey's) and their wild project of a communistic settlement have been already mentioned. The little emigrant society they founded consisted only of themselves and two other members, a young Quaker named Lovell, and George Burnet, a school friend of Southey's. But the God Hymen had decided that the year 1795 should witness the wreck of the plans which boded so ill for society. In 1795 Coleridge went to lecture at Bristol, where he displayed the eloquence which (as in the case of the similarly eloquent and persuasive Welhaven) seems to have sapped his power of poetic production. A young lady in the town of Bristol won his heart; and before the year was over, Sara Fricker was married to Coleridge, her sisters, Edith and Mary, to Lovell and Southey—and the emigration plan was abandoned. Coleridge, who was without will-power all his life, could never have carried out a plan laid so long beforehand. He never succeeded in doing anything except what he had not determined to do, or what, from its nature, could not be determined beforehand.

In 1796 the young man, who was still an enthusiastic Unitarian, allowed himself to be persuaded by some other philanthropists—he is always "persuaded"—to publish a weekly magazine called *The Watchman*, which was to consist of thirty-two pages, large octavo, and to cost the reasonable price of fourpence. Its flaming prospectus bore the motto, "Knowledge is power." With the object of enlisting subscribers, the young and ardent propagandist undertook a tour of the country between Bristol and Sheffield, preaching in most of the great towns, "as an hireless volunteer, in a blue coat and white waistcoat, that not a rag of the woman of Babylon might be seen on me." The description he has given of this, his Odyssey, shows us the young English Romanticist as he was then and as he continued to be—imprudent in worldly matters, enthusiastic in behalf now of this, now of that religious or political half-truth, yet with a humorous appreciation of his own and others' ridiculousness.

"My campaign commenced at Birmingham; and my first attack was on a rigid Calvinist, a tallow-chandler by trade. He was a tall, dingy man, in whom length was so predominant over breadth that he might almost have been borrowed for a foundry poker. O that face! I have it before me at this moment. The lank, black, twine-like hair, *pinguinitescent*, cut in a straight line along the black stubble of his thin gunpowder eyebrows, that looked like a scorched after-math from a last week's shaving. His coat collar behind in perfect unison, both of colour and lustre, with the coarse yet glib cordage that I suppose he called his hair, and which with a bend inward at the nape of the neck (the only approach to flexure in his whole figure) slunk in behind his waistcoat; while the countenance, lank, dark, very hard, and with strong perpendicular furrows, gave me a dim notion of some one looking at me through a used gridiron, all soot, grease, and iron! But he was one of the thorough-bred, a true lover of liberty, and (I was informed) had proved to the satisfaction of many, that Mr. Pitt was one of the horns of the second beast in the Revelation, *that spoke like a dragon*." For half-an-hour Coleridge employed all the resources of his eloquence—argued, described, promised, prophesied, beginning with the captivity of nations and ending with the millennium. "My taper man of lights listened with perseverance and praiseworthy patience, though (as I was afterwards told on complaining of certain odours that were not altogether ambrosial) it was a melting-day with him. 'And what, sir,' he said, after a short pause, 'might the cost be?' 'Only fourpence, only fourpence, sir, each number, to be published on every eighth day.' 'That comes to a good deal of money at the end of the year. And how much did you say there was to be for the money?' 'Thirty-two pages, sir! large octavo, closely printed.' 'Thirty and two pages? Bless me, why, except what I does in a family way on the Sabbath, that's more than I ever reads, sir! all the year round. I am as great a one as any man in Brummagem, sir! for liberty and truth and all them sort of things, but as to this, no offence, sir, I must beg to be excused.'"

Thus ended Coleridge's first attempt at recruiting for the war against the Holy Trinity. His second he made in Manchester, where he tried to enlist a stately and opulent wholesale dealer in cottons. This man measured him from top to toe, and asked if he had any bill or invoice of the thing. Coleridge presented him with the prospectus. He rapidly skimmed and hummed over the first side, and still more rapidly the second and concluding page, then most deliberately and significantly rubbed and smoothed one part against the other, put it in his pocket, turned his back with an "Overrun with these articles!" and retired into his counting-house.

After these unsuccessful attempts, the young man gave up the plan of canvassing from house to house, but nevertheless returned from this memorable tour with almost a thousand names on his list of subscribers. But, alas! the publication of the very first number was, as any one knowing Coleridge might have expected, delayed beyond the day announced for its appearance; the second, which contained an essay against fast-days, lost him nearly five hundred subscribers at a blow; and the two following numbers, which were full of attacks on French philosophy and morals, and directed against those "who pleaded to the poor and ignorant instead of pleading for them," made enemies of all his Jacobin and democratic patrons. Coleridge, who communicates all these details himself, does not seem to have any suspicion that he was only receiving a natural punishment for his indecision—an indecision which consisted in never being prepared to accept the consequences of his own theories. He was undecided in politics, undecided in religion. Writing, as an old man, of this time, he himself says: "My head was with Spinoza, though my whole heart remained with Paul and John;" and he hastens to provide his readers with those convincing proofs of the existence of God and the Holy Trinity which he had not been capable of perceiving in his youth.[2] After the appearance of about a dozen numbers, *The Watchman* had to be given up, and Coleridge took to writing for the newspapers. He began by attacking Pitt's Government, but in course of time, his opinions tending ever more in a conservative direction, he became its ardent supporter, and also, after the occupation of Switzerland by the French, an enemy of France. So hostile to that country were his articles in the *Morning Post*, that they even attracted the attention of Napoleon, and Coleridge became the object of the First Consul's special enmity. He would probably have been arrested during his residence in Italy, if he had not received timely warning from the Prussian ambassador, Wilhelm von Humboldt, and, through an inferior official, from Napoleon's own uncle, Cardinal Fesch.

The year 1797, in the course of which Coleridge became acquainted with Wordsworth, was, as regards his poetry, the most important in his life; for it was in this year that he wrote his famous ballad, *The Ancient Mariner*, and *Christabel*, the fragment which marks a new era in English poetry.

Christabel was planned as the first of a series of poetical romances, the remainder of which never came into being. It is, without doubt, the first English poem which is permeated by the genuine Romantic spirit; and the new cadences, the new theme, the new style of versification, the novelty generally, made a powerful impression on contemporary poets. The irregular and yet melodious metre appealed so strongly to Scott that he employed it in his first Romantic poem, *The Lay of the Last Minstrel*. He frankly confesses how much he owed to the beautiful and tantalising fragment, *Christabel*, which he, like the other poets of the period, made acquaintance with in manuscript; for Coleridge read it aloud in social gatherings for twenty years before it saw the light as public property. Byron, too, heard it first on one of these occasions. Before hearing it he had, in one of his longer poems (*The Siege of Corinth*, xix.), written some lines which were not unlike some in *Christabel*. To these lines he, on a future occasion, appended a note in which he praises Coleridge's "wild and singularly original and beautiful poem." But we see from Moore's *Life and Letters* that there were critics who refused the meed of admiration accorded to *Christabel* by Scott and Byron, and still more freely by Wordsworth. Jeffrey and Moore himself consider it affected (*Memoirs*, ii. 101; iv. 48). Danish critics, thoroughly initiated into the mysteries of this style by Tieck and the brothers Schlegel, and by their own poet Ingemann, cannot possibly attach so much importance to this fragment. Its excessive naïveté and simplicity, the intentional childishness in style and tone, are to us what buns are to bakers' children. The chief merit of the poem, apart from its full-toned, sweet melody, lies in the peculiar power with which the nature of the wicked fairy is presented to us, the *daemonic* element, which had never been present in such force in English literature before. We must, however, remember that, though the first part of the poem was written in 1797, the second was written and the first revised in 1800—that is to say, *after* Coleridge had travelled with Wordsworth in Germany, and there made acquaintance with contemporary German poetry, its medieval ground-work, and its latest tendency.

Coleridge's one other poem of any length, *The Ancient Mariner*, which is even more artificially naïve in style than *Christabel*, and is provided, in the manner of the medieval ballads retailed in the little shops in back streets, with a prose index of contents on the margin of the pages, is now the most popular of all his poems, although it was fiercely attacked on its first appearance. On a very unnatural introduction (three guests on their way to a wedding are stopped, and one of them is led to forget his destination, so eloquent is the ancient mariner—"and on the street, too," as Falstaff says) follows a story of all the horrors, ghostly and material, which ensue, because one of the sailors on a ship has been thoughtless enough to kill an albatross which had alighted on the rigging. The whole crew, with the exception of this one man, die, as a punishment for the act of inhospitality. Swinburne tells that, when the poem was new, the English critics were greatly occupied with the question whether its moral (that one should not shoot albatrosses) was not so preponderant that it destroyed the fantastic effect of the poem; whilst others maintained that the defect of the poem was its want of a practical moral. Long afterwards the same matter formed the subject of a dispute between Freiligrath and Julian Schmidt. Modern criticism would willingly excuse the absence of any moral in the ballad if it could find a poetic central idea in it.

A comparison may serve to show its chief shortcoming. In a collection of poems by the Austrian lyric poet, Moritz Hartmann, entitled *Zeitlosen*, there is to be found one which, although it does not profess to owe its origin to *The Ancient Mariner*, at first sight strikes the reader as being a direct imitation of it. The metrical form is the same, and in the theme there is a close resemblance. *Der Camao* is the title of the poem. The Camao, which answers to Coleridge's albatross, is a bird which, in the Middle Ages, was kept in every house in the Pyrenean Peninsula, and treated with a reverence which had its source in a widespread superstition. It was believed, namely, that this bird could not thrive in a house on which rested the stain of a wife's infidelity; it died if there was even the slightest spot on the honour of its master. Its beautiful cage generally hung in the entrance chamber. In Hartmann's poem the old, deranged man who answers to Coleridge's demented mariner, tells how he, as a page, was seized with a violent passion for his master's wife, and how, every time he rushed from her presence, in despair at her coldness and displeasure, he was tortured as he left her apartments by the bird's song in honour of the chastity of the lady to whom it owed its life. The master of the house returns from the war bringing with him his friend, a handsome young minstrel and hero, whom the lady honours with her friendship, and who is, in consequence, soon hated by the jealous page. Quite beside himself, the young man denounces the lady and her friend to his master; but the latter calmly answers that Camao is still alive, and at that moment singing in his mistress's honour. In his jealous, vindictive rage the page kills the bird; Vasco kills his wife; and thenceforward the criminal wanders, demented and restless, from country to country, seeking rest, but finding it nowhere.

As regards virtuosity and originality in the matter of diction, *Der Camao* is not for a moment to be compared with *The Ancient Mariner*; but as regards the poetic central idea, the German poem is not only much superior to its English model, but is in itself a complete, satisfactory criticism of Coleridge's ballad and all the artificial English theories which it represents. In *Der Camao* the slaughter of the bird is a real human action performed with a real human motive; the punishment is not a caprice, but a just and natural consequence of the misdeed. The misfortune which the killing of the bird brings to Vasco and his wife has a natural cause and effect connection with that deed, whilst the death of the whole ship's crew, as the result of the cruelty shown to the albatross, is folly. The comparison assists us to a clear understanding of the difference between a true poetical conception of the superstitious idea and a Romantic treatment of it. The story in both poems is founded on a superstition. Hartmann has no desire to submit the superstition to the criticism of reason; but he forces it upon no one; the beauty of his poem is quite independent of the belief or disbelief of his reader in the miraculous susceptibility of the Camao. Romantic extravagance, on the other hand, proclaims reverence for the marvellous and inexplicable to be the sum and substance of all wisdom and of all poetry.

But though *The Ancient Mariner* may not take a high place when compared with poetry which has extricated itself from Romantic swaddling-bands, it stands high above most of the kindred productions of German Romanticism. In spite of all its Romantic fictitiousness, it breathes of the sea, the real, natural sea, whose changing moods and whose terrifying, menacing immensity it describes. The fresh breeze, the seething foam, the horrible fog, and the hot, copper-coloured evening sky with its blood-red sun—all these elements are nature's own; and the misery of the men tossing helplessly on the ocean, the starvation, the burning thirst that drives them to suck the blood from their own arms, the pallid countenances, the terrible death-rattle, the horrible putrefaction—all these elements are realities, represented with English realistic force.

And it is a very English trait that Coleridge himself should have been thoroughly capable of seeing the weak points of such a poem as his own famous ballad. The national quality of humour assisted him to this independence of judgment. We have the following anecdote from his own pen. "An amateur performer in verse expressed a strong desire to be introduced to me, but hesitated in accepting my friend's immediate offer, on the score that he was, he must acknowledge, the author of a confounded severe epigram on my *Ancient Mariner*, which had given me great pain. I assured my friend that if the epigram was a good one, it would only increase my desire to become acquainted with the author, and begged to hear it recited, when, to my no less surprise than amusement, it proved to be one which I had myself inserted in the *Morning Post*." When Coleridge tells us, too, that he himself wrote three sonnets expressly for the purpose of exciting a good-natured laugh at the artificial simplicity and doleful egotism of the new poetical tendency, and that he took the elaborate and swelling language and imagery of these sonnets from his own poems, we cannot deny that his endeavours to keep free from the entanglement in theories which was the weak point in German Romanticism, bespeak rare intellectual superiority.

It was, nevertheless, from Germany that Coleridge's intellect received its most invigorating and essential nourishment. He was the first Englishman who penetrated into the forest of German literature, which was as yet unexplored by foreigners; he made his way into it about the same time as Madame de Staël, the pioneer of the Latin races. Whilst he was producing the famous poems just described, he began the study of German. Schiller and Kant attracted him first. In 1798 he and Wordsworth went to Germany on a literary voyage of discovery. In Hamburg they visited the patriarch Klopstock, who praised Bürger to them, but spoke coldly and disparagingly of the rest of the younger literary men, and especially of Coleridge's idols, Kant and Schiller. The latter's *Die Räuber* he professed himself unable to read. But he had plenty to say on the subject of *The Messiah* and his extreme satisfaction with the English translations of it. While in Germany, Coleridge studied the Gothic language, and read the Meistersingers and Hans Sachs; and on his return he published a translation of Schiller's *Wallenstein*, the play which Benjamin Constant was soon afterwards to adapt for the French stage.

It was about this time that Coleridge settled in the Lake district, where Wordsworth and Southey had already taken up their abode—the district which gave its name to the literary school constituted, as their contemporaries chose to consider, by these three poets. The name, as a matter of fact, does not mean much more than if, in Denmark in 1830, Hauch, Ingemann, Wilster, and Peder Hjort, had been dubbed Sorists. The English poets of the Lake School were quite as unlike each other in their gifts as were these Sorö professors. But the criticism of the day always coupled Coleridge's name with Wordsworth's and Southey's because it was known that he was on intimate and friendly terms with them, because he never missed an opportunity of praising them, nor they of praising him, and because he and the other Lakists were crowned every three months with fresh laurels in the *Quarterly Review*, whilst the sinner Byron was chastised with fresh scorpions. Though Coleridge published almost nothing, Wordsworth and Southey were hardly ever under the cascade of criticism without some drops of it falling upon him. The circumstance that the Lake poets aimed (in much the same manner as the Pre-Raphaelite and the Nazarene painters) at poetic intensity, a childlike disposition and a childlike faith, pious blandness and priestly unction, exposed the man who could not but be regarded as the teacher of the school to much satire and derision. As a youth, in his poem *Fire, Famine, and Slaughter*, Coleridge had made all the horrors, one by one, reply to the question: Who bid you rage? with the following refrain, applying to Pitt:—

"Who bade you do't?
The same! the same!
Letters four do form his name.
He let me loose, and cried Halloo!
To him alone the praise is due."

Now he was Mr. Pitt's journalistic henchman, and, like all the other members of the Lake School, a strict Tory, the enemy of liberal opinions in everything relating to church and state. What wonder that he was classed along with the others in the constant party attacks made by the Liberals! And yet it would have been so easy and so natural to distinguish him as a poet from all the others, and to pay him the honour which was due to his originality. The few poems which he wrote in the course of a comparatively long life are distinguished by the exquisite melodiousness of their language; their harmonies are not only delicate and insinuating like Shelley's, but contrapuntally constructed and rich; they have a peculiar, ponderous sweetness; each line has the taste and weight of a drop of honey. In poems such as *Love* and *Lewti*, which are the two sweetest, and in an Oriental fantasy like *Kubla Khan*, which was inspired by a dream, we hear Coleridge flute and pipe and sing with all the changing cadences of the most exquisite nightingale voice. It is Swinburne who makes the apt remark that, in the matter of harmonies, Shelley is, compared with Coleridge, what a lark is compared with a nightingale.

But Coleridge's poetry is as unplastic as it is melodious, and as unimpassioned as it is mellifluous. It is of the fantastic Romantic order; that is to say, it neither expresses strong, personally experienced emotions, nor reproduces what the author has observed in the surrounding world. In this last connection it is interesting to know that Coleridge's long tour in the south was altogether without results as far as his poetry was concerned. The only poem he brought home with him, the *Hymn Before Sunrise in the Vale of Chamouni*, a valley in which he never set foot, was composed with the assistance of the description of the locality given by the well-known Danish authoress, *Friederike Brun*. His historic sense was as defective as his sense of locality. He says himself: "Dear Sir *Walter Scott* and myself are exact, but harmonious opposites in this—that every old ruin, hill, river, or tree called up in his mind a host of historical or biographical associations .... whereas for myself, I believe I should walk on the plain of Marathon without taking more interest in it than in any other plain of similar features. ... Charles Lamb wrote an essay on a man who lived in past time:—I thought of adding another to it on one who lived not *in time* at all, past, present, or future—but beside or collaterally."[3] His poetry is, thence, in the literal sense of the word, visionary; the poem which the best critics consider the finest, he composed in a dream.

In his own life there was as little of will and plan as in a dream. Somewhat indolent by nature, he became more and more procrastinating as years went on; and the result of his procrastination was an accumulation of difficulties which he had not energy and application enough to overcome. To relieve physical suffering he had recourse to opium, and soon became a confirmed opium-eater, thereby increasing his incapacity to carry out any plan. After a period of wandering, living first in one, then in another friend's house, and either writing for magazines or giving lectures on the history of literature, he decided that he was unfit to manage himself and his affairs, and from 1816 onwards he lived at Highgate in the house and under the control of a doctor named Gillman—separated from his own family, whom he left to the care of his friend and brother-in-law, Southey.

On the indulgence in opium followed remorse and self-reproach and increasingly orthodox piety. Most of what Coleridge now wrote was written with the object of refuting the heresies of his youth and defending the doctrine of the Trinity and the Church of England against all attacks.[4] Emerson, who paid him a visit, describes him as "old and preoccupied"; enraged by the effrontery with which a handful of Priestleians dared to attack the doctrine of the Trinity propounded by Paul and accepted unchallenged for centuries; and falling in his talk into all manner of commonplaces. Eighteen years passed, spent in dreaming, talking, and composing edifying essays. His influence during this period was due much less to his productive power than to the manner in which he incited to production. He stimulated and goaded others to the pitch of expressing themselves publicly. Residing close to London, and constantly visited, because of his conversational powers, by the best writers of the day—Charles Lamb, Wordsworth, Southey, Leigh Hunt, Hazlitt, Carlyle—he was a looker-on on life during the years when the great representatives of the opposite intellectual tendency to his, Shelley and Byron, were pouring forth their fiery denunciations of the order of society and state which he considered so excellent. Without will of his own, under control, and himself protected like a child, Coleridge became ever more and more the would-be protector of society, whilst the two great poets of liberty, banished from their homes and thrown entirely on their own resources, developed an independence unexampled in the history of literature, and, protected neither by themselves nor any one else, were shattered long before their time by the ardour of conflict. The right of personal investigation and personal liberty were as precious treasures to them as the Church of England was to Coleridge.

Notes

1. "Being at a loss, when suddenly asked my name, I answered Cumberback; and verily my habits were so little equestrian, that my horse, I doubt not, was of that opinion."
2. See *Biographia Literaria*.
3. *Specimens of the Table Talk of the Late Samuel T. Coleridge*, ii.225.
4. "On the Constitution of Church and State according to the Ideal of Each"; *Lay Sermons*.

—George Brandes, "Naturalistic Romanticism," from *Naturalism in England*, vol. 6 of *Main Currents in Nineteenth Century Literature*, New York: The Macmillan Company, 1905, pp. 72–84.

LANE COOPER "THE ABYSSINIAN PARADISE IN COLERIDGE AND MILTON" (1906)

In his *Poems of Coleridge*, p. 292, Dr. Garnett annotates the allusion to Abyssinia in *Kubla Khan* as follows:

> L. 40. *Singing of Mount Abora.* There seems to be no mountain of this name in Abyssinia at the present day, though one may be mentioned by some ancient traveler. Whether this be the case, or whether the mountain be Coleridge's invention, the name must be connected with the river Atbara, the Astaboras of the ancients, which rises in Abyssinia and falls into the Nile near Berber. The principal affluent of this river is the Tacazze = *terrible*, so called from the impetuosity of its stream. If Coleridge knew this, an unconscious association with the impetuosity of the river he had been describing may have led to the apparently far-fetched introduction of the Abyssinian maid into a poem of Tartary.

Abora might be a variant spelling, not only of *Atbara*, but of *Amara* in some old itinerary or, say, in one of the seventeenth- and eighteenth-century books that touch on the location of the paradise terrestrial. I have not, however, been able to find the variant in anything that Coleridge read. Presumably he read many both of the earlier and of the later travelers. One of the later, the best authority that he could have for his knowledge of Abyssinia, was James Bruce, whose *Travels to Discover the Sources of the Nile* fell into

Coleridge's hand perhaps as early as 1794.[1] It is barely possible that Coleridge borrowed the book from Southey, for the latter's library in 1844 contained a copy of the Dublin (1790) edition. Bruce, of course, mentions the river *Astaboras* or *Atbara*, as well as Atbara, a peninsula, and *Amhara* (compare *Amara*), a "division of country." He speaks of the *Tacazzu* also, remarking on the contrast between its placidity at one season[2] and its turbulence when swollen with rain:

> But three fathoms it certainly had rolled in its bed; and this prodigious body of water, passing furiously from a high ground in a very deep descent, tearing up rocks and large trees in its course, and forcing down their broken fragments scattered on its stream, with a noise like thunder echoed from a hundred hills, these very naturally suggest an idea, that, from these circumstances, it is very rightly called the *terrible*.[3]

Some of the diction and imagery here reminds one of Coleridge's tumultuous river *Alph*. However, there is in general not enough of the fabulous about Bruce to warrant the supposition that Coleridge is indebted to him for much of *Kubla Khan*, full though that poem be of the spirit of the "old travellers." In any case, I cannot believe that Dr. Garnett has hit upon the "unconscious association" that brought Abyssinia into "a poem of Tartary."

For that matter, I cannot regard "poem of Tartary" as an entirely fitting name for Coleridge's sensuous vision. This might preferably be termed a dream of the terrestrial, or even of the "false," paradise; since, aside from its unworthy, acquiescent admission of demoniac love within so-called "holy" precincts,[4] it reads like an arras of reminiscences from several accounts of natural[5] or enchanted parks, and from various descriptions of that elusive and danger-fraught garden which mystic geographers have studied to locate from Florida to Cathay.[6] Like the Tartar paradise at the beginning of *Kubla Khan* and the bewitched inclosure of the Old Man of the Mountain which seems to appear toward the end,[7] this Abyssinian hill in the middle is simply one of those "sumptuous" retreats whose allurements occupied the imagination of a marvel-hunter like Samuel Purchas. It is certainly not "Coleridge's invention." The Portuguese Alvarez passed by the mountain *Amara* in Abyssinia and was acquainted with the myth concerning it.[8] Incidentally he speaks of a city in that region, called *Abra*, the name of which may in some way be connected with Coleridge's *Abora*.

However, if we do not demand unusual exactitude in the poet's handling of proper names, we need not go far afield to discover his mountain; no farther, in fact, than the volume which he says he was reading before he fell asleep and dreamed his *Kubla Khan*. Purchas has an entire chapter of his *Pilgrimage*, entitled "Of the Hill Amara," in which he has collected the substance of the stories about that fabulous spot. An excerpt or two from him may serve in identification:

> The hill Amara hath alreadie been often mentioned, and nothing indeed in all Ethiopia more deserueth mention. . . . This hill is situate as the nauil of that Ethiopian body, and center of their Empire, vnder the Equinoctiall line, where the Sun may take his best view thereof, as not encountering in all his long iourny with the like Theatre, wherein the Graces & Muses are actors, no place more graced with Natures store, . . . the Sunne himself so in loue with the sight, that the first & last thing he vieweth in all those parts is this hill. . . . Once, Heauen and Earth, Nature and Industrie, have all been corriuals to it, all presenting their best presents, to make it of this so louely presence, some taking this for the place of our Fore-fathers Paradise. And yet though thus admired of others, as a Paradise, it is made a Prison to some [i. e., the princes of Abyssinia], on whom Nature had bestowed the greatest freedome. . . .[9]

This, then, is the *Mount Abora* of which Coleridge (or his slave-girl) sings, a paradise which he is led to compare with that of Tartary by the most intimate of mental associations. It is also the *Mount Amara* of Milton's *Paradise Lost*, occurring in a section of that poem with which I can fancy the author of *Kubla Khan* as especially familiar; in the fourth book, where Milton offers his marvelous description of the authentic paradise terrestrial, distinguishing it carefully from sundry false claimants:

> Nor, where Abassin kings their issue guard,
> Mount Amara (though this by some supposed
> True Paradise) under the Ethiop line
> By Nilus' head, enclosed with shining rock
> A whole day's journey high, but wide remote
> From this Assyrian garden. . . .[10]

When the industrious Todd[11] pointed out a connection between these lines and Purchas' chapter on Mount Amara, quoting the passage given below from the *Pilgrimage*, he failed to note that later on in the fourth book Milton had, in spite of his distinction, to all appearances levied on Purchas' description of the false Abyssinian garden for embellishment of the true "Assyrian." Purchas goes on with the account of his "hill."

It is situate in a great Plaine largely extending it selfe every way, without other hill in the same for the space of 30. leagues, the forme thereof round and circular, the height such, that it is a daies worke to ascend from the foot to the top; round about, the rock is cut so smooth and euen, without any vnequall swellings, that it seemeth to him that stands beneath, like a high wall, whereon the Heauen is as it were propped and at the top it is over-hanged with rocks, iutting forth of the sides the space of a mile, bearing out like mushromes, so that it is impossible to ascend it. . . . It is above twenty leagues in circuit compassed with a wall on the top, well wrought, that neither man nor beast in chase may fall downe. The top is a plaine field, onely toward the South is a rising hill, beautifying this plaine, as it were with a watch-tower, not seruing alone to the eye, but yeelding also a pleasant spring which passeth through all that Plaine . . . and making a Lake, whence issueth a River, which hauing from these tops espied Nilus, never leaves seeking to find him, whom he cannot leave both to seeke and finde. . . . The way vp to it is cut out within the Rocke, not with staires, but ascending by little and little, that one may ride vp with ease; it hath also holes cut to let in light, and at the foote of this ascending place, a faire gate, with a *Corpus du Guarde*. Halfe way vp is a faire and spacious Hall cut out of the same rocke, with three windowes very large upwards: the ascent is about the length of a lance and a halfe: and at the top is a gate with another gard. . . . There are no Cities on the top, but palaces, standing by themselves, in number four and thirtie, spacious, sumptuous, and beautifull, where the Princes of the Royall bloud have their abode with their Families. The Souldiers that gard the place dwell in Tents.[12]

This sunlit and symmetrical hill, with its miracle of inner carven passages, may partially explain Coleridge's "sunny dome" and "caves of ice" (why of *ice*?) which must have puzzled more than one reader in *Kubla Khan*. The preceding lines from Milton should also be compared, and, as I have hinted, the following as well:

. . . the setting Sun
Slowly descended, and with right aspect
Against the eastern gate of Paradise
Levelled his evening rays. It was a rock
Of alabaster, piled up to the clouds,
Conspicuous far, winding with one ascent

Accessible from Earth, one entrance high;
The rest was craggy cliff, that overhung
Still as it rose, impossible to climb.
Betwixt these rocky pillars Gabriel sat,
Chief of the angelic guards. . . . [13]

There are, it is true, too many points of similarity in the various paradises
of The Fathers and geographers to permit the critic to say with great assurance
that Milton or Coleridge borrowed this or that embellishment of his mystical
inclosure from any one prior writer. We are dealing here, I presume, with
a world-old effort of imagination showing certain reappearing essentials
of an inherited conception, such as a fountain with outflowing "sinuous
rills," a symmetrical mountain, a disappearing "sacred river," all within a
wall of measured circuit, and the like, the chief of which may be found in
a poem of small compass like *Kubla Khan*[14]—probably all of them in the
fourth book of *Paradise Lost*. In how far Milton may be indebted to Purchas'
compendium for all sorts of quasi-geographical lore, in addition to the slight
obligations already indicated, is a question lying rather in the province of the
professed student of Milton. For the present writer, whose interest here is
more particularly in Coleridge, it seems enough to point out the relationship
between Coleridge's beautiful fragment and Milton's completed masterpiece;
to indicate, in passing, Milton's greater distinctness and mastery in handling
his material; finally, to suggest, on the basis of this brief paper, that, instead of
continuing to treat *Kubla Khan* as a sort of incomparable *hapax legomenon*,
wholly unexplainable, because incomparable, we shall understand it and
its author better if we seek to trace the subtle, yet no less real, connection
between them and the literature to which they belong. Specifically, let the
reader of Coleridge be also a reader of Coleridge's master, Milton, and the
lover of *Kubla Khan* a lover also of that "pleasant soil" in which "his far more
pleasant garden God ordained."[15]

Notes

1. *Coleridge's Poems: Facsimile Reproduction*, p. 173.
2. Edinburgh edition (1790), Vol. III, p. 157.
3. Edinburgh edition (1790), Vol. III, p. 158.
4. A savage place! as holy and enchanted
    As e'er beneath a waning moon was haunted
    By woman wailing for her demon-lover!
                    —*Kubla Khan*, ll. 14–16
5. For example, Bartram's descriptions of Georgia and Florida in his *Travels*,
    etc. (Philadelphia, 1791).

6. See the authorities cited in Pierre Daniel Huet's *La situation du paradis terrestre* (Paris, 1711).

7. Compare *Purchas his Pilgrimage* (1617), p. 428.

8. See his account (chap. 54) in Ramusio.

9. Purchas (1617), p. 843.

10. *Paradise Lost*, Book IV, ll. 280–86.

11. *Milton's Poetical Works*, ed. Todd (1809), Vol. III, pp. 101, 108.

12. Purchas (1617), p. 844.

13. *Paradise Lost*, Book IV, ll. 540–49.

14. Compare, for example, Coleridge's "mighty fountain," "sinuous rills," and "meandering" river with the following, quoted by Todd: "In ipso hortorum apice *fons* est eximius, qui primam argenteis aquarum vorticibus ebulliens, mox diffusus in fluvium sinuosis flexibus, atque maeandris concisus oberrat, et felicia arva perennibus foecundat rivulis."—P. Causinus, *de Eloq.*, lib. XI., edit. 1634 (Todd, *Milton's Poetical Works* [1809], Vol. III, pp. 95, 96). Cf. Milton, *Paradise Lost*, Book IV, ll. 223 ff., and the first part of *Kubla Khan*.

15. *Paradise Lost*, Book IV, l. 215.

—Lane Cooper, "The Abyssinian Paradise
in Coleridge and Milton," *Modern Philology*,
vol. 3, no. 3, January 1906, pp. 327–332

W.J. Dawson "Coleridge" (1906)

W.J. Dawson's essay expresses great appreciation of Coleridge. From the start, Dawson's purpose is clear, namely to present Coleridge in the best possible light. This he does by highlighting only those aspects of the poet's life that support the argument that Coleridge was never meant to be a part of the everyday world of commerce and financial concerns. As further evidence of Coleridge's special status, Dawson mentions that, even in his earliest days at Christ's Hospital, Coleridge exuded a "romantic charm" that set him apart from his contemporaries. Having established Coleridge as a lifelong idealist who rejected offers of employment as a journalist in order to remain devoted to literary and philosophical concerns, Dawson respects him as a man of sincerity and courage, the latter quality being one characteristic that other critics fail to recognize. Dawson views Coleridge as a poet who lived in pure imagination, citing the virtues of *Christabel, The Ancient Mariner,* and "Kubla Khan," and argues that *The Friend* and *Biographia Literaria* contain elements of wisdom. While Dawson admits that Coleridge's opium addiction was a tragic flaw, he nevertheless states that all his great poetry was produced prior to his addiction, thus responding to those critics who claim the drug enhanced his poetic imagination. Nevertheless, Dawson sees Coleridge's greatest achievement, despite all his fine written works, to be his eloquence and laments that there are scarcely any examples of this. Dawson's only regret is that Coleridge chose to be a metaphysician more often than a poet.

If the greatness of a man could be measured by the estimate of his contemporaries, there is no man who loomed before his age with a larger majesty of outline than Coleridge. Wordsworth described him as the most wonderful man he had ever known; De Quincey, as the man of most spacious intellect; Hazlitt, as the one man who completely fulfilled his idea of genius. Carlyle's striking description of Coleridge in his last days is likely to become as immortal as Lamb's description of "the inspired charity-schoolboy," who filled him with wonder and astonishment, when he wrote, "Come back into memory like as thou wert in the dayspring of thy fancies, with hope like a fiery column before thee—the dark pillar not yet turned,—Samuel Taylor Coleridge, logician, metaphysician, bard!" Rarely has a man of genius received such a perfect consensus of admiration from his contemporaries as Coleridge. There was, indeed, about him something of that "ocean-mindedness" which he finely attributes to Shakespeare; and, apart from the fascination of his eloquence, and the spell of an alluring individuality, what most impressed all who knew Coleridge was the comprehensiveness of his vision, and the profundity of his thought.

The noble friendship which existed between Lamb and Coleridge, and the less intimate but equally beautiful intimacy of Coleridge with Southey and Wordsworth, are among the brightest chapters of literary history. Coleridge first met Lamb at Christ's Hospital, and the schoolboy friendship then formed lasted a lifetime. His acquaintance with Wordsworth and Southey came later, and sprang rather out of literary comradeship than spiritual fellowship. In one essential respect Coleridge differed entirely from his great contemporaries. From first to last there was a certain romantic charm about his character. He was an idealist of the purest type, and never seemed at home in the rough commerce of the world. Lamb humbly submitted himself to the yoke of drudgery, and made his literary work the luxury and solace of a life of uncomplaining suffering heroically borne. He once jokingly remarked that his real "works" were to be found in the ponderous ledgers of the East India Office, and there is something to us infinitely pathetic in the spectacle of so rare a spirit as Lamb's chained to the galley-oar of lifelong toil in a London office. Wordsworth, with all his real and noble unworldliness, had a certain shrewdness of character; which served him well in the ultimate disposition of his life. Southey, when once the fervour of youth, with its unconsidered hopes and unfulfilled ambitions, settled down, became one of the most industrious of men, toiling with a pertinacious energy in every walk of literature, and often in ways that gave little scope for the exercise of his true literary gift. But Coleridge ended as he began, an idealist, careless of worldly fame, and unable to master the merest rudiments of worldly success. He had none of that natural discernment which takes a correct measurement of life, and none of that natural pride which preserves men from the insolence and imposition of the men of this world who have their portion in this life. When he left Christ's he actually asked to be apprenticed to a shoemaker; and later on, when he left Cambridge, he enlisted as a soldier. With an unlimited faith in human nature, a curious childlikeness of spirit, an imagination that clothed at will the most prosaic prospects with alluring brilliance, he found himself in the great streets of the crowded world, as virtually a stranger to the common order of human life as though he had been born upon another planet. He walked in a world of dreams, and never bartered them for the sordid grossness of reality. If we can imagine some angelic child, or some simple shepherd of Grecian myth and poetry, suddenly set down in the "central roar" of London, ignorant of every custom of the complex civilization of to-day, and heedless of its forces, we have a tolerably accurate picture of Coleridge, as he stepped into the whirl of the million-peopled life of ordinary men. He had every sense save common sense, every faculty save the faculty of worldly shrewdness. He was like some splendid galleon, laden with a precious argosy, from whose decks there rose the unearthly melodies of singing-men and singing-women, and harpers harping with their harps, but at whose helm no one stood, to whose course upon the widening waters none paid heed. He never learned to adjust himself to his environment. He drew from his lofty idealism a mystic joy, which seemed ample compensation for the loss of worldly honour, and ignorance of the paths of worldly victory. Had the days of patronage still existed, Coleridge was precisely the poet who would have gained most from the protection they afforded against the rude buffetings of an unsympathetic world. When he left Cambridge, he was thrown upon the world, with genius indeed, with intellectual riches incomparable and unique, with infinite literary enthusiasm and aptitude, but with none of those equipments which enable lesser men of all grades to secure advancement and success in life.

To yoke the idealist to the tasks of common life is a difficult and almost impossible task, and the worldly failure of Coleridge's life is mainly attributable to this cause. It is only fair, however, to remember that in his early career at least Coleridge did what in him lay to harness his genius to the lowliest literary labours. He sought drudgery as though he loved it, and never complained of its degradations or penurious rewards. A dreamer of dreams he might be, but a selfish idler he was not. He never lost a chance of work; the fact is, he seldom had a chance. And yet this statement needs modification, for while it is true that he eagerly seized on every opportunity of casual literary employment, when the one great opportunity of competence in journalism came to him he at once refused it. At the age of twenty-eight an offer was made to him of half-shares in the *Courier* and *Post*, on condition that he devoted himself entirely to these journals. To most young men this would have been a sufficiently brilliant offer, for it meant not less than £2,000 per annum. Coleridge rejected it, and has given us his reasons for rejecting it. He would not give up the country for the town, he would not spend the strength of his brains on journalism, and, moreover, he avowed his opinion that any income beyond £350 per annum was a real evil, and one which he dared not incur. Yet at this period he was able to make only a modest income from journalism, and whatever mere worldly prudence may suggest, there is surely something very noble in Coleridge's refusal of a munificent income which, according to his view of things, entailed wealth which he did not desire, at the sacrifice of higher aims which he could not renounce. Long afterwards, in the troubled close of life, he said that poetry had been for him its "own exceeding great reward." And we cannot doubt that Coleridge chose wisely, with a just and perfect apprehension of his own powers, when he renounced journalism for literature. It was the same temptation which in later days was presented to Carlyle, and was refused with the same noble promptitude and decision. To both men ephemeral and anonymous success, attended by whatsoever munificence of present reward, seemed odious, compared with the more remote and uncertain gain of literary fame. So each turned calmly to the steep ways of renunciation in which genius has always found its training, and prepared to do the one thing which he was born to do. This action of Coleridge's is significant of the sincerity of his nature, and reveals to us a strength of manly fibre and courage not usually associated with his name.

The cardinal defect in Coleridge's life was in one accursed habit—opium-taking. The first half of his life is without flaw or serious blemish. He is poor, but noble thoughts console him, noble work enchants him, and true love sweetens all his lot, and casts above his hours of drudgery its rainbow bridge of hope. Coleridge had great animal spirits, unfailing buoyancy, and even "unusual physical energy." He was amiable to a fault, and, indeed, his one cardinal fault of irresolution sprang from the sensitive tenderness of his nature. At twenty-one he had "done the day's work of a giant"; he had won reputation, he had fought the world at great odds, and not altogether unsuccessfully. Then all changes, and what Lamb pathetically calls the "dark pillar" begins to cast its gloom on Coleridge, and the brightness of the fiery column of hope begins slowly to revolve, and pass away. Coleridge's first taking of opium was accidental. He was recommended to take for his rheumatic pains—the Keswick Black Drop. It acted like the distillation of an alchemist; instantly his pain fled as by magic. In a few weeks the habit had become a despotism; in six months Coleridge was a shattered man. He was degraded, and he knew it: his power of free-will was paralyzed. From that moment the life of Coleridge becomes a tragedy. His power of thought was broken, his strength for toil impaired, his joy in life poisoned, his domestic peace shattered: his old bright buoyancy departed, leaving only unutterable despair, the agony of impotence, the spasmodic struggles of a will that knows itself infirm, and which after each attempt at freedom sinks lower in its corrupting bondage.

There is good reason for thinking that in the end Coleridge broke his bondage, but it was not till the treasuries of domestic love were closed to him, and he had lost power to open those further doors of the treasuries of wisdom to which his youthful genius had led him. It has indeed been stupidly alleged that the habit of opium-taking gave fineness and ethereal brilliancy to the poetry of Coleridge, but this is wholly false. The noblest work of Coleridge was done before he acquired the fatal habit. From that moment the fountain of his genius became intermittent in flow, and deficient in quality. No one knew it, no one felt it, more keenly than he. Years after, when he again met Wordsworth in the zenith of his powers, and thought of his own lost opportunities, he wrote those pathetic lines in which we seem to hear the sighings of a breaking heart:

> O great Bard!
> Ere yet that last strain dying awed the air,
> With steadfast eye I viewed thee in the choir
> Of ever-enduring men.
> Ah! as I listened with a heart forlorn,
> The pulses of my being beat anew!

Of De Quincey's famous *Confessions* he says: "Oh, may the God to whom I look for mercy through Christ, show mercy on the author of *The Confessions of an Opium-eater* if, as I have too strong reason to believe, his book has been the occasion of seducing others into the withering vice through wantonness. From this aggravation I have, I humbly trust, been free. Even to the author of that work I pleaded with flowing tears, and with an agony of forewarning."

There is no mistaking the meaning of these pathetic words. If the later life of Coleridge stands out in painful contrast to the earlier; if it appear desultory, aimless, brilliant only with an intermittent splendour, the fiery pillar only at rare intervals turning its Divine radiance towards him, there is one explanation for it all—sad, tragic, and sufficient—"the accursed drug."

What of the works of Coleridge? It may be said briefly that it is upon his poetry that the fame of Coleridge is built. His *Friend* is full of the ripest wisdom; his *Biographia Literaria* of isolated passages of great beauty; his lectures on Shakespeare have long held their place as masterpieces of critical insight; but it is, after all, by his poetry that future generations will know him. *The Ancient Mariner* and *Christabel* stand alone in English literature. Coleridge has an extraordinary power of interpreting the supernatural, the night-side of Nature, that weird, subtle, spiritual undercurrent of life which invests with mysterious significance this hard outer world. In doing this he has done superbly what no other has attempted with more than partial success. He possesses force of imagination and felicity of epithet, and each in an extraordinary degree. His words are music, and his power of producing on the ear the effect of fine music merely by the assonance of words is unrivalled. No great poet has written less, but the best of what he has written is so perfect of its kind that there can be no mistaking the superscription of immortality with which it is stamped.

The real wealth of Coleridge's mind, however, was poured out in his conversations, and of these we have but scanty examples. Yet these are enough to indicate that the man was greater than anything he achieved. Coleridge's conversation was an overpowering stream, wise, witty, profound, embracing all subjects, astonishing all hearers. He once asked Lamb if he had ever heard him preach. "I have never heard you do anything else," said Lamb. It was a perfectly just description of Coleridge's conversations. Any subject gave him a text, and, once started, he would maintain for hours a sort of inspired monologue, often mystical, occasionally incomprehensible, but always most impressively eloquent. He needed a Boswell, and no man since Johnson would have so well repaid the assiduity of that prince of eavesdroppers. The few specimens of table-talk which are ours are not less marked by their incisiveness than by their luminous and sorrowful wisdom. In all Coleridge's later utterances the accent of suffering is very pronounced. We feel that, like Dante, he is "a man who has been in hell." He inspires in us a tenderness and sympathy which arrest judgment, and hush the voice of censure, for which there was but too much ground of justification. It is impossible to think of Coleridge without a mingled sense of pity and affection, and we may say of him, as Mrs. Browning said of Napoleon, but with greater truth

I do not praise him: but since he had
The genius to be loved, why let him have
The justice to be honoured in his grave.

He himself has appealed yet more effectually to our sympathy in his own pathetic epitaph:

Stop, Christian passer-by; stop, child of God,
And read with gentle breast. Beneath this sod
A poet lies, or that which once seemed he.
O lift one thought in prayer for S. T. C.,
That he who many a year with toil of breath
Found death in life, may here find life in death,
Mercy for praise,—to be forgiven for fame,—
He asked and hoped through Christ. Do thou the same.

The faults of Coleridge's style are its occasional turgidity and diffuseness. This, however, is most apparent in his political poems, and is probably attributable to the fact that Coleridge found the theme uncongenial. It was in the world of pure imagination he was most at home, and it was there he attained his highest literary excellence. In delicate and airy fancy, not less than in imaginative intensity, he has few rivals. Such a poem as *Kubla Khan*,—a mere dream within a dream, may illustrate the one, and the *Ancient Mariner* the other. His force as a thinker and metaphysician is a waning force, but his poetic fame has never stood so high as now. This result was accurately perceived immediately on his death by the review that had persistently ridiculed him for many years when it wrote: "Coleridge, of all men who ever lived, was always a poet,—in all his moods, and they were many, inspired." It is so the best poems of Coleridge still impress us, and when the logician and the metaphysician weary us, we turn with ever fresh delight to the bard. The pity of it is that Coleridge was so seldom the bard, and so often the metaphysician; for who would not give all the prose writings of Coleridge for another twenty pages of poetry like the *Ancient Mariner*?

—W.J. Dawson, "Coleridge," from
The Makers of English Poetry, 1906, pp. 80–89

Lane Cooper "The 'Forest Hermit' in Coleridge and Wordsworth" (1909)

The romantic imagination, we are to understand, lays emphasis upon the part as against the whole; upon the poetic detail as against the large and unified poetical conception; upon the individual element in poetry—so Aristotle might put it—as against the universal; upon the individual man also as against the state in and for itself. Hence, in a measure, arises the phenomenon of the beautiful fragment, like *Christabel* or *Kubla Khan*, which its author is powerless to finish; for want of a dominant architectonic idea, for want of an original and compelling unity, he is unable to subordinate each separate phrase, each accretion of images, to the inexorable evolution of a complete and harmonious masterpiece. Hence also, if we may make such a leap, comes in part the romantic idealization of the solitary, the anchoret, the recluse; of the individual who withdraws from the social organism and tries to exist alone and for himself.

His retreat, of course, must be voluntary. If it is forced, or forcibly prolonged, he will shortly be heard lamenting with Cowper's Selkirk:

O Solitude! where are the charms
That sages have seen in thy face?

And even if it be altogether of his own volition, he can by no means deny himself the social joy of telling others about his preference. Thus in a dozen places De Quincey reveals the secret of his carefully nourished "passion" for solitude. His passion, of course, represents a mood that every one feels now and then. But undoubtedly the air was surcharged with the mood after the time of that natural man Rousseau. Even Charles Lamb, most affable and accessible of mortals, confesses to a like "passion," though his confession has the faintest aroma of literary inheritance. The mood was a part of the literary bequest from a generation preceding.

Undoubtedly, too, there is an element here of revived medievalism. The romantic solitary carries about him some reminder of the cloister or the staff and scrip. In any case, retire or wander as far as he will, he can never quite succeed in being a creature sundered from the generality, for after all there are many like him; and in spite of his cry, "I am myself, myself alone!" if we drag him and his nearest neighbor from their respective mossy cells, the sunlight may disclose similarities between them amounting to the fixed characteristics of a type.

In reading *The Rime of the Ancient Mariner*, the present writer long imagined that the Hermit who appears in Part VI to shrive the hero had an original in some real personage. And this may still be true. The moment the Mariner reaches shore, he enters a landscape, along the Somerset coast of the Severn Sea, with which Coleridge and his erstwhile collaborator, Wordsworth, were thoroughly familiar; it may be that somewhere in their ramblings among the Quantock Hills one or both of the poets had seen a recluse corresponding, after a fashion, to the Hermit of the Wood. At the same time, this Hermit has such first-class literary antecedents, and such clear and occasionally artificial parallels in Wordsworth and Coleridge themselves, as to shake one's belief that either poet necessarily had "his eye on the object" when the holy man of the *Rime* was taking shape. The hermits in English literature are numerous. It might be interesting to compare this one with a Spenserian character whom he greatly resembles (albeit the latter is a pious fraud); for it will be recalled that both Coleridge and Wordsworth were eagerly reading Spenser in Quantockian days. First, however, it may be well to compare him and his habitat with other hermits as conceived by the two modern poets; since, whatever his origin, he is without doubt a stereotyped figure in both, and for Wordsworth a stock poetical resource, not unlike several of the pseudo-classic devices which Wordsworth eschewed.

Save for a traditional slip in the printing,[1] the description of the "forest Hermit" in the final text of the *Ancient Mariner* (lines 508–541, 560–563, 570–577) is substantially the same as that first given in the *Lyrical Ballads* of 1798. Coleridge had indeed introduced a touch of something similar in a poem which Dykes Campbell assigns to the year 1793, entitled *Lines to a Beautiful Spring in a Village*:

> Nor thine unseen in cavern depths to dwell,
> The Hermit-fountain of some dripping cell![2]

—where the context savors of an influence from Virgil or even Theocritus. And it is believed that he had in mind the same scene as that just cited from the *Ancient Mariner*, when he put together certain lines in a "ballad-tale" for which Wordsworth gave him the subject in 1797, *The Three Graves*:

> 'Tis sweet to hear a brook, 'tis sweet
>   To hear the Sabbath-bell,
>   Deep in a woody dell.
>
> His limbs along the moss, his head
>   Upon a mossy heap,
> With shut-up senses, Edward lay
> That brook e'en on a working day
>   Might chatter one to sleep.[3]

Again, we may not be far from the holy Hermit's cushion plump, when we are taken in the midnight wood to watch Christabel praying under the traditional mossy oak

The sighs she heaved were soft and low,
And nought was green upon the oak
But moss and rarest mistletoe
She kneels beneath the huge oak tree,
And in silence prayeth she.[4]

Finally, there is a direct reference to the traditional hermit, with a general reminiscence of his sylvan dwelling, in Coleridge's *Mad Monk*, a poem written about three years after the *Ancient Mariner*, and like the *Lines to a Beautiful Spring in a Village*, indebted to a bucolic source in the classics. The familiar oak has changed to a tree of equally good literary parentage, the Sicilian chestnut:

I heard a voice from Etna's side;
    Where o'er a cavern's mouth
    That fronted to the south
A chestnut spread its umbrage wide
A hermit or a monk the man might be;
    But him I could not see
And thus the music flow'd along,
In melody most like to old Sicilian song

"There was a time when earth, and sea, and skies,
    The bright green vale, and forest's dark recess,
With all things, lay before mine eyes
    In steady loveliness:
But now I feel, on earth's uneasy scene,
    Such sorrows as will never cease;—
    I only ask for peace;
If I must live to know that such a time has been!"

The rest is not now to the point. The tale closes abruptly, with a hint of the hermit's customary environment:

Here ceased the voice. In deep dismay,
Down through the forest I pursu'd my way.[5]

So much for sylvan hermits in Coleridge; now for a few in Wordsworth. The first that we come upon in the latter poet is scarcely typical—he is a man with a family; but he is fairly artificial. He dwells on the border of Lake Como, where Wordsworth with careful circumstantiality pictures him in the *Descriptive Sketches* of 1793:

Once did I pierce to where a cabin stood,
The red-breast peace had bury'd it in wood,
There, by the door a hoary-headed sire
Touch'd with his wither'd hand an aged lyre;
Beneath an old-grey oak as violets lie,
Stretch'd at his feet with stedfast, upward eye,
His children's children join'd the holy sound,
A hermit—with his family around.[6]

Whatever reality lay beneath this description, the artificial side of it becomes apparent the instant we examine Wordsworth's subsequent revision. For example, the Popian lyre gives place to a "rude viol," which may or may not have been a real element in the original "delicious scene":

But once I pierced the mazes of a wood
In which a cabin undeserted stood;
There an old man an olden measure scanned
On a rude viol touched with withered hand.
As lambs or fawns in April clustering lie
Under a hoary oak's thin canopy,
Stretched at his feet, with stedfast upward eye,
His children's children listened to the sound;
—A Hermit with his family around.[7]

However, so far as I have observed, the typical Hermit of the Wood does not appear in Wordsworth until after his emancipation from the general artificiality of *Descriptive Sketches*, or until his alliance with Coleridge in *Lyrical Ballads*. We have noted the type in the first of the *Ballads*, that is, in the *Ancient Mariner*; we may note it also in the poem with which the collection closes—in *Tintern Abbey*. Revisiting the sylvan Wye, the devotee of nature glances over a pastoral landscape, descrying here and there

wreaths of smoke
Sent up, in silence, from among the trees!
With some uncertain notice, as might seem,
Of vagrant dwellers in the houseless woods,
Or of some Hermit's cave, where by his fire
The Hermit sits alone.[8]

Here, one might fancy, is the identical holy man of the *Ancient Mariner*, dwelling, not along the sylvan Wye, but somewhere among the Quantock Hills, and transferred for the nonce to the neighborhood of Tintern Abbey.

And in the following description one might be tempted to find the same holy man's woodland chapel; for the "sheltering cove" or recess in the mountains is almost certainly in the vicinity of Alfoxden or Nether Stowey:

> A spot where, in a sheltering cove
> A little chapel stands alone.
> With greenest ivy overgrown,
> And tufted with an ivy grove.[9]

—only this happens to be the chapel of Wordsworth's fervent Methodist in *Peter Dell*. Very likely it may be identified with the woodland chapel in *The Three Graves*.

Is there, then, no hermit in *Peter Bell?* Wordsworth himself seems to expect one. Having conducted his hero to a suitable glade in the very heart of the woods, he inquires:

> And is there no one dwelling here,
> No hermit with his beads and glass?[10]

No, there is no hermit; none, at least, in the ordinary sense. The sole inhabitant of this deep and quiet spot is—

> A solitary Ass.

Peter himself is surprised. It was just the place for a real, *human* eremite. Wordsworth's query supplies one of the many points of contact between his poem and the *Ancient Mariner;* for *Peter Bell* is the ballad of the supernatural which Wordsworth was constrained to write when he found himself unable to proceed conjointly with Coleridge in making the *Rime.*

Still other poems of Wordsworth describe this character in terms that remind us of Coleridge. In both poets, of course, the really curious thing about these holy men is the fact that they always dwell in the woods. They do not perch on pillars; they are not enamored of the heath or the sandy waste. They are lovers of shade, of ivy, moss, and oak. They are amateurs in the contemplation of foliage. Thus the confessor of the *Ancient Mariner* likens those sails, so thin and sere, to

> Brown skeletons of leaves that lag
> My forest-brook along;

and thus Wordsworth, rebelling against the complicated life of London, observes that

> living men
> Are ofttimes to their fellow-men no more

Than to the forest Hermit are the leaves
That hang aloft in myriads.[11]

These lines were written in the year 1800. No especial connection is to be traced between the thought in them and that in the familiar sonnet commencing:

Nuns fret not at their convent's narrow room;
And hermits are contented with their cells;[12]

—the date of which has not been ascertained. Nor does it seem possible to establish any precise relation between the *Inscriptions supposed to be found in and near a Hermit's Cell* (five of them composed in 1818) and the earlier material that we have been studying. The lines, again, *For the Spot where the Hermitage stood on St. Herbert's Island, Derwentwater*, which belong to the earlier, Grasmere period, are contemporary with the *Recluse*; yet their atmosphere does not seem closely allied to that of the *Recluse* or *Tintern Abbey*. St. Herbert is interesting because he gives a local habitation and a name to one of Wordsworth's hermits, and because Wordsworth knew something of his history. But as yet I see no ground for imagining that either he or any other particular recluse of the middle ages underlies the general conception in Wordsworth and Coleridge. St. Herbert, for example, was not a forest type; he lived on an island.

The holy men of the type here examined appear in Coleridge and Wordsworth chiefly in poems written between 1797 and 1804. A final example, representing the latter date, might be taken from the *Prelude*, where Wordsworth is relating his experiences in France during the year 1792, when he walked along the Loire in company with Beaupuy:

From earliest dialogues I slipped in thought,
And let remembrance steal to other times,
When, o'er those interwoven roots, moss-clad,
And smooth as marble or a waveless sea,
Some Hermit, from his cell forth-strayed, might pace
In sylvan meditation undisturbed.[13]

All these passages would gain in significance, if we set beside them several stanzas from Spenser, a few well-known lines from Milton, and a quotation from some eighteenth-century poet—say Parnell. The hermit of the nineteenth-century romantic poets is necessarily in large part the creature of tradition. How much of him is an inheritance, and how much is due to the originality of Wordsworth and Coleridge, may be learned as well, perhaps, by a brief as by an extended comparison. I would call particular attention to the similarity between the first two stanzas in Part VII of the *Ancient Mariner* and the following stanza from the *Faerie Queene*:

> A litle lowly Hermitage it was,
> Down in a dale, hard by a forests side,
> Far from resort of people that did pas
> In traveill to and froe: a litle wide
> There was an holy chappell edifyde,
> Wherein the Hermite dewly wont to say
> His holy thinges each morne and eventyde
> Thereby a christall streame did gently play,
> Which from a sacred fountaine welled forth alway.[14]

Were there space, two passages from Milton might be added: *Il Penseroso*, 167–172, *Comus*, 385–992. There are reminiscences from both in Wordsworth's *Ecclesiastical Sonnets* XXIi, XXII.

We may close our list with the first six lines of Parnell's *Hermit*, in many ways a fair example of what Wordsworth is supposed to have disliked in the age of Pope:

> Far in a wild, unknown to public view,
> From youth to age a reverend hermit grew;
> The moss his bed, his drink the crystal well
> Remote from man, with God he pass'd the
> Prayer all his business, all his pleasure praise.[15]

Here is artificiality with a vengeance. Yet, after all, is not the type in Wordsworth almost as conventional?

Notes

1. This slip is worth noting. In most of the recent versions, including the standard text of Dykes Campbell, lines 529–530 of the *Ancient Mariner* are made to run:

   > The planks looked warped! and see those sails,
   > How thin they are and sere!

   Aside from the impossible past tense, *looked warped* is an odd bit of cacophony to foist upon the author of *Christabel*; it is about as melodious as the celebrated elegiac line composed—says De Quincey—by Coleridge's old pedagogue, Jemmy Boyer:

   > 'Twas thou that smooth'd'st the rough-rugg'd bed of pain.

2. Coleridge, *Poetical Works*, 1893, p. 24.

3. *The Three Graves* 492–500, *Poetical Works*, p. 92; see Hutchinson's edition of *Lyrical Ballads*, pp. 217, 258.

4. *Christabel* 32–36, *Poetical Works*, p. 116.

5. *The Mad Monk* 1–16, 46–47. This poem, by the way, ought sometime to be compared with Wordsworth's *Intimations of Immortality* and Coleridge's *Dejection*; for the discovery will yet be made that they are all three

> In melody most like to old Sicilian song.

The conventional turn, "There was a time . . . . But now . . . ." (cf. *Dejection*, Stanza 6, *Intimations of Immortality*, Stanza 1) is the same modulation that we find in *Lycidas*:

> But O the heavy change, now thou art gon.

6. *Descriptive Sketches*, 1793, lines 168–175, *Poetical Works*, ed. Dowden, 7. 285; cf. *An Evening Walk* 219, *Poetical Works* 7. 272.

7. *Descriptive Sketches* (final version) 145–153, *Poetical Works*, 1. 27.

8. *Lines Composed a few Miles above Tintern Abbey* 17–22, *Poetical Works*, 2. 146.

9. *Peter Bell*, 852–855, *Poetical Works*, 2. 248.

10. *Peter Bell*, 376–377, *Poetical Works*, 2. 232.

11. *Ancient Mariner* 533–534; *Recluse* 605–608, Wordsworth, *Poetical Works*, ed. Morley, p. 342. Cf. *Iliad* 6. 146–149; Dante, *Paradiso* 26. 137–138.

12. Wordsworth, *Poetical Works*, ed. Dowden, 3. 3.

13. *Prelude* 9. 438–443, *Poetical Works*, 7. 182.

14. *F. Q.* 1. 1. 34. Compare Tasso, *Ger. Lib.* 8. 27, 28, 41, 42; Ariosto, *Orl. Fur.* 8. 29 ff.

15. Parnell, *Poetical Works*, Aldine Edition, p. 100.

—Lane Cooper, "The 'Forest Hermit' in Coleridge
and Wordsworth," from *Modern Language Notes*,
vol. 24, no. 2, February 1909, pp. 33–36

B.H. Lehman "The Doctrine of Leadership in the Greater Romantic Poets" (1922)

Using Coleridge's phrase "the permanent politics of human nature," Lehman's essay focuses on the nature and sources of the poet's idea of leadership, an understanding of which then provides a critical framework for judging his works. Lehman begins by pointing out that the political basis for Coleridge's earlier radicalism was not completely dropped in his conservative years but, rather, was harmonized with and integrated into his shifting political beliefs. Though Coleridge adopted the best of Burke's conservatism following his profound disappointment with the French Revolution and its failure to bring about a reformation of society, he went on to view a leader as one who has the power to affirm or forbid and so direct the popular will. Stating that Coleridge clearly recognized that all men were not created equal in intelligence and that there were in fact common men and men of genius, Lehman believes that the poet not only understood this hierarchy but that he subscribed to a Machiavellian scheme in which three levels of intelligence are identified: the first in which a man understands himself and thus exhibits genius, the second in which man understands to the extent that it is shown by others, and the third in which man knows neither himself nor what he is shown. He cites Coleridge's introduction to *The Friend* as evidence of this influence. For Coleridge it is members of this first class only who are fit to become leaders, as they are the ones who can think for themselves and form judgments. Moreover, a defining characteristic of this premier class of intellectuals is the ability to "comprehend" all things in unity. Lehman is certain that Coleridge saw himself as a first-class thinker, fit to lead. Thus, according to Lehman, Coleridge conceives an organic model of the superior thinker. Lehman then proceeds to discuss various works, from early to late, to chart the evolution of Coleridge's doctrine of leadership: from *Religious Musings*, in which the French Revolution is viewed as the dawn of a new era of liberty for the oppressed and there are "eloquent men" who guide the masses, to *The Destiny of Nations*, which defines freedom as "the unfettered use / Of all the powers which God for use had given"; "France, an Ode," in which the poet's soul is in crisis following France's assault on Switzerland; and *Fears in Solitude*, which is a call to Britons to recognize the wrongs their country has committed and return to true faith and spirituality.

⸻ ⸺ ⸻

In his interesting discussion of the politics of the greater romantic poets, Mr. Walter Graham[1] throws light not so much upon the work of the poets as upon the men themselves. The illumination is biographical rather than critical. Is it not possible to carry the analysis of the material further, to view the problem involved in the political doctrines of Wordsworth, Coleridge, Byron, and Shelley in such a way as to give a literary as well as a biographical significance to the data? The importance of such analysis for Scott, Southey, and Keats is less, and in any case cannot be undertaken in the present paper. With respect to Wordsworth, Coleridge, Shelley, and Byron, however, such a consideration has not only its own value but would confirm and also perhaps offer a correction of the biographical view.

In "the permanent politics of human nature"—to use Coleridge's phrase—as distinguished from party politics and domestic policies, the central fact for any political theory is its doctrine of leadership. To discover successively in the case of each of the four poets the nature and sources of authority, to fix the conception of leader explicit or implied and to indicate the importance of the result for a critical reading of the work of each poet is the object of this discussion. . . .

II
COLERIDGE: THE STATESMAN AND THE 'CLERISY'

For Coleridge's change from an early radicalism to a more conservative position, Mr. Graham's case is clear. Yet in themselves the earlier doctrines are not soluble in the later. So much is certain. We must examine the evidence to see what new idea harmonized these oppositions, and what influence of idea or of event moved him from one position to the other.

The psychology of the situation is simple. Coleridge, like others who once held faith in the wisdom and righteousness of the proletariat, found himself convinced by the French events that the theories upon which he had once explained them were not true. He inherited at this juncture the best of Burke's conservatism. The people were not compact of vision and the power to initiate achieving action. The Voice of God was, at the least, not always in residence in the people. The more unquestioning heard the voice, no longer audible in that quarter, speak from the Man of Destiny. Men of thought, like Wordsworth and Coleridge, with unerring logic brought themselves to a new, founded position. What the new position was, exactly, and how, in the case of Coleridge, it was arrived at is clear from the following passage. On April 29, 1832, to whatever auditors were at Highgate, Coleridge said:

> I never said that the *vox populi* was of course the *vox Dei*. It may be; but it may be, and with equal probability, *a priori, vox Diaboli*. That the voice of ten millions of men calling for the same thing is a spirit, I believe; but whether that be a spirit of heaven or hell, I can only know by trying the thing called for by the prescript of reason and God's will.[17]

The new doctrine, then, does not desert for good and all the old, that *vox populi* is *vox Dei*. But it subjects the popular will to the test of reason and divine intent in the mind of one who has knowledge of the high and holy prescript. In other words the new idea of leader is introduced, a leader with power to affirm or forbid.

Coleridge, indeed, pretty freely recognizes that there are men of a common order and men of genius.[18] He without question sets aside as a superior the gifts and services of "the Cranmers, Hampdens, and Sidneys."[19] And he recognizes with some explicitness, though not with rigorous consistency, the three orders of mental capacity that Machiavelli designates.[20] He translates: "There are brains of three races. The one understands of itself; the other understands as much as is shown it by others; the third neither understands of itself, nor what is shown it by others."[21] In *The Friend* he introduces the quotation with "Machiavelli has well observed." The first order is genius. Its capacity to "understand of itself" is a gloss on the cryptic "the greatest and best of men is but an aphorism."[22] Genius is "the action of reason and imagination."[23] This action affords "one of the most characteristic and infallible criteria of the different ranks of men's intellects . . . . the instinctive habit which all superior minds have of endeavouring to bring, and of never resting till they have brought into unity the scattered facts which occur in conversation, or in the statements of men of business."[24] The second order—the taught—finds itself illustrated by those persons, for example, who in philosophy are incapable of pushing back the frontiers in speculative science but to whom the charted science need not therefore be a *terra incognita*.[25] The distinction between these two orders is made perfectly clear by the phrase: "the few men of genius among the learned class."[26] The nature of the third class, the not-learned, is set beyond doubt by a passage in *The Statesman's Manual*: "To the immense majority of men, even in civilized countries, speculative philosophy has ever been, and must ever remain, a *terra incognita*."[27] The whole matter under consideration is neatly touched off by the "*profaccia* with a desponding sigh" in *The Statesman's Manual*: "From a popular philosophy and a philosophic populace, Good Sense deliver us!"[28]

The basis for Coleridge's idea of a great man lies in that "contradistinction of the understanding from reason—for which," he writes in 1825, "during twenty years I have been contending."[29] "By the 'understanding,' I mean the faculty of thinking and forming judgments on the notices furnished by the sense, according to certain rules existing in itself, which rules constitute its distinct nature. By the pure 'reason,' I mean the power by which we become possessed of principles."[30] "The reason itself is the same in all men, yet the means of exercising it, and the materials,—that is, the facts and conceptions—on which it is exercised, being possessed in very different degrees by different persons, the practical result is, of course, equally different."[31]

The greatness of the mind, then, depends upon its bringing into unity with themselves and all things *all* the facts and conceptions, that is, upon the power to make the understanding serve the reason and the reason subserve the understanding. It is the function of reason in this reference "to comprehend," that is, to subordinate the notions of sense and the rules of the understanding's experience to absolute principles or necessary laws. Thus the reason "comprehends" all in the unity.[32]

If, now, we bring together the elements so far set forth we find that the laws or principles of reason and the regulations of prudence or understanding can make contact only in the unifying mind of superior men. This indeed, in practice, is Coleridge's conception. Pure reason in its fullness is Almighty Wisdom. "The laws of the Hebrew Commonwealth," for example, "which flowed from the pure reason, remain and are immutable." From the statesman "we have a right to expect a sober and meditative accommodation to our own times and country of those important truths declared in the inspired writings *for a thousand generations.*"[33] Here then is that "prescript of reason" by which the leader, Wordsworth, Coleridge, or another, shall try the *vox populi* to discover whether it be *vox Dei* or *vox diaboli*.

The development of Coleridge's conservatism, which is nothing more than the subjection of the vague urges of a populace or a mob to the control of a seer, may be traced at the critical moment in his so-called political poems. In *The Destruction of the Bastille* and the lines *To a Young Lady*, the approval is for the freeing of Freedom—nothing more. Of the twelve sonnets in the juvenile Poems, several exalt individual genius, one or two imply the value of the great leader to the cause of liberty, and the sonnet to Priestley looks with sharp disapproval upon the voice of the people and its result in the special case.

> Though roused by that dark Vizir Riot rude
> Have driven our Priestley o'er the ocean swell; . . . .

In *Religious Musings*, in which the French Revolution is heralded as the beginning of that great upheaval of the innumerable tribes of the oppressed, not only are these tribes roused by "eloquent men" "stung to rage with pity," but "the mad careering of the storm" thus set going is tamed by "Philosophers and Bards,"

> Conscious of their high dignities from God,
> . . . .
> Enamored with the charms of order. . . .

and hating "the unseemly disproportion."[34] These, who realize the charms of order, are "Coadjutors of God," "the elect of Heaven," and their function is to dart their strong eye through the deeds of men and to adore steadfastly, yet humbly, Nature's essence, mind, and energy—in short what Coleridge later designated "Reason."

The Destiny of Nations carries us forward by a definition of freedom.

> For what is freedom but the unfettered use
> Of all the powers which God for use had given?
> But chiefly this, him first, him last to view
> Through meaner powers and secondary things
> Effulgent, as through clouds that veil his blaze.[35]

It is not the possession of those

> who deem themselves most free
> When they within this gross and visible sphere
> Chain down the winged thought, *scoffing* ascent,
> Proud in their meanness.[36]

The Ode to the Departing Year adds nothing. *France, an Ode* is the record of the crisis in the poet's soul, which followed France's assault upon Switzerland. So after all, runs the burden of the conclusion, the great upheaval was the vain rebellion of "the Sensual and the Dark," was not informed by the voice of God. *Fears in Solitude*, written in April of 1798, is a call to Britons. The lines have fed on bitter disappointment, but they confirm the *Ode*.

When we assemble the evidence of the poems, we find, then, that freedom of man, liberty, is through them all the continued object of the poet's devotion. Nevertheless, from the first he does not exclude freedom secured to men by a Kosciusko, let us say; specifically in his most elaborate statement he not only allows to the "Coadjutors of God" the initiation and propulsion of freedom's ideals but also assigns to these "Philosophers and Bards" the task of molding to perfect forms the "confusions" of "the outrageous mass." Finally—and with intensest significance—his own reversal of judgment on the French upheaval is based soundly on his devotion to freedom and illustrates, in his own person, the Philosopher and Bard trying events by the prescript of reason and concluding that *vox populi* is in the instance before him *vox diaboli*.

In the light of the same doctrine, Coleridge's conception of the *jus divinum* of kings becomes an intelligible matter. For the "direct relation of the state and its magistracy to the Supreme Being"[37] is merely the fact of the unity of reason and the access to reason of all men fit to rule. And it is to be remembered that, though "the reason hath faith in itself in its own revelations," by his acts a man of power may write himself down a demagogue,[38] and no leader. Camiola seems almost to have had her eye on this teaching when she addressed the King of Sicily:

Since, when you are unjust, the deity
Which you may challenge as a king, parts from you.

In the same light, too, much of the material interpolated in *The Friend* for entertainment of the reader and refreshment—God save the mark!—after the philosophical disquisitions, becomes significant, taking on for the reader the associative values that it bore in the author's mind. For example: in Essays XI and XII of the *General Introduction* Napoleon is finally ruled out of court as "the mimic and caricaturist of Charlemagne."[39] Charlemagne more or less is accepted at Alcuin's evaluation as the embodiment of the Platonic philosopher become king. Napoleon is no philosopher and no king because he takes to mimicing his predecessor's acts instead of accommodating anew to the circumstances the principles and prescript of Reason. Likely enough, had Coleridge known Eginhard's document he would have ruled out Charlemagne for his attempt at an *Augustus Redivivus*. Nevertheless, though this throws a question at the doctrine itself, the choice and treatment of the material is illuminated.

Of Coleridge's praise of Sir Alexander Ball nothing more need be said than that, if his perspectives were crooked and his judgment wrong, the exaltation of the little great man was orthodox, well within the teaching. In his recondite Royal Society *Essay on the Prometheus of Aeschylus*,[40] even one in the porch of the temple can see the god out of the machine: for Aeschylus, the Eleusinian, has concealed in his tragedy and poetry (so says S. T. C.) a *philosophema*. The mythos of the colossal hero is "the generation of the vows, or pure reason in man!"[41] Upon no other theory can I explain Coleridge's explanation than upon his obsession with the doctrine of leader as already set forth. This Coleridge who uplifted Sir Alexander Ball and degraded the *Prometheus Bound* is, one reminds oneself, the Coleridge who protected his leader against quack competition by telling the Higher Classes of Society how to recognize the demagogue with eleven tests,[42] at least four of which we might here turn upon the analyst himself.

For Coleridge regarded himself as leader, beyond question. It was the basic inconsistency of his earliest addresses that they were "*Conciones ad Populum*"—the discourses of a leader. In *Lines on a Friend*, written in his youth, he says,

To me hath Heaven with bounteous hand assigned
Energic Reason and a shaping mind,
The daring ken of Truth, the Patriot's part . . . . [43]

And long before Coleridge sat upon Highgate Hill mumbling to his disciples, he was leading statesmen to the fountain of political truth, and philosophers to the source of Reason. The Highgate *Table Talk* is proof for the latter end; just as the tone of the addresses is for the first—not to speak of his judgment after the Swiss episode, that the *vox populi* in France was not *vox Dei*, but *vox diaboli*. The serious concern over his success and failure with the distinction of Reason and Understanding is evidence in the interval. The best of all evidence, however, if we hold in mind the relation of the great man to the learned classes, is the correction in Coleridge's own hand upon the title page of a copy of the *Statesman's Manual*.[44] After the words *A Lay Sermon Addressed to the Higher Classes of Society*, the author has added *but more particularly to the Learned.* The asterisk guides to the following footnote: "So it was ordered to be printed, and so, I believe, it was advertised." Furthermore, by merely measuring against his doctrine Coleridge's method of performance—with him so conscious a process!—it would be clear to a child that he conceived himself with some wistfulness but with some complacency, also, as leader.

It still remains to point out that the rights and duties of the early Jacobinical faith, recognized in the problem of government by Rousseau, maintain their place in the new scheme. For since Reason is resident in all men, every man may unite himself to the form of society planned and perfected by the leader in accordance with the prescripts of Reason and yet obey himself only and remain as free as before. Thus with both poets the leader is the interpreter of the will of all.

Notes

1. *P.M.L.A.* XXXVI, 60–78.
17. *The Complete Works of Samuel Taylor Coleridge*, New York, 1854, *Table Talk*, VI, 393.
18. *Ibid.*, VI, *Table Talk*, 318, 380, 415.
19. *Ibid.*, II, *The Friend*, 68.
20. *Ibid.*, I, *The Manual*, 427; II, *The Friend*, 114–115.
21. *Ibid.*, I, *The Manual*, 427.
22. *Ibid.*, I, *Aids*, 129.
23. *Ibid.*, VI, *Table Talk*, 319.
24. *Ibid.*, VI, *Table Talk*, 380.
25. *Ibid.*, I, *Manual*, 428; *Biographia Literaria*, III, 251.
26. *Ibid.*, III, *Biographia Literaria*, 251.
27. *Ibid.*, I, *Statesman's Manual*, 428.
28. *Ibid.*, I, *Statesman's Manual*, 442.
29. *Ibid.*, I, *Aids*, 257.
30. *Ibid.*, II, *The Friend*, 164.
31. *Ibid.*, II, *The Friend*, 148.

32. *Ibid.*, II, *The Friend*, 146.

33. *Ibid.*, I, *Manual*, 423.

34. *Ibid.*, VII, *Poems*, 77.

35. *Ibid.*, VII, 83.

36. *Ibid.*, VII, *Poems*, 83.

37. *Ibid.*, I, *Manual*, 429.

38. *Ibid.*, VI, *Lay Sermon*, 170–1.

39. *Ibid.*, II, *The Friend*, 79 ff.

40. Delivered May 18, 1825.

41. *Complete Works*, IV, *Essay on Prometheus*, 351.

42. *Ibid.*, VI, *Lay Sermon*, 170–1.

43. *Ibid.*, VII, *Poems*, 56.

44. In the Widener Collection, Harvard College Library.

—B.H. Lehman, "The Doctrine of Leadership in
the Greater Romantic Poets," from *PMLA*, vol. 37,
no. 4, December 1922, pp. 639, 644–652

WORKS

LYRICAL BALLADS

James Dykes Campbell
"Nether Stowey—*Lyrical Ballads*" (1896)

When Coleridge's ship arrived at the quarantine ground off Portsmouth on the 11th August, he was ill, and possibly for that reason wrote to no one. Mr. Russell, however, wrote to his own friends at Exeter, who wrote to the Coleridges at Ottery, who wrote to Mrs. Coleridge—the news reaching her on the 15th. Coleridge arrived in London on the 17th, and on the following day, having taken up his quarters with Lamb, wrote to Stuart and to Wordsworth. In both letters[1] he described himself as much better since he landed, but in neither did he say anything about going home. He did not write to Wedgwood for ten months, and when he did, he described himself as having arrived from Italy 'ill, penniless, and worse than homeless.' Almost his first words to Stuart were, 'I am literally afraid, even to cowardice, to ask for any person, or of any person.' Spite of the friendliest and most unquestioning welcome from all most dear to him, it was the saddest of home-comings, for the very sympathy held out with both hands induced only a bitter, hopeless feeling of remorse—a

> Sense of past youth, and manhood come in vain;
> And genius given, and knowledge won in vain;—

of broken promises,—promises to friends and promises to himself; and above all, sense of a will paralysed—dead perhaps, killed by his own hand.

Wordsworth, whose family had outgrown Dove Cottage, was then looking for a house close to Keswick, that he might be near Coleridge, should Coleridge decide on living at Greta Hall. He would do nothing until that was settled, but no answer came to his repeated inquiries by letter. Coleridge seems soon to have left Lamb's chambers for a room at the *Courier* office (348 Strand), and to have settled down as assistant to Stuart and to his editor, Street. He had been sent for by Lord Howick (Foreign Secretary), but had been repulsed by the hall porter, and doubted whether the letter on the state of affairs in the Mediterranean which he had left had ever reached his Lordship. A few days after Fox's death (Sep. 13) he promised Stuart a 'full and severe critique' of that statesman's latest views. About the same time, through Davy or William Smith, M.P. for Norwich, or both, he undertook to deliver a series of lectures on 'Taste' at the Royal Institution. On Sep. 16—just a month after his landing—he wrote his first letter to his wife, to say that he might be expected at Greta Hall on the 29th. Before this, Wordsworth had informed Sir George Beaumont that Coleridge

> dare not go home, he recoils so much from the thought of domesticating with Mrs. Coleridge, with whom, though on many accounts he much respects her, he is so miserable that he dare not encounter it. What a deplorable thing! I have written to him to say that if he does not come down immediately I must insist upon seeing him somewhere. If he appoints London I shall go. I believe if anything good is to be done for him it must be done by me.[2]

It was Wordsworth's letter, doubtless, which drew Coleridge to the North. Dorothy's letter to Lady Beaumont,[3] written on receipt of the announcement of Coleridge's home-coming, goes copiously and minutely into the reasons for the estrangement between the poet and his wife. Miss Wordsworth still had hopes of an improvement.

> We have long known (she writes) how unfit Coleridge and his wife were for each other; but we had hoped that his ill-health, and the present need his children have of his care and fatherly instructions, and the reflections of his own mind during this long absence, would have so wrought upon him that he might have returned home with comfort, ready to partake of the blessings of friendship, which he surely has in an abundant degree, and to devote himself to his studies and his children. . . . Poor soul! he had a struggle of many years, striving to bring Mrs. C. to a change of temper, and something like communion with him in his enjoyments. He is now, I trust, effectually convinced that he has no power of this sort. . . . But suppose him once reconciled to that one great want, an utter

want of sympathy, I believe he may live in peace and quiet. Mrs. C. has many excellent properties, as you observe; she is unremitting in her attentions as a nurse to her children, and, indeed, I believe she would have made an excellent wife to many persons. Coleridge is as little fitted for her as she for him, and I am truly sorry for her.

Of Coleridge during the next three months, the only glimpses we have are in the correspondence of distracted friends who cannot draw a word of reply to the letters they address to him. Josiah Wedgwood is the most persistent inquirer—he craves for the long-promised material for the *Life* of his brother Thomas, then being prepared by Sir James Mackintosh.[4] On Nov. 10th, Wordsworth (who had taken his family to Coleorton farm-house) wrote: 'Alas! we have had no tidings of Coleridge—a certain proof that he continues to be very unhappy.' The truth of the presentiment was soon confirmed. Before the 10th December, the Wordsworths had received four letters from Coleridge, in all of which he spoke

> 'with the same steadiness of his resolution to separate from Mrs. C., and she has fully agreed to it, and consented that he should take Hartley and Derwent and superintend their education, she being allowed to have them at the holidays. I say she has agreed to the separation, but in a letter which we have received tonight he tells us she breaks out into outrageous passions, and urges continually that one argument (in fact the only one which has the least effect upon her mind), that this person and that person, and everybody will talk.'[5]

Wordsworth at once wrote and begged Coleridge to come to Coleorton and bring the two boys with him, and on December 21 Coleridge arrived, bringing, however, only Hartley.[6] On Christmas Day, Miss Wordsworth described him to Lady Beaumont as tolerably well and cheerful, and 'already begun with his books.' He seemed 'more like his old self,' and 'contented in his mind, having settled things at home to his satisfaction.'

It was early in the following month that Wordsworth recited to Coleridge the great autobiographical poem which we know as *The Prelude*. He had carried with him to Malta a transcript of the first five 'Books,' but the poem had been slowly built up and completed during his long absence, and was addressed to himself. How deeply the recital impressed him may be gathered from the touching and beautiful response[7] made while the sound of his friend's voice was still vibrating. The picture which Coleridge draws of himself is too sacred for comment—the companion-portrait of his friend is drawn in lines even more strongly contrasting than those which had been used in *Dejection*.

On January 27, 1807, Miss Wordsworth reports Coleridge as pretty well, 'though ailing at some time in every day. He does not take such strong stimulants as he did, but I fear he will never be able to leave them off entirely.' On February 17 he is still at Coleorton, but it must have been soon after this that he took Hartley up to London on a visit to Basil Montagu. It was probably while then in town that he made preliminary arrangements through Davy for the delivery of the course of lectures which had been spoken of in 1806, for in August we find Davy endeavouring to get a definite answer on the subject.[8] Some time in May, Coleridge and Hartley joined Mrs. Coleridge and the two younger children at Bristol (where they had been since the end of March), and on the 6th June the whole family became the guests of Poole at Stowey. The visit was planned for but a fortnight, after which the Coleridges were to have gone to Ottery[9] to stay with his brother George, but the visit had to be abandoned, owing, it was said, to illness in the house. The true reason was, that when George Coleridge was made aware of the proposed separation of S. T. Coleridge from his wife, he refused to receive them into his house. This proved a lasting rupture with Ottery. The Coleridges remained on with Poole—Mrs. Coleridge and the children until the end of July, when they returned to Bristol; Coleridge himself until the end of September. There is much of the doings of this period in Mrs. Sandford's book. It appears to have been on the whole a happy time for all parties, and it would seem as if, probably through Poole's good offices, some kind of reconciliation, or at least some resolution to 'try again,' had been patched up between Coleridge and his wife, for when Mrs. Coleridge left Stowey for Bristol it had been arranged that she should there be joined by her husband, and that the family party should return intact to Greta Hall. Coleridge appears to have been cheerful enough while he basked in the sunshine of old associations and old friendships, but when his host and constant friend urged him to exert himself in preparing for the proposed lectures at the Royal Institution, poor Coleridge could only respond with a sigh—

Let Eagle bid the Tortoise sunwards soar,
As vainly Strength speaks to a broken Mind![10]

Poole succeeded, however, in overcoming Coleridge's reluctance to resume communication with Josiah Wedgwood. While on a visit from Poole's to his old neighbour, Mr. Brice of Aisholt, Coleridge wrote the letter[11] which contains the statement already quoted as to his having returned from Italy 'ill, penniless, and worse than homeless.' It is a sad letter, differing however but little from many which Coleridge was called on to write—a medley of confessions, promises, projects, and pleas self-justificatory. The long-promised contributions to the estimate of Thomas Wedgwood's philosophical views, and the more recently demanded contribution to the memoir (supposed to be preparing by Sir James Mackintosh), were both among the 'effects which have been most unkindly or injudiciously detained by Stoddart' at Malta. If Josiah Wedgwood only knew Coleridge's grief for the loss of his friend Thomas, and his 'own bad state of health and worse state of mind,' he would pity rather than wonder at the 'day after day procrastinating.' 'The faultiest parts of my conduct (he urged) have arisen from qualities both blameable and pitiable, but yet the very opposite of Neglect or Insensibility.' He flatly denies an accusation of having abused Mackintosh to his (M.'s) relations. 'I am at present,' he adds, 'on the eve of sending two volumes of poems to the press,[12] the work of past years.' *Christabel*, the most greatly admired, has been, he is told, 'anticipated as far as all originality of style and manner goes by a work[13] which he has not read.' If this be true, it is 'somewhat hard, for [Scott] had, long before the composition of his own poem, publicly repeated *Christabel*. Besides' (he goes on), 'I have finished a Greek and English grammar on a perfectly new plan, and have done more than half of a small but sufficiently complete Greek and English Lexicon, so that I can put both to press whenever I can make just terms with any bookseller.'[14] Nothing is said about lectures. Of this apologia, Wedgwood wrote to Poole: 'His letter removed all those feelings of anger which occasionally, but not permanently, existed in my mind towards him.'[15]

It was in the following month that De Quincey appeared on the scene. On the 26th of July, Cottle wrote a letter of introduction[16] for that 'Gentleman of Oxford, a scholar and man of genius' (so he described De Quincey) to Poole, which contained a request that he might be introduced to Coleridge. The Opium-eater's story[17] is too well known to require more than brief mention here. When he arrived at Stowey, Coleridge was at Bridgwater, and thither the neophyte pursued him. He found Coleridge standing in reverie, under his host's gateway: 'In height he might seem to be about five feet eight (he was in reality about an inch and a half taller) .... his person was broad and full, and tended even to corpulence; his complexion was fair, though not what painters technically call fair, because it was associated with black hair; his eyes were large and soft in their expression; and it was from the peculiar appearance of haze or dreaminess which mixed with their light, that I recognised my object.'

As soon as it had been arranged that De Quincey should join a dinner-party which Coleridge's host, Mr. Chubb, was to entertain on that evening,

Coleridge began to talk 'in a continuous strain of eloquent dissertation,' which, after about three hours, was arrested by the entrance of Mrs. Coleridge. 'She was in person full and rather below the common height; whilst her face showed, to my eye, some prettiness of rather a common order.' When De Quincey had been 'frigidly' introduced, Mrs. Coleridge retired, and no doubt the dissertation was resumed. But with all this copious talk, De Quincey declares that 'never had he beheld so profound an expression of cheerless despondency' as that which sat on the talker's countenance. At the large dinner-party in the evening, Coleridge seemed to talk with an effort, and to give no heed when his hearers misrepresented what he said. At ten,—dinner had probably begun at five or six,—De Quincey left the party, and 'feeling that he could not easily go to sleep after the excitement of the day, and fresh from the sad spectacle of powers so majestic already besieged by decay,' he mounted his horse, and through the divine calm of the summer night rode back to Bristol. He states that in the course of their conversation 'Coleridge told him of the over-clouding of his life' by the abuse of opium, and warned him against forming the habit, with so 'peculiar an emphasis of horror' as to impress upon the young man's mind 'a feeling that he never hoped to liberate himself from the bondage.' As to this alleged confession, I feel almost persuaded that De Quincey's memory deceived him, and that he learned the secret and received the warning at some later period. Such a lapse in groping back through a past of seven-and-twenty years, is much more probable than that Coleridge should have divulged to a perfect stranger a hitherto jealously-guarded secret. It struck the generous young man that Coleridge might be hampered in many ways by pecuniary difficulties. Immediately after his return to Bristol, he learned that such was the case, 'and in consequence' (he says) 'of what I heard, I contrived that a particular service should be rendered to Mr. Coleridge, a week after, through the hands of Mr. Cottle.'

Such is De Quincey's delicate way of telling the story of his own impulsive generosity. Cottle's account[18] is familiar. De Quincey proposed to give Coleridge five hundred pounds, but Cottle prudently induced the young man to make the sum three hundred. The gift was professedly accepted as an unconditional loan, which (as he told Cottle) Coleridge trusted to be able to restore in two years, and as removing the pecuniary pressures which alone stood in the way of the completion of works, which, if completed, would make him easy. In one year he hopes to ask the name of his benefactor, that he may show him good fruits of the 'tranquillity of mind which his kindness' has rendered possible.[19] I do not doubt the perfect sincerity with which this letter was written, but in view of the events which followed, it can only be read with a pang. Of the use to which De Quincey's gift was put by Coleridge, nothing, I believe, is known. One hopes that part went to repay Wordsworth's loan of £100 made in 1804; but, at all events, soon afterwards, it was all gone. 'Heaven knows, of the £300 received through you,' wrote Coleridge to Cottle in 1815, 'what went to myself!'

Coleridge left Stowey for Bristol about the 12th September. On the 11th he had written a long letter to Davy[20] in reply to an urgent message regarding the proposed lectures. He is better, and his 'will acquiring some degree of strength and power of reaction.'

> I have received such manifest benefit from horse exercise, and gradual abandonment of fermented, and total abstinence from spirituous, liquors, and by being alone with Poole, and the renewal of old times, by wandering about my dear old walks of Quantock and Alfoxden, that I have seriously set about composition with a view to ascertain whether I can conscientiously undertake what I so very much wish, a series of Lectures at the Royal Institution.

He has, however, changed his mind as to the subject. If he lectures, it will not be on 'Taste,' but on 'the Principles of Poetry,' and he will 'not give a single lecture till he has in fair writing at least one-half of the whole course, for as to trusting anything to immediate effort, he shrinks from it as from guilt, and guilt in him it would be.' He concludes by asking Davy to await his final decision, at the end of the month. During the months (September–November) which Coleridge spent in Bristol, he seems to have given himself up very much to talk about religion, surprising his friends there with the change which had taken place in his beliefs. A long and deeply interesting letter[21] printed by Cottle shows that he was no longer a Unitarian—he probably never had been one, in the strictest sense—but a fully-developed Trinitarian. In a letter[22] to Poole from 'Keswick, Dec. 28, 1807,' Mrs. Coleridge says that when her husband joined her at Bristol, 'in such excellent health and improved looks, she thought of days "lang syne," and hoped and prayed it might continue.'

> Alas! (she adds), in three or four days it was all over. He said he must go to town *immediately*, about the Lectures, yet he stayed three weeks without another word about removing, and I durst not speak lest it should *disarrange* him. Mr. De Quincey, who was a frequent visitor to C. in College Street, proposed accompanying me and the children into Cumberland, as he much wished to pay Wordsworth and Southey a visit. . . . Towards the end of October, accordingly, I packed up everything, C.'s things (as I thought, for London) and our own, and left Bristol.[23] . . . I left him (as I thought)

ready to jump into the mail for London. Lo! three weeks after I received a letter from him from White Horse Stairs, Piccadilly; he was just arrived in town, had been ill, owing to sitting in wet cloaths, had passed three weeks at the house of a Mr. Morgan, and had been nursed by his wife and her sister in the kindest manner. C. found Davy very ill. The Lectures on that account were postponed. Stuart had insisted on his being at the *Courier* office during his stay in town.... Wordsworth obtained a few lines from him ten days ago. Davy was better, and the Lectures were to commence in a fortnight. Since then we have heard nothing. Dr. Stoddart is arrived from Malta. He has brought with him C.'s papers. C. wrote to him to expostulate with him for having detained them so long. He received an abusive answer, saying he would deliver up the papers to a person properly documented, with £50 for expenses, etc. C. has since found that he [Stoddart] is writing a book himself.... Southey is enraged at his [Stoddart's] conduct, and foretold this about the book, and gave it as a reason why C.'s documents were not forthcoming.... He [Coleridge] has published a poem in the *Courier* lately—*The Wanderer's Farewell*.[24]

This very interesting letter of Mrs. Coleridge gives a succinct account of her husband up to the end of 1807. It will be observed that it contains no mention of De Quincey's bounty. He, of course, would say nothing to Mrs. Coleridge, and Coleridge himself had evidently been equally reticent. His detention at Bristol, we may assume, was not unconnected with the delay in receiving the three hundred pounds which was paid on November 12, at least a fortnight after Mrs. Coleridge's departure.

Coleridge returned to his old quarters at the top of the *Courier* building in the Strand. 'He sits up in a two pair of stairs room at the *Courier* office and receives visitors,' writes Lamb to Manning (Feb. 28); and De Quincey, in his *Lake Poets*, gives a dismal account of Coleridge's situation at this period:—

I called upon him daily, and pitied his forlorn condition. There was no bell in the room, which for many months answered the double purpose of bed-room and sitting-room. Consequently I often saw him picturesquely enveloped in night-caps surmounted by handkerchiefs indorsed upon handkerchiefs, shouting .... down three or four flights of stairs, to a certain 'Mrs. Brainbridge,' his sole attendant, whose dwelling was in the subterranean regions of the house [the *Courier* office].

His sole duty being to prepare his lectures, he gave much time to the assistance of Stuart and Street in the conduct of their newspaper. Of this, the first[25] course of lectures delivered by Coleridge, but a scanty and fragmentary record remains.[26] Lamb writes to Manning on February 26, 1808: 'Coleridge has delivered two lectures at the R.I.; two more were attended,[27] but he did not come. It is thought he has gone sick upon them. He ain't well, that's certain. Wordsworth[28] is coming to see him.' This sounds a little unfeeling, as coming from Lamb; but it was mainly a letter from Mary Lamb,[29] which was bringing Wordsworth to town. I gather that Lamb suspected opium to be largely responsible for his friend's illness, and that Wordsworth's moral influence would be more powerful than his own. Wordsworth came, and Southey followed; and during their stay in town Coleridge recovered, and before Wordsworth left on the 3rd April he had heard two lectures, which (he says) 'seemed to give great satisfaction,' although Coleridge 'was not in spirits, and suffered much during the week both in body and mind.'[30] About this time Coleridge reviewed his friend Clarkson's 'History of the Abolition of the Slave-trade' in the *Edinburgh*. He had begged Jeffrey to be merciful to an imperfect book for the sake of the almost perfect character of the author; on which Jeffrey asked Coleridge to be himself the critic. Coleridge afterwards complained of gross mutilation of his MS. and of inversion of some of his sentiments, especially as regards Pitt, whose sincerity in the matter of Abolition, he had asserted.[31] He proposed to republish his review, corrected and augmented, but he did not, and it has never been reprinted.[32] In May, Coleridge writes[33] of himself as correcting and revising Wordsworth's *White Doe of Rylstone*, then ready for the press. He is hampered by 'the heat and bustle of these disgusting lectures,' the next of which will be his first on 'Modern Poetry,' to be followed, later on, by one on Wordsworth's 'System and Compositions.' The lectures came to an end late in June.[34] De Quincey's statements[35] respecting Coleridge's condition during the period of the lectures, and of his *frequent* failure to appear at Albemarle Street, have much appearance of exaggeration. They are in no way corroborated by Crabb Robinson, and the two failures reported by Lamb were probably all that took place.

When the lectures were over, Coleridge went to Bury St. Edmunds on a visit to the Clarksons. Mrs. Clarkson was one of his most devoted and sympathetic friends, and one whose high qualities of mind and heart were greatly appreciated by him. It was no doubt owing to her good influence that he at this time relinquished laudanum, or at least the abuse of it. The abuse was no longer a secret from his intimates, for soon after this visit he wrote thus to Stuart:—

I am hard at work, and feel a pleasure in it which I have not
known for years; a consequence and reward of my courage in at
length overcoming the fear of dying suddenly in my sleep, which,
Heaven knows, alone seduced me into the fatal habit, etc. . . .
If I entirely recover I shall deem it a sacred duty to publish my
cure, tho' without my name, for the practice of taking opium is
dreadfully spread.[36]

This was written from 'Allan Bank,' Wordsworth's recently-entered and very
uncomfortable house at Grasmere. 'Coleridge has arrived at last' (wrote
Southey to his brother Tom, September 9, 1808), 'about half as big as the
house. He came with Wordsworth on Monday, and returned with him on
Wednesday. His present scheme is to put the boys to school at Ambleside and
reside at Grasmere himself.'[37] At Stowey, a year before, some such arrangement
had been discussed as a contingency, but up to June 1808 nothing further had
been said regarding it to Mrs. Coleridge. She was anxious, 'on the children's
account,' that Greta Hall might be decided on, and the landlord, Jackson, was
seconding her efforts by building some additional accommodation, fearing
that, owing to the presence of the Southey family, Coleridge found too little
privacy. On December 4, Miss Wordsworth writes from Allan Bank to Mrs.
Marshall: 'At the time of the great storm, Mrs. Coleridge and her little girl[38]
were here, and Mr. Coleridge is with us constantly. . . . Mr. Coleridge and his
wife are separated, and I hope they will both be the happier for it. They are
upon friendly terms, and occasionally see each other. In fact, Mrs. Coleridge
was more than a week at Grasmere [Allan Bank] under the same roof with
him. Coleridge intends to spend the winter with us. On the [other] side of this
paper you will find the Prospectus of a work which he is going to undertake;
and I have little doubt but that it will be well executed if his health does not
fail him; but on that score (though he is well at present) I have many fears.'[39]

The 'prospectus' was, of course, that of *The Friend*. Coleridge and his
associates of this period must have used up a ream or two of it in their
correspondence—one fly-leaf of the foolscap sheet having been left blank
expressly for this advertising purpose. Early in December Coleridge wrote
of his project to Davy[40]: 'My health and spirits are improved beyond my
boldest hopes. A very painful effort of moral courage has been remunerated
by tranquillity—by ease from the sting of self-disapprobation. I have done
more for the last ten weeks than I had done for three years before. . . . I
would willingly inform you of my chance of success in obtaining a sufficient
number of subscribers, so as to justify me prudentially in commencing the
work, but I do not possess grounds even for a sane conjecture. It will depend

in a great measure on the zeal of my friends.' To Stuart and to Poole he wrote in the same strain, and to them he added an intimation that he had consulted a physician. To Poole he says he is now feeling 'the blessedness of walking altogether in the light,' which, taken in conjunction with the letter to Davy, we may interpret it as meaning that opium-eating had been suspended for 'a time.'[41]

The 'prospectus' mentioned by Miss Wordsworth was sent out without consultation with any one,[42] and the first number was announced for 'the first Saturday in January 1809,' 'in case of a sufficient number of subscribers being obtained.'

Of course *The Friend* did not appear on January 7. On January 18, Southey told Rickman: 'Meantime a hundred difficulties open upon him [Coleridge] in the way of publication, and doubtless some material changes must be made in the plan. . . . [*The Friend*] is expected to start in March.' At first *The Friend* was to be printed and published in London; next, in Kendal; but in February Coleridge arranged with 'a clever young man,' Mr. John Brown, to print and publish for him in Penrith. Then it was discovered that this clever young man had not type enough, and Coleridge had to buy £38 worth. On the 23rd March, Wordsworth, who had become very anxious, thus wrote to Poole[43]: 'I give it to you as my deliberate opinion, founded upon proofs which have been strengthening for years, that he neither will nor can execute anything of important benefit to himself, his family, or mankind'; all is 'frustrated by a derangement in his intellectual and moral constitution. In fact, he has no voluntary power of mind whatsoever, nor is he capable of acting under any *constraint* of duty or moral obligation.' *The Friend* may appear, 'but it cannot go on for any length of time. I am *sure* it cannot. C, I understand, has been three weeks at Penrith,' and will answer no letters. And then he calls on Poole to come to the rescue—in summer, for it is of no use to attempt to stop Coleridge *now*. A week later (March 30) Wordsworth wrote again to Poole— Coleridge, he says, has not been at Grasmere for a month. He is now at Keswick, 'having had a great deal of trouble about arranging the publication of *The Friend*. . . . I cannot say that Coleridge has been managing himself well.' Probably he had heard from Southey that opium was again in the ascendant. Poole, Stuart, Montagu, and Clarkson were advancing money for the stamped paper.[44] It was sent, unfortunately, by the wrong route and did not arrive till May 8. At last, but *not until June 1st, The Friend No.* I. appeared.[45] 'The mode of payment by subscribers will be announced in a future number,' promised Coleridge, and in No. II. this promise was fulfilled—characteristically, by a vague proposal that payment should be made 'at the close of each twentieth week.' The third number will be deferred for a fortnight (instead of a week) to allow lists of subscribers to come in, and arrangements to be made for mode of payment. Nothing more was said about the matter until after the issue of the twentieth number, at the end of the year.

Having seen No. II. despatched on June 8, Coleridge returned from Penrith to Grasmere and wrote to Stuart[46]: 'I printed 620 of No. I. and 650 of No. II., and so many more are called for that I shall be forced to reprint both as soon as I hear from Clarkson [regarding fresh stocks of paper].[47] The proof-sheet of No. III. goes back to-day, and with it the "copy" of No. IV., so that henceforth we shall be secure of regularity.' Alas! No. III. appeared on August 10—seven weeks late; and No. IV. on September 7—again three weeks late. And no wonder. The conditions were impossible. There was Coleridge himself; there were the imperfect arrangements for supplies of paper; and, as if these hindrances were not enough, there were the relative situations of Grasmere and Penrith. The mere distance, 28 miles, was nothing; but there was no direct post, and Kirkstone Pass lay, a veritable lion, in the path. The defective postal system was only ameliorated by the passage of chance chaises either way, but once when the printing-house rats had devoured a page-long motto from Hooker, and two fresh transcripts were entrusted by Coleridge to two drivers, both failed of delivery to the printer; and No. VIII. was, in consequence, issued a week after due date. Then the subscription-list plan proved a bad one, as Coleridge publicly confessed in after years.[48] In January 1810 he made the same confession in a letter to Lady Beaumont[49]—many subscribers withdrew their names, and many of those who did not, withheld the money. Nearly all complained that the contents were too dull, and an attempt was made to enliven the pages by printing 'Satyrane's Letters.' These, with contributions in prose and verse from Wordsworth, practically filled up the numbers from November 23 to January 25 (1810), when the 'Sketches and Fragments of the Life and Character of the late Sir Alexander Ball'[50] began—a series, too long indeed, but destined never to be completed.

While *The Friend* was being abandoned to Satyrane and Wordsworth, Coleridge was contributing a series of letters to the *Courier*[51] 'On the Spaniards,' with the view of exciting British sympathy in the struggles of that nation against Napoleon. His own feelings were thoroughly roused—'for this' (he wrote) 'is not a quarrel of Governments, but the war of a people against the armies of a remorseless invader, usurper, and tyrant.' 'Coleridge's spirits have been irregular of late,' wrote Miss Wordsworth to Lady Beaumont at the beginning of March 1810.[52] 'He was damped after the twentieth number by the slow arrival of payments,[53] and half persuaded himself that he ought not to go on. We laboured hard against such a resolve, and he seems determined to fight onwards.' And she proceeds to describe how, from the commencement,

The Friend had been produced by fits and starts—sometimes a number in two days, sometimes not a line composed for 'weeks and weeks'; the papers being generally dictated to Miss Sarah Hutchinson, and never retranscribed.[54] In the same letter Miss Wordsworth announces that Miss Hutchinson's prolonged visit was to come to an end in a fortnight. 'Coleridge most of all will miss her, as she has transcribed almost every paper of *The Friend* for the press.' So much did Coleridge miss his devoted secretary, that *The Friend* came to an end with her visit to Allan Bank—flickering out with 'No. XXVII., Thursday March 15, 1810'—the last printed words, '(To be concluded in our next number),' referring to the articles about Ball.

So perished, one cannot say untimely, a work which Hazlitt not inaptly described as 'an enormous title-page .... an endless preface to an imaginary work.' But it was, like all that came from Coleridge, an integral part of himself, and therefore a heap of ore rich in finest metal. *The Friend* of Highgate and 1818, which he himself described as a '*rifacimento*' of the original, was practically a new work. The original would bear reprinting, for it is now unknown except to the curious book-collector.

During the long period of Coleridge's domestication with the Wordsworths a good deal of friendly intercourse was kept up between Allan Bank and Greta Hall; and the Coleridge boys, who were at school at Ambleside, spent most of their weekly holidays with the Wordsworths. The following passage from a letter[55] of Mrs. Coleridge to Miss Betham is pleasant reading, not only for the tone in which her husband and the Wordsworths are mentioned, but as showing that Coleridge and Lloyd no longer shunned each other. 'Brathay' was Lloyd's home. 'My dear friend, I know it will give you [pleasure] to hear that I was very comfortable during my visits in Westmoreland. C[oleridge] came often to Brathay, before I went to Grasmere, and kindly acceded to my wish of taking my little daughter home again with me after she had passed a fortnight with him at Allan Bank. His first intention was to keep her with him until Christmas, and then to bring her home with her brothers. ... C. is to spend the last week of the boys' holidays here, and take them back with him [to Ambleside]. ... I hope you will soon come again to see us, and I will introduce you to C., and *he* to his invaluable friends.'

Coleridge's movements after the cessation of *The Friend* in the middle of March are not easy to trace. On the 15th April he wrote to Lady Beaumont from Ambleside, excusing himself for inattention to a letter which had arrived at Grasmere when his depression of spirits 'amounted to little less than absolute despondency.' He had only that day found courage to open the letter, which contained an 'enclosure.' He must not accuse himself of idleness, for he has been 'willing to exert energy, only not in anything which the duty of the day demanded.' The next glimpse is in a letter from Mrs. Coleridge to Poole, dated October 3.[56] The poor wife knows not 'what to think or what to do.' Coleridge has been at Greta Hall for four or five months 'in an almost uniform kind disposition towards us all.' His spirits have been better than for years, and he has been reading Italian to both the Saras—only, he has been doing nothing else. 'The last number of *The Friend* lies on his desk, the sight of which fills my heart with grief and my eyes with tears,' and the writer never ceases to pray that 'Mr. Poole were here.'

Notes

1. *Letters from the Lake Poets*, p. 54; *Mem. of Coleorton*, i. 157. These books are the main authorities for this period.
2. Knight's *Life*, ii. 74.
3. *Mem. of Coleorton*, i. 162.
4. Sir James Mackintosh was more diplomatic than Coleridge, for he proved as faithless to his trust and his promises, without sharing the just displeasure of the Wedgwood family.
5. Miss Wordsworth to Lady Beaumont in *Mem. of Coleorton*, i. 182. 'Dec. 10, 1806,' is the post-mark. The date printed at the head of the letter, 'Nov. 16,' is an impossible one.
6. Two days previous Miss Wordsworth wrote thus to Lady Beaumont: 'He [Coleridge] writes calmly and in better spirits. Mrs. C. had been outrageous; but for the last two or three days she had become more quiet, and appeared to be tolerably reconciled to his arrangements. I had a letter from her last week—a strange letter! She wrote just as if all things were going on as usual, and we knew nothing of the intentions of Coleridge. She gives but a very gloomy account of Coleridge's health, but this in her old way, without the least feeling or sense of his sufferings.' *Mem. of Coleorton*, i. 187.
7. *To a Gentleman* [William Wordsworth], *composed on the night of his recitation of a Poem on the growth of an Individual Mind.*

	I quote from the original version chiefly for the sake of including the seventeen lines beginning 'Dear shall it be to every human heart,' which were first printed in the *Mem. of Coleorton*, i. 215. The original version is given entire in *Poet. Works*, 1893, Appendix H, p. 525.

> O Friend! O Teacher! God's great gift to me!
> Into my heart have I received that lay
> More than historic, that prophetic lay
> Wherein (high theme by thee first sung aright)
> Of the foundations and the building up

Of thy own Spirit thou hast loved to tell
What *may* be told, by words revealable:

. . . .

       Thy work
Makes audible a linked song of Truth—
Of Truth profound a sweet continuous song,
Not learnt, but native, her own natural notes!
Dear shall it be to every human heart,
To me how more than dearest! me, on whom
Comfort from thee, and utterance of thy love,
Came with such heights and depths of harmony,
Such sense of wings uplifting, that its might
Scatter'd and quell'd me, till my thoughts became
A bodily tumult; and thy faithful hopes,
Thy hopes of me, dear Friend, by me unfelt!
Were troublous to me, almost as a voice,
Familiar once, and more than musical;
As a dear woman's voice to one cast forth,
A wanderer with a worn-out heart forlorn,
Mid strangers pining with untended wounds.

O Friend, too well thou know'st, of what sad years
The long suppression had benumb'd my soul,
That, even as life returns upon the drown'd,
The unusual joy awoke a throng of pains—
Keen pangs of Love, awakening, as a babe
Turbulent, with an outcry in the heart!
And fears self-will'd, that shunn'd the eye of Hope;
And Hope that scarce would know itself from Fear;
Sense of past youth, and manhood come in vain,
And genius given, and knowledge won in vain;
And all, which I had cull'd in wood-walks wild,
And all which patient toil had rear'd, and all
Commune with Thee had open'd out—but flowers
Strew'd on my corse, and borne upon my bier,
In the same coffin, for the self-same grave!

But the 'orphic song' brought to the listener something more wholesome than despairing remorse—it brought, for the moment at least, hope, and something else which could not be defined. 'Thought was it?' he asks himself, 'or aspiration? or resolve?'—

The tumult rose and ceas'd: for peace is nigh
Where Wisdom's voice has found a list'ning heart.
Amid the howl of more than wintry storms,
The halcyon hears the voice of vernal hours
Already on the wing!

8. *Frag. Rem.* p. 98.

9. 'In less than a week I go down to Ottery, with my children and their mother, from a sense of duty as it affects myself, and from a promise made to Mrs. Coleridge as far as it affects her, and indeed as a debt of respect to her, for her many praiseworthy qualities.' (*Unpublished Letter of S.T.C.*)

10. *T. Poole and his Friends*, ii. 195.

11. To Josiah Wedgwood, June 27, 1807, in *A Group of Englishmen*, pp. 324–328.

12. In Cottle's *Early Recoil* (ii. 130, but not in his *Rem.*) is printed an extract from a letter written by Coleridge to Wade at this time. Its exact date cannot now be ascertained, for of the original only a fragment remains, but it must belong to the early days of September 1807. Some unprinted passages indicate that Coleridge's poems were being transcribed for the press by Mrs. Coleridge at Bristol, that he was under contract with Messrs. Longman for a book (possibly these poems), and that he had received the offer of a regular engagement on some provincial newspaper, and had declined it, under the belief that its acceptance would displease the Wedgwoods. In the same letter he describes himself as under unfulfilled obligations to Wade: 'penniless, resourceless, in heavy debt, his health and spirits absolutely broken down, and with scarce a friend in the world'—an obvious exaggeration, seeing that in Wordsworth and Poole alone he had a host, and that he had been reconciled to Wedgwood. Cottle, as usual, darkens knowledge by garbling the extract he gives. Coleridge did not write '*I have* too much reason' to fear the loss of the annuity; but that at a previous time, when another grief was weighing on him, he *had had* reason to fear for the continuance of the annuity.

13. He is referring to Scott, and *The Lay of the Last Minstrel*.

14. One of these statements had some foundation, for it was from a Greek grammar of his own making that Coleridge taught his little boys. The projects—they were never more—are mentioned again, a year and a half later, in a letter to Davy: 'As soon as I have a little leisure I shall send my Greek accidence and vocabulary of terminations to the press with my Greek–English Lexicon, which will be followed by a Greek Philosophical grammar' (*Frag. Rem.* p. 106).

15. *T. Poole and his Friends*, ii. 183.

16. *Ib.* ii. 190.

17. It began to appear in *Tait's Magazine* for Sep. 1834, two months after Coleridge's death; and has been reprinted (with many alterations) in De Quincey's collected *Works* (1863, ii. 38–122). The whole article bristles with blunders of every description. Even the portions which relate the author's own experience and observation require a large allowance for refraction.

18. *Rem*, pp. 341–344. The narrative is, as usual, full of inaccuracies—as is shown by a comparison with the correspondence printed in *De Quincey's Memorials* (2 vols. 1891), but the latter gives no new complexion to the *conduct* of the parties. Both De Quincey and Cottle write as if the transaction had been carried through at once, but the correspondence explains how it came to drag on from July till November. This was not De Quincey's fault, for he found difficulties in raising the whole of the money at once. Cottle prints Coleridge's receipt: 'November 12, 1807—Received from Mr. Joseph Cottle the sum of Three hundred pounds, presented to me, through him, by an unknown friend. S. T. Coleridge, Bristol.'

19. S.T.C. to Cottle (n.d.), *Rem.* p. 342.

20. *Frag. Rem.* p. 99.

21. *Rem.* pp. 314–325. I have not seen the original, but it was, no doubt, carefully revised by Cottle before printing. The reports of conversations on these topics are more completely given in Cottle's *Early Recoll.*, ii. 99–124. These are, even more than the letter, open to the suspicion of severe editing. Southey wrote thus to W. Taylor, July 11, 1808: 'Had Middleton been now at Norwich, it is possible that you might have seen Coleridge there, for M. called upon him in London. It has been his humour for [some] time past to think, or rather to call, the Trinity a philosophical and most important Truth, and he is very much delighted with Middleton's work on the subject. Dr. Sayers would not find him now the warm Hartleyan that he has been; Hartley was ousted by Berkeley, Berkeley by Spinoza, and Spinoza by Plato; when last I saw him Jacob Behmen had some chance of coming in. The truth is that he plays with systems, and any nonsense will serve him for a text from which he can deduce something new and surprising' (*Mem. of W. T.* i. 215).

22. Partly printed in *T. Poole and his Friends*, ii. 202–204.

23. For De Quincey's account of the journey, see *Works* (1863, ii. 128); Art. 'William Wordsworth.'

24. 'To Two Sisters: A Wanderer's Farewell' printed in the *Courier*, Dec. 10, 1807. The signature was *Siesti*, but this disguise of ESTEESI proved too

thin for Mrs. Coleridge's jealous eyes. 'The wanderer' was Coleridge, and the 'two sisters' were Mrs. J. J. Morgan, and Miss Brent, and Mrs. Coleridge was highly displeased. Coleridge wrote:—

> Even thus did you call up before mine eyes
> Two dear, dear Sisters, prized all price above;

and Mrs. Coleridge well knew that these were not herself and Mrs. Southey. The poem in its integrity was first reprinted in *Poet.* and *Dram. Works*, 1877–80. It will be found also in *Poet. Works*, 1893, p. 179. A few lines adapted from it were published in ed. 1834 (and after) with the heading, 'On taking leave of——, 1817' (the date a misprint for '1807').

25. It was really the first, notwithstanding statements by Coleridge and his editors to the contrary.

26. The following is a list of all the lectures of this course, of which there is any general or particular record, printed and unprinted: I. Jan. 12, 1808; II. Feb. 5; III. and IV. before April 3. At least three more were given before May 15, and several more in the course of the succeeding five or six weeks. Notes of four were made by H. Crabb Robinson—see his *Diary*, etc., 1872, i. 140; and Mrs. H. N. Coleridge's *Notes and Lectures on Shakespeare* [by S.T.C.] 1849. These are not included in *Lectures and Notes on Shakspere and other English Poets*, by S.T.C., now first collected by T. Ashe (Bell, 1883), a useful, and in many respects an excellent compilation.

27. To the confusion of the sense, this word has hitherto been printed 'intended.' I quote from the original letter.

28. On this, see *Mem. of Coleorton*, ii. 35.

29. Coleridge had been ill and better again in December 1807 (*Mem. of Coleorton*, ii. 41). On Feb. 18, 1808, he reports to Beaumont that he has been 'very ill' for many weeks, with only two 'day-long intervals.' He has been able to do nothing except to write 'a moral and political defence of the Copenhagen business,' which requires only a concluding paragraph. This no doubt was for the *Courier* (see H. C. Robinson's *Diary*, etc., 1872, i. 138). 'I shall disgust many friends,' he adds, 'but I do it from *my conscience*. What other motive have I?' (*M. of C.* ii. 47). There is not a word about lectures.

30. *Mem. of Coleorton*, ii. 48.

31. Allsop's *Letters*, etc., p. 185. The article was printed in the *Edinburgh Review* for July 1808. In a letter to Jeffrey (printed in the *Illustrated London News* for June 10, 1893), dated 'Grasmere, Dec. 8, 1808,' Coleridge expresses his thanks for the insertion of the article as an act of personal kindness and attention to the request of one a stranger

except by name, and says that the 'pecuniary remuneration' he had received was a surprise to him. He mildly points out that the alterations the article had undergone have not been very skilfully made; and complains of the inversion of the remarks on Pitt's favourable attitude towards Abolition. Coleridge declares that 'such is his detestation of that pernicious minister, such his contempt of the cowardice and fatuity of his measures, and his Horror at the yet unended Train of their direful consequences, that if obedience to Truth could ever be painful to him, this would have been.' He acted well in praising Pitt, but was pleased that Jeffrey 'acted equally well in altering' the passage 'according to his convictions.' The only explanation of Coleridge's far-stretched complaisance is that he was at the time endeavouring to enlist Jeffrey's aid in getting subscribers for *The Friend*, and meekly accepted two out of three emendations in the phrasing of the Prospectus, which Jeffrey had suggested.

32. *Letters from the Lake Poets*, p. 180; Allsop's *Letters*, etc., p. 185; *Frag. Rem.* p. 102.

33. Knight's *Life of W. W.* ii. 100.

34. Whether he delivered the full contract number of sixteen, I know not, but it seems probable he did, for he received the full fee of a hundred pounds—£40 advanced in October 1808 and £60 in March 1809. In April 1808 he had applied for the £60, and been refused. This lack of confidence was much resented by him, and he immediately borrowed £100 from Stuart, part of which was required to pay the premium on his life-policy (*Gent. Mag.* June 1838, p. 581; *Letters from the Lake Poets*, p. 135).

35. *Works* (1863), ii. 99.

36. *Letters from the Lake Poets*, p. 181, where the passage appears to be given incompletely.

37. *Life and Corr.* iii. 16.

38. See Sara Coleridge's recollections of this visit, printed in her *Memoirs* (1873), pp. 17–20. The two boys had been placed at school at Ambleside.

39. Knight's *Life*, ii. 120.

40. *Frag. Rem.* p. 101.

41. In all these letters of December, Coleridge writes of *The Friend* as of something of which they had been previously aware. Can it have been to some such project that Coleridge alluded in a mutilated passage of his letter to Wordsworth of May 1808? He has been writing of Wordsworth's pecuniary anxieties, and goes on: 'Indeed, before my fall .... I had indulged the hope that, by division of labour, you would have no occasion to think about .... [*sic* in *Life*] as, with very warm and zealous patronage,

I was fast ripening a plan which secures from £12 to £20 a week (the prospectus, indeed, going to the press as soon as Mr. Sotheby and Sir G. Beaumont had read it).' Knight's *Life*, ii. 102.

42. *Letters of R. S.* ii. 120. See an interesting letter from Coleridge to Thomas Wilkinson (Wordsworth's friend of the 'Spade') Dec. 31, 1799, on the prospectus of *The Friend* in the *Friend's Quarterly Examiner* for July 1893—Art. 'S. T. Coleridge on Quaker Principles'; and *Athenaeum* for Sept. 16, 1893—Art. 'Coleridge on Quaker Principles.'

43. Knight's *Life of W. W.* ii. 124.

44. The stamp on each number was 3½d., but there were discounts which reduced the cost to little more than 3d.

45. 'THE FRIEND; a Literary, Moral, and Political Weekly Paper, excluding Personal and Party Politics and Events of the Day. Conducted by S. T. Coleridge of Grasmere, Westmoreland. Each number will contain a stamped sheet of large Octavo, like the present; and will be delivered free of expence, by the Post, throughout the Kingdom, to Subscribers. The Price each Number One Shilling. . . . Penrith: Printed and Published by J. Brown.' The continuity of issue was frequently broken—thus there were eight blank weeks between II. and III.; three between III. and IV.; one between XI. and XII.; one between XX. and XXI.; and one between XXVI. and XXVII. and last.

46. *Letters from the Lake Poets*; p. 166. 'June 13.'

47. A collation of a set of stamped, with the set of unstamped, numbers issued with a title-page in 1812, shows that the first twelve numbers in the volume were *revised reprints* done in 1809.

48. *Biog. Lit.* 1817, i. 162. The real facts of the story there given about 'the gentleman who procured nearly a hundred names' will be found in *Mem. of Coleorton*, ii. 99. A comparison of the two versions will repay the curious student.

49. *Mem. of Coleorton*, ii. 96–108.

50. It is commonly stated, on what authority I know not, that Coleridge and Ball had got on very badly, and that the laudation in *The Friend* was insincere. All the evidence derivable from Coleridge's correspondence and diaries of the period points in the opposite direction. I suspect that Stoddart spread reports about Coleridge which were coloured by his resentment of real or imaginary injuries.

51. No. I. appeared on December 7, 1809, and No. VIII. and last on January 20, 1810. Reprinted in *Essays on his own Times*, pp. 593–676.

52. *Mem. of Coleorton*, ii. 109–115.

53. 'Of the small number who have paid in their subscriptions, two-thirds, nearly, have discontinued the work.' S.T.C. to Lady Beaumont, January 21 1810 (*Mem. of Coleorton*, ii. 97).

54. The MSS. with some correspondence therewith connected are preserved in the Forster Collection at South Kensington.

55. Unprinted. 'Greta Hall, December 19, 1809.'

56. *T. Poole and his Friends*, ii. 241. The date is printed 'August 3,' but the month must have been October.

—James Dykes Campbell, "Nether Stowey— *Lyrical Ballads*," from *Samuel Taylor Coleridge: A Narrative of the Events of His Life*, New York: The Macmillan Co., 1896, pp. 62–93

Charles Wharton Stork (1914)

Charles Wharton Stork's essay focuses on the divergent ways in which Wordsworth and Coleridge made use of the ballad tradition. Stork's discussion of the ballad influence goes beyond an examination of the poems in the *Lyrical Ballads* to include many of their later works, although he begins his discussion with Wordsworth's famous preface to that work. Wordsworth was attracted to both the simplicity of the genre and its subject matter, which focused mainly on the lives of the lower social classes, and the space it allowed for sentimentality and domestic concerns, whereas Coleridge was drawn to the ballad's medieval characteristics and supernatural trappings. For all of Wordsworth's describing many of his poems as ballads, however, Stork maintains that few were actually in the tradition and supports his argument by defining the ballad as a genre animated by action and suspense, treating its characters imperson-ally and objectively, all qualities that were antithetical to Wordsworth's poetic goals. Simply stated, the ballad aimed at telling a vivid, dramatic, and fast-paced story. Wordsworth, while purposefully rejecting any idea of a melodramatic poem that could produce alarming effects, was more interested in the individual character's life and emotions as conveyed in a slower-paced narrative that afforded the reader the space and pace in which to reflect. For Wordsworth, the characters' feelings were the heart of the matter, not the situational trappings of the traditional ballad. While Stork credits Wordsworth's genius in reworking the tradition by pointing out his originality and departure from both older conceptions and eigh-teenth-century conventions, Stork nevertheless finds inherent weaknesses in Wordsworth's reworking of the ballad. He sees them as centering on a triviality born of an aim at absolute simplicity, finding "insipidities in the poems which they inspired," poems in which "a simple style more than any other demands an unusual inspiration in its matter to raise it above the commonplace." He identifies a type of narcissism on Wordsworth's part to the extent that the poet's faithful portrayal of his characters' feelings are actually subjective manifestations of how he saw them. Nevertheless, Stork finds a great deal of virtue in Wordsworth's reworking of the traditional ballad in that his efforts serve as a counterstatement to the Della Cruscans and other forms of eighteenth-century artificiality. The Della Cruscans were a school of late-eighteenth-century English and Italian sentimental poets founded by the English poet Robert Merry (1755–98). They took their name from the Florentine Accademia della Crusca, a society dating back to 1583 that sought to "purify" their language and considered by Wordsworth and other critics to be insincere, sensational, and working within an outmoded tradition of courtly poetry.

According to Stork, Coleridge's engagement with the ballad tradition was more straightforward with respect to a dramatic story and stunning effects, but his contribution was equally as important as Wordsworth's, most especially in *The Rime of the Ancient Mariner*. Stork dubs Coleridge a master of strange beauty and remote times, and he emphasizes Coleridge's style in experimenting with new combinations of language, something Wordsworth did not focus on. Consequently, for Coleridge, the ballad was a platform for playing with a variety of poetic devices in the service of creating dramatic effects. Nevertheless, Stork supports Traill's opinion that Coleridge's poetry in general lacked substance and singleness of purpose and that, by virtue of writing in the "tenacity" of ballad genre, Coleridge was compelled to produce a finished work. Stork then seeks to answer the question as to why Coleridge was willing to forfeit abstract arguments in the *Ancient Mariner* and contends that the poet, as a modern man, felt a certain respect for the tradition and, consequently, remains faithful to "strangely pervasive and enduring power." In a word, Stork maintains that Coleridge "yielded" to the convention and that it is only in this instance that he remained faithful to their agreed-upon responsibilities in composing the *Lyrical Ballads*.

Beyond this particular work, Stork attributes Coleridge's failure to produce complete poems to the poet's abstruse critical theories. Though Coleridge sought to clarify and simplify his theories vis-à-vis his poetry, he never managed to translate his philosophical genius into his poetic practice. Ironically, Wordsworth's philosophical theories, which were far simpler, were successfully expressed in his poetry, most especially in the *Ode: Intimations of Immortality*. As to *The Three Graves*, which cannot be compared to *The Rime of the Ancient Mariner,* Coleridge claimed that the story was taken from real life and, further, that its style is reminiscent of Wordsworth by having the tale narrated by an "unnecessary third person, and [with] such a prosaic indirectness." However, the subject matter of *The Three Graves,* concerning a mother's guilty love for her future son-in-law, while incompatible with Wordsworth's perspective, was chosen by Coleridge for its imaginative possibilities. It remains a mere fragment. With *Christabel,* though it remained unfinished, Stork's assessment is positive, for he sees the poem as stylistically brilliant, enchanting in color and sound, "in which the lights are always changing like those of moonlight on a waterfall," while "Kubla Khan" is a miniature instance of the same artistry. Simply stated, *The Rime of the Ancient Mariner* works as a true ballad because it was written with the intention of telling a wondrous story, enhanced by Coleridge's powerful imagination, and had nothing to do with the poet's artistic theories.

⸺∿∿⸺ ⸺∿∿⸺ ⸺∿∿⸺

Although both Wordsworth and Coleridge were strongly influenced by the popular ballad, they were attracted by this form for very different reasons and affected by it in very different ways. The one point in common is that this influence was in both cases mainly for good. Wordsworth was drawn to the ballad by its directness and simplicity of style, and by the fact that it often treats of the lower classes of men in what Rousseau would have called a natural state of society. Coleridge took up the ballad for a nearly opposite reason; *i. e.,* because of its remoteness from modern life, a remoteness that left him free play for his imagination. Thus, oddly, Wordsworth cultivated the ballad because it had *once* been close to common life; Coleridge because it was *now* remote from common life and gave him a form remarkably susceptible of that strangeness which the romantic genius habitually adds to beauty. Wordsworth preferred the domestic, or occasionally the sentimental-romantic, ballad; Coleridge markedly adhered to the supernatural ballad.

As the subject is rather complex for a brief survey, the following arrangement will be adopted: to examine in each author separately the influence of the ballad, first generally and in relation to his theory of poetry; secondly, in detail as to the subject, treatment, and form of the poetry itself.

At the outset we encounter Wordsworth's prefaces to the *Lyrical Ballads* and Coleridge's attempts to explain them in his *Biographia Literaria.* Wordsworth's theory of poetry has been such a mooted question that we are certain to overemphasize his statement of it unless we note what he himself thought of the *Prefaces.* In a side-note[1] on the manuscript of Barron Field's

Memoirs of the Life and Poetry of William Wordsworth the poet asserts: "I never cared a straw about the 'theory,' and the 'preface' was written at the request of Mr. Coleridge, out of sheer good nature." And again: "I never was fond of writing prose." Coleridge, too,[2] claims the *Preface* as "half a child of my own brain." We may pause to note that it was rather unfair of the philosopher-critic to tempt his colleague into disadvantageous ground and then fall upon him.

What influence the *Reliques* had upon Wordsworth it may not be easy to determine; that he felt such an influence is proved by the following passage:[3] "I do not think that there is an able writer in verse of the present day who would not be proud to acknowledge his obligations to the '*Reliques*'; I know that it is so with my friends; and, for myself, I am happy on this occasion to make a public avowal of my own."

We may safely assert that the influence of ballad narrative treatment upon Wordsworth's conception of poetry was very slight and very indirect. He wrote but few real ballads, though he wrote a good many poems he called ballads. His theory of poetry clearly and repeatedly disavows the only purpose for which a true ballad can exist, viz., the effective telling of a dramatic story for its own sake.

> The moving accident is not my trade;
>> To freeze the blood I have no ready arts:
> 'Tis my delight, alone in summer shade,
>> To pipe a simple song for thinking hearts.[4]

Again, speaking of the *White Doe*, he writes:[5] "I did not think the poem could ever be popular just because there was nothing in it to excite curiosity, and next because the main catastrophe was not a material but an intellectual one." All the action proceeding from the will of the chief agents is "fine-spun and unobtrusive"; Emily "is intended to be loved for what she *endures*." Let the dramatist "crowd his scene with gross and visible action"; but let the narrative poet "see if there are no victories in the world of spirit," let him bring out the interest in "the gentler movements and milder appearances of society and social intercourse, or the still more mild and gentle solicitations of irrational and inanimate nature." Wordsworth decries[6] the qualities of writing which "startle the world into attention by their audacity and extravagance" or by "a selection and arrangement of incidents by which the mind is kept upon the stretch of curiosity, and the fancy amused without the trouble of thought."

Other passages could be added, but the foregoing will suffice to show why Wordsworth's ballads as ballads are unsatisfying. His entire theory (which, at least in this case, underlay his practice) was opposed to the method of the popular ballad. The ballad depends upon action, Wordsworth upon description and reflection; the ballad is objective and impersonal, Wordsworth maintains[7] that the poet should treat of things not "as they *are*," but "as they *seem*, to exist to the senses, and to the passions." Consequently the ballad proceeds, as Professor Gummere says,[8] by a "leaping and lingering" method, holding the attention by rapid movement, suspense, and adequate climax; whereas Wordsworth disbelieves[9] in "gross and violent stimulants" and says[10] that in his poems "the feeling therein developed gives importance to the action and situation, and not the action and situation to the feelings." The ballad is unconscious, existing in and for itself; but in Wordsworth's opinion[11] poetry should have a purpose and should be the product of a mind which has thought long and deeply.

In general we may say that no other of the great English poets was by temperament so incapable of writing a good ballad as Wordsworth. All that he got from the subject matter of the ballad was the idea of attaching his descriptions and reflections to a story, or, as it often proved, to an incident. What, then, were these "obligations" to the ballad which the poet was so careful to acknowledge?

The truth seems to be that Wordsworth's genius (which, as Coleridge says, was one of the most marked in English poetry) was scarcely at all imitative. The ballad first suggested to the philosopher that he should convey his teaching by means of narrative. Afterwards it suggested something else far more important; namely, that he should adopt a simple style, close to the usage of common people in real life. In any case, when Wordsworth wrote, objectively, he would have written of the peasants who lived around him, but *Percy's Reliques* caused him to write in a more direct and intimate way than Crabbe had done. Yet though the style of *We are Seven* is simple, it is not with a ballad simplicity, but in a manner akin to Blake, whose every phrase must be pondered, even dreamt over, before we realize its full significance. As we read the *Lyrical Ballads* we get not so much the incident that is related, as the personality of the poet; we see things not as they are, but as they seemed to Wordsworth.

It was fortunate that such a profound poet should have early formed a style so lucid, but in other ways the choice of models was not advantageous. Wordsworth evidently thought[12] he was writing as primitive men had written, and justified his deviation from the prevalent fashion by declaring[13] that "poems are extant, written upon humble subjects, and in a more naked and simple style than I have aimed at, which have continued to give pleasure from generation to generation." The foregoing obviously refers to ballads.

Wordsworth wrote of humble people as he thought they might have written of themselves, he strove to be a voice to those

> men endowed with highest gifts,
> The vision and the faculty divine,
> Yet wanting the accomplishment of verse?[14]

Whether or not he succeeded in this, he gave English literature some of its noblest poetry in the attempt, though his most successful narrative form was not the stanza but blank verse or octosyllabic couplets.

The reason why the narrative style of the *Lyrical Ballads* seems to us often so flat, even now that we know its elements of greatness, is easy to explain. The old ballads which the critics, from Sir Philip Sidney to Professor Child, have taught us to admire are elementally tragic and compelling; the ballads Wordsworth preferred were tame and dilute Eighteenth-Century versions. He cultivated the spirit not of "the grand old ballad of Sir Patrick Spence," but of *The Babes in the Wood*;[15] and we may suppose he enjoyed less the stirring tales of Percy and Douglas, than[16] the "true simplicity and genuine pathos" of *Sir Cauline*, principally (as he knew) the product of the "Augustan" Thomas Percy. Without denying a certain merit to Wordsworth's favorites, we need not be surprised to find insipidities in the poems which they inspired. These faults are prominent from the fact that a simple style more than any other demands an unusual inspiration in its matter to raise it above the commonplace, and Wordsworth could never see when his subject fell from the significant to the trivial. The "gross and violent stimulants" of the old ballad narrative gave vitality to many a weak phrase and line; with the modern poet the interest of each passage started from a dead level and, being helped by no poetic convention of any sort, depended solely on the intrinsic power of the given poetic impulse.

Few writers have dared to depend upon pure poetry (re-inforced, however, by deep moral purpose) so entirely as did Wordsworth, who discarded story interest and all the adventitious helps of imagery associated with poetic stimuli. The result was that he earned all he won. It is of course true, as Coleridge says,[17] that in the *Lyrical Ballads* there is a certain "inconstancy of style" (we should call it a lack of integrity in tone) which intrudes because the poet will not choose suitable subjects, or, having chosen,[18] will not raise the weaker portions to the level of the best by the use of poetical conventions of any sort. But in the *Lyrical Ballads* Wordsworth has established the habit of absolute sincerity which has made his greatest passages and poems a model of what Bagehot justly calls "the pure style" in poetry. How large a share the ballad had in forming this habit every reader must judge for himself. The influence of Milton, while it tended to obviate baldness of style, was at the same time a reinforcement to Wordsworth's native sincerity. Perhaps even Pope, with whom he rather unexpectedly asserts that he is familiar,[19] may have helped Wordsworth to clarity and memorable lines. But the ballad influence is always to be reckoned with, particularly in some of the greatest later poems.

Having considered the general influence of the ballad on Wordsworth's poetry and theory of poetry, we shall now take up the specific details of his practice. There are three distinct types of influence to be noted: first, imitations of the Eighteenth-Century domestic ballad, usually built around trifling incidents of the poet's own experience; secondly, ballads proper, impersonal poems with genuine story interest usually taken from tradition; and thirdly, poems founded on old ballad ideas but given a totally new significance.

In the first class the subjects are all modern and realistic. We think at once of *Lucy Gray*, *Peter Bell*, *Ruth*, *The Idiot Boy*, etc., etc. This is the class which illustrates Wordsworth's remark that the situations were only used to bring out the characters. Poetry of this class is very uneven, because the simplified style leaves each theme to stand or fall on its merits. In *Peter Bell* a great deal of incident is used rather unconvincingly to account for a change of heart in the hero. In *Ruth* the story brings out the chastened beauty of a soul ennobled by suffering. These two may stand as types of the poet's failure and success; as to the others, let every reader form his own opinion, remembering, however, that a trivial subject may be developed into a far from trivial poem.

A difficulty that besets us here is to distinguish between the ballad and the lyric in a given case. Where shall we class *The Reverie of Poor Susan*, or *The Childless Father*, or *The Fountain*? As all the poems are in a sense lyrical, *i. e.*, the vehicle of personal feeling, and none strictly a ballad, we shall give up any formal attempt to classify them. In the *Lyrical Ballads* Wordsworth sometimes uses subjects remote in place, but he introduces only two which are set in the traditional past. Of these *Hart-Leap Well* begins with a true narrative swing, but shirks the climax ("I will not stop to tell how far he fled Nor will I mention by what death he died"), runs into description and reflection, and ends with a moral. *Ellen Irwin* belongs to the second class of ballad influence.

Despite the praise given to the *Lyrical Ballads*, Wordsworth hardly ever returned to their method. He may have felt that the blank verse of *The Brothers* and *Michael* was a less dangerous and more dignified medium for the lessons he wished to impart by means of the life around him. At all events, his next attempts in the ballad are ballads proper, objective, set in the past and in story sufficient unto themselves. To this class belong *Ellen Irwin*, *The Seven Sisters*, *The Horn of Egremont Castle*, and *The Force of Prayer*. All of these subjects are medieval and all are on stock ballad themes; that is why they are so easy to classify. The point here to be noted is that, though all of these are respectable poems, never descending to bathos, they have contributed and will contribute very little to their author's reputation. When Wordsworth does with a ballad what a ballad should do, he achieves only mediocrity. Better are his earlier nondescript efforts, with their glaring faults and their characteristic virtues.

The third class is the most interesting of all, uniting as it does the attraction of the old ballad with some of the finest poetry in all of Wordsworth. To this we may perhaps relegate two poems from the Tour in Scotland, *Rob Roy's Grave* and *The Solitary Reaper*. The hero of the former appears in a dramatic monologue which anticipates the manner of Browning; it breathes healthy humor and a fine open-air spirit of liberty. In *The Solitary Reaper* we have a picture as immortal as any by Millet. So, Wordsworth believed, the two principal themes of the ballad were handed down; the "old, unhappy, far-off things" and the "familiar matter of to-day." It was the latter type which the poet had cultivated first; he was later to reflect the spirit of "battles long ago."

If there are any two poems of Wordsworth more strikingly noble than the rest, are they not the *Song at the Feast of Brougham Castle* and *The White Doe of Rylstone*? If we answer yes, the reason will be because in these two poems only is Wordsworth's philosophy of life brought into relief by contrast with its opposite. In Lord Clifford we have opposed glorious action and humble but soul-sufficing patience, and it is because the impulse to action is so splendidly connoted in the lines

Armor rusting in his halls
On the blood of Clifford calls

that the victory of forbearance is so memorable.

In the *White Doe* the case is similar, although the motives are less dramatically contrasted. This poem embodies perhaps the deepest expressions of Wordsworth's belief in the refining power of suffering, especially when it is endured amid "nature's old felicities."[20] The mystic symbolism of the doe is a new effect, slightly anticipated, perhaps, by such lyrics as *The Cuckoo* and by the fish in *Brougham Castle*. It was evidently Wordsworth's hope[21] that the story, taken bodily from the ballad *The Rising in the North*, might serve to present his convictions more clearly and forcibly than they could otherwise be stated, and although Hazlitt[22] thought the narrative part a "drag," the majority of critics have sustained the author's choice. The narrative is very spirited in itself and, as in the case of *Brougham Castle*, the virtues of action bring out most clearly the higher virtues of endurance. It would be out of place to praise further; we may only remark that in *The White Doe* Wordsworth makes his best use, both in style and in substance, of the popular ballad.

As we noted in treating the *Lyrical Ballads*, an accurate classification of ballad influence upon Wordsworth is impossible, but at least a few random cases of the first and third types should here be mentioned. After the *Lyrical Ballads* there are only two important stanzaic narrative poems dealing with the present, viz., *Fidelity* and *The Highland Boy*; a fact showing how far the poet had receded from his earlier practice. Both of these poems contain beauties far more noteworthy than any in the objective medieval ballads. A little-known piece, which is, however, remarkable from our point of view, is *George and Sarah Green*, perhaps the only poem composed as a balladist would have composed it. These lines were not the result of "emotion recollected in tranquillity"; for Wordsworth tells us [23] he "effused them" under the direct emotion caused by the event. They give that impression to the reader; the reflections attached are scarcely more complicated than those of a villager might have been, and the whole has the ballad quality of being more affecting than the sum of its parts—as if the poet had composed too fast to put in all he felt. Similar, but more extended and less poignant, is Wordsworth's last narrative effort, *The Westmoreland Girl*.

For the third class of influence, old ballad motives with modern treatment, we may perhaps claim the Yarrow series, with their haunting sense of ancient wrong and sorrow in the background of the scene. On the other hand, Wordsworth's early and very interesting play *The Borderers*, disappoints the promise of its title by giving us no hint of traditional matter save a passing allusion to the fairies. The classic *Laodamia* is out of our province; so are the medieval romances, *The Egyptian Maid* and *Artegal and Elidure*, both in the manner of Spenser. The faint traces noticeable in blank-verse poems such as *The Brothers* may also be passed by.

Nearly all the ballads of the first (contemporary) class (Part One of *Hart-Leap Well* belongs to the second) are told either by the poet or by some unnecessary third person, as opposed to the popular usage of never bringing in the pronoun "I." Again, Wordsworth's primary interest in character gives us individual figures instead of ballad types, people who merely do things. In his objective medieval ballads he has less chance for intimate analysis, a principal reason why these poems are nugatory. In the more subjective poems of our third class we have for the first time character contrast, that feature essential to all dramatic effects. Lord Clifford in *Brougham Castle* has two natures, the active spirit of the ballad hero and the passive fortitude developed in him by

> The silence that is in the starry sky,
> The sleep that is among the lonely hills.

In *The White Doe* Emily and Francis are represented minutely, the others almost with ballad brevity, but with the more effect in contrast for that very reason.

Wordsworth began with the regular four-line stanza, but soon branched out into variants; e. g., an eight-line stave riming *a b a b c d c d*, in which the "*a's*" have always a double ending. Then there are many original combinations of couplets and alternate rimes, such as those in the ten-line stanza of *Her Eyes are Wild* and the eleven-line stanza of *The Thorn*. It would be out of proportion here to enumerate others; suffice it to say that they are all built upon the two original ballad norms of the rimed couplet and the four-line stanza with alternate rimes. The poet seems to have been experimenting to find a slightly more complex arrangement that would make his lines appear somewhat less bare, in fact he tells you[24] that he thinks the stanza used in *Goody Blake* an improvement on the stereotyped method. In *Ellen Irwin* he imitates Burger's *Lenore*. The foot is nearly always the iambus, notable exceptions being *The Reverie of Poor Susan* and *The Childless Father*, in anapests. In lyric flexibility *The White Doe* is reminiscent, not always happily, of *Christabel*.

The three most marked qualities of popular ballad style[25]—the refrain, repetition of conventional lines and phrases, and "incremental repetition"— are conspicuously rare, diminishing from a moderate importance in *We Are Seven* to negligibility in almost all poems after the *Lyrical Ballads*. We have refrains in *The Thorn* and *The Seven Sisters*, that of the latter, "the solitude of Bennorie," suggesting of course the ballad of *The Two Sisters*. *The Idiot Boy* abounds in repeated phrases, but as a rule Wordsworth followed the modern method of thinking out synonyms and finding original adjectives. Of incremental repetition used for dramatic suspense and climax, as in *Babylon*, *Edward*, and many more of the best popular ballads, there is not one example. There is no conscious alliteration in Wordsworth. His forced use of inversion, borrowed from the imitation ballads, decreases steadily.

As to the language of the *Lyrical Ballads* not being the language of real life, Coleridge[26] is of course right. In a broad sense Wordsworth never wrote of anybody but himself; he gives us[27] not people as they are but people as they appear to him. We cannot, therefore, expect him to make them talk as they really would talk. His creations have a very strong and definite actuality, but it is largely an actuality lent them by their creator. As a penetrating critic has said in another connection, fact plus imagination gives another fact—the final fact being, as Coleridge notes,[28] much more interesting and universal than the original. Had Wordsworth written as he proposed, his poems would have been a little better and a great deal worse. It was in imitation of the Eighteenth-Century ballad style, which Wordsworth supposed was an adaptation of the speech of real life, that Lucy Gray was made to answer, "That, father, will I gladly do," surely a cardinal specimen of the namby-pamby; it was from the poet's own heart that the lines came—

No mate, no comrade Lucy knew;
She dwelt on a wide moor,
—The sweetest thing that ever grew
Beside a human door.

This last is what we may call the Blake note, so much like the ballad—and so much more unlike! Of course the two blend in different proportions, the personal driving out the imitative as time goes on. But if the style of the ballad had done no more than help Wordsworth to find the language of common sense, it would have rendered an infinite service in those days of the Della Cruscans and other continuators of Eighteenth-Century artificiality. The extent of this influence, as already stated, can never be calculated in the case of a poet who so entirely assimilated and so strongly modified all that affected him from outside.

* * *

The question of ballad influence on Coleridge is comparatively simple, but extremely interesting none the less; for although but one poem of importance is directly involved, that happens to be *The Rime of the Ancient Mariner*. *The Three Graves*, the fragment of *The Dark Lathe* and *Alice du Clos* are the only other ballads, though suggestions of the tradition appear elsewhere. And not only is the field of ballad influence in Coleridge very limited, but the character of that influence is almost uniform. As noted at the beginning of this article, it consists of a medieval glamour and remoteness almost invariably tending toward the supernatural. Wordsworth had at first made use of the ballad process somewhat as he conceived a peasant might have done; its closeness to common life and its directness of style had impressed him; he may have liked to think he was keeping the convention alive. Coleridge, on the other hand, was in his best poetry primarily a stylist, or perhaps we should rather say an artist. As with De Quincey and Poe (both of whom, like himself, were a prey to stimulants) his soul was enamoured of a beauty exquisitely strange and terrible, a beauty not of time or place, but dwelling in the utmost regions of the imagination. Now to the generation of Coleridge (and largely to those following) the strange and the terrible seemed to belong of right to the Middle Ages. De Quincey's *Avenger* and Poe's *Fall of the House of Usher* show how these kindred geniuses sought a kindred atmosphere. It was almost inevitable that Coleridge should have anticipated them, and that he should have used the ballad, as Chatterton did, only because in many ways it connoted the medieval.

Coleridge's theory and practice of poetry were instinctively those of art for art's sake. Despite his admiration for Wordsworth's stronger and sounder genius, even despite his preference[29] of his friend's poetry to his own, he could not have written other than he did. Consequently, polemical critics must range themselves under the banner of Arnold or of Swinburne in the dispute as to the priority of the two poets. With this dispute we have here nothing to do. It is, however, important to notice Coleridge's emphasis on style. He maintains[30] that "poetry justifies as poetry new combinations of language, and commands the omission of many others allowable in other compositions. Wordsworth has not sufficiently admitted the former in his system and has in his practice too frequently sinned against the latter." Again,[31] "Every phrase, every metaphor, every personification should have its justifying clause in some passion" of the poet or his characters. He finds Wordsworth's *Preface*[32] "very grand, ... but in parts obscure and harsh in style." Coleridge was evidently a man who justified literature, especially poetry, pretty largely by its style. We need not, then, be surprised to find that the ballad for him was not a method of treating actual life as it appeared to him, but rather an assortment of poetic devices by which to give the effects he was planning.

But the ballad did far more for Coleridge than furnish him with a few pigments by which to obtain what we may call delocalized local color, a coloring which makes real to us the country of his imagination. It is not by a coincidence that his greatest finished poem, the one poem universally known and universally praised, happens to be a ballad. Coleridge's weaknesses were lack of substance, lack of purpose, and lack of virility. The popular ballad exists only by right of substance, because the composer has a story to tell; its purpose is clear and inevitable, to tell the story and be done with it; and its form—in stanza, line, and phrase—is terse and vigorous. Here, then, is the reason why, as Mr. Traill has observed,[33] "*The Ancient Mariner* abounds in qualities in which Coleridge's poetry is commonly deficient"; why here alone we have "an extraordinary[34] vividness of imagery and terse vigor of descriptive phrase"; why we find[35] "brevity and self-restraint" here and not in any other poem by the same author. It was surely the ballad convention that kept the poem going, and it was possibly the ballad tenacity of purpose that caused it to be finished; the incomplete *Dark Ladie* throws some doubt on the latter point.

As to the causes of Coleridge's failure with his other poems, much has been said that need not here be rehearsed. He himself asserted[36] that the alleged obscurity of his poetry came from the uncommon nature of his thought, not from any defect in expression. He said[37] that poetry nearly always consists of thought and feeling blended, and that with him philosophical opinions came in to such an extent as to form a peculiar style that was sometimes a fault and sometimes a virtue. But on this point Coleridge, the subtle specialist in criticism, contradicts himself; for in another place[38] he declares that Milton's definition of poetry as "simple, sensuous, and passionate" sums up the whole matter. The second statement is of course the sounder view. Doubtless Coleridge hoped to write of abstruse subjects in a style that would not be abstruse, but it was impossible to get any simple, sensuous, or passionate results out of such an involved mode of thought as his. One has only to look at his prose, with its continual discriminations, qualifications, and parentheses, to see what so often hindered him from being a poet. On the other hand, Wordsworth's philosophical ideas, though deep, were simple; and his conviction as to their truth was so strong as to become a passion, as witness particularly the *Ode on Intimations of Immortality*.

Why was it, we may ask, that in *The Ancient Mariner* Coleridge forgot his involutions and assumed the virtues he so seldom had?—how could he for this once adopt the methods of the ballad? The answer is to be found in a certain mysticism which the modern man feels in the finest passages of the old ballads, a mysticism far simpler than that of Coleridge, but sufficiently permeating to appeal strongly to his sympathies. This effect is hardly to be described, hardly even to be illustrated—one critic will find it where another will deny that it exists—but every true lover of the ballad will have felt it again and again in favorite passages. Perhaps as safe a selection as any is the stanza of *Sir Patrick Spence* which Coleridge himself prefixed to his *Dejection*:

> Late, late yestreen I saw the new Moon,
>   With the old Moon in her arms;
> And I fear, I fear, my Master dear!
>   We shall have a deadly storm.[39]

Anyone who has tried to teach the ballad knows how difficult it is to bring the latent beauty of such passages before an average mind; but once the beauty is perceived, it has a strangely pervasive and enduring power. This Coleridge felt as no other man has ever felt it. Launching into the story with typical ballad abruptness, he yielded himself to the narrative current and was borne by it safely through the labyrinthine reefs of metaphysics indicated by his own notes in the margin. Though *The Ancient Mariner* is true Coleridge, it is in this case a Coleridge that has given up his own intricate and nebulous mysticism for the more direct and concrete mysticism of the ballad.

Coming to the consideration of Coleridge's ballads in detail, we find the first of these to be *The Three Graves*. The first two parts of this poem seem[40] certainly to antedate *The Ancient Mariner*. In the first place the poet asserts[41] that the story was taken from facts, in the second the style very strongly suggests Wordsworth, especially in its imitation of faults which Coleridge later condemns. As in Wordsworth, the tale is put into the mouth of an unnecessary third person, and such a prosaic indirectness as the following indicates a most inartistic resemblance to its models:

> She started up—the servant maid
>   Did see her when she rose;
> And she has oft declared to me
>   The blood within her froze.

But the story itself was one that would have been abhorrent to Wordsworth; the idea of a mother's guilty love for the affianced husband of her daughter would have repelled him at once. Coleridge professes[42] to have chosen the subject not from "any partiality to tragic, much less to monstrous events," but for its imaginative and psychological interest. This defense, by the way, is exactly that which a modern decadent might use on a similar occasion.

The treatment, too, is distinctly immoral, or, as some critics now prefer to call it, unmoral. That an innocent pair should suffer from the curse of the guilty mother is, at least to an average person, repugnant. Coleridge's *penchant* toward the supernatural appears in his dwelling on this point and even going so far as to imagine that

> the mother's soul to Hell
> By howling fiends was borne,—

an unsatisfactory bit of poetic justice, as her curse lives after her. But there is power in the poem, a power of just the sort that anticipates the success of later pieces. Throughout the stanzas we feel the uncanny genius of the poet struggling in a trammeling element, often rising head and shoulders above it. *The Three Graves* is far from being a good poem, but fragmentary and inchoate though it is, we can hardly understand *The Ancient Mariner* without it.

This brings us to the center of our subject. After the experiment of *The Three Graves* Coleridge selected just the theme that suited him, and in the treatment kept tolerably clear of the hampering influence of his colleague. To be sure, Wordsworth supplied the idea[43] that the suffering of the Mariner should be represented as an atonement for the death of the albatross, and no doubt the concluding moral "He prayeth best" was composed under his influence; but these can easily be detached from the body of the poem. We are all familiar with the agreement[44] in regard to the *Lyrical Ballads* by which Wordsworth was to bring out the supernatural side of natural scenes and Coleridge was to bring out the natural, the humanly comprehensible, side of his supernatural phantasies. It was only in *The Ancient Mariner* that Coleridge definitely carried out his share of the undertaking.

The Ancient Mariner, however, was not written to illustrate a theory or even to carry out a conscious purpose. Few phrases could better sum up the effect of the poem than that of an inspired undergraduate who called Coleridge "a literary Turner." There is in these two the same glorifying brilliance of color, the same triumph of beauty over mere subject, the same marvellous gift of style which raises their respective arts almost to the emotional level of music. Even the human soul living through the scenes of the poem, which Lamb thought the greatest achievement of all, is rendered in a light of unreality; for the Mariner's most passionate outcry awakens no real pain in us. Why, then, if they are so vague, do this poem and (say) Turner's *Ulysses Deriding Polyphemus* exercise such a powerful and enduring influence over us? In the case of Turner we know that it is largely from the firm command of draughtsmanship which he allows us to see more clearly in his water-colors. In Coleridge a similar firmness comes from the groundwork of the ballad, the most marked and dominating of all the conventional forms in poetic narrative. The conciseness of the ballad and its insistent progression demand a relation of the parts to the whole not unlike that required by the laws of perspective. (This, like most analogies, may be carried too far, but in general it seems to be not inaccurate.)

Taking his plot from a dream,[45] Coleridge began his long flight unhampered by the weight of actuality; course and destination indefinite, as it were. Though the Mariner tells the tale, the effect on the reader is almost that of an impersonal narrative. The speaker tells nothing of who he is and little of what he does, he is as a helpless soul passing through strange experiences. Consequently we feel the events of the poem very immediately; we do not watch the hero as we watch Lord Clifford or Emily Norton, we live his adventure with our inmost being. It would seem from this that *The White Doe* is nearer to the old ballad than is *The Ancient Mariner*, but in reality we feel that the Nortons are always illustrating a philosophical idea, whereas the Mariner neither reasons nor causes us to reason. The explanations of his voyage are as mystically simple as are those about death in *The Wife of Usher's Well* or about fairyland in *Thomas Rymer*; the modern poet exercises hardly more arbitrary control than does the nameless bard. In both cases we feel intensely but abstractly. We notice that Coleridge is often tempted to digress, but the ballad inspiration drives him on, just as it drove the author of *Sir Patrick Spence*.

The story exists for its own sake as a work of art; essentially it conveys, or should convey, no moral. Its one weakness in form is its promise of a moral suggested, as we have seen, by Wordsworth. For the shooting of the albatross is an absurdly small offense to bring about such a punishment, and the attempt to make the other sailors responsible by having them approve the deed is even worse; besides, the accomplices are punished with death, whereas the principal expiates his sin. Fortunately we feel these defects but slightly, for we must relinquish our judicial qualities to follow the magical flow of the lines.

We have been somewhat over-accenting the resemblance of *The Ancient Mariner* to the ballad; the differences must not be forgotten. As a poet of the highest imaginative power and the most exquisite technic, Coleridge raises every stanza, every phrase, to a miracle of design. The very absence of apparent effort in the process is the final proof of his perfect art. What we find in a happy stanza here and there among the old ballads is a regular rule with the modern poet. His similes are nearly always brief and his metaphors direct, but the best of ballads is dull and uninspired in comparison. His greater subtlety and sensitiveness make the old forms seem rough and childish; his control of sound and color is like a sixth sense. And yet the balance is not all on one side. If the ballad has no real description, Coleridge has no real narration. What we have called a story is but a succession of descriptions photographed on the receptive soul of the Mariner. No one does anything, least of all the hero. Tried in the heat of normal human interest (the test of the ballad), the story melts away to nothing, its appeal can be only to the few. To the peasant for whom *The Hunting of the Cheviot* was written, the whole would have seemed the "tale of a cock and a bull" that the early reviewers found it. The imagery and verbal music of Coleridge are opposed to the compact statement and strong beat of the ballad not wholly to the advantage of the former. After all, there is a difference between real and acquired simplicity.

The unfinished *Ballad of the Dark Ladie* is closely connected[46] with the more lyrical poem, *Love*. The latter piece, Coleridge tells us, was intended to be an introduction to the *Ballad*. But the incidental story told in *Love* is apparently not that of *The Dark Ladie*. In *Love* the knight wears on his shield a burning brand, whereas the *Dark Ladie* sends her page to find "the Knight that wears / The Griffin for his crest." We have little clue as to what the tale of the *Ballad* is to be, but this little seems to indicate another motive than that used in *Love*. When Lord Falkland speaks to his lady of stealing away to his castle "Beneath the twinkling stars" and she shrinks from the idea of darkness and wishes to be married at noon, we have a foreboding of the Lenore theme, the dead lover returned to claim a living bride. There is a *feel* of the German ballad of terror about the poem noticeable in the rather gushing sentiment and in the effort to arouse a shudder. Farther than this the evidence will not take us. In *Alice du Clos*, however, we have a distinctly German ballad with several passages reminiscent of Scott. The theme is violent and painful, the narrative style labored, the diction overwrought. The fragile strength of Coleridge is sadly strained in handling such material; crude acts, the staple of the ballad, belong to a world outside his knowledge. Nevertheless the poem has beautiful descriptive lines and one stirring passage in Scott's better style:

Scowl not at me; command my skill
To lure your hawk back, if you will,
    But not a woman's heart.

Alice du Clos is at least a better excursion into the territory of the rough and ready school of poetry than is Scott's ballad of *Glenfinlas* into the realm of the fantastic.

Passing on to consider ballad influence in the poems which are not ballads, we begin naturally with *Christabel*. If ever style without substance could make a perfect poem, it would be in the case of this unrivalled piece of filigree work. To Swinburne it seemed the acme of poetic art; but few even of the truest art-lovers can be satisfied by melody without sequence, and color without shape. The poem, if one must define it, is a sort of lyric romance-caprice, in which the lights are always changing like those of moonlight on a waterfall. But there are ballad elements in the misty atmosphere of *Christabel*. Terse and direct phrasing often lends the same vividness to supernatural effects that we have noted in *The Ancient Mariner* and *Sir Patrick Spence*. For instance,

And Christabel saw that lady's eye,
And nothing else saw she thereby.

Quoth Christabel, So let it be!
And as the lady bade, did she.
Her gentle limbs did she undress,
And lay down in her loveliness.

But the steady flow of the ballad narrative and the steady pulse of the ballad stanza are not there to give purpose and consistency to the whole. Perhaps it was because he had no traditional model to sustain him that Coleridge confessed[47] he had "scarce poetical enthusiasm enough to finish Christabel." This at least we know: the story in, *Christabel* forgets itself in long descriptions, loses itself in digressions, changes repeatedly, and never ends.

Kubla Khan in small corresponds to *Christabel* in large, except that in it the element of mystery is oriental instead of medieval; a fact which reminds us that at this period the oriental novel was rivaling the "Gothic" in tales of terror. The only point of interest for us in the shorter poem is the "woman wailing for her demon lover," a figure more indigenous to the medieval ballad[48] than to the Arabian tale. *Dejection* in the line "The grand old ballad of *Sir Patrick Spence*" gives us the only specific mention of a ballad or of *the* ballad which has thus far appeared in Coleridge's published writings. His quotation from *Sir Patrick* at the beginning of such a personal poem shows how sensitive he was to the uncanny *feel* of ballad lines even when they merely displayed a popular belief as to the weather. *The Knight's Tomb* also has a ballad touch. *Love* has been sufficiently treated in connection with *The Dark Ladie. The Water Ballad* is too feeble to deserve the second part of its title. *The Devil's Walk* is an excellent humorous ballad.

It remains only to examine the details of ballad influence on Coleridge. *The Three Graves* is in form an imitation of Wordsworth's early style with but a suggestion of independence. In *Parts One* and *Two* the four-line stanza is unvaried, in *Parts Three* and *Four* occur several of the five and six-line stanzas common in *The Ancient Mariner*. As the story is modern, no medievalism can be brought in.

The original form of the title, which was *The Rime of the Ancyent Marinere*, shows at once what effect the author intended to create, but later Coleridge covered his tracks. In the first version of the text two repetitions and the words "phere," "n'old" and "aventure" were excised, probably to diminish the appearance of borrowing from the ballad; the word "swound" was also changed, but later restored. The spelling was modernised as in the title; the cases were not numerous, "cauld," "Emerauld," "chuse" and "neres" being examples.[49] Coleridge's taste was well-nigh perfect in this point, for the vocabulary of the poem conveys the idea of remoteness and never of affectation. In contrast, the unfortunate phrase "bootless bene" in *The Force of Prayer* is almost the only archaism in Wordsworth.

Ballad repetition, similarly, though much more frequent than in Wordsworth, is used with great discrimination. The echoing of a single word gives a greater physical reality to the idea in

The ice was here, the ice was there
		The ice was all around;

as in "Alone, alone, all, all alone" and "Water, water everywhere." Phrases are repeated and parallelism preserved with the same effect, i. e., the reader's attention is kept on the sensuous object and not diverted to the style by any unnecessary change of the wording. The phenomena of sunrise and sunset are made particularly intimate by this means and by the added touch of personification. Incremental repetition is not carried beyond the progression

He holds him with his glittering eye.

followed at the opening of the next stanza by

He holds him with his glittering eye.

There is no refrain anywhere in Coleridge. Alliteration, rugged in the ballad, is toned down so as not to jar the delicate verbal music of the whole. "The furrow followed free" subtly relieves the insistence of the "f"s by the play of "r"s and "l." There is strong vowel alliteration[50] in "Alone, alone, all, all alone," but the change of shading and the fact that the "glottal catch" is so faint a sound serve again to show how perfect is the poet's ear. Inversion, which is often so awkward in Wordsworth, is handled with the same care that appears in the other details of *The Ancient Mariner*.

That Coleridge was working toward a more purely lyrical metre we see by his variants of the regular ballad stanza. Internal rime is frequent. The five-line stanza *a b c c b* is used sixteen times, so that the following form is nearly typical:

With throats unslaked, with black lips baked
	We could nor laugh nor wail;
Through utter drought all dumb we stood!
	I bit my arm, I sucked the blood,
	And cried, A sail, a sail!

Coleridge also cultivated the six-line stanza (occasionally found in the old ballad), often repeating with a slight variation in lines 5 and 6 the thought of lines 3 and 4, as in

A spring of love gushed from my heart,
	And I blessed them unaware;
Sure my kind saint took pity on me
	And I blest them unaware.

This device is used by Poe in *The Raven, Ulalume,* and *Annabel Lee.* One passage, lines 203–211, is very irregular, suggesting the movement of *Christabel.* Two similes, lines 446–451 and 433–438, are so extended as to divert the eye to the secondary picture, and the description of the hermit at the opening of Part Seven is an absolute digression. All these points show the tendency toward lyric freedom and diffuseness which were to prevail in *Christabel* and *Kubla Khan.*

It seems not worth while to examine the details of ballad influence on other poems more minutely than has already been done. *The Dark Ladie* is very regular, *Alice du Clos* very irregular.

In *The Three Graves* we have a failure in the unmodified ballad, in *Christabel* we have a failure, at least from the point of view of narrative, in the lyrical romance; *The Ancient Mariner* stands between them, combining the merits of tradition with the merits of the poet's individual genius. It is hardly a coincidence, we may repeat, that Coleridge's most famous poem is that in which he made the most well-considered use of the popular ballad.[51]

Notes

1. *Letters of the Wordsworth Family,* ed. Knight, Vol. III, p. 121.
2. *Coleridge's Letters* edited by Ernest Hartley Coleridge, p. 388.
3. *Essay Supplementary to the Preface,* 1815. *Prose Works of William Wordsworth,* ed. Knight, Vol. II, p. 247.
4. *Hart-Leap Well,* opening stanza of *Part Second.*
5. *Letters,* III, pp. 466, 467.
6. *Prose Works,* II, p. 253.
7. *Idem,* II, p. 226.
8. *The Popular Ballad,* p. 91.
9. *Prose Works,* I, p. 52.
10. *Idem,* I, p. 51.
11. *Prose Works,* I, pp. 49, 50.
12. *Prose Works,* I, p. 77.
13. *Idem,* I, p. 66.
14. *The Excursion,* Book I, ll. 78–80.
15. *Prose Works,* I, p. 71.
16. *Prose Works,* III, p. 243.
17. *Biographia Literaria,* chap. XXII.
18. *Idem,* chap. XIV.
19. *Letters,* III, p. 122.
20. From the sonnet, *The Trosachs.*

21. *Letters*, I, p. 343.
22. *Letters*, II, p. 62. Coleridge also says in generalising, "Wordsworth should never have abandoned the contemplative position" (*Table Talk*, July 21, 1832).
23. *Letters*, III, p. 465.
24. *Prose Works*, I, p. 69.
25. *Cf.* Professor G. L. Kittredge's *Introduction* to the Cambridge edition of *English and Scottish Popular Ballads* and his references to Professor Gummere's works.
26. *Biog. Lit.*, chaps. XVII, XX.
27. *Cf.* p. 301, *supra*, and note. Wordsworth expressly says that some of his figures were composites (Dowden, *Studies in Literature*, p. 145 and note).
28. *Biog. Lit.*, chap. XVII.
29. Traill's *Life of Coleridge* (English Men of Letters Series), p. 41.
30. *Letters*, pp. 374–5.
31. *Idem*, p. 374.
32. *Idem*, p. 387.
33. *Life of Coleridge*, p. 47.
34. *Idem*, p. 51.
35. *Idem*, p. 53.
36. *Letters*, pp. 194–5.
37. *Idem*, p. 197.
38. *Idem*, p. 387.
39. The correct form of this line is: "That we will come to harm." Coleridge must have mixed stanzas 7 and 8 of Percy's version.
40. Quoted in Mr. J. D. Campbell's notes, Globe ed., p. 590.
41. *Ibid.*, p. 590.
42. *Ibid.*, p. 590, 589.
43. Quoted in Mr. Campbell's notes, Globe ed., p. 594.
44. *Biog. Lit.*, beginning of chap. XIV.
45. Quoted in Mr. Campbell's notes, Globe ed., p. 594.
46. Quoted in Mr. Campbell's notes to the Globe ed., p. 612–3.
47. *Letters*, p. 317.
48. *Cf.* the ballad *James Harris or The Demon Lover*, Cambridge ed. of *Ballads*.
49. One of Professor Archibald MacMechan's students has discovered that all Coleridge's borrowings came from the first volume of Percy.
50. *Cf.* the paper read by Professor F. N. Scott before The Modern Language Association, Dec. 30th, 1913.
51. In other chapters of a proposed book on ballad influence upon English poetry since 1765 the author hopes to show that the ballad has had in

general a salutary effect in modifying the extreme individualism of the Romantic Poets.

—Charles Wharton Stork, "The Influence of the
Popular Ballad on Wordsworth and Coleridge,"
PMLA, vol. 29, no. 3, 1914, pp. 299–326

THE RIME OF THE ANCIENT MARINER

Thomas Shaw (1847)

Shaw praises *The Rime of the Ancient Mariner* for its wondrous, unearthly landscape, which transports the reader into a dream world made all the more alluring by its beautiful lyricism, a "harmony of tone . . . . scrupulously kept up." Unlike many other critics of the poem, however, Shaw does not see it as a work that straddles the borderline between reality and the supernatural.

Of the poems by which Coleridge is best known, both in England and abroad, the most universally read is undoubtedly *The Rime of the Ancient Marinere*, a wild, mystical, phantasmagoric narrative, most picturesquely related in the old English ballad measure, and in language to which is skilfully given an air of antiquity in admirable harmony with the spectral character of the events. The whole poem is a splendid dream, filling the ear with the strange and floating melodies of sleep, and the eye with a shifting vaporous succession of fantastic images, gloomy or radiant. The wedding-party stopped on their way to the feast by the "bright-eyed marinere," the awful fascination by which the guest is obliged to hear and the wanderer to tell his tale, the skeleton ships and the phantoms which play at dice for the soul of the mariner, the punishment and repentance of the man who "shot the albatross,"—all this is wound up into one splendid tissue of cloudy phantoms. We read on, with that kind of consciousness of half-reality, that sensation of indistinct surprise, with which we are carried onward in our dreams. Extravagant and unreal as it all is, that important quality of harmony of tone is scrupulously kept up; and hence the pleasure we experience: we are placed in a new unearthly atmosphere, and all glimpses of the real world are carefully avoided.

—Thomas Shaw, *Outlines of
English Literature*, 1847

PETER BAYNE "COLERIDGE" (1858)

Peter Bayne's biographical sketch presents us with a sympathetic and colorful portrait of Samuel Taylor Coleridge. At times, Bayne's rhetorical flourishes appear to be competing with his subject matter as he delivers his final eulogy on the poet's life. "We image him to ourselves as a desert-born steed, with hoofs to outrun the wind, and eyes to outgleam the lightning, but smitten, at the bright morning hour . . . . and thenceforward staggering, with eye dimmed and limbs tottering, along the burning sand." It is obvious from the outset that Bayne is enamored of the poet, declaring him the British "genius upon the forehead of the age, [who] molded the intellectual destinies of our time." However, in his synopsis of Coleridge's life, it becomes clear that Bayne is highly selective in the details he wishes to highlight, while he omits many essential ones, such as Coleridge's career-defining friendship and literary collaboration with William Wordsworth. Instead, Bayne focuses on the poet's precocious and bookish days (with an uncle who took him to coffeehouses and taverns where he learned the art of conversation), his troubled childhood at Christ's Hospital, and subsequent successes during his brief tenure at Cambridge, while explaining in the most compassionate and appreciative terms Coleridge's journalistic failures with *The Watchman* and *The Friend.*

Bayne peppers his selective chronology with anecdotes, among them a particular day Coleridge was daydreaming along the Strand, originally a muddy track in London that ran east along the Thames but by the late eighteenth century the site of Somerset House, the duke of Somerset's Tudor Palace, along with many other fine mansions. While unwittingly pushed around in a crowd, the young man's hands had unconsciously found their way into a stranger's pocket and he was accused of stealing. This not being the case, Coleridge, the "simple-hearted little dreamer," related the true facts and was rewarded by his accuser with access to a circulating library. Equally as delightful is Bayne's description of Coleridge and Southey's Pantisocracy project, which was as optimistic as it was fraught with such practical obstacles as a lack of money: "Cottle paid some guineas in advance [for every hundred lines of poetry that Coleridge would produce]; but Pegasus scorned to be yoked, in the provision cart." Bayne consistently maintains, however, that many of Coleridge's failures were due to his steadfast immaturity and lack of discipline. With respect to his discussion of *The Rime of the Ancient Mariner*, Bayne points out a most salient feature that other critics have commented on—the painterly aspects of the poem. "A vision of wildest grandeur. . . . Its graphic power is absolutely wonderful." The point is strongly suggestive of Horace's phrase, "ut pictora poesis," discussed in his *Ars Poetica*. Its translation reads "as is painting so is poetry" and refers to the similarity between these two art forms. Horace's concept of the relationship between poetry and painting would later become an important issue for discussion in the sixteenth, seventeenth, and eighteenth centuries and, though often modified and revised, became a basis for a number of critical commentaries.

When Bayne ultimately turns to Coleridge's decline through opium addiction, it is with compassionate regret for the downfall of a towering imagination, "sorrows that might draw tears from the Seraphim." In a word, Bayne presents himself as Coleridge's apologist far more than his biographer.

Among the men who have led the van of British thought during the present century, who have stamped the impress of their genius upon the forehead of the age, and moulded the intellectual destinies of our time, there is one name preeminently fraught with interest to the student of our internal history. That name is Samuel Taylor Coleridge. In our schools of poetry, of philosophy, of theology—among our critics and our ecclesiastics, our moralists and our politicians—the influence of Coleridge has worked, silently and viewlessly, but with wide-spread and mighty power. As by a verbal talisman, his name opens to our mental gaze vast and varied fields of reflection, invokes grave, important, and thickly-crowding thoughts, and forms the centre round which countless subjects of discussion and investigation group themselves. For these reasons, superadded to the fact, that we know of no easily accessible account of his life and writings at once concise and comprehensive, we purpose to devote some considerable space to a biographic sketch of this celebrated poet and thinker.

Towards the latter half of the last century, there lived at Ottery St. Mary, in the southern quarter of the balmy and beautiful county of Devon, discharging there the duties of vicar and schoolmaster, an eccentric, erudite, and remarkably loveable old man. He was the father of Samuel Taylor Coleridge. "The image of my father," says the latter, "my reverend, kind, learned, simple-hearted father, is a religion to me." Richter expressed pity for the man to whom his own mother had not rendered all mothers sacred. Both the remarks shed a beautiful and kindly light over the characters of their authors.

The vicar of Ottery St. Mary was twice married, and had, in all, thirteen children. Samuel Taylor was the youngest; his day of birth was the 21st of October, 1772, when he appeared "about eleven o'clock in the forenoon." He speedily gave indications of superior capacity, being able, at the completion of his third year, to read a chapter in the Bible. We soon begin to discern the operation of causes, bearing, with rather singular importance, upon the formation of his character and the shaping of his destiny. The youngest of the family, he was the object of peculiar affection to both parents, and, in consequence, excited the envious dislike of his brother Francis, and the malevolence of Molly, the nurse of the latter. Hence arose annoyances and small peevish reprisals; for the power of a boisterous and sturdy brother, and a malignant nurse, to embitter the cup of a bard in pinafore is considerable; so little Samuel became "fretful and timorous, and a tell-tale." A tell-tale is an object of united detestation on all forms of all academies; it was so at Ottery St. Mary, where Coleridge went to school; the future metaphysician was driven from play, tormented, and universally hated by the boys; he sought solace at mamma's knee and in papa's books. He became a solitary, moping child, dependent on himself for his amusements, passionately fond of books, of irritable temper, and subject to extreme variations of spirits. At six he had read "Belisarius," "Robinson Crusoe," and "Philip Quarles," and found boundless enjoyment in the wonders and beauties of that Utopia and Eldorado of all school-boys, the Arabian Nights' Entertainments. The following is a portrait of him, about this time, as he sketched it in after years:—"So I became a dreamer, and acquired an indisposition to all bodily action, and I was fretful, and inordinately passionate; and, as I could not play at anything, and was slothful, I was despised and hated by the boys: and because I could read and spell, and had, I may truly say, a memory and understanding forced into almost unnatural ripeness, I was flattered and wondered at by all the old women. And so I became very vain, and despised most of the boys that were at all near my own age, and, before I was eight years old, I was a *character*. Sensibility, imagination, vanity, sloth, and feelings of deep and bitter contempt for almost all who traversed the orbit of my understanding, were even then prominent and manifest."

This has to us a deep significance, in the psychological consideration of Coleridge's character. The ideas lodged in the mind at this early period of life, and the habits formed, may, in after years, change their forms, and appear in manifold and diversified developments; but they retain their place with extreme obstinacy. This childhood of Coleridge's we cannot, on the whole, pronounce healthy. Little boys are naturally objects of dread, rather than of flattery, to old women. Little Robert Clive, for instance, utterly astonished and startled the old women by exhibiting himself on the steeple of Market Drayton; and turned out a man of clear and decisive mind and adamantine vigor. The playground and the meadow, with the jocund voices of his playmates round him, and in the constant consciousness that his independence has to be maintained and defended amid their boisterous and fearless sports, is the proper place for the development of the future man. It is our belief that, in these years, an almost instinctive knowledge of character, a thorough command of the faculties, and a power of bringing them, on all emergencies, into swift energetic action, are attained; and that no subsequent education can compensate the premature devotion of these early days to mental pursuits. May we not here find the faint and unsuspected commencement of that anomalous and mournful severance between the powers of action and the powers of thought, which the world has deplored, and may so well deplore, in Coleridge?

With all his bookishness, however, with all his indolent inaction and indifference to the sports of childhood, little Samuel had a dash of fierce stubbornness in his composition. The old women, on occasion, found cause for abating their flattery: in proof, take the following anecdote. He was about seven years old, when, one evening, on severe provocation from Frank, he rushed at him, knife in hand. Mamma interfered, and Samuel Taylor, dreading chastisement, and in fiercest fury, ran away to the banks of the river Otter. The cold evening air, it was reasonably calculated, would calm his nerves, and bring him quickly home; but the calculation was incorrect. He sat down in resolute stubbornness on the banks of the river, and experienced "a gloomy inward satisfaction," from reflecting how miserable his mother would be! It was in the end of October: the night was stormy; he lay on the damp ground, with the mournful murmuring of the Otter in his ear; but he flinched not, nor relented; with dogged determination, he resolved to sleep it out. His home, meanwhile, was in a tumult of distress and consternation. Search in all directions was instituted; the village was scared from its slumbers, and, ere morning, the ponds and river were dragged. At five in the morning the little rascal awoke, found himself able to cry but faintly, and was utterly unable to move. His crying, though feeble, attracted Sir Stafford Northcote, who had been out all night, and he was borne home. The joy of his parents was inexpressible; but in rushed a young lady, crying out, "I hope you'll whip him, Mrs. Coleridge!" Coleridge informs us, that neither philosophy nor religion was ever able to allay his inveterate antipathy to that woman.

Just as his youngest son was completing his ninth year, the good old vicar of Ottery St. Mary died. Through the influence of Judge Buller, a presentation to Christ's Hospital, London, was obtained for Samuel Taylor; and about April, 1782, he went to London. Here he was, before entering the hospital, domesticated with an uncle. This uncle looked upon him as a prodigy, and was very proud of him. He took him to taverns and coffee-houses; accustomed him to hear himself called a wonderful boy; taught him to converse and discuss with volubility; and, in short "spoiled and pampered him."

This fast mode of life, however, soon came to an end: a very different regimen and environment awaited him in Christ's Hospital. Here he found himself under the strict discipline of Bowyer; his food was stinted; and he had no friends to encourage him by approbation, or refresh his heart by kind indulgence on a holiday. Though enlivened by occasional swimming matches, and wanderings, somewhat hunger-bitten, in the fields, his existence was, on the whole, a joyless one. "From eight to fourteen," he says, "I was a playless day-dreamer—a *helluo librorum*." The manner of his becoming possessed of sufficient opportunity to indulge his keen and insatiable appetite for books, was singular and characteristic. He was wandering one day along the Strand: physically, he was pacing the hard pavement, jostled by the thronging crowd, stunned by the surrounding noises; mentally, he was breasting the waves of the Hellespont, and gazing, through his vacant but glittering eyes, at a light in the distance. The hands, as in somnambulism, caught impulse from the mind, and were cleaving the smoky air in act of swimming. Suddenly he was awakened. By feeling beneath his feet the hard dry sand on the banks of the moonlit Bosphorus, and the kiss of Hero on his lips? No: but by a sudden grasp of the hand, and an exclamation in his ears, "What! so young and so wicked!" His wandering, unconscious fingers had come into too close proximity with a passenger's pocket, and pocket-picking was suspected. The simple-hearted little dreamer told the whole truth: belief could not be withheld, for the whole, we can well see, was written on his cheek and in his eye; and the man, interested in the boy, obtained him access to a circulating library. Reading was henceforth his constant occupation, his unfailing solace. "My whole being," we quote his own words, "was, with eyes closed to every object of present sense, to crumple myself up in a sunny corner, and read, read, read." He went right through the library. He was ever first in his class, occupying that station not from any impulse of ambition or youthful emulation, but simply by his surpassing powers. His general book knowledge was wonderful. Before fifteen, he had sounded the depths of metaphysics and theology, was a fluent master of the learned languages, and had comparatively lost taste for history and separate facts. How strongly developed, even at that early age, was the unalloyed exercise of the intellectual powers! How clearly can we trace, gradually widening, the lamentable severance of which we have spoken! On the whole, what a wonderful boy was this Samuel Taylor Coleridge! The child, even, is father of the man; and, in the boy, his lineaments, both mental and physical, become ever more conspicuous. Already the dream of fancy, or the abstract effort of thought, had greater charms for Coleridge, than the surrounding, or even the historical, realities of life; already his mind had become its own dwelling-place, and found within its own compass a sufficiency of object to allure and delight; already he had drawn astonishment to his commanding faculties. Whether the extreme development of the receptive powers, and the constant inundation of the mind by the ideas of other men, might not, to some extent, weaken the sinews of the soul, and implant the seeds of that irresolution which clouded his latter days, were a question; we would be disposed to render it an affirmative answer. He soon displayed an inability to tread in beaten paths, to pursue common methods. He might be found, during play hours, reading Virgil "for pleasure;" but he could not give a single rule of syntax, save in a way of his own.

His reading was, as might be supposed, exceedingly varied. It reached Greek and Latin medical books on the one side, and Voltaire's "Philosophical Dictionary" on the other. This latter appeared to the boy conclusive; to Bowyer, it did not. In utter disrespect for freedom of opinion, and the finer feelings of Samuel's bosom, Bowyer did not attempt, by laborious effort of philosophical reasoning, to re-convince him; he gave him a sound flogging! It appears to have acted with potent persuasion; and Coleridge called it, in after life, the only just flogging he ever received from him.

In February, 1791, Coleridge entered at Jesus College, Cambridge. He speedily distinguished himself by winning a gold medal, for a Greek ode on the slave trade; but, in various subsequent competitions, during his university career, his endeavors were not attended with corresponding success. As heretofore, he was by no means a methodic student, but he still continued a voracious and desultory reader. He gave proofs, also, of that astonishing conversational power by which he afterwards became so distinguished. His room was the resort of the gowned politicians; and Coleridge, besides being the life and fire of debate, put them, by means of his wonderful memory and swift reading, in possession of the latest political pamphlets.

It was a time of extreme excitement. The French Revolution was exploding; the most wonderful series of events, since the Reformation, was taking place; the long imprisoned winds had burst their cavern, and their noise was going over the world: Coleridge, as all others, felt the influence. The whole atmosphere, political and literary, vibrated with excitement; the glories of the latter morning were deemed to be arising; and thousands of the fiery-hearted youth of the land hasted to enrol themselves under the banners of the good cause.

Principles are rained in blood: that has long been an ascertained fact. And what a deluge of blood did it require to rain this one principle; yea, may we not, from the general appearance of the world at present, predict that even more blood must be shed ere men are fully convinced of it—namely, that, by simply leaving mankind to the freedom of their own will, they will arrive, not at regeneration and highest felicity, but at destruction, misery, and confusion worse confounded? Surely the French Revolution might have taught us this, and instructed us to look for final regeneration to the heavens. But the lesson, if we are now to esteem it acquired, was, as we say, hard to teach. A whole Egyptian inundation of blood was required to water, and enable to take deep root, this one principle; and, in pursuance of a method which nature very often adopts, its contrary was first shown in full operation. Remove the restraints of tyranny; open wide the floodgates, so long pent up, of human love and sympathy; and all men, throwing up their caps to welcome the time of peace, will, simultaneously and of necessity, rush into each other's arms! Such was the faith of Shelley, embodied in the "Revolt of Islam;" such was the belief, for a brief period, of Robert Southey; such was the faith which threw some method into, and some brilliant hues over, the wild, almost demoniac, but yet heartfelt philanthropy of Byron; such were the hopes which, for a time, fed the enthusiasm, and based the dream-fabrics, of Coleridge.

Of his devotion to this creed, he found means of giving proof when at college; it was a proof characteristic of the man. He was, we must remark, of gentle, truly loveable nature; honest, brave, ardent; but not by any means fierce or truculent. He did not plan a college rebellion, for the regeneration of society; he did not, by fiery and desperate audacity, exasperate the university authorities; he displayed his attachment to new era principles in the following somewhat different manner. On the green lawns before St. John's and Trinity Colleges, a train of gunpowder was to be laid, imprinting the grand watchwords of the new epoch, "Liberty" and "Equality." By the ignition of the gunpowder, the words were to be burned into the grass, and to stand forth there, seen by the sun above, and the college windows farther down, for certain days, a monition and benignant illumination to all the world. A "late chancellor of the exchequer" executed the redoubtable plan; and so Coleridge vindicated his claim to the title of champion of democracy.

At this period of his career, Coleridge was Unitarian in his religious principles. His grounds of belief were not those commonly held by the professors of that creed. He distinctly avowed his conviction, that the Scriptures taught the doctrine of the Trinity; and that the attempts to explain away their statements on the question, in which Unitarians indulged, were utterly unjustifiable. His reasons were almost wholly subjective. Refusing to accede to the doctrine of the atonement, and denying the divinity of our Lord, he calmly pronounced these beliefs the Platonisms or Rabbinisms of the apostles John and Paul. A fuller development of his mental powers; a wider and more searching survey of the realms of truth; and a profounder knowledge of the problems of human history, and the wants and workings of the human heart, led him afterwards to the unwavering conviction that Unitarianism was null and void.

Ere this time, Coleridge had written a considerable quantity of poetry. On the whole, it was not of a very astonishing description. A delicacy of fancy, without singular exuberance of power; a command of soft and brilliant language, at times overladen with ornament; occasional vigorous personation; these comprehend the main beauties and merits of his earliest pieces. "The Songs of the Pixies," is a piece of fine fancy-painting, indicating a true eye for nature, and a power of delicately pencilling her gentlest and fairest forms. This poem seems to lie just on the line of demarcation between the years of youth and those of early manhood.

Various circumstances contributed to embitter and darken the latter part of Coleridge's university career. Some public competitions, as the reader will have gathered, resulted in a way to disappoint his expectations. His Unitarian principles, which he was far too honest to disavow, barred the gates of preferment. And some debts, which his simplicity and want of decision had led him to contract, subjected him to numerous and harassing annoyances. Besides all this, we have found it asserted, that his mild and susceptible heart had been sorely vexed in some love affair. The warm-hearted, dreaming youth was, in fact, peculiarly sensible to the enchantment of female gentleness and beauty; while, of a surety, but few girls were, or ever are, to be found, capable of loving, and of corresponding to the ideal of, the author of "Genevieve."

In November, 1793, he suddenly quitted Cambridge for London. Arrived in the "great brick desert," feeling the loneliness which a stranger may experience when surrounded by thronging myriads of his fellow-men, to him mere automata, and finding himself speedily reduced to pecuniary straits, occasioned partly by his Goldsmithian readiness to give money to any distressed object, he cast about for some means of present subsistence. Shifts there were few; these were none of the choicest, and hunger was menacing; he adopted the singular one of enlisting as a dragoon. Silas Tomken Cumberbatch (S. T. C.) was the imposing designation by which he was known to his fellow-soldiers; and, under such auspices as appeared, he commenced his military career.

Now it soon became manifest, that nature, whatever her generosity or ungenerosity, had not gifted this Silas Tomken Cumberbatch with qualities to enable him to discharge creditably the functions of a dragoon. Far-stretching flights into dreamland on the wings of fancy, imagined beating of the Hellespont waves with a Hero's lamp in view, abstract ponderings on theology and metaphysics, interfere objectionably with the grooming of one's horse! Besides, the man has no "ambition," and seems stupidly callous to the attractions of "glory." Accordingly, he meets with no promotion; never rises out of the awkward squad, and at drill, flounders painfully about, so as to provoke the exclamation of a facetious serjeant, "Take care of that Cumberbatch—take care of him, for he will ride over you!"

What a scene! Was there ever, since the days of the mighty hunter, such a private soldier? What have our painters been about? What more supremely appropriate theme could be imagined, for a national painting than this scene of "Cumberbatch on drill," or "Apollo as a dragoon?" "The rapt one of the godlike forehead;" the man whose impulse has probably gone deeper than that of any other into the vital springs of British thought and general mental development in this nineteenth century; the man at whose feet men of genius and fame sat, like children round a wizard, earnestly regardful of his smallest word; stumbling and staggering about, on his ill-groomed steed; the most awkward of the awkward squad! Talk of Kilmenie among the rustics, after her sojourn by the celestial streams; talk of Apollo amid the gaping herdsmen of Admetus; this of Coleridge among the dragoons beats them all hollow!

"Eheu! quam infortunii miserrimum est fuisse felicem!" This sentence, to the utter surprise of an officer who observed it, and, we doubt not, the sheer uncomprehending amazement of his brother privates, Silas had inscribed on his stable wall. With his brother soldiers he was popular; he wrote their letters; entertained and astonished them with historic narrations, and won their hearts by his gentleness; while they, in return, assisted him to groom his horse. We hear, likewise, of one of the officers—the same, we presume, who made the above discovery—condescendingly—permitting him, when their path lay in the country and not in the town, to walk abreast with himself and enter into conversation. How indulgent! How condescending! He would not find such conversation in the messroom, we daresay; such conversation was probably not to be found in the British Islands; the day was coming when Hazlitt, Lamb, Carlyle, and De Quincey, were to listen, in rapt attention, to the tones of that conversation!

At length, after some four months' drill, the astonishing dragoon was discharged. He returned for some short time to Cambridge, but quitted it soon and forever.

In the summer of 1794, Coleridge, on a visit to Oxford, became acquainted with a young man named Robert Southey; a steady thoroughgoing worker, of strong literary tastes and vast information; who also was under the influence of the Liberty and Equality mania. An acquaintance, which soon ripened into friendship, sprung up between them; there was a strong, perhaps radical, dissimilarity between their characters; but the ethereal spark in either bosom urged them together. This intimacy and this friendship gave tone to much of the subsequent history of Coleridge, and furnish us with one of the raciest and most delicately comic of its episodes. The episode is that of world-renowned Pantisocracy. We shall glance at it.

The scheme, as seems generally agreed, originated with Coleridge; a beautiful dream-poem it was, which he mistook for a reality. The amelioration of the species, the regeneration of the world, the attainment of unmitigated felicity here below, were its objects; the excitement of the French Revolution, with which the air was still tremulous, gave hue to the undertaking. A coterie of choice spirits, free from all stain of selfishness, and, with every energy devoted to the above grand ends, was to be selected: these benign and stainless individuals were to select just as many young ladies of similar perfection, and marry them; the whole were then to take shipping for the banks of the Susquehanna River, beyond the blue Atlantic. This Susquehanna was chosen, Coleridge informed Gillman, on account of the name being pretty and metrical! Here the choice spirits male were to toil, untiring and unselfish, in the supposable manner of their father Adam *before* the fall; the choice spirits female were to do the household work, and perform all the delicate sweetnesses appointed them by nature; all taint of selfishness, all deleterious admixture, of whatever sort, of human failing was to be nonexistent. The unruffled felicity of a second Eden was to be the unquestioned result. Meanwhile, the world, in amazement at its own long stupidity,—and rapt admiration at the dwellers in the new Happy Valley, was to open all its prison gates, fling all its crowns into Limbo, and sheathe sword from pole to pole! Then, by slow degrees or more rapidly, after a gently-brightening silver age or in full and sudden glory, the long-postponed golden age was to gleam upon the world! All living beings were to be embraced in the scheme of love. Hear this:—

"Innocent Foal! thou poor despised Forlorn
I hail thee Brother—spite of the fool's scorn!
And fain would take thee with me, in the Dell
Of Peace and mild Equality to dwell.
Where Toil shall call the charmer Health his bride,
And Laughter tickle Plenty's ribless side!
How thou wouldst toss thy heels in gamesome play,
And frisk about as lamb or kitten gay!"

From bards to donkeys the blessings of Pantisocracy were to extend!

The pleading of this unassailable scheme, and the object of raising the terrestrial element of cash, caused much lecturing in Bristol, whence the world-renovating expedition was to sail. In this town, abode one Joseph Cottle: a man whose nature we can confidently pronounce one of the gentlest, noblest, purest, and most generous to be met with in literary annals, and to whom the world is deeply indebted for his published reminiscences of Coleridge and Southey; he was a bookseller, and warmly patronized genius. Cottle became acquainted with the schemers; enjoyed much their conversation; encouraged their efforts; and lived in hourly expectation of the sailing of the fateful ship, bound for the Elysian Susquehanna. His nerves, one fine morning, were thoroughly and conclusively calmed by the receipt of the following note:—

> "MY DEAR SIR,—Can you conveniently lend me five pounds, as we want a little more than four pounds to make up our lodging bill, which is indeed much higher than we expected; seven weeks, and Burnet's lodging for twelve weeks, amounting to twelve pounds.— Yours affectionately,
> S. T. COLERIDGE."

Four pounds wanting for a lodging-bill, and the regeneration of the world in hand! One begins to fear that the tough old incorrigible is not to be regenerated yet! Pantisocracy vanishes into vacuity, or is drowned in peals of "inextinguishable laughter!"

Did it all vanish then? Did the whole of the elaborate and fairly-schemed plan fleet into nonentity, and the aerial elemental stuff which dreams are made of? Oh no; very decidedly not. The golden age, as usual, hung back; the Eden on the banks of the musically-named Susquehanna could not be set agoing, without fully more than "four pounds to pay our lodging-bill;" but there was one part of the scheme, which, being of the ethereal sort, and flourishing well when fanned by the airs which blow from dreamland, took deep root. This part, as all our fair readers anticipate, was that in which the young ladies figured; Coleridge and Southey were both engaged in marriage. The union of the former with Miss Sarah Fricker took place on the 4th of October, 1795; the provision by which the youthful husband purposed to support himself and his bride being—an engagement, on the part of Cottle, to give him a guinea and a half for every hundred lines of poetry which he delivered him!

This financial scheme, it was found, would not work; in fact, to secure a competency in this way, one would outwrite Homer before his marriage coat, if very carefully preserved, was out at elbow. Cottle paid some guineas in advance; but Pegasus scorned to be yoked, in the provision cart; and, on the whole, some more substantial and certain plan of subsistence was found necessary. The young couple had taken up their abode at Clevedon, a village on the banks of the Severn.

The mind of Coleridge was always scheming, and generally his plans were on a gigantic scale; Cottle tells us of a list of eighteen contemplated works, not one of which was accomplished: his schemes almost invariably, like those of Mithridates, found themselves unduly seconded, and ineffectually actualized, in execution. His schemes on the present occasion, however, were by no means of a singularly romantic or impracticable character. They were chiefly three: to found a school, to become a Unitarian preacher, and to undertake the editing of a magazine. The latter, after consideration, and with somewhat of reluctance, was adopted. The magazine was to be entitled the Watchman; it was to consist of high political writing, of biographical essays, and of reviews; its date of appearance was fixed for Tuesday, 1st March, 1796, and its price was to be fourpence.

Whether the idea of a magazine was congenial or uncongenial to the mind of Coleridge, he entered upon its realization with ardent and manly energy. He undertook a tour to collect subscribers; and accompanied the performance of this primary object with the occasional delivery of pulpit discourses. His religious views were still Unitarian, and his pulpit garb would have somewhat startled an orthodox audience; on one occasion, he appeared in blue coat and white waistcoat. His discourses, too, were "preciously peppered with politics;" and we must shock our readers by informing them, that subjects were afforded for two of them by the corn-laws and the hair-powder tax!

The tour preliminary to the publication of the "Watchman," is one of the most brilliant passages in Coleridge's history. His mind was in the warm glow of opening manhood: full of hope, ardor, courage, love; we can well imagine that the Cherub Contemplation seemed ever to lie and dream in his dark gray eye. His conversation was at the time perhaps at its climax; men hung in wondering silence on the rhythmic stream which, in wild lyric grandeur, or in gentlest lute tones, rolled ever from his lips. His eloquence attracted crowds when he appeared in the pulpit; he was the "figurante" in all companies, and his irresistible powers of persuasion increased his list of subscribers, beyond even his own imaginings. Of his pulpit manner, we may form an idea from Hazlitt's description of him a few years afterwards. Earnest solemnity, despite his dress and politics, seems to have distinguished his mode of delivery; poetic adornment, graphic power, and enthusiastic exuberance, his style. "The tones of his voice were musical and impressive," says Hazlitt; and "he launched into his subject like an eagle dallying with the wind." No wonder that he attracted crowds.

At Nottingham, he had some dealings with Dr. Darwin, who utterly scorned religion, and thought himself in position to banter Coleridge on the subject. His arguments fell of course like snowflakes on a river; they might, Coleridge said, have been of force at fifteen, but provoked only a smile at twenty. "He (Dr. Darwin) boasted that he had never read one book in favor of such stuff, but that he had read all the works of infidels." The impartial, free-thinking man! "Such," adds Coleridge, "are all the infidels whom I have known."

We said above, that his powers of persuasion during this tour were irresistible; but it is unsafe to indulge in such poetic generalizations; the dull tints and dusts of earth so obstinately mingle with all human glories. Coleridge was in Birmingham, beating up for subscribers—enchanting, astonishing, electrifying. In the strict prosecution of his design, he was destined speedily to find his perseverance and courageous scorn of difficulties put to the test. We must give his own description of the scene; it at once indicates the graphic truth of his pencil, and illustrates the fine hearty joviality which lay deep in his bosom:—"My campaign commenced at Birmingham, and my first attack was on a rigid Calvinist, a tallow-chandler by trade. He was a tall, dingy man, in whom length was so predominant over breadth, that he might almost have been borrowed for a foundry poker. Oh that face!. . . . I have it before me at this moment. The lank, black, twine-like hair, pinguinitescent, cut in a straight line, along the black stubble of his thin gunpowder eyebrows, that looked like a scorched aftermath from a last week's shaving. His coat collar behind, in perfect unison, both of color and lustre, with the coarse yet glib cordage that I suppose he called his hair, and which, with a bend inward at the nape of the neck (the only approach to flexure in his whole figure), slunk in behind his waistcoat; while the countenance, lank, dark, very *hard*, and with strong perpendicular furrows, gave me a dim notion of some one looking at me through a *used* gridiron, all soot, grease, and iron!"

This man was a friend of the species, and grand society-regenerator. Attentively he listened to "the heaven-eyed creature," as he poured forth, now like a cataract of sunny foam, now like an Aeolian harp, his eloquent pleadings; the tallow fumes meanwhile wandering intrusively about the nostrils of the wondrous speaker, mournfully reminiscent of earth. Persuasion that might have melted Shylock having had due course, Coleridge paused to become aware of the effect. "And what, sir, might the cost be?" "Only fourpence (oh how I felt the anti-climax, the abysmal bathos of that FOURPENCE), only fourpence, sir, each number, to be published on every eighth day." "That comes to a deal of money at the end of a year; and how much did you say there was to be for the money?" "Thirty-two pages, sir; large octavo, closely printed." "Thirty and two pages? Bless me, why, except what I does in a family way on the Sabbath, that's more than I ever read, sir, all the year round! I am as great a one as any man in Brummagem, sir, for liberty and truth, and all them sort of things, but as to this (no offence, I hope, sir) I must beg to be excused."

From Sheffield, in the January of 1796, Coleridge wrote to a friend reporting progress. In that letter occurs the following sentence:—"Indeed, I want firmness; I perceive I do. I have that within me which makes it difficult to say No, repeatedly, to a number of persons who seem uneasy and anxious." This, so strictly true, we regard as a physiognomic glimpse of importance. With all his brilliancy, with all his marvellous powers, with all the genius which dwelt in his wonderful eye, the great disruption between the powers of thought and the powers of action had begun to be conspicuously manifest in Coleridge. He had not the power of saying No! And yet how necessary, how utterly indispensable, in this world of ours, is the ability to utter, on needful occasions, a clear, defiant No! Mentally or physically it has to be done every hour of our life; and would we not be near the mark, in dating the full development of self-sustained manhood at the thorough attainment of that power?

The "Watchman" did not succeed; the causes of its failure were manifold. Too much was expected by the public; a sufficient staff of talented men was not attached to it; and, finally, the close, accurate drudgery, necessary to the successful superintendence of a magazine, was singularly uncongenial to Coleridge's nature.

Some time after the publication of the "Watchman" ceased, we find its editor stationed at Stowey. Here, though for a brief space he enjoyed tranquillity and comfort, the frustrated hopes of his past life sunk deep into his soul. He was approaching a critical and important epoch in his spiritual development. It can be discerned, with indubitable distinctness, that his mind was in an unhealthy portentous state—feverish, excited, unsettled; now in the whirl of fiery enthusiasm and hilarity, now in the morbid disquietude of hopeless depression; now scheming stupendous epics, now cowering, anxious and trembling, to propitiate the "two Giants, Bread and Cheese." All this points to a shattered nervous state and prompts mournful forebodings.

About this time, Coleridge was of very striking appearance. In person he was somewhat full, and rather above the common size; his complexion inclined to light, but was shaded by dark hair; his eyebrows were large and protruding; his forehead, as Hazlitt describes it, was "broad and high, as if built of ivory;" his large gray eye rolled and gleamed, in the light of mild but mighty genius.

We have arrived, as we said, at a grand crisis in his character and history. We have seen him in his youth; we have marked the swift expansion of his faculties, the first meteoric blaze of his fame. His path hitherto must be pronounced brilliant. Not unshaded by sorrow, not untinctured with error, it is yet encompassed with a grand auroral radiance. The light of genius flashing from his eye, the light of hope and ardor firing his bosom, he has trod along, kindling expectant admiration in all breasts. His very errors have been those of a noble and mighty nature. The banner of human advancement had been thrown abroad upon the winds, inscribed with liberty and with love; and ardent young souls hastened to range themselves beneath it; unweeting that those golden words had been, or were to be, soaked and blotted with blood. With what in the mighty onrushing of the French Revolution was truly noble, with the perennial truths of freedom and advancement, Coleridge had deeply sympathized; in its wild volcanic fury he never shared, and, when murder and despotism sat in its high places, he utterly abjured its cause. For a time, the ardent, all-fusing love in his own bosom, had bathed the world in kindness and beauty; the tones of his own heart were those of tenderness and gentlest sympathy, and he had dreamed that he had heard responsive notes from the bosoms of all his fellow-men. Hence had arisen the Susquehanna scheme, the beautiful morning dream of the Happy Valley. Already, in various ways, he had evinced gigantic powers. In a constellation of rarely gifted youths, he had been the central light, the most dazzling star; his eloquence and his conversation had shed enchantment around him: his "Religious Musings," to specify no other of his juvenile performances, had been the indubitable pledge of power to scale the loftiest heights of thought and of fame, and to sit there crowned among the mightiest.

But his path, dazzling and wonderful as it was, had been strictly that of youth. An element of excitement had encompassed him; the atmosphere of his mind had been tempestuous and fiery; and the grand question which presents itself, at the momentous period of his history at which we have now arrived, is this:—Is his radiance to be merely meteoric, intermittent, and youthful; or is he henceforth, in calmer air and with steadier glory, to shine in the placid majesty of manhood?

Southey, the friend of his youth, and the sharer for a time in his dreams, with powers whose might was never considered so rare or so wonderful as his own, calmly and courageously marched from the dreamland of youth, and in gathered energy commenced life victoriously as a man; Wordsworth, gentle but stalwart-hearted, had virtually done the same; and how was it with him, whose eye gleamed with a more unearthly radiance than that of either, who was among them the acknowledged monarch—Samuel Taylor Coleridge?

What, in our view, marks the full development of manhood, and dissevers it totally from the states of boyhood and youth, is a sustained *self-mastery*. When the energies are not the slaves of excitement; when the fiery impatience of occasional effort has become the perseverent energy of continued work; when the powers are ranged in ordered submission under the will; when the motives are not the faint wavering fatui or meteors of the hour, but the guiding principle of the life is clearly ascertained and resolutely adhered to;—then the boy has passed into the man.

According to this view of the matter, it is manifest that sound healthful manhood does not necessarily presuppose any vastness of mental power, any extraordinary or astonishing genius. A William Burns, for instance, toiling calmly and with stern endurance to find sustenance for himself and his children, may be a sounder, and in stricter terms, a more fully developed man than his world-shaking son the poet, with his wildly-tossing passions and his sadly blasted hopes. The miner, who works resolutely and without flinching in the bowels of the earth, may be more a man than the feverish creature of excitement, who now soars above the clouds, and now lies prostrate and hopeless in the mire. Who ever said Byron was a fully developed man?

Still more, it is precisely where the powers are mightiest, and the passions strongest, that the difficulty of attaining calm manhood is sternest. A comparatively easy task it is for the man of common, everyday powers, to attain their proper command, to restrain them within their due mechanic circle. But when the passions are fierce and mighty as whirlwinds, when the breast heaves with volcanic fire, and the eye rolls in frenzy, when the sensibility is as intensely acute to disappointment as the hopes are bright and certain of failure; then it is, at the momentous crisis when the dreams of youth, whose light has hitherto suffused the world, vanish finally from the soul, that the struggle is tremendous. The bearing of these remarks upon the character of Coleridge will become manifest as we proceed.

After the failure of the "Watchman," we find Coleridge residing at Stowey. The urgency of a regular mode of subsistence had become more imperative, from the fact of his having become a father. Pecuniary affairs, however, wore by no means a hopeless aspect; Charles Lloyd, a young man who had conceived the profoundest admiration for Coleridge's genius, had taken up his abode with him; occasional sums were obtained from Cottle for poetry; and at length, in 1798, Mr. Josiah Wedgewood and his brother, who patriotically desired that Coleridge's marvellous powers should be untrammelled by a profession, bestowed upon him an annuity of £150. One half of this sum ceased to be paid at a subsequent period.

Ere proceeding in our history of Coleridge's character, we must indulge our readers and ourselves with a glance at his Stowey life; a sunny prospect, which we shall soon find enveloped in cloud and darkness. We avail ourselves of the words of kind and honest Cottle, who waxes hilarious and quasi-poetical on the occasion; the time was June 29, 1797. "Mr. C. took peculiar delight in assuring me (at least at that time) how happy he was; exhibiting successively his house, his garden; his orchard, laden with fruit; and also the contrivances he had made to unite his two neighbors' domains with his own .... After the grand circuit had been accomplished, by hospitable contrivance, we approached the "Jasmine Harbor," where, to our gratifying surprise, we found the tripod table laden with delicious bread and cheese, surmounted by a brown mug of true Taunton ale. We instinctively took our seats; and there must have been some downright witchery in the provisions, which surpassed all of its kind; nothing like it on the wide terrene, and one glass of the Taunton settled it to an axiom. While the dappled sunbeams played on our table, through the umbrageous canopy, the very birds seemed to participate in our felicities, and poured forth their selectest anthems. As we sat in our sylvan hall of splendor, a company of the happiest mortals (T. Poole, C. Lloyd, S. T. Coleridge, and J. C.), the bright blue heavens, the sporting insects, the balmy zephyrs, the feathered choristers, the sympathy of friends, all augmented the pleasurable to the highest point this side the celestial! While thus elevated, in the universal current of our feelings, Mrs. Coleridge appeared, with her fine Hartley; we all smiled, but the father's joy was transcendental!"

All this was too bright to last. As yet, indeed, there seemed no great cause for abatement of the hopes of those who, in ever-increasing numbers and in ever-deepening veneration, encircled Coleridge. We might say, in fact, that it was much the reverse. The dreamy disappointments of youth might become matter for a pleasant smile; the poetic fire, in which he had clothed nature and man, might yet warm his own bosom and nerve his own arm.

His political opinions had attained a fuller development; while retaining all the enthusiasm and love of early days, they had settled into assured stability, on a foundation of soundest wisdom. His theological views also—a fact of momentous importance, and fraught with richest hope—had undergone revision. More profoundly and with truer reverence, he had acknowledged, in his inmost soul, that the Bible is, in very truth, the articulate voice of God to man; he had perceived that the whole history of the human race, for the silent but mighty facts of which no youthful imaginings could be substituted, hath, for its centre, its keystone, and its crown, the Lord Jesus Christ; he had begun to discern that religion, if in any sense strictly revealed, must superadd something to the dicta of nature, and be a "religation" or binding again; he had heard the deep and awful words of mystery which rise from the whole frame of nature and the whole inner world of the soul; and, in meekest but manliest adoration, he had bowed down to the triune God. Oh, how Hope now, dashing aside the veil of the shadowing years, seems still, despite our knowledge of the end, with brightest smile to point to Coleridge, as he was at the close of the last century!

In the years of boyhood and youth, Coleridge's constitution, although not peculiarly robust, was unquestionably sound and healthful; not free from weakness, not unvisited by pain, he was yet indubitably the possessor of a buoyant spirit and vigorous frame. But on one occasion, about the close of the century, he had been visited by severe and singular bodily ailment, accompanied by excruciating pain. For relief he had recourse to—opium! Finding the relief he sought, and unaware that he was dallying with a power, whose deadly necromancy withers the arm and palsies the soul, he went on, heedless and unweeting, until resistance was vain.

Here, then, was the blasting of all hope; here was the attainment of calm manhood rendered forever impossible; henceforward the chaining of his energies in ordered submission to the car of will, was hopeless.

Beyond all doubt, this was the proximate and decisive agent in bringing about the tragic anomaly of Coleridge's after life. Yet there were other influences at work, which acted mainly as hindrances and counteracting forces to his at once awakening from his trance, and tearing from his bosom the vampire that drank his life-blood. The shattering of his youthful schemes, and the failure of his youthful hopes, had wakened tones of deepest sorrow in his soul. We hear of a "calm hopelessness," of long days of despairing anticipation and unbrightened foreboding. Besides this, we have reason for thinking it a fact, and we need do no more than mention it, that his marriage had in some respects been an unhappy one.

But for the mighty magic of opium, which, at such a crisis, came in to throw a shade of most mournful gloom over the character and life of Coleridge, these secondary disturbing influences might well have been overborne; but for the depressing effects of these influences, opium might never have succeeded in throwing its withering influence, finally, and irremediably, over his soul: in their mutual operation, they produced what we have called the grand severance in Coleridge's character.

After visiting Germany, in 1798, and making a stay there of fourteen months, Coleridge settled in the Lake country, and engaged largely in newspaper writing. In 1804, he visited Malta. Returning, after a residence of considerable length, to England, we find him, in the year 1809, commencing, once more, the publication of a periodical, this time named, "The Friend." During the period when this paper appeared, the circulating libraries were doubtless in as full operation as ever; the British public of this enlightened age were hanging over their novels, or preparing, perhaps, their ball dresses; commerce was rushing heedless onwards; Mammon was stalking abroad, with all eyes turned towards him in supplication or praise; "The Friend," being sadly over-freighted with wisdom, and having no direct bearing on cash, but only on the eternal destiny of man, and his true and lasting temporal amelioration, could not be carried on for lack of support! This is a fact; and admits of being thus broadly stated. As we peruse those volumes, now promising fair for literary immortality, in which the published numbers of "The Friend" are preserved to us, it appears strange and even humiliating, that such periodical writing should, in our century, under what ever disadvantages, have failed of adequate support. But what, after all, must we say? That, in this defective world, small worms destroy imposing gourds, that, as Richter remarks, though wings are admirable for the azure, we want boots for the paving stones, that the consummate linguistic skill and high metaphysics of Coleridge were rendered unavailing, not solely through the indifference or stupidity of his countrymen, but through such small and undignified shortcomings, as want of punctuality, want of clearness, and want of business tact.

Towards the end of his sojourn at the Lakes, Coleridge's mode of existence, as we learn from Mr. De Quincey, was cheerless and anomalous. Towards the afternoon, he descended from his bedroom; and through the still watches of the night, until the morning struck the stars, his lonely taper burned mournfully in his window. The same writer assures us, that the intense glow of sympathy and joyous admiration, with which Coleridge had once gazed upon Nature, had now well-nigh died away: the magic had passed from stream and lake, from wood and mountain, from the ocean and the stars: they woke no tones of music in his breast, they lit no fire of rapture in his eye. Ah, what a mournful change was here!

In 1810, Coleridge quitted the Lake country forever. In the early part of 1814, we find him lecturing at Bristol. Opium was now in the full exercise of its tyrannic and deadly power. Sternly, and with sincerest effort, he resisted it, but its magic became ever the more irresistible; its necromancy had smitten his energy with fatal paralysis. The effort to free himself from the spell was vain; the thrill of temporary gladness, as of returning youth and rapture, formed so witching a contrast to the remorse and almost despair of his disenchanted hours, that he ever threw himself again into the arms of his destroyer. He seems to us to be sorrowfully, but truly, imaged by his own "miserable knight," haunted by the spectre of a bright and beautiful lady, from the ghastly gleam of whose eye he could not escape, and whom he *knew* to be a fiend.

The wildfire in his eye, and other indications, revealed to Cottle the melancholy state of affairs. In deepest distress, and actuated by his sincere and tender love for Coleridge, he resolved to address to him an expostulating letter. With Cottle, we can find no fault; the voice of duty to his friend and to his God prompted the effort; but, with deep conviction we must say, he was not the man to perform the task. The delicate and reverential kindness which every sentence should have breathed; the admiring and bewailing pity, distinguishing minutely and unremittingly between crime and disease; the manliness of friendly and most earnest advice, with no tone of censorious exhortation or blame;—these were beyond the mental capacity of Cottle. How sad are these words in reply:—"You have poured oil in the raw and festering wounds of an old friend's conscience, Cottle! but it is *oil of vitriol!*" And what an unfathomable sorrow is here:—"I have prayed, with drops of agony on my brow; trembling, not only before the justice of my Maker, but even before the mercy of my Redeemer. 'I gave thee so many talents, what hast thou done with them?'"

Ah! little did Cottle, or even Southey, with his far greater soul, know of the fearful battle which this mighty and valiant spirit had to fight; we must even say that they did not fully attend to what they might plainly have discerned. Does not the whole course of Coleridge's life indicate sternest effort? His newspaper writing, his editing "The Friend," his long researches into metaphysics and theology; do they not show an earnest and noble *effort* to attain "the perennial fireproof joys of constant employment?" do they not show a soul struggling, with Titanic *effort* and deadly perseverance, against a viewless but resistless power? Could aught which Southey or Cottle might say, instil a deeper abhorrence of opium into Coleridge's mind than was there already? Could any human hand portray its effects and influence, in darker hues, than those in which, in his own agonized and blasted soul, they were imaged already to the eye of Coleridge? It was not advice or exhortation which was needed; it was kindliest, tenderest co-operation with the efforts of the sufferer: it was admiring sympathy and respectful assistance. Good conscientious Cottle somewhat mistook his function in addressing Coleridge, and his attempt was, of course, unattended with any important result.

In 1816, Coleridge took up his abode at Highgate, in the immediate vicinity of London, under the roof of Mr. Gillman, a physician. Here he thenceforward remained; and here he terminated his career, in 1834. During this long period, he constantly displayed his astonishing intellectual powers; and exhibited, along with them, the marvellous and melancholy prostration of the powers of action. On the whole, from these years there seems to breathe a wailing cadence of unutterable sorrow. Splendors there were, beautiful, meteoric; but they appear but as the gleaming of nightly meteors over the pale Arctic snow, far different from the calm and brightening beams of morn. His mental powers were still mighty and rampant, as an army of lions; but his will, that should have guided and subdued them, was feeble and wavering as a deer.

Yet how wonderful is the power of genius! Mournfully as the lines of decision had faded from that cheek, sadly as the fire was dimmed in that eye, broken as were the tones of that once soft and melodious voice, ardent and gifted souls were drawn instinctively towards him. Week after week and year after year, did they listen attentively, did they journey patiently; drawn by the weird gleam of the halo of genius round his brow. A sort of undefined glory encompassed him; an influence proceeded from him as of some wizard power, allied to inspiration, and linked in some mysterious manner with infinitude. Round his shrine was ever a brilliant troop of powerful young minds; among the others, we can see William Hazlitt, John Sterling, and Thomas Carlyle.

The last mentioned writer, in his lately published life of John Sterling, has devoted a chapter to Coleridge; and we present to our readers the following sketch of him during his Highgate life, from Carlyle's unequalled pencil:—

"Coleridge sat on the brow of Highgate Hill in those years, looking down on London and its smoke-tumult, like a sage escaped from the inanity of life's battle; attracting towards him the thoughts of innumerable brave souls still engaged there. . . . The good man, he was now getting old, towards sixty perhaps; and gave you the idea of a life that had been full of sufferings; a life heavy-laden, half-vanquished, still swimming painfully in seas of manifold, physical, and other bewilderment. Brow and head were round, and of massive weight, but the face was flabby and irresolute. The deep eyes, of a light hazel, were as full of sorrow as of inspiration; confused pain looked mildly from them, as in a kind of mild astonishment. The whole figure and air, good and amiable otherwise, might be called flabby and irresolute; expressive of weakness under possibility of strength. He hung loosely on his limbs, with knees bent, and stooping attitude; in walking he rather shuffled than decisively stept; and a lady once remarked, he never could fix which side of the garden walk would suit him best, but continually shifted in corkscrew fashion and kept trying both. A heavy-laden, high-aspiring, and surely much suffering man. His voice, naturally soft and good, had contracted itself into a painful snuffle and sing-song: he spoke as if preaching,—you would have said, preaching earnestly and also hopelessly the weightiest things. I still recollect his "object" and "subject," terms of continual recurrence in the Kantean province; and how he sung and snuffled them into "om-m-mject" and "sum-m-mject," with a kind of solemn shake or quaver, as he rolled along." He died, as we have said, in 1834.

There are four aspects under which Samuel Taylor Coleridge presents himself to our gaze:—those of poet, philosopher, critic, and conversationalist. Our glance at him in these capacities must be very hurried. The perusal of Coleridge's poetry is singularly suggestive of the idea of stupendous powers, never exerted to their full extent, and never applied to objects fully worthy of their might. To paint with delicate exactness, until the mimicry produces a titillating delight; to evoke visions from dreamland, and present them, dressed in the gaudy tinsel of fancy, to the eye of ennui-stricken maiden, demanding no effort of thought, inspiring no new and nobler life; such may have been the attempts of some, whom it would be deemed hard to exclude from the confines of Parnassus; but such we must esteem a desecration of poetry, and such could never have been the poetry of Coleridge. To flash new light upon the destiny of man, and to kindle his eye with light from heaven, must ever constitute the true mission of the poet; and to this alone could Coleridge, fully and finally, have devoted his powers.

But to these objects, it cannot be said that he ever, in full measure, devoted them. He has done much; but we are profoundly sensible that he might have done more. Strains of softest, gentlest melody he has left us, strains which will sound in the ears of the latest generations; the gift he bestowed upon his country was precious and marvellous. Yet might not the Titanic powers to which they bear witness have drawn new notes of grandeur from the great unwritten epic of human history, have thrown new and brighter light on the ways of God to man, have spread out a new auroral banner to illumine man's destiny, and lead him nearer to the celestial country? In his youth he schemed an epic, which might have set him on the same starry pinnacle with Milton; but it was his fate to scheme, while Milton, heroic in every fibre, accomplished.

We shall notice, and that but most cursorily, only four of Coleridge's poems: "Religious Musings," "The Ancient Mariner," "Christabel," and "Love."

In the Pickering edition of 1844, the date affixed to the "Religious Musings" is Christmas Eve, 1794. If this is correct, the piece was composed when its author was a dragoon; but Cottle asserts it to have been written at a later period. We are inclined, however, to suspect, that the latter has confounded subsequent revision and addition, with original production. At all events, it was a juvenile effort, and truly it was a mighty one. All through it, there glows the white heat of a noblest and holiest enthusiasm; its tempestuous rapture reminds you of Homer. Some passages gleam with a Miltonic grandeur and sublimity; and the marvellous power with which the poet spreads his vivifying enthusiasm all over nature, is unsurpassed.

The magnificent personifications with which this poem abounds, are perhaps its distinguishing characteristic. The power of personification, we regard as one of the truest and severest tests of poetic genius; and among modern poets Coleridge and Shelley are probably its greatest masters. As a specimen of the ability of the former in this way, and also as a characteristic extract from the poem of which we speak, we quote the following lines; our readers will recollect Coleridge's early political views, and the excitement of the French Revolution:—

> "Yet is the day of retribution nigh;
> The Lamb of God hath open'd the fifth sea
> And upward rush on swiftest wing of fire
> The innumerable multitude of Wrongs
> By man on man inflicted! Rest awhile,
> Children of wretchedness! The hour is nigh
> And lo! the great, the rich, the mighty Men,
> The Kings and the chief Captains of the World,
> With all that fix'd on high like stars of Heaven
> Shot baleful influence, shall be cast to earth,
> Vile and down-trodden, as the untimely fruit
> Shook from the fig-tree by a sudden storm.
> Even now the storm begins; each gentle name,
> Faith and meek Piety, with fearful joy
> Tremble far off—for lo! the giant Frenzy,
> Uprooting empires with his whirlwind arm,
> Mocketh high Heaven; burst hideous from the cell
> Where the old Hag; unconquerable, huge,
> Creation's eyeless drudge, black Ruin, sits,
> Nursing the impatient earthquake."

That "giant Frenzy," we are inclined to pronounce the finest personification in the whole compass of modern poetry; and we are not sure that two such figures as this, and "creation's eyeless drudge, black Ruin," are to be found, in an equally short space, in any poem that ever was written. And this was composed ere Coleridge was twenty-five.

The "Ancient Mariner" is one of the most wonderful products of modern times. So much has been said of it, that little need now be added. It is a vivid and awful phantasmagoria, of weird mystery and terrific sublimity. A vision of wildest grandeur, which passed before the poet's ecstatic eye, it was cast into poetic unity by the vivifying power of imagination, and limned forth by the poetic hand in magical and meteoric tints, to the rivetted eyes of all men. Its graphic power is absolutely wonderful; and we need only remind our readers what an important element of poetic effect this is. What other men *hear* of the poet *sees*; in the intense glow of poetic rapture, annihilating time and space, he gazes one moment into the flames of Tophet, and the next upon the crowns of the Seraphim; what other men speak of, he paints. It is perhaps the mingling of awe, and mystery, and wildest imagining, with terrific distinctness of picturing, that makes the spell, which this poem throws over the reader, so irresistible. What a picture is this:—

"The upper air burst into life!
　　And a hundred fire-flags sheen;
To and fro they were hurried about!
And to and fro, and in and out,
　　The wan stars danced between.

And the coming wind did roar more loud,
　　And the sails did sigh like sedge;
And the rain poured down from one black cloud;
　　The moon was at its edge.

The thick black cloud was cleft, and still
　　The moon was at its side;
Like waters shot from some high crag,
The lightning fell with never a jag,
　　A river steep and wide."

Those wan stars, that black cloud with the moon at its edge, and that river of lightning, make up surely one of the most terrific landscapes ever conceived or portrayed. What a still and awful sublimity, too, is there in these lines:—

"Still as a slave before his lord,
　　The ocean hath no blast;
His great bright eye most silently
　　Up to the moon is cast."

If, again, we consider the imagery of the poem, we find it also perfect:—

"Day after day, day after day,
   We stuck, nor breath nor motion;
As idle as a painted ship
   Upon a painted ocean."

The inexpressible beauty and appropriateness of this image were never surpassed.

   And does not the heart thrill with the aerial melody, and serene loveliness, of these so simple lines?

"It ceased; yet still the sails made on
   A pleasant noise till noon,
A noise like of a hidden brook
   In the leafy month of June,
That to the sleeping woods all night
   Singeth a gentle tune."

But we can particularize the beauties of this poem no farther. We regard it as one of the most wondrous phantasmagorias, one of the most marvellous pieces of imaginative painting, to be met with in ancient or modern poetry.

   "Christabel" is a production by itself. Coleridge wrote no other piece like it, and no man but Coleridge ever could have written it. The idea of satanic enmity and malice, under the garb of angelic innocence and beauty, seems to have been much present to the mind of Coleridge. Geraldine, and the fiend lady beautiful and bright, are personifications of the same thought; and it is one of chilliest horror. We give no excerpts from "Christabel;" its most striking passages have been quoted numberless times. The blending of undefined mystery and awe, with the most vivid bodying forth of each portrait in the picture, and the most delicate minuteness in laying on the tints, perhaps distinguish it as a poem.

   We lack words to speak our admiration of Coleridge's poem called "Love." Its melody rolls trancingly over the soul, raising unutterable emotions; its gentle but mighty enthusiasm, calm as a cloudless summer noon, wraps the whole being in an atmosphere of rapture; its ideally beautiful painting laughs at our power of admiration. There are a few pieces in our language which stand apart from all others, in unapproached, inexhaustible loveliness: among these we place Milton's "Allegro" and "Il Penseroso," Shelley's "Cloud," and Coleridge's "Love." Our readers, of course, all know it; but we must once more recall to their minds its serenely beautiful commencement:—

"All thoughts, all passions, all delights,
   Whatever stirs this mortal frame,

All are but ministers of Love,
  And feed his sacred flame.

Oft in my waking hours do I
  Live o'er again that happy hour,
When midway on the mount I lay,
  Beside the ruin'd tower.

The moonshine, stealing o'er the scene,
  Had blended with the lights of eve;
And she was there, my hope, my joy—
  My own dear Genevieve!"

The pieces we have mentioned are the most wonderful efforts of Coleridge. We have been able to do little more than refer to them as proofs of his gigantic powers, without, in any adequate measure, analyzing or displaying their beauties.

Of Coleridge, as philosopher and critic, we cannot speak, save in the briefest terms. The "Friend," the "Aids to Reflection," the "Biographia Literaria," and the "Method," are his leading contributions to criticism and philosophy. We shall not characterize them separately. They abound in profound wisdom and practical insight; a collection of aphorisms might be made from them, we venture to say, embodying all, or almost all, the great truths, religious, moral, and political, whose proclamation constitutes the spiritual advancement and attainment of the nineteenth century; their style is on all hands considered one of the most perfect of models. Of his distinction between the reason and the understanding, which was the keystone of his philosophy, and which has so widely influenced philosophic thought in our century; and of his distinction between the imagination and the fancy, to which critics have been so much beholden, we shall say nothing. Their importance may be very great; they may have led to new and rich fields of thought; but we are very far from thinking that it is by estimating their precise value, that a correct or adequate idea of the influence which Coleridge has exerted, and the work he has done, is to be obtained. It is in the spiritual impulse which he communicated to British thought; in the new earnestness and elevated enthusiasm with which he inspired the noblest spirits of our age; in the new life which he kindled in thousands of hearts, that the extent and magnitude of his influence are to be seen. From his works, in their whole range, comes a mild but powerful influence, purging the soul of earthliness, turning the eye heavenward, and nerving the arm to noblest endeavor; while mammonism, selfishness, and baseness, like spectres and night-birds at the morning strains of Memnon, are startled and flee away. To perform this work in our gold-worshipping age, Coleridge seems pre-eminently to have been missioned by the Most High. And when the reader conceives to himself the effect of this, in its thousandfold ramifications, through our families, our churches, and our literary schools, to trace which is at present impossible for us, he will agree with us in thinking the work of Coleridge afar extending and mighty work.

To Coleridge's conversational powers, allusion has already been made. On all hands they have been recognized as wonderful; but there has been an important difference of opinion regarding them. Mr. Carlyle, in the work from which we have already quoted, says:—"I have heard Coleridge talk, with eager musical energy, two stricken hours, his face radiant and moist, and communicate no meaning whatever to any individual of his hearers—certain of whom, I for one, still kept eagerly listening in hope," etc. The importance of this is very great, and its weight cannot, by any means, be entirely nullified. It is difficult for any reader of Carlyle to believe, or even conceive, that, in any such case, his earnest and fiery eye would not see into the heart of what matter there was. But we must listen to another authority on the subject, which will also be recognized as of weighty import, that of Mr. De Quincey;—"Coleridge, to many people, and often I have heard the complaint, seemed to wander; and he seemed then to wander the most, when, in fact, his resistance to the wandering instinct was greatest, viz., when the compass and huge circuit by which his illustrations moved, travelled farthest into remote regions, before they began to revolve. Long before this coming round commenced, most people had lost him, and naturally enough supposed that he had lost himself. They continued to admire the separate beauty of the thoughts, but did not see their relations to the dominant theme. . . . I can assert, upon my long and intimate knowledge of Coleridge's mind, that logic, the most severe, was as inalienable from his modes of thinking as grammar from his language."

Under the shield of De Quincey, we venture to suggest, that the practical energy of Carlyle, and the fact that long and subtle trains of abstract speculation are not congenial to his mind, may afford a solution of the circumstance, that he failed to discover order or continuity of argument, where, to the more practised metaphysical intellect of De Quincey, all was beautifully and emphatically perspicuous.

We have finished our cursory survey of the life and works of Samuel Taylor Coleridge. Around his career are glories as of empyrean light; and sorrows that might draw tears from the Seraphim. Of kind and gentle nature, and by constitution and early education ill adapted for the sore buffetings of the life-battle, his intellectual vision was wide as that of the eagle, and piercing as that of the lynx; his love of nature was deep and delicate as a Naiad's that has dwelt forever by a fountain in the silent wood; his youth was bright, and radiant with the beams of promise; his intellectual prowess, in its full expansion, was gazed on with dumb astonishment; while, in beautiful union with this, was a fantastic, almost childish playfulness and geniality of heart. His religion, despite the sad anomaly in his character, and the baleful influence of the power under whose magic he lay, we must, from the whole spirit of his writings, from the deep devotion of his private letters, and from the agonized struggle of his life, declare to have been profound and all-pervasive. In a fatal hour, he quaffed the enchanting draught of opium, and there was not enough of rugged vigor in his soul to break the spell; henceforward it was as if the spirit of an eagle was closed in the heart of a dove. We image him to ourselves as a desert-born steed, with hoofs to outrun the wind, and eyes to outgleam the lightning, but smitten, at the bright morning hour, by the withering Samiel, and thenceforward staggering, with eye dimmed and limbs tottering, along the burning sand.

—Peter Bayne, "Coleridge," from
Essays in Biography and Criticism, Boston:
Gould and Lincoln, 1858, pp. 108–148

GERTRUDE GARRIGUES
"COLERIDGE'S ANCIENT MARINER" (1880)

Garrigues writes in response to those critics who accuse *The Rime of the Ancient Mariner* of being a poem without a purpose, comprised of strange events and fanciful images born of an "unconscious genius." She also strives to set forth her own argument for Coleridge's deep intellect and unique way of thinking at the young age of fifteen. Garrigues begins with a defense of Coleridge's maturity at the time he wrote *The Rime of the Ancient Mariner*, citing his literary accomplishments, which include some minor poems, his contributions to *The Watchman* (which he both edited and lectured on), and finally his historic collaboration with William Wordsworth in what would become a revolutionary work, the *Lyrical Ballads*. As Garrigues also points out, it is essential to understand that each poet agreed to contribute poems according to his own highly individual talent and style, with Coleridge assigned the task of treating fantastic and improbable events. Thus, Garrigues continues her defense by maintaining that *The Rime of the Ancient Mariner* lives up to its avowed aims and designated assignment. Furthermore, she maintains that a far more profound meaning lies submerged in an otherwise inexplicable event—the issue of why an entire ship's crew is made to bear the consequences of one individual's act of killing a sacred albatross and, even more puzzling, the fact that the mariner lives on as the sole survivor of the tragedy. It is Garrigues's opinion that the poem symbolizes a "higher truth," and she advances the idea of Coleridge's ability to distill his extraordinary intellect through the "alembic of his fervid imagination" and thereby produce a poem of complex and hidden meanings. More specifically, Garrigues identifies the overall theme of the Fall of man from ignorance and his eventual return, through suffering, to faith and virtue as the moral story embedded in *The Ancient Mariner*.

Garrigues continues with a lengthy explication of the poem, beginning with the opening scene in which a young wedding guest, concerned with material things and about to participate in a ceremony of sensual indulgence, is compelled to stop and listen to a frail but powerful old man who insists on delivering an important moral lesson he has learned through a miraculous journey. As Garrigues explains, the compulsion to stop is irrepressible, for it is the voice of a soul that will be heard. As further support to the universality of the theme, Garrigues points out that there is, by design, no specific temporality in the time of day, while references to the cycle of man's life from childhood to old age are irrelevant within the context of the poem. "The terms childhood and youth apply to the period of unconsciousness, of the utter indifference of the Me and Not-me; when the Me begins to be conscious of its existence through the pressure upon it of the Not-me, maturity is reached, at whatever age." Ultimately, this disruption of the wedding guest is preparatory to the voyage that the young man must now experience for himself as he is drawn into the elder's narrative of how he fell into a state of sin and negation by killing a sacred bird. Shorn of his spirituality, the mariner is left to find his own way back to redemption.

Left alone and devoid of hope, all motion stops for the mariner, and he experiences a state of death in life. Weary and gazing aimlessly, he grasps at mere illusions of rescue only to find his hopes dashed. According to Garrigues, the telos of the poem is the unmitigated misery of the mariner gazing on his fellow seamen lying dead on deck as the ocean is decaying and he is unable to look up at the heavens for some form of relief from the terrifying seascape, for mercy is forbidden and shut from his view, leaving him in a state of unremitting dread. With this compelling portrait of abject misery now cast before the feet of the wedding guest, the tempo of the poem transitions to a gently moving moon accompanied by a few stars. Having lived through the tempestuous storm, people may once again look to the heavens with reverence and hope, for evil and wickedness have been shaken out. Thus, as Garrigues argues, far from being an individual tale of a lone mariner who had no choice but to live through a fearful trial of guilt and expiation, the poem ends with a universal message. This conclusion is arrived at through a process whereby individual concerns are superseded by an objective world in which God alone is sovereign, just as the mariner is ultimately forced to contemplate the spiritual world of which he is but a minute particle. Garrigues sees one of the poem's messages as being that only through love and prayer can people achieve a union with God.

<hr>

Those who regard the *Ancient Mariner* as an exhibition of unconscious genius—a mere product of exuberant fancy, weird and thrilling in its effect, exquisite in its versification, but without final end or aim—have but a faint comprehension of the deep, subtile, and peculiar mind from which it emanated. He who could say of himself: "I am by the law of my nature a reasoner. I can take no interest whatever in hearing or saying anything merely as a fact—merely as having happened. I must refer it to something within me before I can regard it with any curiosity or care. I require a reason why the thing is at all, and why it is there and then rather than elsewhere or at another time;" who, at a very premature age, even before his fifteenth year, was deeply interested in metaphysics; and who owned that the faults of language observable in his juvenile poems were mostly owing to the effort he made and was always making to give a poetic coloring to abstract and metaphysical truths, was of all men, least likely, in the prime of his poetical period, to write a mere musical farrago, which, whatever may be said of its rhyme, if taken literally, can scarcely be accredited with a superabundance of reason.

Coleridge had already written a number of his minor poems, besides contributing largely in prose to the *Watchman,* which he edited, and had acquired some reputation as a lecturer, when, in 1796, he made the acquaintance of, and shortly after formed a close friendship with, the poet Wordsworth. It was at the beginning of the career of each, and the influence which they exerted upon one another is incalculable. During the following year they entered into an agreement to publish a volume of their joint works, each engaging to treat his subjects after the style which had already become peculiar to him. Wordsworth was to seek to give interest to what is common and usual; in other words, to treat those subjects which are generally considered as more especially belonging to prose; Coleridge was to give to the weird and improbable a charm which was to spring from the truth of the feeling rather than from the truth of the incident portrayed. The volume appeared in 1798, and contained, among other poems by Coleridge, the subject of our sketch.

That the poem fully meets the demand which the author made upon himself will scarcely be questioned. The feeling is undoubtedly true. We are convinced that, under the circumstances, one could not have felt otherwise or suffered less than did the Mariner; but the circumstance, or rather the cause of the train of circumstances, is so slight (a man kills an albatross—a bird—and for that act he and all his comrades—a whole ship's crew—suffer the most unspeakable horrors of body and of mind which he, the offender, alone survives) that it could never, despite its almost unapproachable rhythm, exert the fascination it does if we did not feel that the thin tissue of its fable concealed a deeper meaning; that the whole poem is merely a symbol, which is all that a work of art can ever be, of a higher truth.

Only a short time before the *Ancient Mariner* was written, Wordsworth read Coleridge some cantos of his then unedited poem upon the growth of an individual mind *(The Prelude)*. Coleridge was enthusiastic in its praise, and besought him to continue and expand it, making, at the same time, some suggestions as to how it should be done. We quote Coleridge's account, to be found in his *Table Talk:* "Then the plan laid out and I believe partly suggested by me was, that Wordsworth should assume the station of a man in mental repose—one whose principles were made up and prepared to deliver upon authority a system of philosophy. He was to treat man as man—a subject of eye, ear, touch, and taste—in contact with external nature, and informing the senses from the mind, and not compounding a mind out of the senses; then he was to describe the pastoral and other states of society, assuming something of the Juvenalian spirit as he approached the high civilization of cities and towns, and opening a melancholy picture of the present state of degeneracy and vice; thence he was to infer and reveal the proof of and necessity for the whole state of man and society, being subject to and illustrative of a redemptive process in operation, showing how this idea reconciled all the anomalies, and promised future glory and restoration. Something of this sort was, I think, agreed on. It is, in substance, what I have been all my life doing in my system of philosophy."

Wordsworth never executed the project, but we believe Coleridge did in a measure. The thought, in its passage through the alembic of his fervid imagination, took upon itself something of a personal character, and he has given us the development, not of the race, but of the individual; he has shown us the "macrocosm in the microcosm." What all his life he labored to execute, and for which, for lack of constructive ability, all his genius and all his labor availed him naught—to erect a system of Christian philosophy—we believe he accomplished in his twenty-fifth year, when he wrote the *Ancient Mariner*.

It was the author's intention, in our opinion, to present the Fall from the innocence of ignorance, from the immediacy of natural faith; and the return, through the mediation of sin and doubt, to conscious virtue and belief. Regarded in this light, the poem may be said to have a two-fold character: it may be considered either in a universal or in a particular sense—the Ancient Mariner may represent Life or a life. In either case he offers to the passer-by, selected on account of his fitness to hear, his receptivity, a view of the "terrible discipline of culture" through which man must pass in order to reach self-consciousness and self-determination.

"It is an ancient mariner, and he stoppeth *one* of three." Not to all men is it given to behold the solution of life's deepest problem: "Many are called, but few are chosen." But him to whom, even for a moment, the Eternal Verities are once unveiled, the wedding-feast—the pleasure and profit of mere worldly existence—calls in vain. Strive as he may, "he cannot choose but hear" the voice of his own soul.

"The ship was cheered, the harbor cleared." Man, with all his weakness and all his power, with all his potentialities for good and evil, commences the voyage of life. The journey is bravely begun, childhood and youth pass brightly and cheerily, till, "over the mast at noon," maturity is reached. No specific time is intended. The terms childhood and youth apply to the period of unconsciousness, of the utter indifference of the Me and Not-me; when the Me begins to be conscious of its existence through the pressure upon it of the Not-me, maturity is reached, at whatever age. It is not our intention to dwell upon the consummate art which the poem displays, but we find it difficult altogether to avoid calling attention to the beauty, especially when it also represents the adequacy of its form. Mark, at this point, how significant is the pause which allows time to present the final relinquishment on the part of the wedding-guest of all thought of escape; whatever interruption he makes henceforth is in the interest of the narrative, and betrays its control over him; he no longer seeks to retard or dismiss it. A point of departure is also reached, the preparation is complete, and the motive may now make itself felt. It is the tightening of the belt as the race begins.

"And now the storm-blast came." The world, with its buffets, its sorrow, and care, its wild-beast struggle for mere existence, confronts him. In his horror and fear, he looks wildly around in search of such sympathy and comfort from his fellows as he needs and thinks he shall surely find, only to discover each chased by the same inexorable necessity, and powerless or too utterly lost in his own affairs to afford him aid. Balked of human help he "grows wondrous cold," and is about to perish when faith in a higher than human sympathy—the albatross—crosses his path to save and bless him. For a time the bird brings peace, but only for a time. In a wanton moment, scarce knowing what he does, he strikes the blow by which he loses sight and consciousness of the spiritual—the true sin against the Holy Ghost, which, if persisted in, shall not be forgiven.

Why does he kill the bird? This is the question of questions. It is the problem of Original Sin. Man is, by nature, evil, and his first conscious, merely natural act, is necessarily a sin against the spiritual. He is then in a state of negation. Spirit is too strong not to resist the natural impulse, and thereon commences the battle between good and evil, which must either end in the putting under foot of the natural, in the negating of the negation, or man dies like the beasts that perish. The conflict is the appointed task of man. Each man must of himself work out his own redemption; he must himself prepare the way for that regeneration which is the promised victory over sin and death.

At first the nature of the man recoils before this daring act of the will. "Ah, wretch! said they, the bird to slay." But when the mist and fog of ignorance and unconsciousness disappear at the approach of the glorious sun of knowledge which now arises, "nor dim, nor red, like God's own head," all fear is forgotten, and in a burst of exultation the cry changes: "'Twas right, said they, such birds to slay, that bring the fog and mist." Man has now become as a god, knowing good and evil, and the ship rushes blithely on. Suddenly its course is stayed: "The breeze dropt down, the sails dropt down, 'twas sad as sad could be." Knowledge is not sufficient; man must not only know, but do. He has lost view of the spiritual, and the natural alone cannot content him. He has lost his faith, and with it hope and the power to labor, for the right faith of man not only brings him tranquillity, but helps him to do his work.

A fearful calm follows; life is at a standstill. To add to his misery, he beholds on all sides aspirations, hopes, endeavors, and beliefs; but none which he can make his own. He is isolated and despairing. "There is water, water everywhere, nor any drop to drink." The world around him seems content with a happiness which holds no charm for him. Its pursuit of fame, of wealth, of pleasure, does not allure him. It appears to hold no thought of a conflict such as is wasting him; it lives at ease, encompassed, as he thinks, with wonders and terrors. He grows to distrust its fair outside; the evil within him drives him to see evil in all without him; the world is the shadow of himself, and as such he fears and suspects it. "The very deep did rot." "Yea, slimy things with legs did crawl upon the slimy sea." Still, even this madness has its lucid intervals. "Some in dreams assured were of the spirit that plagued us so;" and there are times when he has a glimpse that his torment is not a useless and vain torture; that there can be no victory without a battle. He has an intuition of the two elements which are at war within him; he feels that there will be no peace until the spiritual conquers. But he has no power and sees no means by which to assist himself. He is sunk and lost in self—mere finite subjectivity. He makes one effort, but it is in the wrong direction: he will conform to the world and its law. The cross—the emblem of true and living faith—is removed from his neck, and the albatross—the dead faith of creeds and rituals—takes its place.

There is, there can be, no peace in a mere outward conformance to customs that are dead to us; there may be stillness, but there is no serenity. Nothing has changed; the ship is still becalmed; all is weariness and distaste. "There passed a weary time, a weary time." The "glazed and weary eye" wanders listlessly toward the west; the moody and miserable mind of man peers hopelessly and indifferently into the future, and sees a "something in the sky." He watches it, carelessly at first, then more and more eagerly, until at last it assumes proportion and a shape. The final stage of his "temptation in the wilderness" is reached. At last he has discovered a solution to his problem: he will negate the spiritual; he will fall down and worship the evil one, and he will be saved, and all the glory of the world shall be given unto him. The thought fills him with a horrible joy, and he calls up his whole being to rejoice in the promised deliverance. His cry, "A sail, a sail!" is answered by a "grin" of joy. "The western wave was all aflame," the future now is glorious with earthly promise, "when the strange shape drove suddenly betwixt us and the sun."

With horror he discovers that it is only a skeleton bark. No kindly, helpful hands are extended from its side to aid him; the only companion of Unbelief is Death—here and hereafter. The game has been played; Unbelief has won the will of man; Death claims his other faculties, and darkness and fear envelope him. To doubt the All is to doubt himself, and this, the worst of unbeliefs, now fastens upon him. "One after one, by the star-dogged moon," every aspiration and noble desire, every power and every purpose, "with heavy thump, a lifeless lump," drops down and perishes, only turning ere they die to curse his negligence to use, or worse, his abuse of them.

"Alone, alone, all, all alone, alone on a wide, wide sea!" The suffering soul of man in the wide expanse, in the crowded immensity of the world, is isolated by its agony in that Gethsemane where the best beloved are left behind, and the bare spirit goes up alone to meet and wrestle with its Maker. And oh! the horror, the shrinking, the bloody sweat of it all! The grace and beauty of life have departed, and only a sickening sense of guilt and wretchedness, of bitter self-loathing and self-disgust remains: "A thousand, thousand slimy things lived on; and so did I."

"I looked upon the rotting sea"—the world which is his shadow, upon which he has projected his Me—"and drew my eyes away!" "I looked upon the rotting deck"—his own inner consciousness—"and there the dead men lay." "I looked to Heaven," but his unbelief has closed that to his prayer. "I closed my lids and kept them closed," but he cannot shut out the view, "for the sky and the sea, the sea and the sky"—doubt of all around and of all above him—"lay like a load on my weary eye, and the dead"—doubt in himself—"were at my feet!" The talent which the lord of the country gave to his laborer to keep for him has been returned, and he hears the well-earned sentence: "Take, therefore, the talent from him, and cast the unprofitable servant into outer darkness." The lowest deep is reached. On this plane there is no more to suffer or to know. Hell is sounded.

This is the culmination of the poem; no higher point, no greater misery is possible. It has been gradually, but powerfully and tempestuously, working up to its climax, and now the change is marked, truly and unmistakably, by the altered movement. Hitherto the transitions have all been sudden, the epithets harsh, and the tone hard and rebellious. The stars have "rushed out;" the breeze "dropt down;" "at one stride" came the dark. We have had "glittering eyes" and "bright" eyes and looks that were "fire;" the "bloody sun," the "broad and burning sun." The moon has been "horned" and "star-dogged." Now:

The moving moon went up the sky,
And nowhere did abide;
Softly she was going up,
And a star or two beside.

The wild tempest of passion and revolt has raged itself out; the warring elements have become quiet from sheer exhaustion. Wrapped in this momentary calm, man now finds time to look away from self and cast his eyes outward. "Beyond the shadow of the ship, I watched the water-snakes." Now that his desire for the earthly has perished, the world is transfigured. All its horror, its wickedness, its coldness, have vanished. It is no longer a "den of lies;" no longer a "charnel-house," for over and through it rushes the eternal stream of life, and power, and purpose. His hard destiny has crushed out of him all warm and hopeful life, but at the same time it has purified him of all particularity. "Within the shadow of the ship, I watched their rich attire." Gradually he grows to feel himself a part of this transcendent movement, and, as the persuasion gains upon him, each particular aim and thought, each selfish purpose and desire, seems poorer and more trivial to his view, till, in a rush of love and humility, he bows his stubborn head; "I blessed them unaware."

"The self-same moment I could pray." The first renunciation of self has been accomplished, and now heaven and its glory open upon his adoring gaze. In his worship, man renounces his particular aims and interests; appealing to the Absolute as absolute, he becomes conscious of their union and his subordination. With the knowledge that the subjective and objective will are one, he attains his freedom: "The albatross fell off, and sank like lead into the sea."

He no longer feels himself a being lonely and apart. He has united himself with the All—making the union his own act by accepting and agreeing with it, by becoming conscious of it—he feels that he is free, because he feels that the necessity, too, is his. In this full confidence he dismisses every private fear and anxiety, and sinks into a healing repose: "The gentle sleep from heaven, that slid into my soul." But contemplation, even of the Highest, is not the true destiny of man. His slumber calms and soothes him, but it is of short duration—the need for action soon returns. He awakes to find that the time, which had seemed to be passing so eventlessly, has not been lost. During its wise silence "the great rain of his strength, which sweepeth away ill-set foundations," has been falling, and it has brought him strength and comfort; he is still wretched and self-distrustful, but he has gained power and patience to endure. He has cast himself into the stream of being, and he is now irresistibly floated onward: "The loud wind never reached the ship, but now the ship moved on." The great and triumphant effort has been made. Man has willed, purely and decidedly, the good; and now the stream of goodness flows in upon him.

The dead faculties are aroused by the same impulse: "Beneath the lightning and the moon, the dead men gave a groan." They perform their accustomed tasks, but in an unconscious way: "They raised their limbs like lifeless tools." The old activity, the old sentient volition has not returned; "'Twas not those souls that fled in pain, that to their corses came again, but a troop of spirits blest."

In his abrogation of self, man has entirely sunk all individuality; practical effort is abandoned, and he lives in the theoretical alone. From an unconscious immersion in the objective, he passed over into the particular phase, in which he went so far as to deny it—the objective—all validity. In this process he attained a consciousness which assisted in his restoration. He knows now that the objective and subjective are one, but knows it only in such a way that the objective is that one, and that in it the subjective is absorbed. His return is into the realm of Abstract Universality, an universality which subjugates the individual and denies all his personal aims. But God himself as Absolute Subjectivity involves the element of particularity, and, therefore, the particular or personal part of man, although on the merely natural side a something to be denied or overcome, on the spiritual or spiritualized natural is a something to be preserved and honored: "It is in the world that spirit is to be realized."

The power of the spirit, which "under the keel, nine fathoms deep," had "made the ship to go," has brought him thus far; it is now time to supplement grace by works: "The sails at noon left off their tune, and the ship stood still also." The new insight which recalls him to the world seems for a moment to loosen the band which binds him to the spiritual. But spirit is itself that band, and "in a moment she 'gan stir, with short uneasy motion."

Now the old movement, on an advanced plane, is duplicated; he passes over into the antithesis again. But this is a concreter phase; a conflict is unavoidable, because it is the sphere of the negative, but the old spirit of revolt is cancelled. Man now is not only willing but anxious to do his work; he is only uncertain as to what that work may be, and whether he is worthy to perform it. Tossed backward and forward by conflicting emotions, and finally overcome by their violence, he sinks into a lethargy. The body is inactive, but the soul is not asleep. It is a council chamber in which a debate is being carried on between doubt (not the old doubt of all things, but doubt of himself, his right to recognition, knowing himself to be chief among guilty sinners, he doubts his call to "preach Christ and him crucified") and the new insight which teaches him that to every man to whom the power is given belongs the right, to every man who has won the victory the triumph is due: "I heard, and in my soul discerned, two voices in the air."

The first voice asks: "Is it he? Is this the man?"—who killed the albatross. Is it he who has cast aside, who has destroyed his natural faith, and thus estranged the unconscious spirit of childlike humility and ignorance: "The spirit who bideth by himself in the land of mist and snow;" is it for him who has suffered all the misery of doubt and denial, who has barely been rescued from utter destruction, to imagine that he has any worth in himself—that his subjectivity has any claim to personality?

The second voice answers: "The man hath penance done." The sin is condoned, for it has been cancelled. Man turned away from the spiritual, it is true; but he has returned, richer and better for the lapse, for it has won him consciousness—"And penance more will do." Sin is no positive thing; it is the disharmony, the drawing apart, the sundering of the attributes of the human soul—pure negativity. Every negative action is followed by its own punishment; the doer is surrounded by the atmosphere of his deed; and until "the mortal puts on immortality" man's life is bound to be a succession of penances. Innocence is effortless; it is spontaneity; virtue is a perpetual struggle. The great distinction between the wicked and the righteous lies in the fact that the fallen human will is in absolute bondage and helplessness, while the righteous man, by his continual struggle, is able to negate his negativity as it arises, to perform for himself the function of negative unity—he is freely self-determined.

"What makes the ship drive on so fast—what is the ocean doing?" But why is this man being now so irresistibly floated onward—what part has the world in his progress? The last question is answered first: "Still as a slave before his lord, the ocean hath no blast." "His great, bright eye most silently up to the moon is cast." Far above all finite differences and determinations, the eternally Positive gazes down upon the world which he at the same time fills and governs—of which he is at once process and product—graciously looking upon his reflection; but seeing no sin, and hiding his face from the wicked because they are not—to him; forever accomplishing the purpose which he forever designs—the realization of himself in the self-consciousness of the "creature." The first voice asks again: "But why drives on the ship so fast, without or wave or wind?" "The air is cut away before and closes from behind." In the realm of the merely natural, God's freedom is shown in the law of necessity. In the world of spirit man's freedom is God's necessity. When man strives with a single heart to attain truth, by the necessity of his nature, God must will that he shall succeed.

"Fly, brother, fly." "For slow and slow that ship must go when the mariner's trance is abated." Between the theoretical and the practical—the thought, the creation of the intellect and the actual performance—how wide, how well-nigh impassable a gulf!

"I woke." "The dead men stood together." One more backward glance which takes in the whole of the wasted past, and then "this spell was snapt, once more I viewed the ocean green." He is done now and forever with all enervating regret; he leaves to the past its dead; the present claims him. He ceases to think of what he has been, and tries to resolve what he shall be; but, still "in fear and dread," the new path is all untried, and his past errors have deprived him of confidence. "Soon there breathed a wind o'er me:" tribulation has taught him patience, and "patience worketh experience, and experience hope."

"Oh, dream of joy!" "Is this mine own countree?" The true self-return of human activity is accomplished. Freed from all prepossessions, he returns into himself, prepared to start anew in his circling movement. He has returned from whence he started, but with what a rich cargo of experience! As he nears his home, as he looks more closely into his own consciousness, he discerns the true meaning of the conflict in which he has been engaged. "Each corse, lay flat, lifeless and flat." Known now in its true relation, as the blank page on which spirit writes its history, the power of the natural is at an end. "A man all light, a seraph man, on every corse there stood." Man no longer supposes himself to be possessed of single and particular faculties, attributes, and powers, for he sees that spirit informs them all with its unity. The soul of man emits its own light, and serves him as "signals to the land."

"But soon I heard the dash of oars, I saw a boat appear." The Hermit—the new faith which is no longer blind, but blessed with insight, which is now belief—comes to "wash away the albatross's blood." As the "skiff-boat" nears the ship the "lights, so many and fair," disappear. Spirit is only visible in the moment of activity. To the outer world the nature of the regenerated man looks "warped;" his faculties "thin and sere." The inner struggle has marred the outer man for those who see no beauty save in perfection of form and delicacy of tint.

"The boat came close beneath the ship, and straight a sound was heard." The time has come for man to make an objective assertion of personality. He is equal to the moment. He allows all finite things to fall away. "The ship went down like lead," and the infinite, the soul—the essential part of man—rises alone to the surface: "Like one who hath been seven days drowned, my body lay afloat." He has died to the world, and been born anew even in this life. To mere sensuous knowing and finite understanding, the Pilot and the Pilot's boy, the change is superhuman; they cannot fathom it, and the appearance fills them with terror: "The pilot shrieked and fell down in a fit." "The pilot's boy who now doth crazy go." But the true faith—the Hermit—which is Reason, investigates. He asks: "What manner of man art thou?"

"And now, all in my own countree, I stood on the firm land." The circle is complete, he has found himself, the return through the object to subject is accomplished. He has hearkened to the lesson: Neither shall ye say, lo here! or lo there! for behold, the kingdom of God is within you."

"At an uncertain hour that agony returns." The necessity for negation of the finite may often return, but man has now learned the potent spell, and the old depths of misery need never again be sounded. "I pass like night from land to land; I have strange powers of speech." Go now whithersoever he must, he will never again leave his home, for he carries it with him—he is at home with himself. He has ceased to regard inaction as the highest good; ceased to distrust his own worth; ceased to struggle with his destiny. He accepts the work and the place appointed him; and, in fulfilling all necessary actions at the same time that he abrogates all merely selfish interests, feels that he commands the universe. In acknowledging necessity he affirms his freedom.

"O, wedding-guest! this soul hath been alone on a wide, wide sea." Wrapped in finite selfhood, he saw nothing of the beauty and glory around and above him, and, faint with self-weariness, his heavy gaze saw not the ineffable image within. Tried seven times by fire, all particularity now has vanished, and he has been given to feel the bliss which flows from the union of each with all, and all with each. "'Tis sweeter far to me to walk together to the kirk," "And all together pray." He has found that prayer—the soliloquy of the beholding soul when its unity with God has become apparent, and by which that unity is perpetuated—is the only happiness.

"He prayeth best who loveth best." He rises most nearly to the height of that union who comprehends it, whether he, through belief and love and lowly listening feels it, or, by the piercing power of reason, knows it. "For, the dear God who loveth us, He made and loveth all." The subjective in absorbing all—in making it its own—in loving it—becomes all. Subject and Object in one—true Universal.

A sordid, solitary thing, 'Mid countless brethren with a lonely heart, Through courts and cities the smooth Savage roams, Feeling himself, his own low Self, the whole; When he by sacred sympathy might make The whole one Self! Self that no alien knows! Self, far diffused as fancy's wing can travel! Self, spreading still! Oblivious of its own, Yet all of all possessing! this is Faith! This the Messiah's destined victory.

—Gertrude Garrigues, "Coleridge's Ancient Mariner," *Journal of Speculative Philosophy*, July 1880, pp. 327–338

HALL CAINE (1883)

Sir Thomas Henry Hall Caine (1853–1931) was a popular British novelist and playwright of the late Victorian and Edwardian eras. Serving as secretary to Dante Gabriel Rossetti and a frequent guest of John Ruskin, Caine was involved with some of the most influential writers and thinkers of his age. Caine discovered Coleridge's poetry at the age of fifteen, and the poet became an important influence on Caine. Later in life, he even attempted to write a completion to Coleridge's *Christabel*. In the following excerpt, Caine maintains that *The Rime of the Ancient Mariner* possesses a genuine and endearing spirituality, characteristics that evince and bring to life the essence of the poet.

The Ancient Mariner is a poem of which (in the experience of most of us) the first impression dates back to those earliest years when the *Bible* and the *Pilgrim's Progress* made up the whole body of serious reading; but if we could encounter it first of all late in life, after the stream of more modern literature had filtered into our minds, it would probably seem to us like meeting for the first time in person some great writer of whom we have known much through his books. For just as in the one case, many qualities of mind and heart which have endeared the writer to us, find to our heightened sense a kind of visible embodiment in the face, voice, gait and gesture of the man in whose work we recognised them; so in the other, many exquisite and original imaginative fantasies which we must have seen wandering through uncertain channels, would find their true place and fitting mission in the beautiful and complete conception from which they were borrowed.

—Hall Caine, *Cobwebs of Criticism*, 1883, p. 59

Henry Duff Traill (1884)

Traill (1842–1900) was a British author and journalist. In a prefatory note to his comprehensive biography, *Men of Letters*, Traill discusses both the daunting task for anyone attempting such an endeavor—to compensate for the many "tantalising gaps in Coleridge's life which refuse to be bridged over"—as well as the need to make the attempt as no adequate biography existed at the time of his writing.

In regard to *The Rime of the Ancient Mariner*, Traill declares it a poem without comparison in the history of English literature but maintains that it must be interpreted in the context of the complete body of Coleridge's poetic output, and from that vantage point, it is a poem difficult to categorize. Traill maintains that this singularly "weird ballad" contains both the worst faults that have been leveled against the poet's work and some of the finest characteristics, which other critics have identified in his work. Traill finds that the *Ancient Mariner* exhibits a newfound restraint from Coleridge's earlier works, a way to contain the "exuberance of immaturity" one finds in such works as *Religious Musings*.

Traill gives an account of the reasons for the project of the *Lyrical Ballads*, mainly Wordsworth and Coleridge's need to raise funds for a trip to Germany. As to the individual sources for the poem, Traill relates how *The Rime of the Ancient Mariner* was born of a dream related by Coleridge's friend, Mr. Cruikshank, though the bulk of the poem can be attributed to Coleridge's capacious imagination. Added to these influences is Wordsworth's reading of George Shelvocke's memoir and suggestion that Coleridge could create his own imaginative reworking of the events related by Shelvocke (1675–1742), an English privateer who published a book in 1723, *A Voyage Round the World by Way of the Great South Sea*, based on his adventures. Most significantly, Wordsworth recounted to Coleridge Shelvocke's story of his second mate, who shot a black albatross as they were sailing around Cape Horn. Coleridge seized on the image and out of it created his own elaborate tapestry of crime and punishment, guilt and expiation. According to De Quincey, Coleridge denied this source about twelve years later, quite possibly because he simply forgot, as Traill suggests. However, above all supernatural considerations, Traill maintains that it is the "realistic force of its narrative" that is perhaps the work's most profound aspect, creating sufficient plausibility to allow for a "willing suspension of disbelief" among its readers. Thus, Traill argues that Coleridge manages to reveal a profound aspect of human nature and the real consequences wrought by a crime against nature. Traill further notes the importance of the painterly effects of the poem, with great admiration for Coleridge's ability to portray the bony structure of a skeletal ship through which the mariner can gaze on the horrors of a hellish oceanscape while his dead crewman lie about on deck. Enamored of the spectacular aspects of the poem and the many ways it plays on our sense of sight and sound, Traill proclaims *The Rime of the Ancient Mariner* to be a consummate work of art.

"During the first year that Mr. Wordsworth and I were neighbours our conversation turned frequently on the two cardinal points of poetry, the power of exciting the sympathy of the reader by a faithful adherence to the truth of nature, and the power of giving the interest of novelty by the modifying colours of the imagination. The sudden charm which accidents of light and shade, which moonlight or sunset diffused over a known and familiar landscape appeared to represent the practicability of combining both. These are the poetry of nature. The thought suggested itself (to which of us I do not recollect) that a series of poems might be composed of two sorts. In the one the incidents and agents were to be, in part at least, supernatural; and the interest aimed at was to consist in the interesting of the affections by the dramatic truth of such emotions as would naturally accompany such situations, supposing them real.... For the second class, subjects were to be chosen from ordinary life; the characters and incidents were to be such as will be found in every village and its vicinity where there is a meditative and feeling mind to seek after them, or to notice them when they present themselves. In this idea originated the plan of the *Lyrical Ballads*, in which it was agreed that my endeavours should be directed to persons and characters supernatural, or at least romantic, yet so as to transfer from our inward nature a human interest and a semblance of truth sufficient to procure for these shadows of imagination that willing suspension of disbelief for the moment which constitutes poetic faith. Mr. Wordsworth, on the other hand, was to propose to himself, as his object, to give the charm of novelty to things of everyday, and to excite a feeling analogous to the supernatural by awakening the mind's attention from the lethargy of custom and directing it to the loveliness and the wonders of the world before us; an inexhaustible treasure, but for which, in consequence of the film of familiarity and selfish solicitude, we have eyes which see not, ears that hear not, and hearts which neither feel nor understand."

We may measure the extent to which the poetic teaching and practice of Wordsworth have influenced subsequent taste and criticism by noting how completely the latter of these two functions of poetry has overshadowed the former. To lend the charm of imagination to the real will appear to many people to be not one function of poetry merely but its very essence. To them it is poetry, and the only thing worthy of the name; while the correlative function of lending the force of reality to the imaginary will appear at best but a superior kind of metrical romancing, or clever telling of fairy tales. Nor of course can there, from the point of view of the highest conception of the poet's office, be any comparison between the two. In so far as we regard poetry as contributing not merely to the pleasure of the mind but to its health and strength—in so far as we regard it in its capacity not only to delight but to sustain, console, and tranquillise the human spirit—there is, of course, as much difference between the idealistic and the realistic forms of poetry as there is between a narcotic potion and a healing drug. The one, at best, can only enable a man to forget his burdens; the other fortifies him to endure them. It is perhaps no more than was naturally to be expected of our brooding and melancholy age, that poetry (when it is not a mere voluptuous record of the subjective impressions of sense) should have become almost limited in its very meaning to the exposition of the imaginative or spiritual aspect of the world of realities; but so it is now, and so in Coleridge's time it clearly was *not*. Coleridge, in the passage above quoted, shows no signs of regarding one of the two functions which he attributes to poetry as any more accidental or occasional than the other; and the fact that the realistic portion of the *Lyrical Ballads* so far exceeded in amount its supernatural element, he attributes not to any inherent supremacy in the claims of the former to attention but simply to the greater industry which Wordsworth had displayed in his special department of the volume. For his own part, he says, "I wrote the *Ancient Mariner*, and was preparing, among other poems, the *Dark Ladie* and the *Christabel*, in which I should have more nearly realised my ideal than I had done in my first attempt. But Mr. Wordsworth's industry had proved so much more successful, and the number of the poems so much greater, that my compositions, instead of forming a balance, appeared rather an interpolation of heterogeneous matter." There was certainly a considerable disparity between the amount of their respective contributions to the volume, which, in fact, contained nineteen pieces by Wordsworth and only four by Coleridge. Practically, indeed, we may reduce this four to one; for, of the three others, the two scenes from *Osorio* are without special distinction, and the *Nightingale*, though a graceful poem, and containing an admirably-studied description of the bird's note, is too slight and short to claim any importance in the series. But the one long poem which Coleridge contributed to the collection is alone sufficient to associate it for ever with his name. *Unum sed leonem.* To any one who should have taunted him with the comparative infertility of his Muse he might well have returned the haughty answer of the lioness in the fable, when he could point in justification of it to the *Rime of the Ancient Marinere.*

There is, I may assume, no need at the present day to discuss the true place in English literature of this unique product of the human imagination. One is bound, however, to attempt to correlate and adjust it to the rest of the poet's work, and this, it must be admitted, is a most difficult piece of business. Never was there a poem so irritating to a critic of the "pigeon-holing" variety. It simply defies him; and yet the instinct which he obeys is so excusable, because in fact so universal, that one feels guilty of something like disloyalty to the very principles of order in smiling at his disappointment. Complete and symmetrical classification is so fascinating an amusement; it would simplify so many subjects of study if men and things would only consent to rank themselves under different categories and remain there; it would, in particular, be so inexpressibly convenient to be able to lay your hand upon your poet whenever you wanted him by merely turning to a shelf labelled "Realistic" or "Imaginative" (nay, perhaps, to the still greater saving of labour—Objective or Subjective), that we cannot be surprised at the strength of the aforesaid instinct in many a critical mind. Nor should it be hard to realise its revolt against those single exceptions which bring its generalisations to nought. When the pigeon-hole will admit every "document" but one, the case is hard indeed; and it is not too much to say that the *Ancient Mariner* is the one document which the pigeon-hole in this instance declines to admit. If Coleridge had only refrained from writing this remarkable poem, or if, having done so, he had written more poems like it, the critic might have ticketed him with a quiet mind, and gone on his way complacent. As it is, however, the poet has contrived, in virtue of this performance, not only to defeat classification but to defy it. For the weird ballad abounds in those very qualities in which Coleridge's poetry with all its merits is most conspicuously deficient, while on the other hand it is wholly free from the faults with which he is most frequently and justly chargeable. One would not have said in the first place that the author of *Religious Musings*, still less of the "Monody on the Death of Chatterton," was by any means the man to have compassed triumphantly at the very first attempt the terseness, vigour, and naivete of the true ballad-manner. To attain this, Coleridge, the student of his early verse must feel, would have rather more to retrench and much more to restrain than might be the case with many other youthful poets. The exuberance of immaturity, the want of measure, the "not knowing where to stop," are certainly even more conspicuous in the poems of 1796 than they are in most productions of the same stage of poetic development; and these qualities, it is needless to say, require very stern chastening from him who would succeed in the style which Coleridge attempted for the first time in the *Ancient Mariner*.

The circumstances of this immortal ballad's birth have been related with such fulness of detail by Wordsworth, and Coleridge's own references to them are so completely reconcilable with that account, that it must have required all De Quincey's consummate ingenuity as a mischief-maker to detect any discrepancy between the two.

In the autumn of 1797, records Wordsworth in the MS. notes which he left behind him, "Mr. Coleridge, my sister, and myself started from Alfoxden pretty late in the afternoon with a view to visit Linton and the Valley of Stones near to it; and as our united funds were very small, we agreed to defray the expense of the tour by writing a poem to be sent to the *New Monthly Magazine*. Accordingly we set off, and proceeded along the Quantock Hills towards Watchet; and in the course of this walk was planned the poem of the *Ancient Mariner*, founded on a dream, as Mr. Coleridge said, of his friend Mr. Cruikshank. Much the greatest part of the story was Mr. Coleridge's invention, but certain parts I suggested; for example, some crime was to be committed which should bring upon the Old Navigator, as Coleridge afterwards delighted to call him, the spectral persecution, as a consequence of that crime and his own wanderings. I had been reading in Shelvocke's *Voyages*, a day or two before, that while doubling Cape Horn they frequently saw albatrosses in that latitude, the largest sort of sea-fowl, some extending their wings twelve or thirteen feet. 'Suppose,' said I, 'you represent him as having killed one of these birds on entering the South Sea, and that the tutelary spirits of these regions take upon them to avenge the crime.' The incident was thought fit for the purpose, and adopted accordingly. I also suggested the navigation of the ship by the dead men, but do not recollect that I had anything more to do with the scheme of the poem. The gloss with which it was subsequently accompanied was not thought of by either of us at the time, at least not a hint of it was given to me, and I have no doubt it was a gratuitous afterthought. We began the composition together on that to me memorable evening. I furnished two or three lines at the beginning of the poem, in particular–

> "'And listened like a three years' child:
> The Mariner had his will.'

.... The *Ancient Mariner* grew and grew till it became too important for our first object, which was limited to our expectation of five pounds; and we began to think of a volume which was to consist, as Mr. Coleridge has told the world, of poems chiefly on supernatural subjects." Except that the volume ultimately determined on was to consist only "partly" and not "chiefly" of poems on supernatural subjects (in the result, as has been seen, it consisted "chiefly" of poems upon natural subjects), there is nothing in this account which cannot be easily reconciled with the probable facts upon which De Quincey bases his hinted charge against Coleridge in his *Lake Poets*. It was not Coleridge who had been reading Shelvocke's *Voyages*, but Wordsworth, and it is quite conceivable, therefore, that the source from which his friend had derived the idea of the killing of the albatross may (if indeed he was informed of it at the time) have escaped his memory twelve years afterwards, when the conversation with De Quincey took place. Hence, in "disowning his obligations to Shelvocke," he may not by any means have intended to suggest that the albatross incident was his own thought. Moreover, De Quincey himself supplies another explanation of the matter, which we know, from the above-quoted notes of Wordsworth's, to be founded upon fact. "It is possible," he adds, "from something which Coleridge said on another occasion, that before meeting a fable in which to embody his ideas he had meditated a poem on delirium, confounding its own dream-scenery with external things, and connected with the imagery of high latitudes." Nothing, in fact, would be more natural than that Coleridge, whose idea of the haunted seafarer was primarily suggested by his friend's dream, and had no doubt been greatly elaborated in his own imagination before being communicated to Wordsworth at all, should have been unable, after a considerable lapse of time, to distinguish between incidents of his own imagining and those suggested to him by others. And, in any case, the "unnecessary scrupulosity," rightly attributed to him by Wordsworth with respect to this very poem, is quite incompatible with any intentional denial of obligations.

Such, then, was the singular and even prosaic origin of the *Ancient Mariner*—a poem written to defray the expenses of a tour; surely the most sublime of "pot-boilers" to be found in all literature. It is difficult, from amid the astonishing combination of the elements of power, to select that which is the most admirable; but, considering both the character of the story and of its particular vehicle, perhaps the greatest achievement of the poem is the simple realistic force of its narrative. To achieve this was of course Coleridge's main object: he had undertaken to "transfer from our inward nature a human interest and a semblance of truth sufficient to procure for these shadows of imaginations that willing suspension of disbelief for the moment which constitutes poetic faith." But it is easier to undertake this than to perform it, and much easier to perform it in prose than in verse—with the assistance of the everyday and the commonplace than without it. Balzac's *Peau de Chagrin* is no doubt a great feat of the realistic-supernatural; but no one can help feeling how much the author is aided by his "broker's clerk" style of description, and by the familiar Parisian scenes among which he makes his hero move. It is easier to compass verisimilitude in the Palais-Royal than on the South Pacific, to say nothing of the thousand assisting touches, out of place in rhyme and metre, which can be thrown into a prose narrative. The *Ancient Mariner*, however, in spite of all these drawbacks, is as real to the reader as is the hero of the *Peau de Chagrin*; we are as convinced of the curse upon one of the doomed wretches as upon the other; and the strange phantasmagoric haze which is thrown around the ship and the lonely voyager leaves their outlines as clear as if we saw them through the sunshine of the streets of Paris. Coleridge triumphs over his difficulties by sheer vividness of imagery and terse vigour of descriptive phrase—two qualities for which his previous poems did not prove him to possess by any means so complete a mastery. For among all the beauties of his earlier landscapes we can hardly reckon that of intense and convincing truth. He seems seldom before to have written, as Wordsworth nearly always seems to write, "with his eye on the object;" and certainly he never before displayed any remarkable power of completing his word-picture with a few touches. In the *Ancient Mariner* his eye seems never to wander from his object, and again and again the scene starts out upon the canvas in two or three strokes of the brush. The skeleton ship, with the dicing demons on its deck; the setting sun peering "through its ribs, as if through a dungeon-grate;" the water-snakes under the moonbeams, with the "elfish light" falling off them "in hoary flakes" when they reared; the dead crew, who work the ship and "raise their limbs like lifeless tools"—everything seems to have been actually *seen*, and we believe it all as the story of a truthful eye-witness. The details of the voyage, too, are all chronicled with such order and regularity, there is such a diary-like air about the whole thing, that we accept it almost as if it were a series of extracts from the ship's "log." Then again the execution—a great thing to be said of so long a poem—is marvellously equal throughout; the story never drags or flags for a moment, its felicities of diction are perpetual, and it is scarcely marred by a single weak line. What could have been better said of the instantaneous descent of the tropical night than

> The Sun's rim dips; the stars rush out:
> At one stride comes the dark;

what more weirdly imagined of the "cracks and growls" of the rending iceberg than that they sounded "like noises in a swound?" And how beautifully steals in the passage that follows upon the cessation of the spirit's song—

> It ceased; yet still the sails made on
> A pleasant noise till noon,
> A noise like to a hidden brook
> In the leafy month of June,
> That to the sleeping woods all night
> Singeth a quiet tune.

Then, as the ballad draws to its close, after the ship has drifted over the harbour-bar—

> And I with sobs did pray—
> O let me be awake, my
> God; Or let me sleep alway,

with what consummate art are we left to imagine the physical traces which the mariner's long agony had left behind it by a method far more terrible than any direct description—the effect, namely, which the sight of him produces upon others—

> I moved my lips—the Pilot shrieked
> And fell down in a fit;
> The holy Hermit raised his eyes,
> And prayed where he did sit.
> I took the oars: the Pilot's boy,

Who now doth crazy go,
Laughed loud and long, and all the while
His eyes went to and fro.
"Ha! ha!" quoth he, "full plain I see
The Devil knows how to row."

Perfect consistency of plan, in short, and complete equality of execution, brevity, self-restraint, and an unerring sense of artistic propriety—these are the chief notes of the *Ancient Mariner*, as they are not, in my humble judgment, the chief notes of any poem of Coleridge's before or since. And hence it is that this masterpiece of ballad minstrelsy is, as has been said, so confounding to the "pigeon-holing" mind.

—H.D. Traill, *Coleridge,* 1884, pp. 46–53

WILLIAM WATSON
"COLERIDGE'S SUPERNATURALISM" (1893)

William Watson introduces the topic of Coleridge's supernaturalism by way of speculative philosophical theories, a metaphysical predisposition that Watson expresses in liquid terms and that he maintains was evident from the poet's childhood days at Christ's Hospital. There Coleridge "drank" from the waters of an "authentic Castaly," a reference to a fountain of Parnassus believed to be sacred to the poetic Muses and thus a source of poetic inspiration to all who drank from it. Watson cites other influential fountains of wisdom: Ploitnus (considered the founder of neoplatonism, who taught, among other things, that there is a supreme, indivisible, and totally transcendent being) and Jamblichus (a Syrian philosopher who was a leading proponent of neoplatonism and profoundly influenced by Plotinus's teachings). Hence, Coleridge vacillated since his childhood between the poetic and philosophical impulses.

In Watson's discussion of *The Rime of the Ancient Mariner*, he points out that any attentive reading of the poem will show that Coleridge maps out precise geographical settings for the poem before introducing any supernatural elements. According to Watson, Coleridge had a particular strategy in that he first sought to transport the reader to an unearthly realm where the conditions of the known world were left behind. In other words, Coleridge set the scene, something that Watson finds objectionable to the extent that it is an inartistic gesture. "Coleridge very astutely takes pains to avoid anything like geography. We reach that silent sea into which we are the first that ever burst, and that is sufficient for imaginative ends." With natural law thus suspended, Coleridge has now created a vast open space in which he is free to pile on one fantastic detail after another, as the reader is fully drawn into a dreamland. For Watson, what then follows is ironic, as the dream world can no longer be judged from a realistic framework, so there is no actual blending of the real and the supernatural. The world of the *Ancient Mariner*, then, appears to be perfectly constructed and credible on its own. However, there is a crack in this seeming perfection, for the reader must return to the world of human experience and, thus, the poem is flawed. "But at last we quit this consistently, unimpeachably, most satisfactorily impossible world; we are restored to the world of common experience; and when so restoring us, the poet makes his first and only mistake." As to the final miracle when angelic forms appear, the reader is once again jarred from the natural world of harbors, rocks, and weathercocks but able to identify with the character of the Ancient Mariner who prays for resolution: to remain in the mortal world or become "naturalised citizens of a self-governing dreamland."

Watson holds the first part of *Christabel* in a similarly high regard for its artistry. He can find nothing inappropriate or overly extravagant in Coleridge's aims: to create a poem of elusive beauty. However, Watson finds the second part of the poem to be flawed, as Coleridge nudges his way toward the light of common day, thereby breaking the spell of this magical realm with "the clumsy foot of Fact" and allowing the impression of "mere unreality" to enter.

It is usual to think of Coleridge the metaphysician as directly responsible for the gradual supersession, if not extinction, of Coleridge the bard; and it is clear that he himself, at a comparatively early date, was conscious of—and not unalarmed at—the growing ascendancy exercised by his philosophical over his creative powers. It is in 1802, when he has still thirty-two years of life before him, that he acknowledges himself in the singular position of a man unable, so to speak, to get at his own genius or imagination except by a circuitous route,—*via* his intellect.

> 'By abstruse research to steal
> From my own nature all the natural man,—'

this, he says, has become his 'sole resource,' his 'only plan,'

> 'Till that which suits a part infects the whole,
> And now is almost grown the habit of my soul.'

But although his speculative faculty did ultimately dominate and overbear his poetic powers, we are inclined to think there was a time when it co-operated with them not disloyally. One is a little apt to forget that his metaphysical bent was no less innate than his poetical,—even at Christ's Hospital, his spiritual potation was a half-and-half in which the waters of a more or less authentic Castaly, and the 'philosophic draughts' from such fountains as Jamblichus and Plotinus, were equally mingled. Whether or not a born 'maker,' he was certainly a born theorist; and we believe not only that under all his most important artistic achievements there was a basis of intellectual theory, but that the theory, so far from being an alien and disturbing presence, did duty as the unifying principle which co-ordinated the whole. We think we can see such a theory underlying *The Ancient Mariner*, and securing the almost unqualified imaginative success of that poem; and we further think we can see it departed from in one isolated instance, with temporary artistic disaster as the result.

Anyone examining the poem with a critical eye for its machinery and groundwork, will have noticed that Coleridge is careful not to introduce any element of the marvellous or supernatural until he has transported the reader beyond the pale of definite geographical knowledge, and thus left behind him all those conditions of the known and the familiar, all those associations with recorded fact and experience, which would have created an inimical atmosphere. Indeed, there is perhaps something rather inartistic in his undisguised haste to convey us to the aesthetically necessary region. In some half-dozen stanzas, beginning with 'The ship was cleared,' we find ourselves crossing the Line and driven far towards the Southern Pole. Beyond a few broad indications thus vouchsafed, Coleridge very astutely takes pains to avoid anything like geography. We reach that silent sea into which we are the first that ever burst, and that is sufficient for imaginative ends. It is enough that the world, as known to actual navigators, is left behind, and a world which the poet is free to colonise with the wildest children of his dreaming brain, has been entered. Forthwith, to all intents and purposes, we may say, in the words of Goethe as rendered by Shelley:—

'The bounds of true and false are passed;—
Lead us on, thou wandering gleam.'

Thenceforth we cease to have any direct relations with the verifiable. Natural law is suspended; standards of probability have ceased to exist. Marvel after marvel is accepted by us, as by the Wedding-Guest, with the unquestioning faith of 'a three years' child.' We become insensibly acclimatised to this dreamland. Nor is it the chaotic, anarchic, incoherent world of arabesque romance, where the real and unreal by turns arbitrarily interrupt and supplant each other, and are never reconciled at heart. On the contrary, here is no inconsistency, for with the constitution of *this* dream-realm nothing except the natural and the probable could be inconsistent. Here is no danger of the intellect or the reason pronouncing an adverse judgment, for the venue has been changed to a court where the jurisdiction of fantasy is supreme. Thus far then, the Logic of the Incredible is perfect, and the result, from the view point of art, magnificent. But at last we quit this consistently, unimpeachably, most satisfactorily impossible world; we are restored to the world of common experience; and when so restoring us, the poet makes his first and only mistake. For the concluding miracle, or rather brace of miracles—the apparition of the angelic forms standing over the corpses of the crew, and the sudden preternatural sinking of the ship—take place just when we have returned to the province of the natural and regular, to the sphere of the actual and the known; just when, floating into harbour, we sight the well-remembered kirk on the rock, and the steady weathercock which the moonlight steeps in silentness. A dissonant note is struck at once. We have left a world where prodigies were normal, and have returned to one where they are monstrous. But prodigies still pursue us with unseasonable pertinacity, and our feeling is somewhat akin to that of the Ancient Mariner himself, whose prayer is that he may either 'be awake' or may 'sleep away.' We would fain either surrender unconditionally to reality, or remain free, as naturalised citizens of a self-governing dreamland.

If *The Ancient Mariner* is the finest example in our literature, of purely fantastic creation—and we think it is—the First Part of *Christabel* is not less wonderful in its power of producing an equally full and rich effect by infinitely more frugal means. In *Christabel*, there is nothing extravagant or bizarre, no mere imaginative libertinism, nothing that even most distantly suggests a riot of fancy. The glamour, everywhere present, is delicate, elusive, impalpable, curiously insidious,—the glamour of 'enchantments drear, where more is meant than meets the ear.' Acute critics seem to have felt from the first that the very essence of the unique attraction exercised by this poem lay in its obscurity, its enigmatical character,—that its fascination was pre-eminently the fascination of the impenetrable. Charles Lamb dreaded a 'continuation' which should solve the riddle—and break the spell: which should light up—and destroy—this costly and faultless fabric of mystery. His fears (he was eventually reconciled to the 'continuation' by the inimitable passage on divided friendship) were only too well justified. In the Second Part, Coleridge does not actually vulgarise his shadowland by letting in commonplace daylight; but he distinctly goes some little way in that direction. It is not merely a falling-off in the quality of the workmanship—(although there *is* a falling off of that sort, the poetry, as such, is still very fine)—but the whole basis, environment, and atmosphere of the First Part were magical,—and were homogeneous. The conditions of time and place were purely ideal; there was no uncomfortable elbowing of Wonder by Familiarity; the clumsy foot of Fact did not once tread upon the rustling train of Romance. But we turn to the continuation—we enter the second chamber of this enchanted palace—and we are met at the threshold by the dull and earthy imp, Topography. Since writing his First Part, Coleridge has removed to Keswick, and so, forsooth, when he resumes his story, we hear of Borrowdale and Langdale, of Bratha-Head and Dungeon-Ghyll. The subtlest part of the illusion is gone: the incursion of accidents has commenced, and the empire of fantasy is threatened. The notable thing is, that the point where the air of fine strangeness and aloofness ceases to be sustained, is precisely the point where the impression of *mere unreality* begins to make itself obtrusively felt. There has been conceded to us just that foothold in *terra firma* which affords a basis for the leisurely delimitation of *terra incognita*. And, truth to tell, the poet has not really taken up again his abandoned thread. How could he? It was a filament of fairy gossamer, and he has endeavoured to piece it with what is, after all, only the very finest silk from the reel.

—William Watson, "Coleridge's Supernaturalism,"
Excursions in Criticism, 1893, pp. 97–103

RICHARD GARNETT "THE 'ANCIENT MARINER' AS AN EXEMPLAR OF COLERIDGE'S GENIUS" (1904)

Richard Garnett's essay contextualizes the *Ancient Mariner* within two eighteenth-century tendencies he identifies as a wider perspective on the ethical responsibility men have toward one another to include all sentient beings, in this case the albatross, and "the renascence of wonder." As to the first trend, a heightened awareness of social responsibility, Garnett traces this issue to the eighteenth-century age of philanthropy and its notion of the "virtue of humanity." For Garnett, Coleridge was revolutionary in expanding the notion to include an obligation to care for the well-being of animals and, further, to no longer perceive of animals as being a form of rational being but, rather, as part of a "pervading life" shared by all. Recent critics have discussed the general movement in England in the second half of the eighteenth century that saw the rise of many animal rights advocates. This movement was so pervasive that it entered all forms of written works, from children's literature to scientific works and poetry. For these early advocates, the issues surrounding animal rights included the various harms inflicted on wild birds.

As to the second tendency, a revitalization of the supernatural, Garnett explains that, though there were earlier eighteenth-century influences on Coleridge such as Walpole's gothic novel, *The Castle of Otranto* (1764), which was in part in jest, Coleridge's treatment of the supernatural was momentous for he intended his readers to consider it a credible story, an aspect that aligns the poet with Shakespeare, who implicitly demanded the trust of his audience: "[I]f the ghost of Hamlet's father were not as real an existence as any of the mortal personages, the tragedy would become a farce." Garnett also gives much credit to Coleridge in that he considers this poem to be the first genuine example of the reawakening of the tale of wonder and, thus, credits *The Rime of the Ancient Mariner* with being the inaugural poem in a new literary era. Garnett points out, however, two defects in questioning the necessity for the ghost ship with its description of the Death and Life-in-Death; this he finds excessive and what he perceives to be a "violation of poetical justice." In this last point, Garnett is suggesting the unfairness of punishing the ship's crew, who simply approved of the mariner's actions, while the mariner lives on despite his crime.

———   ———   ———

There is more difficulty in the case of Coleridge than in that of almost any other writer of his rank in selecting, as the plan of our work requires, the most typical and characteristic of his more important writings. Judged from the point of view of literature, which must be ours, his poetry takes precedence of his prose; but among all his poems there is not one of any considerable length, and the longest and most laboured, and the one written with the most deliberate consciousness of a mandate from heaven above and a message to men below ("Religious Musings") belongs to his immature period, both as poet and thinker. "Christabel" being unfinished, nothing with any pretension to poetical greatness, as determined by the scale of execution, remains except "The Ancient Mariner," and insignificant as is even its bulk in comparison with the productions on which his chief poetical contemporaries would be most willing to rest their fame, and utterly inadequate as it is to represent the general cast of so opulent and versatile an intelligence, it does happen to be in close alliance with some of those tendencies of his own age with which Coleridge was most completely sympathetic.

These especial tendencies are the extension of the virtue of humanity so as to comprise not mankind only, but all sentient nature; and the reaction against what threatened to become the despotism of mere good sense devoid of any spiritual illumination, through what a distinguished critic has aptly termed the "renascence of wonder." The eighteenth century had been pre-eminently the age of philanthropy, more so than any epoch in history since the age of the Antonines. Man's duty to man had never been so emphatically set forth, and the pauper, the slave, the savage, the debtor, the convict even, were tasting, or were about to taste the fruits of this new and practical "enthusiasm of humanity."

But it had scarcely extended beyond mankind. It was something quite novel for a poet to take up an offence committed against an irrational creature as entailing a curse upon the perpetrator only to be eluded by severest penance. Such legends had existed before, but they had been related as picturesque tales; it was entirely a new departure to hold them up as embodiments of sound ethical rule. The inculcation of the duty of kindness to animals was a minor matter, but most momentous was the assumption upon which the poet's attitude was grounded, that sentient nature was not divided into the two sharply demarcated classes of beings rational, and beings irrational, but that one pervading life was common to all. Poetry is always in advance of Science. The maxims of the evolutionary school of naturalists may be said to have been implicitly comprehended in this proposition, which Coleridge did not at the time openly enunciate as Goethe, Schiller, and other Germans had done and were doing,[1] but without which the teaching of the Ancient Mariner cannot be justified. To the poet, the slaughter of the unoffending albatross was a crime crying for vengeance: those who admitted no kinship between the slayer and his victim might from their point of view rationally inquire, *"Tant de bruit pour une omelette?"*

The renascence of wonder, to employ Mr. Watts-Dunton's appellation for what he justly considers the most striking and significant feature in the great romantic revival which has transformed literature, is proclaimed by this very appellation not to be the achievement of any one innovator, but a general reawakening of mankind to a perception that there were more things in heaven and earth than were dreamt of in Horatio's philosophy. For a long time the supernatural had been almost excluded from imaginative literature, save occasionally in the avowed imitation of the antique or exotic. Horace Walpole's "Castle of Otranto" (1764), though but half in earnest, marks an epoch as a serious endeavour to revive it, but the supernatural machinery is clearly introduced for the sake of literary effect. Whether it were, or were not, explained as an illusion, could make no difference to the story. Far otherwise is it with Shakespeare: if the ghost of Hamlet's father were not as real an existence as any of the mortal personages, the tragedy would become a farce. Coleridge identifies himself entirely with Shakespeare's position, and demands implicit trust in the veracity of the ancient man's narrative, thus rehabilitating the supernatural as no less legitimate for poetical treatment than the natural, provided that the poet complies with the indispensable preliminary condition of believing in it himself.

The poem was to have been jointly written by Wordsworth and Coleridge, but, save for a single stanza and a line here and there claimed by the former, belongs entirely to the latter so far as the actual composition is concerned. Wordsworth had nevertheless exerted great influence upon his companion by his suggestion of the incident of the killing of the albatross, without which the piece, originally founded upon a dream of a friend of Coleridge's, would have been a mere ballad of the wild and wonderful. This incident he derived from Shelvocke's "Voyage Round the World by way of the Great South Sea" (1726). And here a curious question arises. In Shelvocke's narrative the slaughter of the albatross does not appear as a piece of wanton cruelty, but as prompted by a not unnatural superstition. The bird was a *black* albatross. So long as it accompanied the ship bad weather prevailed, and the seaman who shot it, a melancholy, hypochondriacal person, Shelvocke says, did so under the impression that it was an inauspicious creature, bringing ill luck. Did Coleridge know this? Wordsworth doubts whether he ever saw Shelvocke's narrative, but the circumstances may well have been related to him along with the other particulars, and his statement that the Ancient Mariner's companions, who had at first condemned, afterwards justified his conduct:

'Twas right, they averred, to slay the bird
That brought the fog and mist—

affords some presumption that he did know it. If so, he showed admirable judgement in discarding a circumstance at first sight so picturesque, but which would have been ruinous to his moral, to which it is essential that no stain should sully the innocence of the victim, and that nothing but repentance should extenuate the fault of the Ancient Mariner.

In the ancient man Coleridge has added one to that gallery of typical figures created by poets and writers of imaginative prose who impersonate a particular class of men or a particular order of ideas. The Mariner represents the glamour attaching to the old man who, having from his youth sailed the seas, returns to spend his old age among his fellows on shore, and is naturally and justly regarded by them as the depositary of mysterious knowledge respecting a world unfamiliar to themselves. Such a personage must, from the nature of the case, be venerable, weather-beaten, and more or less oracular; he may well be endowed with a glittering eye; possibly, though less probably, with an eloquent tongue also; and, dealing with a region unknown to his hearers, must feel himself entitled to claim from them "that suspension of disbelief which constitutes poetic faith." Should any mysterious circumstance or dark rumour attach to his own character or history, he may himself become a legendary figure in his own lifetime. Lancelot Blackburne, having made a voyage to the West Indies in his youth, took the character of a buccaneer along with him to the archiepiscopal throne of York; and the veteran seaman, Owen Parfit, having voyaged on the West African coast and there had, as was not questioned, dealings in slaves and with the devil, left his neighbours in no doubt how to account for his disappearance when, one summer afternoon, paralyzed as he was and unable to move a step by himself, he vanished without leaving a trace behind him.

It is possible that some reminiscence of this inexplicable affair, which occurred in the adjacent county of Somersetshire a few years before Coleridge's birth, may have contributed something to his conception of the Mariner. However this may be, he has in this typical personage embodied whatever is most characteristic of the glamour of ocean,

Its living sea by coasts uncurbed,
    Its depth, its mystery and its might,
Its indignation if disturbed,
    The glittering peace of its delight.

An affinity may also be remarked between the Ancient Mariner and another legendary figure more ancient and more celebrated still, the Wandering Jew. Both are aged, both range the earth in expiation of a crime; both are always ready to narrate their histories, and, these once told, vanish without a trace. In dealing with the incidents of seafaring life and the portraiture of his principal character, Coleridge, while always correct in essentials, has avoided the realism of detail which, while it well becomes a novelist like Herman Melville or Joseph Conrad, whose object it is to make us live on shipboard, would not befit a poem which aims at being a selection of picturesque circumstances, and not an indiscriminate transcript of whatever an observing eye might find to note upon or around a vessel. When the "Ancient Mariner" was written, Coleridge had never been at sea. When at last he made a voyage, he discovered an inaccuracy in one of his most beautiful descriptions, and amended this in the next edition, but, to the contentment of the modern reader, beauty and melody eventually prevailed over strict accuracy, and the passage returned to its original form.[2]

Coleridge himself has given us an analysis of "The Ancient Mariner" in the shape of a marginal summary set against the text in the second edition (1800), and our object of providing the poem with a running commentary cannot be better accomplished than by a reprint of this exposition with a few inconsiderable omissions. This summary was an afterthought, the first edition having merely a brief prose argument. It was probably suggested by imputations of obscurity which the poem was far from deserving, but may well have seemed a necessary condescension to the dullness of average readers at a time when imaginative perception had fallen to so low an ebb. In our day this gloss is almost an annoyance when travelling in company with the verse, but may serve a useful purpose in the absence of the latter.

An ancient Mariner meeteth three gallants bidden to a wedding feast, and detaineth one.

The Wedding Guest is spell-bound by the eye of the old seafaring man, and constrained to hear his tale.

The Mariner tells him the ship sailed southward with a good wind and fair weather, until it reached the Line.

The ship driven by a storm toward the South Pole.

The land of ice, and of fearful sounds where no living thing was to be seen.

Till a great sea-bird, called the Albatross, came through the snow-fog, and was received with great joy and hospitality.

And lo! the Albatross proveth a bird of good omen, and followeth the ship as it returned northward through fog and floating ice.

The ancient Mariner inhospitably killeth the pious bird of good omen.

His shipmates cry out against him.

But when the fog cleared off they justify the same, and thus make themselves accomplices in the crime.

The fair breeze continues; the ship enters the Pacific Ocean, and sails northward, even till it reaches the Line.

The ship hath been suddenly becalmed, and the Albatross begins to be avenged.

A Spirit had followed them; one of the invisible inhabitants of this planet, neither departed souls nor angels.

The shipmates, in their sore distress, would fain throw the whole guilt on the ancient Mariner; in sign whereof they hang the dead sea-bird around his neck.

The ancient Mariner beholdeth a sign in the element afar off.

At its nearer approach, it seemeth him to be a ship; and at a dear ransom he freeth his speech from the bonds of thirst.

A flash of joy; and horror follows; for can it be a ship that comes onward without wind or tide?

It seemeth him but the skeleton of a ship; and its ribs are seen as bars on the face of the setting Sun.

The Spectre-Woman and her Death-mate, and no other on board the skeleton ship,

Death and Life-in-Death have diced for the ship's crew, and she winneth the ancient Mariner.

At the rising of the Moon, one after another, his shipmates drop down dead: but Life-in-Death begins her work upon the ancient Mariner.

The Wedding Guest feareth that a spirit is talking to him; but the ancient Mariner assureth him of his bodily life, and proceeded to relate his horrible penance.

By the light of the Moon he beholdeth God's creatures of the great calm, their beauty and their happiness.

He blesseth them in his heart; the spell begins to break.

By grace of the holy Mother, the ancient Mariner is refreshed with rain.

He heareth sounds, and seeth strange sights and commotions in the sky and the element.

The bodies of the ship's crew are inspired, and the ship moves on.

But not by the souls of the men, nor by daemons of earth or middle air, but by a blessed troop of angelic spirits.

The lonesome Spirit from the South Pole carries on the ship as far as the Line in obedience to the angelic troop, but still requireth vengeance.

The Polar Spirit's fellow-daemons, the invisible inhabitants of the element, take part in his wrong; and two of them relate one to the other that penance long and heavy for the ancient Mariner hath been accorded to the Polar Spirit, who returneth southward.

The Mariner hath been cast into a trance; for the angelic power causeth the vessel to drive northward faster than human life could endure.

The supernatural motion is retarded; the Mariner awakes, and his penance begins anew.

The curse is finally expiated; and the ancient Mariner beholdeth his native country.

The angelic spirits leave the dead bodies, and appear in their own forms of light.

The Hermit of the Wood approacheth the ship with wonder.

The ship suddenly sinketh.

The ancient Mariner is saved in the Pilot's boat.

The ancient Mariner earnestly entreateth the Hermit to shrive him, and the penance of life falls on him.

And ever and anon throughout his future life an agony constraineth him to travel from land to land, and to teach by his own example reverence to all things that God hath made and loveth.

We thus learn from Coleridge himself what the moral of his poem was intended to be. It was a republication with vast extension of one of the most characteristic contributions of the eighteenth century to human progress. What the philanthropists of that century had eloquently enforced with respect to man's duty to man Coleridge extended to embrace all living beings, and this not upon the mere ground of the moral beauty of compassion, which the eighteenth-century thinkers would have admitted equally with himself, but upon that of kinship, the entire sentient creation being regarded equally with mankind as an effluence of the Divine energy.[3] He thus introduced a mystical element unintelligible to merely rational thinkers. Mrs. Barbauld, who, reading the poem in the first edition, lacked the guidance of the running commentary subsequently added, deplored the absence of a moral, so entirely had what seems to us its obvious purport escaped her. Coleridge replied that there was too much moral. If he meant that this was unduly obtruded he did himself injustice; but if he had simply stated what the moral was, as he afterwards did in his marginal note, Mrs. Barbauld would probably have told him that this was too trivial; and he himself was far from apprehending at the time what momentous consequences were enfolded, not so much in his proposition itself, as in the grounds on which he rested it.

The other great distinction of "The Ancient Mariner," its character as almost the first authentic proclamation of "the renascence of wonder," is not of course insisted upon, or even clearly expressed in the poem itself. In this department it asserts nothing, it simply proves its case by its own existence. The instinct for the wonderful had indeed never died out of the soul of man, and, like a captive subsisting upon scraps and windfalls, had of late been nourished upon translations and imitations of Oriental tales, upon Percy ballads and Ossian; and on the Continent, though hardly in England, by that violent reaction against the unimaginative deadness of the time which produced the illuminism which in life embodied itself most conspicuously in Count Saint Germain and Cagliostro, and in literature in a powerful fiction, Schiller's "Ghost-seer." In England, however, "The Ancient Mariner" was perhaps the first publication which had not merely the characteristics that denoted the existence of a new movement, but the literary force that could urge it onward. Blake, indeed, had begun to sing, but had not succeeded in making himself audible. "Vathek," regarded as a tale of wonder, is a masterpiece, but it was originally written in French, and its spirit of mockery and persiflage is wholly that of a French *conte* of the eighteenth century.

Neither the idea of all-embracing humanity, nor the revival of the passion for the wild and wonderful, nevertheless, would preserve "The Ancient Mariner" from oblivion if it were not at the same time a work of exquisite poetry. On this point the *vox populi* and the *vox Dei* sound the same note. The delight of all imaginative readers since its first publication, it has always maintained its popularity with the generality, and is known to multitudes to whom the rest of Coleridge is a sealed book. The cause is no doubt to be found in the deep human interest of the story, notwithstanding its wildness, and in the perfect simplicity of both style and thought. Shelley, Keats and Tennyson present formidable difficulties to the reader of inferior or even medium culture, but though the leisure of a deep thinker would not be misapplied in expounding "The Ancient Mariner," it has with perfect propriety and general acceptance been inserted into poetry books designed for children. Its poetical beauty, moreover, is even and continuous; it is indeed no exception to Johnson's just remark, that no poem of any length can be one entire diamond, but it is a chain of jewels so closely strung as to conceal the connecting links. In seeking to illustrate it by a succession of passages, we shall hardly find one which has not already gained the popular ear and become common property.

> The western wave was all a-flame,
>   The day was well nigh done:
> Almost upon the western wave
>   Rested the broad, bright sun;
> When that strange shape drove suddenly
>   Betwixt us and the sun.
>
> And straight the sun was flecked with bars
>   (Heaven's Mother send us grace!)
> As if through a dungeon-grate he peered
>   With broad and burning face.
>
> Alas! (thought I, and my heart beat loud)
> How fast she nears and nears!
> Are those her sails that glance in the sun,
>   Like restless gossamers?

Are those her ribs through which the sun
Did peer, as though a grate?
And is that Woman all her crew?
Is that a Death? and are there two?
Is Death that woman's mate?

Her lips were red, her looks were free,
Her locks were yellow as gold:
Her skin was as white as leprosy,
The night-mare Life-in-Death was she,
Who thicks man's blood with cold.

The naked hulk alongside came,
And the twain were casting dice;
"The game is done! I've won, I've won!"
Quoth she, and whistles thrice.

The sun's rim dips; the stars rush out;
At one stride comes the dark;
With far-heard whisper, o'er the sea,
Off shot the spectre bark.

                    *   *   *

The moving moon went up the sky,
And no where did abide:
Softly was she going up,
And a star or two beside

Her beams bemocked the sultry main,
Like April hoar-frost spread;
But where the ship's huge shadow lay,
The charmed water burnt alway,
A still and awful red.

Beyond the shadow of the ship
I watched the water-snakes:
They moved in tracks of shining white,
And when they reared, the elfish light
Fell off in hoary flakes.

Within the shadow of the ship
I watched their rich attire:
Blue, glossy green, and velvet black,

They coiled and swam, and every track
Was a flash of golden fire.

O happy living things! no tongue
Their beauty might declare:
A spring of love gushed from my heart,
And I blessed them unaware!
Sure my kind saint took pity on me,
And I blessed them unaware.

The selfsame moment I could pray;
And from my neck so free
The Albatross fell off, and sank
Like lead into the sea.

But soon there breathed a wind on me,
Nor sound nor motion made;
Its path was not upon the sea,
In ripple or in shade.

It raised my hair, it fanned my cheek
Like a meadow-gale of spring
It mingled strangely with my fears,
Yet it felt like a welcoming

Swiftly, swiftly flew the ship
Yet she sailed softly too;
Sweetly, sweetly blew the breeze
On me alone it blew.
Oh! dream of joy! is this indeed
The lighthouse top I see?
Is this the hill? is this the kirk?
Is this mine own countree?

We drifted o'er the harbour-bar,
And I with sobs did pray
"O let me be awake, my God!
Or let me sleep alway."

The harbour-bay was clear as glass,
So smoothly was it strewn!
And on the bay the moonlight lay,
And the shadow of the moon.

The rock shone bright, the kirk no less,
That stands above the rock:
The moonlight steeped in silentness
The steady weathercock.

And the bay was white with silent light,
Till rising from the same,
Full many shapes that shadows were,
In crimson colours came.

It will be observed how completely Coleridge has solved two difficult problems, that of relating the most surprising events and embodying the most imaginative conceptions in language of transparent simplicity; and, conversely, of investing this familiar speech with a dignity becoming the grandeur of the tale and the half unearthly character of the narrator.

In diction and metre the "Ancient Mariner" is not only faultless but is far above the ordinary standard of good poetry. This was not the case with the first edition of 1798. Coleridge had begun to compose under the mistaken impression that it behoved him to be archaic, and the poem in its original shape is much infested with quaint and obsolete spellings and locutions. These disappeared in the second edition, which is also so greatly improved by revision throughout as to render the comparison of the two versions a most interesting study. This impeccability does not entirely extend to the conduct of the story. Although we would on no account part with the description of the spectre ship with Death and Life-in-Death on board, it must be owned that this is a superfluity as regards the development of the narrative, and seems somewhat discordant with the general tone of the poem. It would have been in better keeping with that other typical figure of nautical legend, "The Flying Dutchman." It must be remembered in palliation that the apparent excrescence is closely related to the foundation of the poem, which originated in the dream of a friend of Coleridge's in which he saw a ship worked by dead men. The introduction of Death and his mate thus came naturally to Coleridge, though he has not succeeded in so interweaving it with his action as to make it appear indispensable.

A more serious defect is the violation of poetical justice in the penalties meted out to the mariner and his shipmates. The offenders whose crime is the mere approval of a bad action, perish; the actual perpetrator returns to his "own countree" and moralizes upon their doom. It can only be pleaded that the revivification of so many corpses would have bordered upon the ludicrous, and that Poetical Justice must give way when she comes into collision with Poetry herself.

Paris, in "Troilus and Cressida," reminds Diomed that chapmen "dispraise the thing that they desire to buy." It is not usual to find them dispraising the thing that they desire to sell. Wordsworth, nevertheless, when reprinting "The Ancient Mariner" with Coleridge's alterations in the second edition of "Lyrical Ballads," added a note in which he disparaged the poem on several grounds, mostly imaginary or trivial. He adds, notwithstanding, that it has a value "not often possessed by better poems." Where he had found a better poem than "The Ancient Mariner" in its own class he does not tell us, nor can we conjecture. In thus depreciating Coleridge's work he was sawing off the branch upon which he himself was sitting. He might in a measure have claimed to be himself the author of "The Ancient Mariner," for although the poem lay outside his sphere, he by his new views and the contagion of his inspiration had raised Coleridge from the levels of Thomson and Akenside to the higher regions where alone such an achievement was possible. But Coleridge had amply repaid the obligation by providing the less exalted if infinitely significant performances of his friend with a prelude of such dignity that it might serve as a fit portal, not merely to them, but to the age of great poetry then commencing for Britain:

> The eastern gate
> Where the great sun begins his state.

Notes

1. On the contrary, he opposed Lord Erskine's bill for suppressing cruelty to animals on metaphysical grounds, thus establishing his thesis that the reason differs from the understanding.

2. He had written "The furrow followed free," "but I had not been long on board a ship before I perceived that this was the image as seen by a spectator from the shore, or from another vessel. From the ship itself the water appears like a brook flowing off from the stern." He therefore substituted "The furrow streamed off he&" in the edition of 1816, but the original reading was restored in the collected edition of his works in 1828.

3. Shelley puts the pith of the whole matter into two lines and a half:

> If no bright bird, insect, or gentle beast
> I consciously have injured, but still loved
> And cherished these my kindred. Alastor.

—Richard Garnett, "The 'Ancient Mariner' as
an Exemplar of Coleridge's Genius," from *Bell's
Miniature Series of Great Writers*, Coleridge,
London: George Bell & Sons, 1904, pp. 82–99

A.W. Crawford "On Coleridge's Ancient Mariner" (1919)

It seems now to be generally accepted that *The Ancient Mariner* is a sort of allegory, picturing human life as a Pilgrim's Progress upon the sea. The poem contains not only a mysterious or supernatural element, which none can fail to see, but also carries a deep mystical and symbolic meaning which requires careful interpretation. The larger part of the poem lends itself readily to such an interpretation, and its meaning has become tolerably clear. The mariner starts out on the voyage of life, only to find himself at once getting into all sorts of trouble. This seems symbolic of the sins that overtake men in life. After penance he starts on his return home, rounding out his voyage at the port from which he embarked. There are, however, certain difficult points in the interpretation. On his return voyage the Mariner is aided by the Pilot, the Pilot's boy, and the Hermit. These come out in the Pilot's boat to welcome him as he draws near, and finally rescue him from the sea as his ship goes down. Little is given in the poem to indicate the meaning of these, but of the Hermit the Mariner says

> It is the Hermit good!
> He singeth loud his godly hymns
> That he makes in the wood.
> He'll shreve my soul, he'll wash away
> The Albatross's blood.

He further speaks of him as living in the wood, where "He kneels at morn, and noon, and eve—," praying beside the trees in the forest. In the margin Coleridge calls him "The Hermit of the Wood," and evidently intends to portray in him Nature's High Priest, who shrives the Mariner from his sins against Nature. The Mariner has sinned primarily against God's creatures, or Nature, as symbolized by the Albatross, and only the Hermit, as Priest of Nature, can shrive him from this sin.

The Pilot and the Pilot's boy, however, are not so easily interpreted. They perform no such function in the poem as the Hermit. The boat they come in, which rescues the Mariner, is called "the Pilot's boat," though neither the Pilot nor the Pilot's boy seems to give any real assistance to the Mariner. On the contrary, they seem only to add to the confusion, for when the crisis came the Pilot said, "I am a-feard," and after the ship went down and they had picked up the Mariner's body,

> the Pilot shrieked
> And fell down in a fit.

And to make matters worse, when the Mariner himself took the oars, as the Hermit prayed,

> the Pilot's boy,
> Who now doth crazy go,
> Laughed loud and long, and all the while
> His eyes went to and fro.

Then he added further embarrassment and revealed his utter inability to appreciate anything of the real situation by suggesting that the Mariner is no other than the Devil himself.

Few writers have made any attempt to explain the allegory at these points, and none so far as I know has offered a satisfactory explanation. One editor, however, suggests that the Pilot represents "in some sense practical wisdom," and that the Hermit acts "as the bearer of the truths of Christianity." But these suggestions do not seem to meet the difficulty, and are in fact too indefinite to be of value.

As an attempt at explanation, one of my students[1] some time ago ventured the suggestion that perhaps the Pilot may represent the Church and the Pilot's boy the clergy. And a careful consideration of both the poem and the mind of the poet at this period of his work leads me to believe that this is the real solution of the difficulty and the true explanation of the persons. As all students of Coleridge know, he was not well satisfied with the condition of the Church of his day, and not averse to passing criticism on both the Church and the Clergy.

Coleridge was brought up in the established church, as the son of a clergyman, but for a period covering the time of the writing of *The Ancient Mariner*, and several succeeding years, he separated himself from that church and identified himself with the Unitarians. Only the annuity from the Wedgwoods in 1798 prevented him accepting a call to become minister of the Unitarian Church at Shrewsbury. At a later date, however, he repudiated the doctrines of Unitarianism, and became more sympathetic toward the orthodox churches. When writing his poem he believed that the Church was devoid of spiritual power or religious leadership, and was unable to render any assistance in the spiritual crises of men's lives; he deplored the Church's lack of religion, and the spiritual barrenness of the eighteenth century. Romanticism, indeed, put new emphasis upon the spiritual life. But the Pilot in the poem could provide only the boat, or the empty form and institution of the Church, while the Hermit alone could render any real spiritual assistance. At the very climax of the crisis the Pilot himself was utterly confused and "fell down in a fit." Then, when the Mariner took up the oars, the Pilot's boy went "crazy," and with an idiotic laugh called the Mariner a "devil." This seems to imply that to the clergy of the day spiritual phenomena looked like forms of lunacy, or the work of evil spirits, so unfamiliar were they with anything of the sort. The great religious revival of the century had not yet accomplished its work. With no aid from the church, then, the Mariner passed through the greatest spiritual crisis of his life. And after completing his voyage back to his home harbor, he felt constrained to travel from land to land telling the "ghastly tale" of his new and wonderful experience.

The Ancient Mariner, then, is not only Coleridge's interpretation of man's deepest spiritual experiences, but also his criticism of the spiritual feebleness of the Church of his day. The poet, fortunately, lived to see a day when he could think better of the Church.

Note

1. Mr. Vernon B. Rhodenizer, now Professor of English in Acadia College, Wolfville, Nova Scotia.

—A.W. Crawford, "On Coleridge's
Ancient Mariner," from *Modern Language Notes*,
vol. 34, no. 5, May 1919, pp. 311–313

"KUBLA KHAN"

THOMAS LOVE PEACOCK (1818)

Thomas Love Peacock was an accomplished classicist and scholar of French and Italian literature. A contemporary of Coleridge and a close friend of Percy Bysshe Shelley, Peacock continued the eighteenth-century satirical tradition in a series of novels in which a group of argumentative characters discourse on philosophical issues of the day. The works were parodies of the philosophical and social subject matter with which the romantic poets were so consumed. The following excerpt is taken from Peacock's third novel, *Nightmare Abbey*, which features the irreverent Mr. Ferdinando Flosky, a transcendental philosopher, whom Peacock identified in a footnote as a reference to the Greek term for one who is "a lover, or spectator, of shadows." In *Nightmare Abbey*, Flosky serves as a satirical portrait of Samuel Taylor Coleridge, and he implicitly pokes fun at Coleridge's account of the composition of "Kubla Khan" by punning on the name of one of Shakespeare's most comical characters, Bottom the Weaver, because the poem lacks a "bottom" and is devoid of purpose. In *A Midsummer Night's Dream*, Nick Bottom is one of a group of craftsmen who decide to put on a play for Theseus's wedding. During rehearsal for the play, Bottom is transformed into a creature with an ass's head, though he does not know it. When he is changed back to his former physical being, he is unsure of what has happened, exemplifying one of the major themes of *A Midsummer Night's Dream*, that things are never quite what they appear to be.

Mr Flosky: That is strange: nothing is so becoming to a man as an air of mystery. Mystery is the very key-stone of all that is beautiful in poetry, all that is sacred in faith, and all that is recondite in transcendental psychology. I am writing a ballad which is all mystery; it is "such stuff as dreams are made of," and is, indeed, stuff made of a dream; for, last night I fell asleep as usual over my book, and had a vision of pure reason. I composed five hundred lines in my sleep; so that, having had a dream of a ballad, I am now officiating as my own Peter Quince, and making a ballad of my dream, and it shall be called Bottom's Dream, because it has no bottom.

—Thomas Love Peacock,
Nightmare Abbey, 1818, chapter 8

GEORGE CALVERT (1880)

George Calvert extols the virtues of "Kubla Khan," likening it to a megatherium, an extinct genus of large, plant-eating, ground-dwelling sloths that lived from approximately two million to 8,000 years ago. Calvert thus revels in the otherworldly and exotic lushness of imagery that is the poem's self-justification. Calvert's zoological metaphor is striking in that he heaps the highest praise on Coleridge's fantastic imagination by comparing him to a scientist who studies the origins of the Earth to discover the enormous transformations wrought by the passage of time. It is important to note that at the time Calvert was writing, zoology had become a modern scientific area of inquiry in British universities, primarily established by Thomas Henry Huxley (1825–1895). He was a known supporter of many of Charles Darwin's theories of evolution and considered by some to be one of the best comparative anatomists of the second half of the nineteenth century. Continuing the evolutionary metaphor, Calvert observes that "[m]etrical talent must be there to handle the molten words as they flow from the furnace of genius, shaping and placing them while still swollen with genial warmth." In paying attention to such minute details as punctuation—as when Coleridge places a colon at the end of the line "in tumult to a lifeless ocean"—Calvert argues that, instead of stopping with this image, Coleridge meant to further awaken the attentive reader to new associations and, ultimately, to a transcendent consciousness of human destiny. Calvert suggests that a careful reader will be thus transported and led to participate in the poetic process along with Coleridge, as the breathless pace of image upon image propels the reader forward while, simultaneously, compelling her or him to look back at human history.

Were there left of Coleridge nothing but *Kubla Khan*, from this gem one might almost reconstruct, in full brightness, its great author's poetic work, just as the expert zoologist reconstructs the extinct megatherium from a single fossil bone. Of this masterpiece, the chief beauty is not the noted music of the versification, but the range and quality of the imaginings embodied in this music. Were there in these no unearthly breathings, no mysterious grandeur, the verse could not have been made to pulsate so rhythmically. The essence of the melody is in the fineness of the conception, in the poetic imaginations. In this case, as in all cases, the spirit not only controls but creates the body. Metrical talent must be there to handle the molten words as they flow from the furnace of genius, shaping and placing them while still swollen with genial warmth. Genius, the master, cannot do without talent, the servant.

> Five miles meandering with a mazy motion
> Through wood and dale the sacred river ran,
> Then reached the caverns measureless to man,
> And sank in tumult to a lifeless ocean:

To present of a sudden to the mind a signal thought, which springs unexpectedly but appropriately out of another, the meeting of the two striking a light that flashes a new and brilliant ray upon the attention,—to do this is to perform a high poetic feat. The sacred river running through wood and dale, then gliding into the earth through caverns measureless to man, to sink "in tumult to a lifeless ocean:" this mysterious picture sets the mind a brooding, awakens its poetic sensibility. Suppose the passage had stopped here. Regaled by such a fresh, impressive presentation, the mind would have grasped it as an inward boon, to be held tightly hold of by the susceptible reader, awakening in him, through quick affinities, thoughts of human fate and woe. But the passage does not stop here; in the poet's mind, as in the capable reader's, are generated associations with human destiny: and so, instead of a full stop at "ocean," there is only a colon, the poet's thought springing forward into the two wonderful lines,—

> And mid this tumult Kubla heard from far
> Ancestral voices prophesying war.

And the passage, instead of leaving on the reader an impression of calm, strange beauty, kindles into a startling splendor. The physical tumult passes into human tumult; the vague, hoarse swell of a torrent grows articulate, the "caverns measureless to man" deepen into the abode of former kings, who, from the subterranean darkness to which their warrior-ambition has doomed them, throw upon the ear of their Sardanapalean descendant doleful, menacing predictions. All this, and more, is in those two lines, so laden with meaning and music, whereby the physical picture is magnified, deepened, vivified, through psychical participation. The poetical is ever an appeal to the deepest in the human mind, and a great burst of poetic light like this lays bare, for the imagination to roam in, a vast indefinite domain.

In another part of the short poem is a similar sudden heightening of effect by the introduction of humanity into a scene of purely terrene features:

> But oh! that deep romantic chasm which slanted
> Down the green hill athwart a cedarn cover!
> A savage place! as holy and enchanted
> As e'er beneath a waning moon was haunted

These lines could have been written only by a poet with the finest ear, an internal ear. When we come to the last word of the fourth line, we pass into a higher region: "haunted!" Haunted by what?

> By woman wailing for her demon lover.

On this single line is stamped the power of a great poet; that is, a poet in whom breadth and depth of intellectual and sympathetic endowment give to the refining aspiring poetic faculty material to work upon drawn from the grander, subtler, remoter resources of the human soul,—material beyond the reach of any but poets of the first order, whose right, indeed, to a place in this order rests upon their power of higher spiritual reach united to wider intellectual range. How much is involved in this short passage! A landscape gift, to present in two lines a clear picture of the "savage place;" then, by a leap of the poet's imagination, the scene is overhung by an earthly atmosphere that makes it so holy and enchanted that (and here the poet takes the final great leap) it is fit, "under a waning moon," to be haunted

> By woman wailing for her demon lover.

That is a poetically imaginative leap of the boldest and most beautiful. What an ethereal springiness, what an intellectual swing, in the mind that could make such a leap! That particular one Coleridge's friend Wordsworth could not have made, strong as he was in poetic imagination. It implies almost something spectral, superearthly, something uncanny. And what an exquisitely musical rhythm the thought weaves about itself for its poetic incarnation.

—George H. Calvert, *Coleridge, Shelley, Goethe:
Biographic Aesthetic Studies*, 1880, pp. 12–16

CHRISTABEL

GEORGE GORDON, LORD BYRON (1816)

Christabel—I won't have you sneer at *Christabel*—it is a fine wild poem.

—George Gordon, Lord Byron, letter to
John Murray, September 30, 1816

JOHN GIBSON LOCKHART "ON THE LAKE SCHOOL OF POETRY: III. COLERIDGE" (1819)

While admitting that Coleridge has displayed his abilities as a talented poet, capable of writing an accomplished and carefully crafted work such as *The Rime of the Ancient Mariner*, John Gibson Lockhart's review is primarily focused on *Christabel*. In it, he delivers mostly negative commentary, accusing Coleridge of suffering from a serious lack of determination and failing to have formulated a cohesive plan for its completion, content to leave it as a mere fragment. Lockhart suggests that Coleridge has not really been present to himself while working on the poem: "It does not appear that even the language of a poem can arise spontaneously throughout like a strain of music, any more than the colours of the painter will go and arrange themselves on his canvass, while he is musing on the subject in another room." However, Lockhart mitigates, ever so slightly, some of the condemnation he has leveled at *Christabel*, in admitting that the finished product might have been a strong work. All in all, though, Lockhart delivers a scathing review, warning the unwary reader that "[h]e that is determined to try every thing by the standard of what is called common sense .... had better not open this production."

Christabel, as our readers are aware, is only a fragment, and had been in existence for many years antecedent to the time of its publication. Neither has the author assigned any reason either for the long delay of its appearance—or for the imperfect state in which he has at last suffered it to appear. In all probability he had waited long in the hope of being able to finish it to his satisfaction; but finding that he was never revisited by a mood sufficiently genial—he determined to let the piece be printed as it was. It is not in the history of *Christabel* alone that we have seen reason to suspect Mr. Coleridge of being by far too passive in his notions concerning the mode in which a poet ought to deal with his muse. It is very true, that the best conceptions and designs are frequently those which occur to a man of fine talents, without having been painfully sought after: but the exertion of the Will is always necessary in the worthy execution of them. It behooves a poet, like any other artist, after he has fairly conceived the idea of his piece, to set about realising it in good earnest, and to use his most persevering attention in considering how all its parts are to be adapted and conjoined. It does not appear that even the language of a poem can arise spontaneously throughout like a strain of music, any more than the colours of the painter will go and arrange themselves on his canvass, while he is musing on the subject in another room. Language is a material which it requires no little labour to reduce into beautiful forms,—a truth of which the ancients were, above all others, well and continually aware. For although vivid ideas naturally suggest happy expressions, yet the latter are, as it were, only insulated traits or features, which require much management in the joining, and the art of the composer is seen in the symmetry of the whole structure. Now, in many respects Mr Coleridge seems too anxious to enjoy the advantages of an inspired writer, and to produce his poetry at once in its perfect form—like the palaces which spring out of the desert in complete splendour at a single rubbing of the lamp in the Arabian Tale. But carefulness above all is necessary to a poet in these latter days, when the ordinary medium through which things are viewed is so very far from being poetical—and when the natural strain of scarcely any man's associations can be expected to be of that sort which is most akin to high and poetical feeling. There is no question there are many, very many passages in the poetry of this writer, which shew what excellent things may be done under the impulse of a happy moment—passages in which the language—above all things—has such aerial graces as would have been utterly beyond the reach of any person who might have attempted to produce the like, without being able to lift his spirit into the same ecstatic mood. It is not to be denied, however, that among the whole of his poems there are only a few in the composition of which he seems to have been blessed all throughout with the same sustaining energy of afflatus. The Mariner—we need not say—is one of these. The poem "Love" is another—and were Christabel completed as it has been begun, we doubt not it would be allowed by all who are capable of tasting the merits of such poetry, to be a third—and, perhaps, the most splendid of the three.

It is impossible to gather from the part which has been published any conception of what is the meditated conclusion of the story of *Christabel*. Incidents can never be fairly judged of till we know what they lead to. Of those which occur in the first and second cantos of this poem, there is no doubt many appear at present very strange and disagreeable, and the sooner the remainder comes forth to explain them, the better. One thing is evident, that no man need sit down to read Christabel with any prospect of gratification, whose mind has not rejoiced habitually in the luxury of visionary and superstitious reveries. He that is determined to try every thing by the standard of what is called common sense, and who has an aversion to admit, even in poetry, of the existence of things more than are dreamt of in philosophy, had better not open this production, which is only proper for a solitary couch and a midnight taper. Mr Coleridge is the prince of superstitious poets; and he that does not read *Christabel* with a strange and harrowing feeling of mysterious dread, may be assured that his soul is made of impenetrable stuff.

—John Gibson Lockhart, "On the Lake School
of Poetry: III. Coleridge," *Blackwood's Edinburgh
Magazine*, October 1819, pp. 8–9

John Sterling
"On Coleridge's Christabel" (1828)

John Sterling's commentary on *Christabel* is written in defense of a poem he believes has been outrageously attacked by those who cannot appreciate its beauty. Sterling congratulates Coleridge for being the first English poet in 150 years to revive the fantasy and magic of the medieval romance. For Sterling, Coleridge is a man of genius who addressed his poem to a readership that welcomed a return to the mystical qualities of that tradition.

It is common to hear everything which Mr. Coleridge has written condemned with bitterness and boldness. His poems are called extravagant; and his prose works, poems too, and of the noblest breed, are pronounced to be mystical, obscure, metaphysical, theoretical, unintelligible, and so forth; just as the same phrases have over and over been applied, with as much sagacity, to Plato, St. Paul, Cudworth, and Kant. But *Christabel* is the only one of his writings which is ever treated with unmingled contempt; and I wish to examine with what justice this feeling has been excited. In the first place it should be remembered, that, at the time when it was written, the end of the last century, no attempt had been made in England by a man of genius for a hundred and fifty years to embody in poetry those resources which feudal manners and popular superstitions supply to the imagination. To those who care not for the mythology of demoniac terrors and wizard enchantment, Mr. Coleridge did not write. He did not write for Bayles and Holbachs; nor did he write for Glanvils or Jameses: but for those who, not believing the creed of the people, not holding that which was in a great degree the substantial religion of Europe for a thousand years, yet see in these superstitions the forms under which devotion presented itself to the minds of our forefathers, the grotesque mask assumed for a period, like the veil on the face of Moses, as a covering for the glory of God. Persons who think this obsolete faith to be merely ridiculous, will of course think so of *Christabel*. He who perceives in them a beauty of their own, and discovers all the good to which in those ages they were necessary accompaniments, will not object to have them represented, together with all the attributes and associations which rightly belong to them, and in which genius, while it raises them from their dim cemetery, delights again to array them.

—John Sterling, "On Coleridge's Christabel,"
1828, *Essays and Tales*, ed. Julius Charles Hare,
1848, vol. 1, pp. 101–102

Edgar Allan Poe
"The Rationale of Verse" (1848)

Out of a hundred readers of Christabel, fifty will be able to make nothing of its rhythm, while forty-nine of the remaining fifty will, with some ado, fancy they comprehend it, after the fourth or fifth perusal. The one out of the whole hundred who shall both comprehend and admire it at first sight—must be an unaccountably clever person—and I am by far too modest to assume, for a moment, that that very clever person is myself.

—Edgar Allan Poe, "The Rationale of Verse," 1848

WILLIAM WATSON "LINES IN A
FLYLEAF OF CHRISTABEL" (1893)

Inhospitably hast thou entertained,
O Poet, us the bidden to thy board,
Whom in mid-feast, and while our thousand mouths
Are one laudation of the festal cheer,
Thou from thy table dost dismiss, unfilled.
Yet loudlier thee than many a lavish host
We praise, and oftener thy repast half-served
Than many a stintless banquet, prodigally
Through satiate hours prolonged; nor praise less well
Because with tongues thou hast not cloyed, and lips
That mourn the parsimony of affluent souls,
And mix the lamentation with the laud.

—William Watson, "Lines in a
Flyleaf of Christabel," 1893

CRITICAL WRITINGS

WILLIAM HAZLITT "MR. COLERIDGE" (1825)

An opposing point of view on Coleridge's combination of scientific knowledge with literary interpretation is William Hazlitt's assessment of Coleridge's criticism. Rather than seeing the romantic era as a revitalized age, Hazlitt complains that the enormous influx of new ideas has become dazzling, though not understood or mastered. "We are like those who have been to see some noble monument of art, who are content to admire without thinking of rivalling it." Though he admits that Coleridge possesses a fantastic imagination and unique understanding, Hazlitt views his criticism as marginal, finding it fragmentary and lacking purpose. In a word, Hazlitt sees Coleridge's critical writings as impressionistic and therefore missing the point. Hazlitt is also of the opinion that Coleridge wasted his critical-writing talents by becoming a public lecturer, preferring to revel in the applause of his audience. While Hazlitt is impressed with Coleridge's talent for extemporaneous lectures on any given topic, "from Peter Abelard down to Thomas Moore, from the subtlest metaphysics to the politics of the *Courier*," he nevertheless pronounces Coleridge's literary productivity to have ended some twenty years before Hazlitt composed the essay. Hazlitt goes so far to suggest that Coleridge, like all brilliant thinkers, become the victims of their own unchecked curiosity; in their enormous range of interests, "amidst the infinite variety of the universe," they simply cannot focus on any one particular issue and instead consider all the various points within their compass.

Having established Coleridge's genius, Hazlitt then proceeds to sketch briefly the evolution of a true scholar, beginning with his youthful endeavors in "Ode on Chatterton" and his ability to become the idol of schoolfellows drawn to his charming and inspiring conversation. According to Hazlitt, one of the finest instances of Coleridge's mesmerizing talks was on the Greek tragedians, during which he expounded on the passions of Euripides and the honeyed language of Aeschylus. Yet, despite all his youthful achievements and recognition at school, Hazlitt maintains that the poet was so far immersed in his studies that he never thought of himself as a superior being. Without providing any dates, Hazlitt then proceeds to delineate the beginning of Coleridge's most inauspicious career as a critic, which began with his dabbling in several new philosophical schools, both English and German, followed by lectures on the Trinity in which he "pared religion down to the standard of reason, and stripped faith of mystery." Nevertheless, at this unspecified juncture, Hazlitt maintains that poetry could still come to Coleridge's rescue and reanimate his lyrical imagination as he looked to such predecessors as Milton, Bowles, and Cooper to supplement his great familiarity with the most important English, German, and French writers of the eighteenth century. His crowning achievement, in Hazlitt's opinion, is *The Rime of the Ancient Mariner* as an extravagant celebration of imagination. Hazlitt also mentions some admirable qualities to be found in *Christabel*'s passage on divided friendship as well as in Coleridge's inspired translation of Schiller's *Wallenstein*.

After rendering a tribute to Coleridge for being a source of inspiration, Hazlitt then spends the rest of this essay lamenting how the poetic genius fell prey to opium and an unmitigated disappointment with life. Hazlitt is truly sympathetic to the fact that Coleridge became bogged down with daily burdens and the problems wrought by society, as he sees the poet suffering from a broken heart, "too romantic for the herd of vulgar politicians."

In Hazlitt's estimation, Coleridge's greatest talent was in the art of conversation, followed by a few poetic works of extraordinary beauty and, lastly, his prose works, which Hazlitt believes were a failure, for this last category of writing in no way reflects Coleridge's vast knowledge and learning, and instead the poet lapses into long-winded and abstruse arguments. As a result of what Hazlitt perceives to be a hierarchy of talents, he predicts that Coleridge has bequeathed little to a posterity that will not have the privilege of hearing his eloquent lectures. Moreover, Coleridge's lectures are really a tapestry of fragments and digressions born of an undisciplined thought process that never sees the argument brought to completion. Nevertheless, Hazlitt concludes that Coleridge was a genius who was forced to live in a most inhospitable age following the enormous disappointment with and loss of hope in the French Revolution, a war fought between power and reason. When the British government made life impossible for those associated with the radical movement, Coleridge turned to lecturing to his disaffected colleagues, "who turned back disgusted and panic-struck from the dry desert of unpopularity." Though his fellow Lake School poets were able to establish themselves on firm ground, Coleridge was destined to remain an eternal wanderer.

The present is an age of talkers, and not of doers; and the reason is, that the world is growing old. We are so far advanced in the Arts and Sciences, that we live in retrospect, and doat on past achievements. The accumulation of knowledge has been so great, that we are lost in wonder at the height it has reached, instead of attempting to climb or add to it; while the variety of objects distracts and dazzles the looker-on. What *niche* remains unoccupied? What path untried? What is the use of doing anything, unless we could do better than all those who have gone before us? What hope is there of this? We are like those who have been to see some noble monument of art, who are content to admire without thinking of rivalling it; or like guests after a feast, who praise the hospitality of the donor 'and thank the bounteous Pan'—perhaps carrying away some trifling fragments; or like the spectators of a mighty battle, who still hear its sound afar off, and the clashing of armour and the neighing of the war-horse and the shout of victory is in their ears, like the rushing of innumerable waters!

Mr. Coleridge has 'a mind reflecting ages past': his voice is like the echo of the congregated roar of the 'dark rearward and abyss' of thought. He who has seen a mouldering tower by the side of a crystal lake, hid by the mist, but glittering in the wave below, may conceive the dim, gleaming, uncertain intelligence of his eye: he who has marked the evening clouds uprolled (a world of vapours) has seen the picture of his mind, unearthly, unsubstantial, with gorgeous tints and ever-varying forms—

That which was now a horse, even with a thought
The rack dislimns, and makes it indistinct
As water is in water.

Our author's mind is (as he himself might express it) *tangential*. There is no subject on which he has not touched, none on which he has rested. With an understanding fertile, subtle, expansive, 'quick, forgetive, apprehensive,' beyond all living precedent, few traces of it perhaps remain. He lends himself to all impressions alike; he gives up his mind and liberty of thought to none. He is a general lover of art and science, and wedded to no one in particular. He pursues knowledge as a mistress, with outstretched hands and winged speed; but as he is about to embrace her, his Daphne turns—alas! not to a laurel! Hardly a speculation has been left on record from the earliest time, but it is loosely folded up in Mr. Coleridge's memory, like a rich, but somewhat tattered piece of tapestry: we might add (with more seeming than real extravagance) that scarce a thought can pass through the mind of man, but its sound has at some time or other passed over his head with rustling pinions.

On whatever question or author you speak, he is prepared to take up the theme with advantage—from Peter Abelard down to Thomas Moore, from the subtlest metaphysics to the politics of the *Courier*. There is no man of genius, in whose praise he descants, but the critic seems to stand above the author, and 'what in him is weak, to strengthen, what is low, to raise and support': nor is there any work of genius that does not come out of his hands like an illuminated Missal, sparkling even in its defects. If Mr. Coleridge had not been the most impressive talker of his age, he would probably have been the finest writer; but he lays down his pen to make sure of an auditor, and mortgages the admiration of posterity for the stare of an idler. If he had not been a poet, he would have been a powerful logician; if he had not dipped his wing in the Unitarian controversy, he might have soared to the very summit of fancy. But, in writing verse, he is trying to subject the Muse to *transcendental* theories: in his abstract reasoning, he misses his way by strewing it with flowers.

All that he has done of moment, he had done twenty years ago: since then, he may be said to have lived on the sound of his own voice. Mr. Coleridge is too rich in intellectual wealth, to need to task himself to any drudgery: he has only to draw the sliders of his imagination, and a thousand subjects expand before him, startling him with their brilliancy, or losing themselves in endless obscurity—

And by the force of blear illusion,
They draw him on to his confusion.

What is the little he could add to the stock, compared with the countless stores that lie about him, that he should stoop to pick up a name, or to polish an idle fancy? He walks abroad in the majesty of an universal understanding, eyeing the 'rich strond' or golden sky above him, and 'goes sounding on his way,' in eloquent accents, uncompelled and free!

Persons of the greatest capacity are often those, who for this reason do the least; for surveying themselves from the highest point of view, amidst the infinite variety of the universe, their own share in it seems trifling, and scarce worth a thought; and they prefer the contemplation of all that is, or has been, or can be, to the making a coil about doing what, when done, is no better than vanity. It is hard to concentrate all our attention and efforts on one pursuit, except from ignorance of others; and without this concentration of our faculties no great progress can be made in any one thing. It is not merely that the mind is not capable of the effort; it does not think the effort worth making. Action is one; but thought is manifold. He whose restless eye glances through the wide compass of nature and art, will not consent to have 'his own nothings monstered'; but he must do this before he can give his whole soul to them. The mind, after 'letting contemplation have its fill,' or

Sailing with supreme dominion
Through the azure deep of air,

sinks down on the ground, breathless, exhausted, powerless, inactive; or if it must have some vent to its feelings, seeks the most easy and obvious; is soothed by friendly flattery, lulled by the murmur of immediate applause: thinks, as it were, aloud, and babbles in its dreams!

A scholar (so to speak) is a more disinterested and abstracted character than a mere author. The first looks at the numberless volumes of a library, and says, 'All these are mine': the other points to a single volume (perhaps it may be an immortal one) and says, 'My name is written on the back of it.' This is a puny and grovelling ambition, beneath the lofty amplitude of Mr. Coleridge's mind. No, he revolves in his wayward soul, or utters to the passing wind, or discourses to his own shadow, things mightier and more various!—Let us draw the curtain, and unlock the shrine.

Learning rocked him in his cradle, and while yet a child,

He lisped in numbers, for the numbers came.

At sixteen he wrote his 'Ode on Chatterton,' and he still reverts to that period with delight, not so much as it relates to himself (for that string of his own early promise of fame rather jars than otherwise) but as exemplifying the youth of a poet. Mr. Coleridge talks of himself without being an egotist; for in him the individual is always merged in the abstract and general. He distinguished himself at school and at the University by his knowledge of the classics, and gained several prizes for Greek epigrams. How many men are there (great scholars, celebrated names in literature) who, having done the same thing in their youth, have no other idea all the rest of their lives but of this achievement, of a fellowship and dinner, and who, installed in academic honours, would look down on our author as a mere strolling bard! At Christ's Hospital, where he was brought up, he was the idol of those among his schoolfellows, who mingled with their bookish studies the music of thought and of humanity; and he was usually attended round the cloisters by a group of these (inspiring and inspired) whose hearts even then burnt within them as he talked, and where the sounds yet linger to mock Elia on his way, still turning pensive to the past!

One of the finest and rarest parts of Mr. Coleridge's conversation is, when he expatiates on the Greek tragedians (not that he is not well acquainted, when he pleases, with the epic poets, or the philosophers, or orators, or historians of antiquity)—on the subtle reasonings and melting pathos of Euripides, on the harmonious gracefulness of Sophocles, tuning his love-laboured song, like sweetest warblings from a sacred grove; on the high-wrought, trumpet-tongued eloquence of Aeschylus, whose *Prometheus,* above all, is like an Ode to Fate and a pleading with Providence, his thoughts being let loose as his body is chained on his solitary rock, and his afflicted will (the emblem of mortality)

Struggling in vain with ruthless destiny.

As the impassioned critic speaks and rises in his theme, you would think you heard the voice of the Man hated by the Gods, contending with the wild winds as they roar; and his eye glitters with the spirit of Antiquity!

Next, he was engaged with Hartley's tribes of mind, 'etherial braid, thought-woven,'—and he busied himself for a year or two with vibrations and vibratiuncles, and the great law of association that binds all things in its mystic chain, and the doctrine of Necessity (the mild teacher of Charity) and the Millennium, anticipative of a life to come; and he plunged deep into the controversy on Matter and Spirit, and, as an escape from Dr. Priestley's Materialism, where he felt himself imprisoned by the logician's spell, like Ariel in the cloven pine-tree, he became suddenly enamoured of Bishop Berkeley's fairy-world,[1] and used in all companies to build the universe, like a brave poetical fiction, of fine words. And he was deep-read in Malebranche, and in Cudworth's *Intellectual System* (a huge pile of learning, unwieldy, enormous) and in Lord Brook's hieroglyphic theories, and in Bishop Butler's Sermons, and in the Duchess of Newcastle's fantastic folios, and in Clarke and South, and Tillotson, and all the fine thinkers and masculine reasoners of that age; and Leibnitz's *Pre-established Harmony* reared its arch above his head, like the rainbow in the cloud, covenanting with the hopes of man. And then he fell plumb, ten thousand fathoms down (but his wings saved him harmless) into the *hortus siccus* of Dissent, where he pared religion down to the standard of reason, and stripped faith of mystery, and preached Christ crucified and the Unity of the Godhead, and so dwelt for a while in the spirit with John Huss and Jerome of Prague and Socinus and old John Zisca, and ran through Neal's History of the Puritans and Calamy's Non-Conformists' Memorial, having like thoughts and passions with them. But then Spinoza became his God, and he took up the vast chain of being in his hand, and the round world became the centre and the soul of all things in some shadowy sense, forlorn of meaning, and around him he beheld the living traces and the sky-pointing proportions of the mighty Pan; but poetry redeemed him from this spectral philosophy, and he bathed his heart in beauty, and gazed at the golden light of heaven, and drank of the spirit of the universe, and wandered at eve by fairy-stream or fountain,

> When he saw nought but beauty,
> When he heard the voice of that Almighty One
> In every breeze that blew, or wave that murmured—

and wedded with truth in Plato's shade, and in the writings of Proclus and Plotinus saw the ideas of things in the eternal mind, and unfolded all mysteries with the Schoolmen and fathomed the depths of Duns Scotus and Thomas Aquinas, and entered the third heaven with Jacob Behmen, and walked hand in hand with Swedenborg through the pavilions of the New Jerusalem, and sang his faith in the promise and in the word in his *Religious Musings*.

And lowering himself from that dizzy height he poised himself on Milton's wings, and spread out his thoughts in charity with the glad prose of Jeremy Taylor, and wept over Bowles's Sonnets, and studied Cowper's blank verse, and betook himself to Thomson's *Castle of Indolence,* and sported with the wits of Charles the Second's days and of Queen Anne, and relished Swift's style and that of the *John Bull* (Arbuthnot's we mean, not Mr. Croker's), and dallied with the British Essayists and Novelists, and knew all qualities of more modern writers with a learned spirit: Johnson, and Goldsmith, and Junius, and Burke, and Godwin, and the *Sorrows of Werter,* and Jean Jacques Rousseau, and Voltaire, and Marivaux, and Crebillon, and thousands more: now 'laughed with Rabelais in his easy chair' or pointed to Hogarth, or afterwards dwelt on Claude's classic scenes, or spoke with rapture of Raphael, and compared the women at Rome to figures that had walked out of his pictures, or visited the Oratory of Pisa, and described the works of Giotto and Ghirlandaio and Massaccio, and gave the moral of the picture of the Triumph of Death, where the beggars and the wretched invoke his dreadful dart, but the rich and mighty of the earth quail and shrink before it; and in that land of siren sights and sounds, saw a dance of peasant girls, and was charmed with lutes and gondolas,—or wandered into Germany and lost himself in the labyrinths of the Hartz Forest and of the Kantean philosophy, and amongst the cabalistic names of Fichte and Schelling and Lessing, and God knows who. This was long after; but all the former while he had nerved his heart and filled his eyes with tears, as he hailed the rising orb of liberty, since quenched in darkness and in blood, and had kindled his affections at the blaze of the French Revolution, and sang for joy, when the towers of the Bastille and the proud places of the insolent and the oppressor fell, and would have floated his bark, freighted with fondest fancies, across the Atlantic wave with Southey and others to seek for peace and freedom—

In Philarmonia's undivided dale!

Alas! 'Frailty, thy name is *Genius!*'—What is become of all this mighty heap of hope, of thought, of learning and humanity? It has ended in swallowing doses of oblivion and in writing paragraphs in the *Courier*. Such and so little is the mind of man!

It was not to be supposed that Mr. Coleridge could keep on at the rate he set off. He could not realize all he knew or thought, and less could not fix his desultory ambition. Other stimulants supplied the place, and kept up the intoxicating dream, the fever and the madness of his early impressions. Liberty (the philosopher's and the poet's bride) had fallen a victim, meanwhile, to the murderous practices of the hag Legitimacy. Proscribed by court-hirelings, too romantic for the herd of vulgar politicians, our enthusiast stood at bay, and at last turned on the pivot of a subtle casuistry to the *unclean side*: but his discursive reason would not let him trammel himself into a poet-laureate or stamp-distributor; and he stopped, ere he had quite passed that well-known 'bourne from whence no traveller returns'— and so has sunk into torpid, uneasy repose, tantalized by useless resources, haunted by vain imaginings, his lips idly moving, but his heart for ever still, or, as the shattered chords vibrate of themselves, making melancholy music to the ear of memory! Such is the fate of genius in an age when, in the unequal contest with sovereign wrong, every man is ground to powder who is not either a born slave, or who does not willingly and at once offer up the yearnings of humanity and the dictates of reason as a welcome sacrifice to besotted prejudice and loathsome power.

Of all Mr. Coleridge's productions, the *Ancient Mariner* is the only one that we could with confidence put into any person's hands, on whom we wished to impress a favourable idea of his extraordinary powers. Let whatever other objections be made to it, it is unquestionably a work of genius—of wild, irregular, overwhelming imagination, and has that rich, varied movement in the verse, which gives a distant idea of the lofty or changeful tones of Mr. Coleridge's voice. In the *Christabel,* there is one splendid passage on divided friendship. The Translation of Schiller's *Wallenstein* is also a masterly production in its kind, faithful and spirited. Among his smaller pieces there are occasional bursts of pathos and fancy, equal to what we might expect from him; but these form the exception, and not the rule. Such, for instance, is his affecting Sonnet to the author of the *Robbers.*

> Schiller! that hour I would have wish'd to die,
> If through the shudd'ring midnight I had sent
> From the dark dungeon of the tower time-rent,
> That fearful voice, a famish'd father's cry—
> That in no after-moment aught less vast
> Might stamp me mortal! A triumphant shout
> Black horror scream'd, and all her goblin rout
> From the more with'ring scene diminish'd pass'd.
> Ah! Bard tremendous in sublimity!
> Could I behold thee in thy loftier mood,
> Wand'ring at eve, with finely frenzied eye,
> Beneath some vast old tempest-swinging wood!
> Awhile, with mute awe gazing, I would brood,
> Then weep aloud in a wild ecstasy.

His Tragedy, entitled *Remorse,* is full of beautiful and striking passages; but it does not place the author in the first rank of dramatic writers. But if Mr. Coleridge's works do not place him in that rank, they injure instead of conveying a just idea of the man; for he himself is certainly in the first class of general intellect.

If our author's poetry is inferior to his conversation, his prose is utterly abortive. Hardly a gleam is to be found in it of the brilliancy and richness of those stores of thought and language that he pours out incessantly, when they are lost like drops of water in the ground. The principal work, in which he has attempted to embody his general views of things, is the *Friend,* of which, though it contains some noble passages and fine trains of thought, prolixity and obscurity are the most frequent characteristics.

No two persons can be conceived more opposite in character or genius than the subject of the present and of the preceding sketch. Mr. Godwin, with less natural capacity and with fewer acquired advantages, by concentrating his mind on some given object, and doing what he had to do with all his might, has accomplished much, and will leave more than one monument of a powerful intellect behind him; Mr. Coleridge, by dissipating his, and dallying with every subject by turns, has done little or nothing to justify to the world or to posterity the high opinion which all who have ever heard him converse, or known him intimately, with one accord entertain of him. Mr. Godwin's faculties have kept at home, and plied their task in the workshop of the brain, diligently and effectually: Mr. Coleridge's have gossiped away their time, and gadded about from house to house, as if life's business were to melt the hours in listless talk. Mr. Godwin is intent on a subject, only as it concerns himself and his reputation; he works it out as a matter of duty, and discards from his mind whatever does not forward his main object as impertinent and vain.

Mr. Coleridge, on the other hand, delights in nothing but episodes and digressions, neglects whatever he undertakes to perform, and can act only on spontaneous impulses without object or method. 'He cannot be constrained by mastery.' While he should be occupied with a given pursuit, he is thinking of a thousand other things: a thousand tastes, a thousand objects tempt him, and distract his mind, which keeps open house, and entertains all comers; and after being fatigued and amused with morning calls from idle visitors he finds the day consumed and its business unconcluded. Mr. Godwin, on the contrary, is somewhat exclusive and unsocial in his habits of mind, entertains no company but what he gives his whole time and attention to, and wisely writes over the doors of his understanding, his fancy, and his senses—'No admittance except on business.' He has none of that fastidious refinement and false delicacy, which might lead him to balance between the endless variety of modern attainments. He does not throw away his life (nor a single half hour of it) in adjusting the claims of different accomplishments, and in choosing between them or making himself master of them all. He sets about his task (whatever it may be), and goes through it with spirit and fortitude. He has the happiness to think an author the greatest character in the world, and himself the greatest author in it.

Mr. Coleridge, in writing an harmonious stanza, would stop to consider whether there was not more grace and beauty in a *Pas de trois,* and would not proceed till he had resolved this question by a chain of metaphysical reasoning without end. Not so Mr. Godwin. That is best to him, which he can do best. He does not waste himself in vain aspirations and effeminate sympathies. He is blind, deaf, insensible to all but the trump of Fame. Plays, operas, painting, music, ball-rooms, wealth, fashion, titles, lords, ladies, touch him not. All these are no more to him than to the magician in his cell, and he writes on to the end of the chapter through good report and evil report. *Pingo in eternitatem* is his motto. He neither envies nor admires what others are, but is contented to be what he is, and strives to do the utmost he can. Mr. Coleridge has flirted with the Muses as with a set of mistresses: Mr. Godwin has been married twice, to Reason and to Fancy, and has to boast no short-lived progeny by each.

So to speak, he has valves belonging to his mind, to regulate the quantity of gas admitted into it, so that like the bare, unsightly, but well-compacted steam-vessel, it cuts its liquid way, and arrives at its promised end: while Mr. Coleridge's bark, 'taught with the little nautilus to sail,' the sport of every breath, dancing to every wave,

Youth at its prow, and Pleasure at its helm,

flutters its gaudy pennons in the air, glitters in the sun, but we wait in vain to hear of its arrival in the destined harbour. Mr. Godwin, with less variety and vividness, with less subtlety and susceptibility both of thought and feeling, has had firmer nerves, a more determined purpose, a more comprehensive grasp of his subject; and the results are as we find them. Each has met with his reward: for justice has, after all, been done to the pretensions of each; and we must, in all cases, use means to ends!

It was a misfortune to any man of talent to be born in the latter end of the last century. Genius stopped the way of Legitimacy, and therefore it was to be abated, crushed, or set aside as a nuisance. The spirit of the monarchy was at variance with the spirit of the age. The flame of liberty, the light of intellect, was to be extinguished with the sword—or with slander, whose edge is sharper than the sword. The war between power and reason was carried on by the first of these abroad, by the last at home. No quarter was given (then or now) by the Government-critics, the authorized censors of the press, to those who followed the dictates of independence, who listened to the voice of the tempter Fancy. Instead of gathering fruits and flowers, immortal fruits and amaranthine flowers, they soon found themselves beset not only by a host of prejudices, but assailed with all the engines of power: by nicknames, by lies, by all the arts of malice, interest and hypocrisy, without the possibility of their defending themselves 'from the pelting of the pitiless storm,' that poured down upon them from the strongholds of corruption and authority.

The philosophers, the dry abstract reasoners, submitted to this reverse pretty well, and armed themselves with patience 'as with triple steel,' to bear discomfiture, persecution, and disgrace. But the poets, the creatures of sympathy, could not stand the frowns both of king and people. They did not like to be shut out when places and pensions, when the critic's praises, and the laurel wreath were about to be distributed. They did not stomach being sent to Coventry, and Mr. Coleridge sounded a retreat for them by the help of casuistry and a musical voice.—'His words were hollow, but they pleased the ear' of his friends of the Lake School, who turned back disgusted and panic-struck from the dry desert of unpopularity, like Hassan the camel-driver,

> And curs'd the hour, and curs'd the luckless day,
> When first from Shiraz' walls they bent their way.

They are safely inclosed there. But Mr. Coleridge did not enter with them; pitching his tent upon the barren waste without, and having no abiding place nor city of refuge!

Notes

1. Mr. Coleridge named his eldest son (the writer of some beautiful Sonnets) after Hartley, and the second after Berkeley. The third was called Derwent, after the river of that name. Nothing can be more characteristic of his mind than this circumstance. All his ideas indeed are like a river, flowing on for ever, and still murmuring as it flows, discharging its waters and still replenished—

And so by many winding nooks it strays,
With willing sport to the wild ocean!

—William Hazlitt, "Mr. Coleridge,"
The Spirit of the Age, 1825

CHARLES KNIGHT (1849)

Charles Knight praises Coleridge for his invaluable contribution to Shakespearean criticism, for having written his opinions in brief snippets rather than in the form of cumbersome and unwieldy essays. Knight also credits Coleridge for the same mode of writing for which other critics have faulted him, maintaining that the fragmentary nature of the critical writings enabled Shakespeare to be introduced to and understood by the popular mind.

What that great man did for Shakspere during the remainder of his valuable life can scarcely be appreciated by the public. For his opinions were not given to the world in formal treatises and ponderous volumes. They were fragmentary; they were scattered, as it were, at random; many of them were the oral lessons of that wisdom and knowledge which he poured out to a few admiring disciples. But they have had their effect. For ourselves, personally, we owe a debt of gratitude to that illustrious man that can never be repaid. If in any degree we have been enabled to present Shakspere to the popular mind under new aspects, looking at him from a central point, which should permit us, however imperfectly, to comprehend something of his wondrous SYSTEM, we owe the desire so to understand him ourselves to the germs of thought which are scattered through the works of that philosopher; to whom the homage of future times will abundantly compensate for the partial neglect of his contemporaries. We desire to conclude this outline of the opinions of others upon the works of Shakspere, in connection with the imperfect expression of our own sense of those opinions, with the name of COLERIDGE.

—Charles Knight, *Studies of Shakspere*,
1849, p. 560

GEORGE GILFILLAN
"JEFFREY AND COLERIDGE" (1854)

Assessing Coleridge's critical writings only, George Gilfillan (1813–78), sees them as appearing at a time when criticism had sunk to a low level with Hayley, a moralistic poet best remembered for his association with the visual arts, and Hugh Blair, a Scottish author and rhetorician who was considered the reigning critic. In comparison, Gilfillan finds Coleridge a brilliant and passionate orator with a new message to deliver.

It is not our purpose to enter on the *mare magnum* of the Coleridgean question as a whole; but to speak simply and shortly of him in his critical function and faculty. That partook of the vast enlargement and varied culture of his mind. He arose at a time when criticism had fallen as low as poetry. Hayley was then the leading poet, and Blair the ruling critic! The *Edinburgh Review* had not risen, when a dark-haired man, "more fat than bard beseems," with ivory forehead, misty eye, boundless appetite for Welsh mutton, turnips, and flip, "talking like an angel, and doing nothing at all," commenced to talk and lecture on poetry all along the Bristol Channel—in Shropshire and in

Shrewsbury, in Manchester and in Birmingham; and so new and striking were his views, and so eloquent his language, and so native his enthusiasm, that all men's hearts burned.

—George Gilfillan, "Jeffrey and Coleridge,"
A Third Gallery of Portraits, 1854, pp. 223–226

WALTER PATER "COLERIDGE" (1865)

Walter Pater argues that Coleridge's involvement with transcendental philosophy via the Germany philosophers, most particularly Schelling, was fortuitous for the time in which he lived. This interest exerted its most profound influence in the aesthetic realm, in both Coleridge's imaginative works and his artistic criticism. Pater further asserts that transcendental philosophy enabled Coleridge to apply a system of rules to account for individual genius as well as the simplest of artistic ideas, such as being able to explain creativity. Philosophy enabled Coleridge to bring artistic genius down to earth by revealing its connection to simpler processes of the mind. Coleridge's application of a philosophical system, which Pater refers to as Schelling's "Philosophy of Nature," is traced back to an ancient Greek tradition in which nature was conceived as a reflection of human intelligence. That tradition was built on two different paradigms: nature as evidence of divine plan or nature as an energetic manifestation of human intelligence.

Regrettably for Pater, science replaced the aesthetic consciousness. Still, there were those who never completely gave up the Greek model, "the suspicion of a mind latent in nature, struggling for release, and intercourse with the intellect of man through true ideas, has never ceased to haunt a certain class of minds." For Pater, this suspicion is aligned with a "poetic inwardness," and Coleridge, as a critic, serves as a type of organic medium through which this classical notion was brought back to life. Pater adds a new perspective in which he viewed science as an evolutionary discipline in which ideas that are inherent to nature need to be discovered by such minds as Newton or Cuvier who are in sympathy with the natural world, and whose ideas in turn led to creative genius. "At last, in imaginative genius, ideas become effective: the intelligence of nature, all its discursive elements now connected and justified, is clearly reflected; the interpretation of its latent purposes being embodied in the great central products of creative art." Coleridge thus presented recent German metaphysics as a return to an expansion of the classical paradigm, urging readers to see the soul that resides within the tangible work of art just as it has always existed in nature. Ironically, as Pater points out, this same critical mission provided a unifying and motivating force for Coleridge whose life was otherwise in disarray. Furthermore, this critical agenda underscores two other important talents in that it revealed Coleridge as both a philologist, as he appreciated the ways in which individual words had their own histories of meaning, and as a psychologist, in that he was a keen and sympathetic observer of human nature. Pater further points out that characteristics of Coleridge's unique personality, a combination of emotional turmoil and an inherent dreamy languor, led to the production of some highly original visionary poetry.

With respect to Coleridge's poetry, Pater places the greatest emphasis on his Nether Stowey years (1797–98), when all the principal works on which his poetic fame rests were written. Unlike other poets whose powers evolve over time, Pater maintains that Coleridge's powers both blossomed and became extinct during this brief interval. To this period belongs both *The Rime of the Ancient Mariner* and *Christabel*, although the latter was not published until 1816; both of these Pater considers to be Coleridge's crowning achievements. Though both are aligned with the ballad, they are marked by a daring originality in that their supernaturalism is informed by his arcane interests, "odd and out-of-the-way reading in the old-fashioned literature of the marvellous." Though he considers *Christabel* to be a beautiful fragment reminiscent of old romantic ballads, Pater maintains that it nevertheless possesses a modern quality through its psychological insights, a "gift of handling the finer passages of human feeling, at once with power and delicacy." *The Rime of the Ancient Mariner*, on the other hand, is a thoroughly complete and consummate work of art that exhibits Coleridge's artistic mastery in blending the fantastic with the real to create an uncanny sense of the plausible.

In sum, Walter Pater pays tribute to a brilliant and sensitive genius who returned a spirituality to the understanding of human life and its relationship to nature, one who rescued aesthetic consiousness from the deleterious effects of scientific inquiry, rooted in experience and compartmentalized in focus, and taught people once again to dwell on the totality of all living things in both their physical and spiritual dimensions. "The relative spirit," Pater asserts, "by its constant dwelling on the more fugitive conditions or circumstances of things, breaking through a thousand rough and brutal classifications, and giving elasticity to inflexible principles, begets an intellectual *finesse* of which the ethical result is a delicate and tender justice in the criticism of human life."

Coleridge's intellectual sorrows were many; but he had one singular intellectual happiness. With an inborn taste for transcendental philosophy, he lived just at the time when that philosophy took an immense spring in Germany, and connected itself with an impressive literary movement. He had the good luck to light upon it in its freshness, and introduce it to his countrymen. What an opportunity for one reared on the colourless analytic English philosophies of the last century, but who feels an irresistible attraction towards bold metaphysical synthesis! How rare are such occasions of intellectual contentment! This transcendental philosophy, chiefly as systematised by the mystic Schelling, Coleridge applied with an eager, unwearied subtlety, to the questions of theology, and poetic or artistic criticism. It is in his theory of poetry, of art, that he comes nearest to principles of permanent truth and importance: that is the least fugitive part of his prose work. What, then, is the essence of his philosophy of art—of imaginative production?

Generally, it may be described as an attempt to reclaim the world of art as a world of fixed laws, to show that the creative activity of genius and the simplest act of thought are but higher and lower products of the laws of a universal logic. Criticism, feeling its own inadequacy in dealing with the greater works of art, is sometimes tempted to make too much of those dark and capricious suggestions of genius, which even the intellect possessed by them is unable to explain or recall. It has seemed due to the half-sacred character of those works to ignore all analogy between the productive process by which they had their birth, and the simpler processes of mind. Coleridge, on the other hand, assumes that the highest phases of thought must be more, not less, than the lower, subject to law.

With this interest, in the *Biographic Literaria*, he refines Schelling's "Philosophy of Nature" into a theory of art. "There can be no plagiarism in philosophy," says Heine:—*Es giebt kein Plagiat in der Philosophie*, in reference to the charge brought against Schelling of unacknowledged borrowing from Bruno; and certainly that which is common to Coleridge and Schelling and Bruno alike is of far earlier origin than any of them. Schellingism, the "Philosophy of Nature," is indeed a constant tradition in the history of thought: it embodies a permanent type of the speculative temper. That mode of conceiving nature as a mirror or reflex of the intelligence of man may be traced up to the first beginnings of Greek speculation. There are two ways of envisaging those aspects of nature which seem to bear the impress of reason or intelligence. There is the deist's way, which regards them merely as marks of design, which separates the informing mind from its result in nature, as the mechanist from the machine; and there is the pantheistic way, which identifies the two, which regards nature itself as the living energy of an intelligence of the same kind as though vaster in scope than the human. Partly through the influence of mythology, the Greek mind became early possessed with the conception of nature as living, thinking, almost speaking to the mind of man. This unfixed poetical prepossession, reduced to an abstract form, petrified into an idea, is the force which gives unity of aim to Greek philosophy. Little by little, it works out the substance of the Hegelian formula: "Whatever is, is according to reason: whatever is according to reason, that is." Experience, which has gradually saddened the earth's colours for us, stiffened its motions, withdrawn from it some blithe and debonair presence, has quite changed the character of the science of nature, as we understand it. The "positive" method, in truth, makes very little account of marks of intelligence in nature: in its wider view of phenonema, it sees that those instances are a minority, and may rank as happy coincidences: it absorbs them in the larger conception of universal mechanical law. But the suspicion of a mind latent in nature, struggling for release, and intercourse with the intellect of man through true ideas, has never ceased to haunt a certain class of minds. Started again and again in successive periods by enthusiasts on the antique pattern, in each case the thought may have seemed paler and more fantastic amid the growing consistency and sharpness of outline of other and more positive forms of knowledge. Still, wherever the speculative instinct has been united with a certain poetic inwardness of temperament, as in Bruno, in Schelling, there that old Greek conception, like some seed floating in the air, has taken root and sprung up anew. Coleridge, thrust inward upon himself, driven from "life in thought and sensation" to life in thought only, feels already, in his dark London school, a thread of the Greek mind on this matter vibrating strongly in him. At fifteen he is discoursing on Plotinus, as in later years he reflects from Schelling that flitting intellectual tradition. He supposes a subtle, sympathetic co-ordination between the ideas of the human reason and the laws of the natural world. Science, the real knowledge of that natural world, is to be attained, not by observation, experiment, analysis, patient generalisation, but by the evolution or recovery of those ideas directly from within, by a sort of Platonic "recollection"; every group of observed facts remaining an enigma until the appropriate idea is struck upon them from the mind of a Newton, or a Cuvier, the genius in whom sympathy with the universal reason becomes entire. In the next place, he conceives that this reason or intelligence in nature becomes reflective, or self-conscious. He fancies he can trace, through all the simpler forms of life, fragments of an eloquent prophecy about the human mind. The whole of nature he regards as a development of higher forms out of the lower, through shade after shade of systematic change. The dim stir of chemical atoms towards the axis of crystal form, the trance-like life of plants, the animal troubled by strange irritabilities, are stages which anticipate consciousness. All through the ever-increasing movement of life that was shaping itself; every successive phase of life, in its unsatisfied susceptibilities, seeming to be drawn out of its own limits by the more pronounced current of life on its confines, the "shadow of approaching humanity" gradually deepening, the latent intelligence winning a way to the surface. And at this point the law of development does not lose itself in caprice: rather it becomes more constraining and incisive. From the lowest to the very highest acts of the conscious intelligence, there is another series of refining shades. Gradually the mind concentrates itself, frees itself from the limitations of the particular, the individual, attains a strange power of modifying and centralising what it receives from without, according to the pattern of an inward ideal. At last, in imaginative genius, ideas become effective: the intelligence of nature, all its discursive elements now connected and justified, is clearly reflected; the interpretation of its latent purposes being embodied in the great central products of creative art. The secret of creative genius would be an exquisitely purged sympathy with nature, with the reasonable soul antecedent there. Those associative conceptions of the imagination, those eternally fixed types of action and passion, would come, not so much from the conscious invention of the artist, as from his self-surrender to the suggestions of an abstract reason or ideality in things: they would be evolved by the stir of nature itself, realising the highest reach of its dormant reason: they would have a kind of prevenient necessity to rise at some time to the surface of the human mind. . . .

Coleridge's prose writings on philosophy, politics, religion, and criticism, were, in truth, but one element in a whole lifetime of endeavours to present the then recent metaphysics of Germany to English readers, as a legitimate expansion of the older, classical and native masters of what has been variously called the a priori, or absolute, or spiritual, or Platonic, view of things. His criticism, his challenge for recognition in the concrete, visible, finite work of art, of the dim, unseen, comparatively infinite, soul or power of the artist, may well be remembered as part of the long pleading of German culture for the things "behind the veil." To introduce that spiritual philosophy, as represented by the more transcendental parts of Kant, and by Schelling, into all subjects, as a system of reason in them, one and ever identical with itself, however various the matter through which it was diffused, became with him the motive of an unflagging enthusiasm, which seems to have been the one thread of continuity in a life otherwise singularly wanting in unity of purpose, and in which he was certainly far from uniformly at his best. Fragmentary and obscure, but often eloquent, and always at once earnest and ingenious, those writings, supplementing his remarkable gift of conversation, were directly and indirectly influential, even on some the furthest removed from Coleridge's own masters; on John Stuart Mill, for instance, and some of the earlier writers of the "high-church" school. Like his verse, they display him also in two other characters—as a student of words, and as a psychologist, that is, as a more minute observer or student than other men of the phenomena of mind. To note the recondite associations of words, old or new; to expound the logic, the reasonable soul, of their various uses; to recover the interest of older writers who had had a phraseology of their own—this was a vein of inquiry allied to his undoubted gift of tracking out and analysing curious modes of thought. A quaint fragment of verse on "Human Life" might serve to illustrate his study of the earlier English philosophical poetry. The latter gift, that power of the "subtle-souled psychologist," as Shelley calls him, seems to have been connected with some tendency to disease in the physical temperament, something of a morbid want of balance in those parts where the physical and intellectual elements mix most closely together, with a kind of languid visionariness, deep-seated in the very constitution of the "narcotist," who had quite a gift for "plucking the poisons of self-harm," and which the actual habit of taking opium, accidentally acquired, did but reinforce. This morbid languor of nature, connected both with his fitfulness of purpose and his rich delicate dreaminess, qualifies Coleridge's poetic composition even more than his prose; his verse, with the exception of his avowedly political poems, being, unlike that of the "Lake School," to which in some respects he belongs, singularly unaffected by any moral, or professional, or personal effort or ambition,—"written," as he says, "after the more violent emotions of sorrow, to give him pleasure, when perhaps nothing else could;" but coming thus, indeed, very close to his own most intimately personal characteristics, and having a certain languidly soothing grace or cadence, for its most fixed quality, from first to last. After some Platonic soliloquy on a flower opening on a fine day in February, he goes on—

> Dim similitudes
> Weaving in mortal strains, I've stolen one hour
> From anxious self, life's cruel taskmaster!
> And the warm wooings of this sunny day
> Tremble along my frame and harmonise
> The attempered organ, that even saddest thoughts
> Mix with some sweet sensations, like harsh tunes
> Played deftly on a sweet-toned instrument.

The expression of two opposed, yet allied, elements of sensibility in these lines, is very true to Coleridge:—the grievous agitation, the grievous listlessness, almost never entirely relieved, together with a certain physical voluptuousness. He has spoken several times of the scent of the bean-field in the air:—the tropical touches in a chilly climate; his is a nature that will make the most of these, which finds a sort of caress in such things. *Kubla Khan*, the fragment of a poem actually composed in some certainly not quite healthy sleep, is perhaps chiefly of interest as showing, by the mode of its composition, how physical, how much of a diseased or valetudinarian temperament, in its moments of relief, Coleridge's happiest gift really was; and side by side with *Kubla Khan* should be read, as Coleridge placed it, the "Pains of Sleep," to illustrate that retarding physical burden in his temperament, that "unimpassioned grief," the source of which lay so near the source of those pleasures. Connected also with this, and again in contrast with Wordsworth, is the limited quantity of his poetical performance, as he himself regrets so eloquently in the lines addressed to Wordsworth after his recitation of *The Prelude*. It is like some exotic plant, just managing to blossom a little in the somewhat un-english air of Coleridge's own south-western birthplace, but never quite well there.

In 1798 he joined Wordsworth in the composition of a volume of poems—the *Lyrical Ballads*. What Wordsworth then wrote already vibrates with that blithe impulse which carried him to final happiness and self-possession. In Coleridge we feel already that faintness and obscure dejection which clung like some contagious damp to all his work. Wordsworth was to be distinguished by a joyful and penetrative conviction of the existence of certain latent affinities between nature and the human mind, which reciprocally gild the mind and nature with a kind of "heavenly alchemy."

> My voice proclaims
> How exquisitely the individual mind
> (And the progressive powers, perhaps, no less
> Of the whole species) to the external world
> Is fitted; and how exquisitely, too,
> The external world is fitted to the mind;
> And the creation, by no lower name
> Can it be called, which they with blended might
> Accomplish.

In Wordsworth this took the form of an unbroken dreaming over the aspects and transitions of nature—a reflective, though altogether unformulated, analysis of them.

There are in Coleridge's poems expressions of this conviction as deep as Wordsworth's. But Coleridge could never have abandoned himself to the dream, the vision, as Wordsworth did, because the first condition of such abandonment must be an unvexed quietness of heart. No one can read the "Lines composed above Tintern" without feeling how potent the physical element was among the conditions of Wordsworth's genius—"felt in the blood and felt along the heart."

My whole life I have lived in quiet thought!

The stimulus which most artists require of nature he can renounce. He leaves the ready-made glory of the Swiss mountains that he may reflect glory on a mouldering leaf. He loves best to watch the floating thistledown, because of its hint at an unseen life in the air. Coleridge's temperament, ... with its faintness, its grieved dejection, could never have been like that.

My genial spirits fail;
And what can these avail
To lift the smothering weight from off my breast?
It were a vain endeavour,
Though I should gaze for ever
On that green light that lingers in the west:
I may not hope from outward forms to win
The passion and the life whose fountains are within.

Wordsworth's flawless temperament, his fine mountain atmosphere of mind, that calm, sabbatic, mystic, wellbeing which De Quincey, a little cynically, connected with worldly (that is to say, pecuniary) good fortune, kept his conviction of a latent intelligence in nature within the limits of sentiment or instinct, and confined it to those delicate and subdued shades of expression which alone perfect art allows. In Coleridge's sadder, more purely intellectual, cast of genius, what with Wordsworth was sentiment or instinct became a philosophical idea, or philosophical formula, developed, as much as possible, after the abstract and metaphysical fashion of the transcendental schools of Germany.

The period of Coleridge's residence at Nether Stowey, 1797–1798, was for him the annus mirabilis. Nearly all the chief works by which his poetic fame will live were then composed or planned. What shapes itself for criticism as the main phenomenon of Coleridge's poetic life, is not, as with most true poets, the gradual development of a poetic gift, determined, enriched, retarded, by the actual circumstances of the poet's life, but the sudden blossoming, through one short season, of such a gift already perfect in its kind, which thereafter deteriorates as suddenly, with something like premature old age. Connecting this phenomenon with the leading motive of his prose writings, we might note it as the deterioration of a productive or creative power into one merely metaphysical or discursive. In his unambitious conception of his function as a poet, and in the very limited quantity of his poetical performance, as I have said, he was a contrast to his friend Wordsworth. That friendship with Wordsworth, the chief "developing" circumstance of his poetic life, comprehended a very close intellectual sympathy; and in such association chiefly, lies whatever truth there may be in the popular classification of Coleridge as a member of what is called the "Lake School." Coleridge's philosophical speculations do really turn on the ideas which underlay Wordsworth's poetical practice. His prose works are one long explanation of all that is involved in that famous distinction between the Fancy and the Imagination. Of what is understood by both writers as the imaginative quality in the use of poetic figures, we may take some words of Shakespeare as an example.—

> My cousin Suffolk,
> My soul shall thine keep company to heaven:
> Tarry, sweet soul, for mine, then fly abreast.

The complete infusion here of the figure into the thought, so vividly realised, that, though birds are not actually mentioned, yet the sense of their flight, conveyed to us by the single word "abreast," comes to be more than half of the thought itself:—this, as the expression of exalted feeling, is an instance of what Coleridge meant by Imagination. And this sort of identification of the poet's thought, of himself, with the image or figure which serves him, is the secret, sometimes, of a singularly entire realisation of that image, such as makes these lines of Coleridge, for instance, "imaginative"—

> Amid the howl of more than wintry storms,
> The Halcyon hears the voice of vernal hours
> Already on the wing.

There are many such figures both in Coleridge's verse and prose. He has, too, his passages of that sort of impassioned contemplation on the permanent and elementary conditions of nature and humanity, which Wordsworth held to be the essence of a poet; as it would be his proper function to awaken such contemplation in other men—those "moments," as Coleridge says, addressing him—

Moments awful,
Now in thy inner life, and now abroad,
When power streamed from thee, and thy soul received
the light reflected, as a light bestowed.

The entire poem from which these lines are taken, "composed on the night after Wordsworth's recitation of a poem on the growth of an individual mind," is, in its high-pitched strain of meditation, and in the combined justice and elevation of its philosophical expression—

high and passionate thoughts
To their own music chaunted;

wholly sympathetic with *The Prelude* which it celebrates, and of which the subject is, in effect, the generation of the spirit of the "Lake poetry." The "Lines to Joseph Cottle" have the same philosophically imaginative character; the "Ode to Dejection" being Coleridge's most sustained effort of this kind. . . .

Christabel, though not printed till 1816, was written mainly in the year 1797: *The Rhyme of the Ancient Mariner* was printed as a contribution to the *Lyrical Ballads* in 1798; and these two poems belong to the great year of Coleridge's poetic production, his twenty-fifth year. In poetic quality, above all in that most poetic of all qualities, a keen sense of, and delight in beauty, the infection of which lays hold upon the reader, they are quite out of proportion to all his other compositions. The form in both is that of the ballad, with some of its terminology, and some also of its quaint conceits. They connect themselves with that revival of ballad literature, of which Percy's *Reliques*, and, in another way, Macpherson's Ossian are monuments, and which afterwards so powerfully affected Scott—

Young-eyed poesy
All deftly masked as hoar antiquity.

The Ancient Mariner, as also, in its measure, *Christabel,* is a "romantic" poem, impressing us by bold invention, and appealing to that taste for the supernatural, that longing for *le frisson,* a shudder, to which the "romantic" school in Germany, and its derivations in England and France, directly ministered. In Coleridge, personally, this taste had been encouraged by his odd and out-of-the-way reading in the old-fashioned literature of the marvellous—books like Purchas's *Pilgrims,* early voyages like Hakluyt's, old naturalists and visionary moralists, like Thomas Burnet, from whom he quotes the motto of *The Ancient Mariner,* "*Facile credo, plures esse naturas invisibiles quam visibiles in rerum universitate, etc."* Fancies of the strange things which may very well happen, even in broad daylight, to men shut up alone in ships far off on the sea, seem to have occurred to the human mind in all ages with a peculiar readiness, and often have about them, from the story of the stealing of Dionysus downwards, the fascination of a certain dreamy grace, which distinguishes them from other kinds of marvellous inventions. This sort of fascination *The Ancient Mariner* brings to its highest degree: it is the delicacy, the dreamy grace, in his presentation of the marvellous, which makes Coleridge's work so remarkable. The too palpable intruders from a spiritual world in almost all ghost literature, in Scott and Shakespeare even, have a kind of crudity or coarseness. Coleridge's power is in the very fineness with which, as by some really ghostly finger, he brings home to our inmost sense his inventions, daring as they are—the skeleton ship, the polar spirit, the inspiriting of the dead corpses of the ship's crew. *The Rhyme of the Ancient Mariner* has the plausibility, the perfect adaptation to reason and the general aspect of life, which belongs to the marvellous, when actually presented as part of a credible experience in our dreams. Doubtless, the mere experience of the opium-eater, the habit he must almost necessarily fall into of noting the more elusive phenomena of dreams, had something to do with that: in its essence, however, it is connected with a more purely intellectual circumstance in the development of Coleridge's poetic gift. Some one once asked William Blake, to whom Coleridge has many resemblances, when either is at his best (that whole episode of the re-inspiriting of the ship's crew in *The Ancient Mariner* being comparable to Blake's well-known design of the "Morning Stars singing together") whether he had ever seen a ghost, and was surprised when the famous seer, who ought, one might think, to have seen so many, answered frankly, "Only once!" His "spirits," at once more delicate, and so much more real, than any ghost—the burden, as they were the privilege, of his *temperament*—like it, were an integral element in his everyday life. And the difference of mood expressed in that question and its answer, is indicative of a change of temper in regard to the supernatural which has passed over the whole modern mind, and of which the true measure is the influence of the writings of Swedenborg. What that change is we may see if we compare the vision by which Swedenborg was "called," as he thought, to his work, with the ghost which called Hamlet, or the spells of Marlowe's *Faust* with those of Goethe's. The modern mind, so minutely self-scrutinising, if it is to be affected at all by a sense of the supernatural, needs to be more finely touched than was possible in the older, romantic presentment of it. The spectral object, so crude, so impossible, has become plausible, as

The blot upon the brain,
That *will* show itself without;

and is understood to be but a condition of one's own mind, for which, according to the scepticism, latent at least, in so much of our modern philosophy, the so-called real things themselves are but *spectra* after all.

It is this finer, more delicately marvellous supernaturalism, fruit of his more delicate psychology, that Coleridge infuses into romantic adventure, itself also then a new or revived thing in English literature; and with a fineness of weird effect in *The Ancient Mariner,* unknown in those older, more simple, romantic legends and ballads. It is a flower of medieval or later German romance, growing up in the peculiarly compounded atmosphere of modern psychological speculation, and putting forth in it wholly new qualities. The quaint prose commentary, which runs side by side with the verse of *The Ancient Mariner,* illustrates this—a composition of quite a different shade of beauty and merit from that of the verse which it accompanies, connecting this, the chief poem of Coleridge, with his philosophy, and emphasising therein that psychological interest of which I have spoken, its curious soul-lore.

Completeness, the perfectly rounded wholeness and unity of the impression it leaves on the mind of a reader who fairly gives himself to it—that, too, is one of the characteristics of a really excellent work, in the poetic as in every other kind of art; and by this completeness, *The Ancient Mariner* certainly gains upon *Christabel*—a completeness, entire as that of Wordsworth's "Leech-Gatherer," or Keats's *Saint Agnes' Eve,* each typical in its way of such wholeness or entirety of effect on a careful reader. It is Coleridge's one great complete work, the one really finished thing, in a life of many beginnings. *Christabel* remained a fragment. In *The Ancient Mariner* this unity is secured in part by the skill with which the incidents of the marriage-feast are made to break in dreamily from time to time upon the main story. And then, how pleasantly, how reassuringly, the whole nightmare story itself is made to end, among the clear fresh sounds and lights of the bay, where it began, with

The moon-light steeped in silentness,
The steady weather-cock.

So different from *The Rhyme of the Ancient Mariner* in regard to this completeness of effect, *Christabel* illustrates the same complexion of motives, a like intellectual situation. Here, too, the work is of a kind peculiar to one who touches the characteristic motives of the old romantic ballad, with a spirit made subtle and fine by modern reflection; as we feel, I think, in such passages as—

But though my slumber had gone by,
This dream it would not pass away—
It seems to live upon mine eye;—

and—

For she, belike, hath drunken deep
Of all the blessedness of sleep;

and again—

With such perplexity of mind
As dreams too lively leave behind.

And that gift of handling the finer passages of human feeling, at once with power and delicacy, which was another result of his finer psychology, of his exquisitely refined habit of self-reflection, is illustrated by a passage on Friendship in the Second Part—

Alas! they had been friends in youth;
But whispering tongues can poison truth;
And constancy lives in realms above;
And life is thorny; and youth is vain;
And to be wroth with one we love,
Doth work like madness in the brain.
And thus it chanced, as I divine,
With Roland and Sir Leoline.
Each spake words of high disdain
And insult to his heart's best brother:
They parted—ne'er to meet again!
But never either found another
To free the hollow heart from paining—
They stood aloof the scars remaining,
Like cliffs which had been rent asunder;
A dreary sea now flows between;
But neither heat, nor frost, nor thunder,
Shall wholly do away, I ween,
The marks of that which once hath been.

I suppose these lines leave almost every reader with a quickened sense of the beauty and compass of human feeling; and it is the sense of such richness and beauty which, in spite of his "dejection," in spite of that burden of his morbid lassitude, accompanies Coleridge himself through life. A warm poetic joy in everything beautiful, whether it be a moral sentiment, like the friendship of Roland and Leoline, or only the flakes of falling light from the water-snakes—this joy, visiting him, now and again, after sickly dreams, in sleep or waking, as a relief not to be forgotten, and with such a power of felicitous expression that the infection of it passes irresistibly to the reader— such is the predominant element in the matter of his poetry, as cadence is the predominant quality of its form. "We bless thee for our creation!" he might have said, in his later period of definite religious assent, "because the world is so beautiful: the world of ideas—living spirits, detached from the divine nature itself, to inform and lift the heavy mass of material things; the world of man, above all in his melodious and intelligible speech; the world of living creatures and natural scenery; the world of dreams." What he really did say, by way of "A Tombless Epitaph," is true enough of himself—

> Sickness, 'tis true,
> Whole years of weary days, besieged him close,
> Even to the gates and inlets of his life!
> But it is true, no less, that strenuous, firm,
> And with a natural gladness, he maintained
> The citadel unconquered, and in joy
> Was strong to follow the delightful Muse.
> For not a hidden path, that to the shades
> Of the beloved Parnassian forest leads,
> Lurked undiscovered by him; not a rill
> There issues from the fount of Hippocrene,
> But he had traced it upward to its source,
> Through open glade, dark glen, and secret dell,
> Knew the gay wild flowers on its banks, and culled
> Its med'cinable herbs. Yea, oft alone,
> Piercing the long-neglected holy cave,
> The haunt obscure of old Philosophy,
> He bade with lifted torch its starry walls S
> parkle, as erst they sparkled to the flame
> Of odorous lamps tended by saint and sage.
> O framed for calmer times and nobler hearts!
> O studious Poet, eloquent for truth!
> Philosopher! contemning wealth and death,
> Yet docile, childlike, full of Life and Love.

The student of empirical science asks, Are absolute principles attainable? What are the limits of knowledge? The answer he receives from science itself is not ambiguous. What the moralist asks is, Shall we gain or lose by surrendering human life to the relative spirit? Experience answers that the dominant tendency of life is to turn ascertained truth into a dead letter, to make us all the phlegmatic servants of routine. The relative spirit, by its constant dwelling on the more fugitive conditions or circumstances of things, breaking through a thousand rough and brutal classifications, and giving elasticity to inflexible principles, begets an intellectual *finesse* of which the ethical result is a delicate and tender justice in the criticism of human life. Who would gain more than Coleridge by criticism in such a spirit? We know how his life has appeared when judged by absolute standards. We see him trying to "apprehend the absolute," to stereotype forms of faith and philosophy, to attain, as he says, "fixed principles" in politics, morals, and religion, to fix one mode of life as the essence of life, refusing to see the parts as parts only; and all the time his own pathetic history pleads for a more elastic moral philosophy than his, and cries out against every formula less living and flexible than life itself.

"From his childhood he hungered for eternity." There, after all, is the incontestable claim of Coleridge. The perfect flower of any elementary type of life must always be precious to humanity, and Coleridge is a true flower of the *ennuye,* of the type of Rene. More than Childe Harold, more than Werther, more than Rene himself, Coleridge, by what he did, what he was, and what he failed to do, represents that inexhaustible discontent, languor, and home-sickness, that endless regret, the chords of which ring all through our modern literature. It is to the romantic element in literature that those qualities belong. One day, perhaps, we may come to forget the distant horizon, with full knowledge of the situation, to be content with "what is here and now"; and herein is the essence of classical feeling. But by us of the present moment, certainly—by us for whom the Greek spirit, with its engaging naturalness, simple, chastened, debonair, . . . is itself the Sangrail of an endless pilgrimage, Coleridge, with his passion for the absolute, for something fixed where all is moving, his faintness, his broken memory, his intellectual disquiet, may still be ranked among the interpreters of one of the constituent elements of our life.

—Walter Pater, from "Coleridge,"
1865, *Appreciations,* 1889

Algernon Charles Swinburne
"Coleridge" (1869)

Swinburne's essay introduces Coleridge as a brilliant and receptive man who nevertheless was destined to live an eminently lonely life. While acknowledging Coleridge's greatest gift as having taught Swinburne how to think in a highly original way, he appraises Coleridge's life and work as fraught with complications. While the work Coleridge produced was in part superb, Swinburne does not hesitate in describing the many ways in which he was burdened by debilitating character flaws.

With respect to Coleridge's younger days, Swinburne remembers him as a gentle and sensitive boy, as reflected in his earliest verse, which was only to be followed by such failures as *Religious Musings*. For Swinburne, Coleridge's creative path was always a difficult one to navigate, filled with many obstacles and stumbling blocks, which accounted for unevenness in his juvenilia.

Among the personality traits that placed Coleridge at a disadvantage in his poetry, Swinburne points out Coleridge's lack of focus or clear purpose. In turning to *The Rime of the Ancient Mariner*, however, Swinburne holds this poem to be sui generis; though it bears resemblance to the ballad tradition, it is nevertheless far beyond any expectations of that genre. Swinburne responds to those critics who complained that the work lacked a clear moral or was overburdened by imaginative trappings, stating that it is a forceful poem of vibrant color that has taken on a life of its own, to the delight of many, both young and old. Nevertheless, Swinburne is especially enamored with *Christabel* and "Kubla Khan," paying tribute to the exquisite beauty to be found in these two poems, for he believes no one other than Coleridge could have written them. "There is a charm upon these poems which can only be felt in silent submission of wonder. Any separate line has its own heavenly beauty, but to cite separate lines is intolerable. They are to be received in a rapture of silence." Swinburne feels transported to the lush landscape of "Kubla Khan," a work he deems has achieved a seamlessness and a delicacy that belie its craftsmanship. *Christabel* is admired for its blending of terror and simple enchantment made all the more alluring by its incomparable lyricism. "The very terror and mystery of magical evil is imbued with this sweetness; the witch has no less of it than the maiden; their contact has in it nothing dissonant or disfiguring, nothing to jar or to deface the beauty and harmony of the whole imagination." Rather than viewing *Christabel* as a charming fragment, as many other critics had labeled it, Swinburne admires the poem as a fully integrated, organic entity in which image and meter work in complete tandem.

Swinburne contends that Shelley's poetry possesses the greater spiritual clarity, without the sensuous indulgences that cloud the moral meaning in Coleridge. Yet, Swinburne does not hold this as a fault, merely a fact. "This is neither blameable nor regrettable; none of these [Dante or Shelley, Milton or Hugo] could have done his work; nor could he have done it had he been in any way other or better than he was." Swinburne does not believe that

Coleridge had any aptitude for dramatic poetry, citing *Remorse* and *Zapolya* as containing only snippets of nobility or memorability. With respect to Coleridge's talent in writing odes, Swinburne declares the "Ode to France" the finest of his work in the genre, admiring its celebration of liberty, though, once again, less spirited in comparison with Shelley's fiery odes.

"Fears in Solitude" is branded as "hysterical" and spineless, a poem that pales in comparison to Wordsworth's more masculine and restrained sonnet on the same subject, though Swinburne thinks Coleridge the greater poet of the two. "This debility of mind and manner is set off in strong relief by the loveliness of landscape touches in the same poem." What Swinburne admires most is Wordsworth's strength and stability over Coleridge's effeminate mannerisms.

In sum, Swinburne presents a balanced view of Coleridge's life and work, admiring some of his finest poems but reminding us of the poet's lack of self-discipline, which caused him to lose sight of his subject and get tangled in abstruse arguments. "Out of that holy and pestilential jungle [of transcendental metaphysics] he emerged but too rarely into sunlight and clear air. It is not depth of thought which makes obscure to others the work of a thinker; real and offensive obscurity comes merely of inadequate thought embodied in inadequate language." Of Coleridge's poetic achievement, Swinburne has no doubt that Coleridge is one of the finest of his age and of all time.

The great man of whom I am about to speak seems to me a figure more utterly companionless, more incomparable with others, than any of his kind. Receptive at once and communicative of many influences, he has received from none and to none did he communicate any of those which mark him as a man memorable to all students of men. What he learnt and what he taught are not the precious things in him. He has founded no school of poetry, as Wordsworth has, or Byron, or Tennyson; happy in this, that he has escaped the plague of pupils and parodists. Has he founded a school of philosophy? He has helped men to think; he has touched their thought with passing colours of his own thought; but has he moved and moulded it into new and durable shapes? Others may judge better of this than I, but to me, set beside the deep direct work of those thinkers who have actual power to break down and build up thought, to construct faith or destroy it, his work seems not as theirs is. And yet how very few are even the great names we could not better afford to spare, would not gladlier miss from the roll of 'famous men and our fathers that were before us'. Of his best verses I venture to affirm that the world has nothing like them, and can never have: that they are of the highest kind, and of their own.

They are jewels of the diamond's price, flowers of the rose's rank, but unlike any rose or diamond known. In all times there have been gods that alighted and giants that appeared on earth; the ranks of great men are properly divisible, not into thinkers and workers, but into Titans and Olympians. Sometimes a supreme poet is both at once: such above all men is Aeschylus; so also Dante, Michel Angelo, Shakespeare, Milton, Goethe, Hugo, are gods at once and giants; they have the lightning as well as the light of the world, and in hell they have command as in heaven; they can see in the night as by day. As godlike as these, even as the divinest of them, a poet such as Coleridge needs not the thews and organs of any Titan to make him greater. Judged by the justice of other men, he is assailable and condemnable on several sides; his good work is the scantiest in quantity ever done by a man so famous in so long a life; and much of his work is bad. His genius is fluctuant and moonstruck as the sea is, and yet his mind is not, what he described Shakespeare's to be, 'an oceanic mind'. His plea against all accusers must be that of Shakespeare, a plea unanswerable:

> I am that I am; and they that level
> At my abuses reckon up their own.

'I am that I am'; it is the only solid and durable reply to any impertinence of praise or blame. We hear too much and too often of circumstances or accidents which extenuate this thing or qualify that; and such, no doubt, there always may be; but usually—at least it seems so to me—we get out of each man what he has in him to give. Probably at no other time, under no other conditions, would Coleridge for example have done better work or more. His flaws and failures are as much ingrained in him as his powers and achievements.

For from the very first the two sides of his mind are visible and palpable. Among all verses of boys who were to grow up great, I remember none so perfect, so sweet and deep in sense and sound, as those which he is said to have written at school, headed 'Time, Real and Imaginary'. And following hard on these come a score or two of 'poems' each more feeble and more flatulent than the last. Over these and the like I shall pass with all due speed, being undesirous to trouble myself or any possible reader with the question whether *Religions Musings* be more damnable than 'Lines to a Young Ass', or less damnable. Even when clear of these brambles, his genius walked for some time over much waste ground with irregular and unsure steps. Some poems, touched with exquisite grace, with clear and pure harmony, are tainted with somewhat of feeble and sickly which impairs our relish; 'Lewti' for instance, an early sample of his admirable melody, of tender colour and dim grace as of clouds, but effeminate in build, loose-hung, weak of eye and foot. Yet nothing of more precious and rare sweetness exists in verse than that stanza of the swans disturbed. His style indeed was a plant of strangely slow growth, but perfect and wonderful in its final flower. Even in the famous verses called 'Love' he has not attained to that strength and solidity of beauty which was his special gift at last. For melody rather than for harmony it is perfect; but in this oenomel there is as yet more of honey than of wine.

Coleridge was the reverse of Antaeus; the contact of earth took all strength out of him. He could not handle to much purpose any practical creed; his political verse is most often weak of foot and hoarse of accent. There is a graceful Asiatic legend cited by his friend Southey of 'the footless birds of Paradise' who have only wings to sustain them, and live their lives out in a perpetual flight through the clearest air of heaven. Ancient naturalists, Cardan and Aldrovandus, had much dispute and dissertation as to the real or possible existence of these birds, as to whether the female did in effect lay her eggs in a hollow of the male's back, designed by nature to that end; whether they could indeed live on falling dew; and so forth. These questions we may presume to be decided; but it is clear and certain enough that men have been found to live in much this fashion. Such a footless bird of Paradise was Coleridge; and had his wings always held out it had been well for him and us. Unhappily this winged and footless creature would perforce too often furl his wings in mid air and try his footing on earth, where his gait was like a swan's on shore.

Of his flight and his song when in the fit element, it is hard to speak at all, hopeless to speak adequately. It is natural that there should be nothing like them discoverable in any human work; natural that his poetry at its highest should be, as it is, beyond all praise and all words of men. He who can define it could 'unweave a rainbow'; he who could praise it aright would be such another as the poet. The *Christabel,* the *Kubla Khan,* with one or two more, are outside all law and jurisdiction of ours. When it has been said that such melodies were never heard, such dreams never dreamed, such speech never spoken, the chief thing remains unsaid, and unspeakable. There is a charm upon these poems which can only be felt in silent submission of wonder. Any separate line has its own heavenly beauty, but to cite separate lines is intolerable. They are to be received in a rapture of silence; such a silence as Chapman describes; silence like a god 'peaceful and young', which

Left so free mine ears,
That I might hear the music of the spheres,
And all the angels singing out of heaven.'

More amenable to our judgment, and susceptible of a more definite admiration, the *Ancient Mariner,* and the few other poems cast in something of a ballad type which we may rank around or below it, belong to another class. The chief of these is so well known that it needs no fresh comment. Only I will say that to some it may seem as though this great sea-piece might have had more in it of the air and savour of the sea. Perhaps it is none the worse; and indeed any one speaking of so great and famous a poem must feel and know that it cannot but be right, although he or another may think it would be better if this were retrenched or that appended. And this poem is beyond question one of the supreme triumphs of poetry. Witness the men who brought batteries to bear on it right and left. Literally: for one critic said that the 'moral sentiment' had impaired the imaginative excellence; another, that it failed and fell through for want of a moral foothold upon facts. Remembering these things, I am reluctant to proceed—but desirous to praise, as I best may. Though I doubt if it be worth while, seeing how the *Ancient Mariner*—praised or dispraised—lives and is like to live for the delight equally of young boys and old men; and seeing also that the last critic cited was no less a man than Hazlitt. It is fortunate—among many misfortunes—that for Coleridge no warning word was needed against the shriek of the press-gang from this side or that. He stooped once or twice to spurn them; but he knew that he stooped. His intense and overwrought abstraction from things of the day or hour did him no ill service here.

The *Ancient Mariner* has doubtless more of breadth and space, more of material force and motion, than anything else of the poet's. And the tenderness of sentiment which touches with significant colour the pure white imagination is here no longer morbid or languid, as in the earlier poems of feeling and emotion. It is soft and piteous enough, but womanly rather than effeminate; and thus serves indeed to set off the strange splendours and boundless beauties of the story. For the execution, I presume no human eye is too dull to see how perfect it is, and how high in kind of perfection. Here is not the speckless and elaborate finish which shows everywhere the fresh rasp of file or chisel on its smooth and spruce excellence; this is faultless after the fashion of a flower or a tree. Thus it has grown: not thus has it been carved.

Nevertheless, were we compelled to the choice, I for one would rather preserve *Kubla Khan* and *Christabel* than any other of Coleridge's poems. It is more conceivable that another man should be born capable of writing the *Ancient Mariner* than one capable of writing these. The former is perhaps the most wonderful of all poems. In reading it we seem rapt into that paradise revealed to Swedenborg, where music and colour and perfume were one, where you could hear the hues and see the harmonies of heaven. For absolute melody and splendour it were hardly rash to call it the first poem in the language. An exquisite instinct married to a subtle science of verse has made

it the supreme model of music in our language, a model unapproachable
except by Shelley. All the elements that compose the perfect form of English
metre, as limbs and veins and features a beautiful body of man, were more
familiar, more subject as it were, to this great poet than to any other. How, for
instance, no less than rhyme, assonance and alliteration are forces, requisite
components of high and ample harmony, witness once for all the divine
passage[2] which begins—

Five miles meandering with a mazy
motion, &c.

All these least details and delicacies of work are worth notice when the
result of them is so transcendent. Every line of the poem might be subjected
to the like scrutiny, but the student would be none the nearer to the master's
secret. The spirit, the odour in it, the cloven tongue of fire that rests upon its
forehead, is a thing neither explicable nor communicable.

Of all Coleridge's poems the loveliest is assuredly *Christabel*. It is not so
vast in scope and reach of imagination as the *Ancient Mariner*; it is not so
miraculous as *Kubla Khan*; but for simple charm of inner and outer sweetness
it is unequalled by either. The very terror and mystery of magical evil is
imbued with this sweetness; the witch has no less of it than the maiden;
their contact has in it nothing dissonant or disfiguring, nothing to jar or to
deface the beauty and harmony of the whole imagination. As for the melody,
here again it is incomparable with any other poet's. Shelley indeed comes
nearest; but for purity and volume of music Shelley is to Coleridge as a lark
to a nightingale; his song heaven-high and clear as heaven, but the other's
more rich and weighty, more passionately various, and warmer in effusion of
sound.[3] On the other hand, the nobler nature, the clearer spirit of Shelley, fills
his verse with a divine force of meaning, which Coleridge, who had it not in
him, could not affect to give. That sensuous fluctuation of soul, that floating
fervour of fancy, whence his poetry rose as from a shifting sea, in faultless
completion of form and charm, had absorbed—if indeed there were any to
absorb—all emotion of love or faith, all heroic beauty of moral passion, all
inner and outer life of the only kind possible to such other poets as Dante
or Shelley, Milton or Hugo. This is neither blameable nor regrettable; none
of these could have done his work; nor could he have done it had he been
in any way other or better than he was. Neither, for that matter, could we
have had a *Hamlet* or a *Faust* from any of these, the poets of moral faith and
passion, any more than a *Divina Commedia* from Shakespeare, a *Prometheus
Unbound* from Goethe. Let us give thanks for each after their kind to nature
and the fates.

Alike by his powers and his impotences, by his capacity and his defect, Coleridge was inapt for dramatic poetry. It were no discredit to have fallen short of Shelley on this side, to be overcome by him who has written the one great English play of modern times; but here the very comparison would seem a jest. There is little worth praise or worth memory in the *Remorse* except such casual fragments of noble verse as may readily be detached from the loose and friable stuff in which they lie imbedded. In the scene of the incantation, in the scene of the dungeon, there are two such pure and precious fragments of gold. In the part of Alhadra there are lofty and sonorous interludes of declamation and reflection. The characters are flat and shallow; the plot is at once languid, violent, and heavy. To touch the string of the spirit, thread the weft of evil and good, feel out the way of the soul through dark places of thought and rough places of action, was not given to this the sweetest dreamer of dreams. In *Zapolya* there are no such patches of imperial purple sewn on, but there is more of air and motion; little enough indeed of high dramatic quality, but a native grace and ease which give it something of the charm of life. In this lighter and more rapid work, the song of Glycine flashes out like a visible sunbeam; it is one of the brightest bits of music ever done into words.

The finest of Coleridge's odes is beyond all doubt the 'Ode to France'. Shelley declared it the finest of modern times, and justly, until himself and Keats had written up to it at least. It were profitless now to discuss whether it should take or yield precedence when weighed with the 'Ode to Liberty' or the 'Ode to Naples'. There is in it a noble and loyal love of freedom, though less fiery at once and less firm than Shelley's, as it proved in the end less durable and deep. The prelude is magnificent in music, and in sentiment and emotion far above any other of his poems; nor are the last notes inadequate to this majestic overture. Equal in force and sweetness of style, the 'Ode on Dejection' ranks next in my mind to this one; some may prefer its vaguer harmonies and sunset colours to the statelier movement, the more august and solemn passion of the earlier ode.

It is noticeable that only his supreme gift of lyrical power could sustain Coleridge on political ground. His attempts of the kind in blank verse are poor indeed:—

Untimely breathings, sick and short assays.

Compare the nerveless and hysterical verses headed 'Fears in Solitude' (exquisite as is the overture, faultless in tone and colour, and worthy of a better sequel) with the majestic and masculine sonnet of Wordsworth, written at the same time on the same subject: the lesser poet—for, great

as he is, I at least cannot hold Wordsworth, though so much the stronger
and more admirable man, equal to Coleridge as mere poet—speaks with a
calm force of thought and resolution; Coleridge wails, appeals, deprecates,
objurgates in a flaccid and querulous fashion without heart or spirit. This
debility of mind and manner is set off in strong relief by the loveliness of
landscape touches in the same poem. The eclogue of 'Fire, Famine, and
Slaughter', being lyrical, is worthier of a great name; it has force and motion
enough to keep it alive yet and fresh, impeded and trammelled though it
usually be by the somewhat vain and verbose eloquence of a needlessly
'Apologetic Preface'. Blank verse Coleridge could never handle with the
security of conscious skill and a trained strength; it grows in his hands
too facile and feeble to carry the due weight or accomplish the due work. I
have not found any of his poems in this metre retouched and reinvigorated
as a few have been among his others. One such alteration is memorable
to all students of his art; the excision from the *Ancient Mariner* of a
stanza (eleventh of the Third Part) which described the Death-mate of the
Spectre-Woman, his bones foul with leprous scurf and green corruption
of the grave, in contrast to the red lips and yellow locks of the fearfuller
Nightmare Life-in-Death. Keats in like manner cut off from the 'Ode on
Melancholy' a first stanza preserved for us by his biographer, who has duly
noted the delicate justice of instinct implied by this rejection of all ghastly
and violent images, however noble and impressive in their violence and
ghastliness, from a poem full only of the subtle sorrow born of beauty.
The same keen and tender sense of right made Coleridge reject from his
work the horrors while retaining the terrors of death. But of his studies
in blank verse he seems to have taken no such care. They remain mostly
in a hybrid or an embryonic state, with birthmarks on them of debility or
malformation. Two of these indeed have a charm of their own, not shallow
or transient: the 'Nightingale' and 'Frost at Midnight'. In colour they are
perfect, and not (as usual) too effusive and ebullient in style. Others,
especially some of the domestic or religious sort, are offensive and grievous
to the human sense on that score. Coleridge had doubtless a sincere belief
in his own sincerity of belief, a true feeling of his own truth of feeling;
but he leaves with us too often an unpleasant sense or taste—as it were
a tepid dilution of sentiment, a rancid unction of piety. A singular book
published in 1835 without author's name—the work, as I find, of a Mr.
Allsop, long after to be advertised for on public placards as an accomplice
in the enterprise which clouded the fiery fame and closed the heroic life of
Felice Orsini—gives further samples of this in *Letters, Conversations and
Recollections;* samples that we might well have spared.[4] A selection from

his notes and remains, from his correspondence and the records of his *Table-Talk*, even from such books as Cottle's and this anonymous disciple's, would be of real interest and value, if well edited, sifted and weeded of tares and chaff. The rare fragments of work done or speech spoken in his latter years are often fragments of gold beyond price. His plastic power and flexible charm of verse, though shown only in short flashes of song, lose nothing of the old freshness and life. To the end he was the same whose 'sovereign sway and masterdom' of music could make sweet and strong even the feeble and tuneless form of metre called hexameters in English; if form of metre that may be called which has neither metre nor form. But the majestic rush and roll of that irregular anapaestic measure used once or twice by this supreme master of them all, no student can follow without an exultation of enjoyment. The 'Hymn to the Earth' has a sonorous and oceanic strength of harmony, a grace and a glory of life, which fill the sense with a vigorous delight. Of such later work as the divine verses on 'Youth and Age', 'The Garden of Boccaccio', sun-bright and honey-sweet, 'Work without Hope' (what more could be left to hope for when the man could already do such work?)—of these, and of how many more! what can be said but that they are perfect, flawless, priceless? Nor did his most delicate and profound power of criticism ever fail him or fall off. To the perfection of that rare faculty there were but two things wanting: self-command and the natural cunning of words which has made many lesser men as strong as he was weak in the matter of verbal emendation. In that line of labour his hand was unsure and infirm. Want of self-command, again, left him often to the mercy of a caprice which swept him through tangled and tortuous ways of thought, through brakes and byways of fancy, where the solid subject in hand was either utterly lost and thrown over, or so transmuted and transfigured that any recognition of it was as hopeless as any profit. In an essay well worth translating out of jargon into some human language, he speaks of "the holy jungle of transcendental metaphysics." Out of that holy and pestilential jungle he emerged but too rarely into sunlight and clear air. It is not depth of thought which makes obscure to others the work of a thinker; real and offensive obscurity comes merely of inadequate thought embodied in inadequate language. What is clearly comprehended or conceived, what is duly thought and wrought out, must find for itself and seize upon the clearest and fullest expression. That grave and deep matter should be treated with the fluency and facility proper to light and slight things, no fool is foolish enough to desire: but we may at least demand that whatever of message a speaker may have for us be delivered without impediment of speech. A style that stammers and rambles and stumbles, that stagnates here, and there overflows into waste marsh relieved only by thick patches of powdery bulrush and such bright flowerage of barren blossom as is bred of the fogs and the fens—such a style gives no warrant of depth or soundness in the matter thus arrayed and set forth. What grains of truth or seeds of error were borne this way or that on the perpetual tide of talk concerning 'subject and object', 'reason and understanding', those who can or who care may at their leisure determine with the due precision. If to the man's critical and philosophic faculty there had been added a formative power as perfect as was added to his poetic faculty, the fruit might possibly have been wellnigh as precious after its kind. As it is, we must judge of his poetic faculty by what is accomplished; of the other we must judge, not by what is accomplished, but by what is suggested. And the value of this is sometimes great, though the value of that be generally small: so great indeed that we cannot weigh or measure its influence and its work.

Our study and our estimate of Coleridge cannot now be discoloured or misguided by the attraction or repulsion to which all contemporary students or judges of a great man's work cannot but be more or less liable. Few men, I suppose, ever inspired more of either feeling than he in his time did. To us his moral or social qualities, his opinion on this matter and his action in that, are nothing except in so far as they affect the work done, the inheritance bequeathed us. With all fit admiration and gratitude for the splendid fragments so bequeathed of a critical and philosophic sort, I doubt his being remembered, except by a small body of his elect, as other than a poet. His genius was so great, and in its greatness so many-sided, that for some studious disciples of the rarer kind he will doubtless, seen from any possible point of view, have always something about him of the old magnetism and magic. The ardour, delicacy, energy of his intellect, his resolute desire to get at the roots of things and deeper yet, if deeper might be, will always enchant and attract all spirits of like mould and temper. But as a poet his place is indisputable. It is high among the highest of all time. An age that should forget or neglect him might neglect or forget any poet that ever lived. At least, any poet whom it did remember such an age would remember as something other than a poet; it would prize and praise in him, not the absolute and distinctive quality, but something empirical or accidental. That may be said of this one which can hardly be said of any but the greatest among men; that come what may to the world in course of time, it will never see his place filled. Other and stronger men, with fuller control and concentration of genius, may do more service, may bear more fruit; but such as his was they will not have in them to give. The highest lyric work is either passionate or imaginative; of passion Coleridge's has nothing; but for height and perfection of imaginative quality he is the greatest of lyric poets. This was his special power, and this is his special praise.

Notes

1. Euthymioe Raptus; *The Tears of Peace* (1609).
2. Witness also the matchless fragments of metrical criticism in Coleridge's *Remains*, which prove with what care and relish the most sweet and perfect melodist among all our poets would set himself to examine and explain the alternations and sequences of sound in the noblest verse of others.
3. From this general rule I except of course the transcendent anti-phonal music which winds up the *Prometheus* of Shelley, and should perhaps except also the 'Ode to the West Wind', and the close of the 'Ode to Naples'. Against *Christabel* it would for example be fairer to set 'The Sensitive Plant' for comparison of harmonies.
4. It contains however among others one elaborate letter of some interest and significance, in which Coleridge, not without a tone of contempt, falls foul of the orthodox vulgarity of Wordsworth's theism ('what Hartley,' his son, I presume, 'calls the popping in of the old man with a beard') in a fashion showing how far apart his own theosophic mysticism, though never so daintily dressed up in cast church-clothes, had drifted from the more clear and rigid views of a harder and sounder mind.

—Algernon Charles Swinburne, "Coleridge,"
1869, *Essays and Studies*, 1875, pp. 259–275

JAMES RUSSELL LOWELL "COLERIDGE" (1885)

James Russell Lowell (1819–1891), an American romantic poet and critic, writes a sympathetic review of Coleridge, whose reputation he seeks to rescue from the wrongs to which it has been subjected. Lowell seeks to present, in a brief overview, a fitting memorial, basing his opinion on Coleridge's literary rather than his philosophical works. Lowell speaks of Coleridge's capacious imagination and bids readers to remember that many great minds found solid ground amid his fanciful images, "his cloud castles solid habitations." Lowell contends that Coleridge liberated the English mind from the oppression of common sense by demonstrating the humanity and freedom to be found in the imagination offered to those with a willingness to be open to it. The poet showed that a receptiveness to the imagination is a liberating process. Above any debt to German philosophical thought, Coleridge owed the most to his own imaginative powers.

Surely there are no friends so constant as the poets, and among them, I think, none more faithful than Coleridge. I am glad to have a share in this reparation of a long injustice, for as we looked about us hitherto in Poet's Corner we were tempted to ask, as Cavalcante dei Cavalcanti did of Dante, If these are here through loftiness of genius, where is he? It is just fifty-one years ago that I became the possessor of an American reprint of Galignani's edition of Coleridge, Shelley, and Keats in one volume. It was a pirated book, and I trust I may be pardoned for the delight I had in it. I take comfort from the thought that there must be many a Scottish minister and laird now in Heaven who liked their claret none the less that it had paid no tribute to the House of Hanover. I have heard this trinity of poets taxed with incongruity. As for me, I was grateful for such infinite riches in a little room, and never thought of looking a Pegasus in the mouth whose triple burden proved a stronger back than that even of the Templars' traditional steed. Much later, but still long ago, I read the *Friend,* the *Biographic Literaria,* and other prose works of Coleridge. In what may be given me to say I shall be obliged to trust chiefly to a memory which at my time of life is gradually becoming one of her own reminiscences, and is forced to compound as best she may with her inexorable creditor, Oblivion. But perhaps she will serve me all the better for the matter in hand, for what is proper here is at most a rapid generalization rather than a demonstration in detail of his claims to grateful remembrance. I shall naturally trust myself to judge him by his literary rather than by his metaphysical achievement. In the latter region I cannot help being reminded of the partiality he so often betrays for clouds, and see him, to use his own words, "making the shifting clouds seem what you please," or "a traveller go from mount to mount through cloudland, gorgeous land." Or sometimes I think of him as an alchemist in search of the philosopher's stone, and stripping the lead, not only from his own roof, but from that of the parish church itself, to quench the fiery thirst of his alembic. He seems never to have given up the hope of finding in the imagination some universal solvent, some *magisterium majus,* by which the lead of scepticism should be transmuted into the pure gold of faith, or, at least, persuaded to believe itself so. But we should not forget that many earnest and superior minds found his cloud castles solid habitations, nor that alchemy was the nursing mother of chemistry. He certainly was a main influence in showing the English mind how it could emancipate itself from the vulgarizing tyranny of common sense, and teaching it to recognize in the imagination an important factor not only in the happiness but in the destiny of man. In criticism he was, indeed, a teacher and interpreter whose service was incalculable. He owed much to Lessing, something to Schiller, and more to the younger Schlegel, but he owed most to his own sympathetic and penetrative imagination. This was the lifted torch (to borrow his own words again) that bade the starry walls of passages, dark before to the apprehension of even the most intelligent reader, sparkle with a lustre, latent in them to be sure, but not all their own. As Johnson said of Burke, he wound into his subject like a serpent. His analysis was elucidative mainly, if you will, but could not have been so except in virtue of the processes of constructive and philosophical criticism that had gone on so long in his mind as to make its subtle apprehension seem an instinct. As he was the first to observe some of the sky's appearances and some of the shyer revelations of outward nature, so he was also first in noting some of the more occult phenomena of thought and emotion. It is a criticism of parts and passages, and was scattered carelessly in *obiter dicta,* but it was not a bringing of the brick as a specimen of the whole house. It was comparative anatomy, far rather, which from a single bone reconstructs the entire living organism. Many of his hints and suggestions are more pregnant than whole treatises, as where he says that the wit of *Hudibras* is the wit of thought.

But what I think constitutes his great power, as it certainly is his greatest charm, is the perpetual presence of imagination, as constant a quality with him as fancy is with Calderon. She was his lifelong housemate, if not always hanging over his shoulders and whispering in his ear, yet within easy call, like the Abra of Prior—

Abra was with him ere he spoke her name,
And if he called another, Abra came.

It was she who gave him that power of sympathy which made his Wallenstein what I may call the most original translation in our language, unless some of the late Mr. Fitzgerald's be reckoned such. He was not exact any more than Chapman. The molten material of his mind, too abundant for the capacity of the mould, overflowed it in gushes of fiery excess. But the main object of translation he accomplishes. Poetry is reproduced as poetry, and genius shows itself as genius, patent even in the march of the verse. As a poet, the impression he made upon his greater contemporaries will, I believe, be the ultimate verdict of criticism. They all thought of him what Scott said of him, "No man has all the resources of poetry in such profusion. . . . His fancy and diction would long ago have placed him above all his contemporaries had they been under the direction of a sound judgment and a steady will."

No doubt we have in Coleridge the most striking example in literature of a great genius given in trust to a nerveless will and a fitful purpose. But I think the secret of his doing no more in poetry is to be found in the fact that the judgment, so far from being absent, grew to be there in excess. His critical sense rose like a forbidding apparition in the path of his poetic production. I have heard of a military engineer who knew so well how a bridge should be built that he could never build one. It certainly was not wholly indolence that was to blame in Coleridge's case, for though he used to say early in life that he had no "finger industry," yet he left behind him a mass of correspondence, and his letters are generally long. But I do not care to discuss a question the answer to which must be left mainly to conjecture or to the instinct of individual temperament. It is enough for us here that he has written some of the most poetical poetry in the language, and one poem, the *Ancient Mariner*, not only unparalleled, but unapproached in its kind, and that kind of the rarest. It is marvellous in its mastery over that delightfully fortuitious inconsequence that is the adamantine logic of dreamland. Coleridge has taken the old ballad measure and given to it by an indefinable charm wholly his own all the sweetness, all the melody and compass of a symphony. And how picturesque it is in the proper sense of the word. I know nothing like it. There is not a description in it. It is all picture. Descriptive poets generally confuse us with multiplicity of detail; we cannot see their forest for the trees; but Coleridge never errs in this way. With instinctive tact he touches the right chord of association, and is satisfied, as we also are. I should find it hard to explain the singular charm of his diction, there is so much nicety of art and purpose in it, whether for music or meaning. Nor does it need any explanation, for we all feel it. The words seem common words enough, but in the order of them, in the choice, variety, and position of the vowel-sounds they become magical. The most decrepit vocable in the language throws away its crutches to dance and sing at his piping. I cannot think it a personal peculiarity, but a matter of universal experience, that more bits of Coleridge have imbedded themselves in my memory than of any other poet who delighted my youth—unless I should except the sonnets of Shakespeare. This argues perfectness of expression. Let me cite an example or two:—

The sun's rim dips, the stars rush out,
  At one stride comes the dark;
With far-heard whisper through the dark
  Off shot the spectre barque.

Or take this as a bit of landscape:—

> Beneath yon birch with silver bark
> And boughs so pendulous and fair,
> The brook falls scattered down the rock,
> And all is mossy there.

It is a perfect little picture and seems so easily done. But try to do something like it. Coleridge's words have the unashamed nakedness of Scripture, of the Eden of diction ere the voluble serpent had entered it. This felicity of speech in Coleridge's best verse is the more remarkable because it was an acquisition. His earlier poems are apt to be turgid, in his prose there is too often a languor of profuseness, and there are pages where he seems to be talking to himself and not to us, as I have heard a guide do in the tortuous caverns of the Catacombs when he was doubtful if he had not lost his way. But when his genius runs freely and full in his prose, the style, as he said of Pascal, "is a garment of light." He knew all our best prose and knew the secret of its composition. When he is well inspired, as in his best poetry he commonly is, he gives us the very quintessence of perception, the clearly crystallized precipitation of all that is most precious in the ferment of impression after the impertinent and obtrusive particulars have evaporated from the memory. It is the pure visual ecstasy disengaged from the confused and confusing material that gave it birth. It seems the very beatitude of artless simplicity, and is the most finished product of art. I know nothing so perfect in its kind since Dante. The tiny landscape I have cited reminds me in its laconic adequacy of—

> Li ruscelletti che de' verdi colli
> Del Casentin discendon giuso in Arno,
> Faccendo i lor canali e freddi e molli.

I confess that I prefer the *Ancient Mariner* to *Christabel,* fine as that poem is in parts and tantalizing as it is in the suggestion of deeper meanings than were ever there. The *Ancient Mariner* seems to have come of itself. In "Christabel" I fancy him saying, "Go to, let us write an imaginative poem." It never could be finished on those terms.

This is not the time nor the place to pass judgment on Coleridge the man. Doubtless it would have been happier for him had he been endowed with the business faculty that makes his friend Wordsworth so almost irritatingly respectable. But would it have been happier for us? We are here to-day not to consider what Coleridge owed to himself, to his family, or to the world, but what we owe to him. Let us at least not volunteer to draw his frailties from their dread abode. Our own are a far more profitable subject of contemplation.

Let the man of imaginative temperament, who has never procrastinated, who has made all that was possible of his powers, cast the first stone. The cairn, I think, will not be as tall as Hector's. With Coleridge I believe the opium to have been congenital, and if we may judge by many a profoundly pathetic cry both in his poems and his letters, he answered grievously for his frailties during the last thirty years of his life. In an unpublished letter of his he says, speaking of another, but thinking certainly of himself, "An unfortunate man, enemy to himself only, and like all of that character expiating his faults by suffering beyond what the severest judge would have inflicted as their due punishment." There let us leave it, for nothing is more certain than that our personal weaknesses exact the uttermost farthing of penalty from us while we live. Even in the dilapidation of his powers, due chiefly, if you will, to his own unthrifty management of them, we might, making proper deductions, apply to him what Mark Antony says of the dead Caesar—

He was the ruins of the noblest man
That ever lived in the tide of time.

Whatever may have been his faults and weaknesses, he was the man of all his generation to whom we should most unhesitatingly allow the distinction of genius, that is, of one authentically possessed from time to time by some influence that made him better and greater than himself. If he lost himself too much in what Mr. Pater has admirably called "impassioned contemplation," he has at least left us such a legacy as only genius, and genius not always, can leave. It is for this that we pay him this homage of memory. He himself has said that—

It seems like stories from the land of spirits
If any man obtain that which he merits,
Or any merit that which he attains.

Both conditions are fulfilled to-day.

—James Russell Lowell, from "Coleridge," 1885,
Works, Riverside edition, 1890, vol. 6, pp. 69–77

LAURA JOHNSON WYLIE (1894)

Laura Johnson Wylie has great admiration for Coleridge for having saved criticism from dullness and a very circumscribed set of standards. With his knowledge of history and engagement with the scientific thinking of his age, Coleridge is characterized here as the philosopher of a new age of criticism, contributing a fresh perspective and strategy to the interpretation

of literature. She maintains that, although Coleridge's criticism broke with
the eighteenth-century sense of perfection, his originality and ability to
incorporate different areas of knowledge into his work elevated criticism
to its own version of dignity.

However variously Coleridge's theories be judged, the delicacy of his critical
perception raises him above the limitations of any school. The most musical
and philosophic poet of the century could not bring his poetic intuition to
bear on the critical study of literature without enriching for all time our
conception of its spirit and purpose. This sympathetic understanding of his
peers it is unfair to claim as the exclusive mark of his school; it had already
spiritualized the Classicism of Lessing, and liberalized the culture of St.
Evremond and Addison and Gray. But Coleridge's possession of a sympathetic
temperament made him not only a great interpreter of literature, but a typical
critic of the new Romanticism. Dryden's integrity of thought had never
hindered him from making the greatest of ancients and moderns into the
image of his own age; Coleridge's sensitive and sympathetic appreciation but
reflects the spirit that guided the energies and blurred the judgments of his
contemporaries. In the reaction against monotonous standards and narrow
interests, criticism began to perceive in the most unlike types the expression
of a common and all-powerful force; and if the new enthusiasm for variety
and originality dulled the earlier sense of perfection, it yet first made possible
a true conception of either excellence or relation in the world of art. By the
sensitiveness of his nature and his sympathy with the historic and scientific
spirit of his time, Coleridge was the preacher of these new doctrines; and
his poetic intuitions were thus at once the instrument and the crown of his
intellectual endeavor. His interpretation of literature was founded on the
perception, both spiritual and scientific, of the interdependence of varying
types and expressions, and of the ruling power of the creative imagination—a
perception that touched even the most personal of his judgments with the
light and dignity of philosophy.

—Laura Johnson Wylie, *Studies in the Evolution
of English Criticism*, 1894, pp. 199–200

ALICE SNYDER "A NOTE ON COLERIDGE'S SHAKESPEARE CRITICISM" (1923)

In her essay on Coleridge's Shakespearean criticism, Alice Snyder makes
the case that modern psychology (such as it was in 1923) could provide a

context for classifying Coleridge's eclectic commentary on Shakespeare's plays. The psychological trend to which Snyder refers is the "functional school" that got rid of all externality and, instead, analyzed the patient wholly on the basis of her or his internal thoughts. This approach attempts to explain the conscious mind in terms of the unconscious. Snyder maintains that in his Shakespearean criticism, Coleridge was aware of entering the abnormal arena, when responding to a wide range of characters such as Hamlet and Macbeth, where the answer to the question of motive lies within the individual temperament. In other words, "the difference between the supposed cause and the real germ of action" is to be found in the unconscious. Snyder produces several examples from Coleridge's notes that make a convincing argument for the poet's superb psychological insight into Shakespeare. Moreover, in applying this paradigm of absolute interiority, Snyder offers a resolution to the longstanding criticism that Coleridge's metaphysics got in the way of explaining contradictions in the plays. For instance, in identifying an inherent, tragic weakness in certain characters, such as Richard II, where positive forces compete with some inner flaw or limitation, the negative forces sometimes win out due to some particular circumstance—in Richard's case an "intellectual feminineness." By applying this paradigm of complete interiority to Coleridge's criticism, the problem of explaining the otherwise inexplicable is resolved and, indeed, responds to the point such as that made by J.H. Hanford that Coleridge's notes were sometimes rendered inaccurate by his philosophical arguments.

That Coleridge's literary criticism owes much of its significance to keen psychological analysis is a fact that has now for some time been generally recognized. In 1912 Professor Oliver Elton noted that Coleridge's psychological genius accounted for much of his best aesthetic criticism, mentioning specifically his analyses of the characters of Shakespeare's plays.[1] A little later we find C. E. Vaughan going so far as to assert that Coleridge's "records of the working of the mind, especially under abnormal or morbid conditions, are extraordinarily minute and subtle," and that "it would hardly be too much to say that he is the founder of what has since become a distinct . . . . branch of philosophy: the study of experimental psychology."[2] Other students of Coleridge might be cited. And yet, so far as I am aware, no thorough-going attempt has been made to classify his psychological comments and formulate the underlying principles.

This is not to be wondered at, for Coleridge's variety of eclecticism was such as to baffle most attempts to get at fundamental principles. But recent developments in psychological thinking have been rapidly bringing to consciousness principles that do—we must now admit—to some extent integrate Coleridge's scattered comments, and make classification, at least within a limited field, seem perhaps worth while. Looking at his criticism in the light of our contemporary functional psychology we see interesting anticipations of a fairly definable psychological point of view. Many of Coleridge's comments anticipate, both in substance and in phraseology, the tendency of the functional school to "get rid of *externality* in psychology,"[3] to talk in terms of vital activity rather than externally "given" elements, in terms of significance rather than mere facts. A number of these parallel rather remarkably the utterances of the present-day abnormal psychologists who find significance rather than accident even in errors, and explain the pathological and the vicious in terms of normal vital functions vitiated only by deficiencies, repressions, or some similar interference.

Such passages frequently bear witness to Coleridge's persistent attempt to do away with philosophic dualism, to prove to himself that extremes do meet, to reconcile all opposites.[4] This is entirely natural, for the contemporary thought tendency referred to is really the modern, psychological rather than metaphysical, way of resolving dualism. It shows itself as the attempt, now to explain the objective or external—reality as grasped by the intellect—in terms of vital activity; now to explain the conscious in terms of the subconscious; and now to explain the pathological in terms of the normal, the destructive in terms of the constructive or creative.

I have tabulated Coleridge's comments, taken from the notes on Shakespeare's plays, that anticipate rather strikingly this modern psychological attempt at monism. In each there is evidence that Coleridge was conscious of some dualism to be dealt with; there is always some pair of opposing elements or some contradiction to be reconciled, or something vaguely but truly paradoxical in its implications. But, unlike many of his metaphysical attempts to reconcile opposites, these psychological attempts have given a body of doctrine that must be recognized as relatively sound and significant at the present time.

Since the modern parallels that the comments will suggest are, many times, to be found in the field of abnormal psychology, it is worth while to note at the outset that Coleridge was himself conscious that he was dealing in abnormal psychology. In his comparison of Chaucer and Shakespeare he remarked: "Shakspeare's characters are the representatives of the interior nature of humanity, in which some element has become so predominant as to destroy the health of the mind."[5] This very statement is a significant anticipation of the view of one of our contemporary psychologists who notes that among others Iago, Richard III, Macbeth, Hamlet, Anthony, and Timon "can all be studied like patients suffering from neuroses."[6]

I

In handling the question of motive Coleridge frequently tends to discount the obvious external motive, stressing instead the temperament or predisposition of the individual, once or twice even suggesting that the external motive is deliberately created by what the contemporary abnormal psychologist would probably call the "unconscious." The paradoxical phrase "motive-mongering" used in the following *Hamlet* note gives the essence of his conception. On the King's lines (Act 3, scene 3) "My words fly up, my thoughts remain below: Words, without thoughts, never to heaven go," Coleridge comments:

> "O what a lesson concerning the essential difference between wishing and willing, and the folly of all motive-mongering, while the individual self remains!"[7]

Similarly, to Iago's soliloquy (*Othello*, Act 1, scene 3), "I hate the Moor; . . . . I know not if 't be true; But I, for mere suspicion in that kind, Will do 't as if for surety," Coleridge applies the paradoxical phrase "the motive-hunting of a motiveless malignity."[8] It is possible, of course, that here Coleridge conceived the "motive-hunting" merely as a means of justifying the proposed action to others, not as the attempt of a blind malignity to furnish itself with a motive for action; but that the latter conception was in his mind seems likely from the use of the same phrase in one of the *Anima Poetae* notes, where Coleridge says that in dealing with suicide we usually try to "fish out some *motive* for an act which proceeded from a *motive-making* impulse."[9]

The difference between the supposed cause and the real germ of action lies at the bottom of Coleridge's comments on the dialogue between Banquo and Macbeth just after the disappearance of the witches (*Macbeth*, Act 1, scene 3).

" . . . . Banquo goes on wondering, like any common spectator:

Were such things here as we do speak about?

whilst Macbeth persists in recurring to the self-concerning:—

Your children shall be kings.
Ban. You shall be king.
Macb. And thane of Cawdor too: went it not so?
So surely is the guilt in its germ anterior to the supposed cause, and immediate temptation!"

And later,

> "Then he relapses into himself again, and every word of his soliloquy shows the early birth-date of his guilt."[10]

Finally, in a note on *Romeo and Juliet* Coleridge commends Shakespeare for introducing Romeo as "already love-bewildered" before the introduction of Juliet, for

> "The necessity of loving creates an object for itself," and "no one
> . . . . ever experiences any shock at Romeo's forgetting his Rosaline,
> who had been a mere name for the yearning of his youthful
> imagination, and rushing into his passion for Juliet."[11]

II

Mood, and even intellectual conviction, ordinarily conceived as forced on the individual by something beyond his control, are sometimes seen by Coleridge as the deliberate creations of an inner self. Note the phrasing of the following comment on Macbeth's speech after the death of Lady Macbeth (Act 5, scene 5):

> "Alas for Macbeth! now all is inward with him; he has no more
> prudential prospective reasonings. His wife, the only being who
> could have had any seat in his affections, dies; he *puts on
> despondency, the final heart-armor of the wretched,* and would fain
> think every thing shadowy and unsubstantial, as indeed all things
> are to those who cannot regard them as symbols of goodness:—
>
>   Out, out, brief candle!
>   Life's but a walking shadow; . . . ."[12]

In explaining the contradiction between the weightiness of the occasion and the triviality of mood in *Hamlet* Act 1, scene 4, Coleridge writes:

> "The unimportant conversation with which this scene opens is a
> proof of Shakspeare's minute knowledge of human nature. It is a
> well-established fact, that on the brink of any serious enterprise,
> or event of moment, men almost invariably endeavor to elude the
> pressure of their own thoughts by turning aside to trivial objects and
> familiar circumstances: thus this dialogue on the platform begins
> with remarks on the coldness of the air, and inquiries, obliquely
> connected, indeed, with the expected hour of the visitation, but
> thrown out in a seeming vacuity of topics, as to the striking of the
> clock and so forth. The same desire to escape from the impending
> thought is carried on in Hamlet's account of, and moralizing on,
> the Danish custom of wassailing: he runs off from the particular
> to the universal, and in his repugnance to personal and individual

concerns, escapes, as it were, from himself in generalizations, and smothers the impatience and uneasy feelings of the moment in abstract reasoning."[13]

Of the lines (Act 1, scene 5) "*Mar.* Hillo, ho, ho, my lord! *Ham.* Hillo, ho, ho, boy! come bird, come . . . ." he notes:

"This part of the scene after Hamlet's interview with the Ghost has been charged with an improbable eccentricity. But the truth is, that after the mind has been stretched beyond its usual pitch and tone, it must either sink into exhaustion or inanity, or seek relief by change. It is thus well known, that persons conversant in deeds of cruelty contrive to escape from conscience by connecting something of the ludicrous with them, and by inventing grotesque terms and a certain technical phraseology to disguise the horror of their practices. Indeed, paradoxical as it may appear, the terrible by a law of the human mind always touches on the verge of the ludicrous."[14]

In *The Tempest* Act 2, scene 1, Coleridge says that Shakespeare has,

"as in many other places, shown the tendency in bad men to indulge in scorn and contemptuous expressions, as a mode of getting rid of their own uneasy feelings of inferiority to the good. . . ."[15]

Reading these passages to-day one is half surprised not to find mention of "defense reactions" as such.

III

Nowhere, perhaps, does Coleridge more nearly approach the contemporary standpoint than in some of his explanations of the vices, faults, and tragic weaknesses of Shakespeare's characters. The paradoxical law that certain positive, essentially moral forces may, when coexistent with some inner weakness or some peculiarity of environment, result in anti-social and even criminal acts, was clearly recognized by Coleridge, and we find him explaining such acts as the distortion of what is fundamentally wholesome. His note on Act I, scene 4 of *Richard II* reads:

"In this scene a new light is thrown on Richard's character. Until now he has appeared in all the beauty of royalty; but here, as soon as he is left to himself, the inherent weakness of his character is immediately shown. It is a weakness, however, of a peculiar kind, not arising from want of personal courage, or any specific defect of faculty, but rather an intellectual feminineness, which feels a necessity of ever leaning on the breasts of others, and of reclining on those who are all the while known to be inferiors. To this must be attributed . . . . all Richard's vices, his tendency to concealment, and his cunning, the whole operation of which is directed to the getting rid of present difficulties. . . . Shakspeare has represented this character in a very peculiar manner. He has not made him amiable with counterbalancing faults; but has openly and broadly drawn those faults without reserve, relying on Richard's disproportionate sufferings and gradually emergent good qualities for our sympathy; and this was possible, because his faults are not positive vices, but spring entirely from defect of character."[16]

Lear's attitude toward his daughters is explained as the distortion of a kindly and loving nature. In speaking of the "moral verities" on which the play is founded Coleridge notes

"the strange, yet by no means unnatural, mixture of selfishness, sensibility, and habit of feeling derived from, and fostered by, the particular rank and usages of the individual;—the intense desire of being intensely beloved,—selfish, and yet characteristic of the selfishness of a loving and kindly nature alone;—the self-supportless leaning for all pleasure on another's breast;—the craving after sympathy with a prodigal disinterestedness, frustrated by its own ostentation, and the mode and nature of its claims;—the anxiety, the distrust, the jealousy, which more or less accompany all selfish affections, and are amongst the surest contradistinctions of mere fondness from true love, and which originate Lear's eager wish to enjoy his daughter's violent professions, whilst the inveterate habits of sovereignty convert the wish into claim and positive right, and an incompliance with them into crime and treason."[17]

The distortion of some positive force—a will-to-power as it were—is used to account even for Oliver's apparently wholly vicious speech about Orlando just after his interview with Charles (*As You Like It*, Act 1, scene 1). Of the lines "Yet he's gentle; never school'd, and yet learned; full of noble device; . . . ." Coleridge notes:

"It is too venturous to charge a passage in Shakspeare with want of truth to nature; and yet at first sight this speech of Oliver's expresses truths, which it seems almost impossible that any mind should so distinctly, so livelily, and so voluntarily, have presented to itself in connection with feelings and intentions so malignant, and so contrary to those which the qualities expressed would naturally have called forth. But I dare not say that this seeming unnaturalness is not in the nature of an abused wilfulness, when united with a strong intellect. In such characters there is sometimes a gloomy self-gratification in making the absoluteness of the will (*sic pro ratione voluntas!*) evident to themselves by setting the reason and the conscience in full array against it."[18]

Madness itself is shown to be simply a variation of its opposite. Of *Hamlet* Act 4, scene 2 Coleridge notes:

"Hamlet's madness is made to consist in the free utterance of all the thoughts that had passed through his mind before,—in fact, in telling home-truths."[19]

And in one of the notes on *Macbeth* the opposites *hope* and *fear* are shown to have an identical basis:

"Hope, the master element of a commanding genius, meeting with an active and combining intellect, and an imagination of just that degree of vividness which disquiets and impels the soul to try to realize its images, greatly increases the creative power of the mind; and hence the images become a satisfying world of themselves, as is the case in every poet and original philosopher—but hope fully gratified, and yet the elementary basis of the passion remaining, becomes fear; and, indeed, the general, who must often feel, even though he may hide it from his own consciousness, how large a share chance had in his successes, may very naturally be irresolute in a new scene, where he knows that all will depend on his own act and election."[20]

IV

The general principle of psychological compensation is suggested by Coleridge over and over again, when he tests Shakespeare's characters and finds them tragic characters because of a deficiency in one sphere accompanied by a corresponding proficiency in another. Sometimes he sees a cause and effect relationship between the deficiency and the proficiency, and sometimes mere coexistence. The principle is, naturally, most fully elaborated in his notes on the character of Hamlet.

"I believe the character of Hamlet may be traced to Shakspeare's deep and accurate science in mental philosophy.... In order to understand him, it is essential that we should reflect upon the constitution of our own minds. Man is distinguished from the brute animals in proportion as thought prevails over sense: but in the healthy processes of the mind, a balance is constantly maintained between the impressions from outward objects and the inward operations of the intellect:—for if there be an overbalance in the contemplative faculty, man thereby becomes the creature of mere meditation, and loses his natural power of action. Now one of Shakspeare's modes of creating character is, to conceive any one intellectual or moral faculty in morbid excess, and then to place himself, Shakspeare, thus mutilated or diseased, under given circumstances. In Hamlet he seems to have wished to exemplify the moral necessity of . . . . an *equilibrium* between the real and the imaginary worlds. In Hamlet this balance is disturbed: his thoughts, and the images of his fancy, are far more vivid. than his actual perceptions, and his very perceptions, instantly passing through the *medium* of his contemplations, acquire, as they pass, a form and a color not naturally their own. Hence we see a great, an almost enormous, intellectual activity, and a proportionate aversion to real action, consequent upon it. . . . This character Shakspeare places in circumstances under which it is obliged to act on the spur of the moment:—Hamlet is brave and careless of death; but he vacillates from sensibility, and procrastinates from thought, and loses the power of action in the energy of resolve."[21]

The same inverse ratio Coleridge finds exemplified in Richard II, with his "continually increasing energy of thought, and as constantly diminishing power of acting," and again, his "wordy courage which only serves to betray more clearly his internal impotence."[22]

Macbeth, similarly, he finds to be "all-powerful without strength; he wishes the end, but is irresolute as to the means."[23]

And finally:

"Lady Macbeth, like all in Shakspeare, is a class individualized:—of high rank, left much alone, and feeding herself with day-dreams of ambition, she mistakes the courage of fantasy for the power of bearing the consequences of the realities of guilt. Hers is the mock fortitude of a mind deluded by ambition; she shames her husband with a superhuman audacity of fancy which she can not support, but sinks in the season of remorse, and dies in suicidal agony."[24]

＊ ＊ ＊

In a recent article on Coleridge as a philologian,[25] Professor J. H. Hanford notes that Coleridge's characteristic weaknesses show in his work as commentator as well as elsewhere, that his textual interpretations of Shakespeare were sometimes rendered inaccurate by his philosophical interests. The same might well be said of his character analyses as such. Some of his attempts to make manifest Shakespeare's fidelity to the laws of human nature are obvious struggles to construe facts in terms of theory, and are of dubious value. In any estimate of Coleridge's psychological genius this must be granted.

Moreover, this compilation of notes that seem to have some integrating principle is in no sense evidence of any original formulation of a well defined standpoint. An attempt to get at the origins of the psychological comments quoted would lead one far and wide over the field of recognized sources of Coleridge's philosophic thought. The ideas involved could doubtless be traced back in every case to Aristotle or Leibnitz or Kant, or one or more of a dozen others that should be named. And there is little evidence that Coleridge consciously worked out the relationships involved. Granted all this, however, the notes that have been compiled seem to be significant anticipations, and go far toward justifying the eclecticism from which they result.

Notes

1. *Survey of English Literature, 1830–1880*, Vol. II, pp. 106, 120–121.
2. *Cambridge History of English Literature*, XI, p. 152.
3. The phrase is Professor Dewey's.
4. A more comprehensive survey of Coleridge's attempts to reconcile philosophic opposites will be found in my study, "The Critical Principle of the Reconciliation of Opposites as Employed by Coleridge," No. IX of the *Contributions to Rhetorical Theory*, edited by F. N. Scott, of the University of Michigan.
5. *Works*, N. Y., 1856–75, Vol. IV, p. 246.
6. Mordell, *The Erotic Motive in Literature*.
7. *Works*, IV, 181. The following notes are all taken from the section entitled "Shakspeare, with Introductory Matter on Poetry, the Drama, and the Stage," in Vol. IV of this edition.
8. *Ib.*, p. 181.
9. *Anima Poetae*. London, 1895, p. 196.
10. *Works*. Vol. IV, p. 168.
11. *Ib.*, p. 111.
12. *Ib.*, p. 174. The italics are mine.

13. *Ib.*, p. 154.
14. *Ib.*, p. 155–6.
15. *Ib.*, p. 77.
16. *Ib.*, p. 123–4.
17. *Ib.*, p. 133–4.
18. *Ib.*, p. 88.
19. *Ib.*, p. 162.
20. *Ib.*, p. 165–6.
21. *Ib.*, p. 145.
22. *Ib.*, pp. 125 and 126–7.
23. *Ib.*, p. 168.
24. *Ib.*, p. 170.
25. *Modern Philology*, April, 1919.

—Alice D. Snyder, "A Note on Coleridge's
Shakespeare Criticism," *Modern Language Notes*,
vol. 38, no. 1, January 1923, pp. 23–31

BIOGRAPHIA LITERARIA

GEORGE WATSON "INTRODUCTION" (1906)

I. 1800–1815

The story of the *Biographia Literaria* begins seventeen years before it
appeared as two volumes on the London bookstalls in July 1817: it begins in
a conversation between two friends. In the autumn of 1800 Wordsworth and
Coleridge, both settled in the Lake District after their return from Germany
in the previous year, were debating what form a second edition of the *Lyrical
Ballads* should take to replace the exhausted edition of 1798. In the course of
a walk the idea of replacing the brief Advertisement by a critical preface was
conceived. In the aged memory of Wordsworth many years after, the idea,
and indeed the very substance of the Preface as he came to write it, were all
Coleridge's. 'I never cared a straw about the theory,' he wrote impatiently on
the manuscript of Barron Field's biography of himself, 'and the Preface was
written at the request of Mr Coleridge out of sheer good nature. I recollect
the very spot, a deserted quarry in the Vale of Grasmere, where he pressed the
thing upon me, and but for that it would never have been thought of.'

This is the first recorded moment in the life of this book. For though it
would be an exaggeration to call the Preface a first draft of the *Biographia*,

the exaggeration would be of the slightest. Coleridge himself said it was 'half a child of my own brain,'[1] and admitted to another friend at the same time that he had first suggested writing the Preface himself, but had abandoned it and turned over his notes to Wordsworth.[2] By 1815, of course, when he came to write the *Biographia*, the Preface was 'Wordsworth' and the *Biographia* Coleridge's reply to Wordsworth; but the simplification is much too crude. No doubt there were already real if hidden differences between the two men in 1800, but if so they were hidden from Coleridge himself. It is easy to detect the note of surprise in his letters of 1802–3 when he first speaks of disagreements, and even then he was uncertain what the disagreements were. On the evidence it seems fair to suppose that the attacks upon the Preface in the *Biographia*, sharp as they are, are the sharpness of a middle-aged man disagreeing with his youth. No wonder Wordsworth, who had written the Preface only under persuasion, resented these attacks; but it proves nothing about his part in composing the Preface that he constantly reprinted it. An author may feel as protective of the reputation of commissioned work as of any other.

The Preface of 1800 poses and tries to answer two closely connected questions: first, what relation should the language of poetry bear to that of ordinary life? And secondly, what relation should the subject of poetry bear to life itself? (The order in which the questions are put looks irrational, but it is Wordsworth's own order and there are good reasons for it.) The answers of the Preface are 'the real language of men in a state of vivid sensation' (restated in 1802 as 'a *selection* of the language really spoken by men'), and 'the incidents of common life.' These two questions, or rather Coleridge's attempt to modify and clarify the old answers to them, are together the central theme of the second half of the *Biographia*. It is conventional to call this part of the book (chs. 14–22) the 'critique of Wordsworth,' but the convention is highly misleading. Little or nothing purely Wordsworthian is here under arraignment, though Coleridge seizes the opportunity to use the poetry of Wordsworth, whom he considered the greatest poet of his age, to illustrate his mature views on the language and subject of poetry.

The Coleridge who had turned over to Wordsworth the task of writing a critical preface was a man who was nursing a similar project of his own. His plans for a biography of Lessing, which he had gone to Germany to prepare, were being pushed out of his thoughts by the more seductive idea of a treatise which would combine in some unspecified way his twin interests of philosophy and poetry. On 9 October 1800 he wrote to Humphry Davy: 'The works which I gird myself up to attack as soon as money concerns will permit me are the life of Lessing and the essay on poetry. The latter is still more at my heart than the former: its title would be *An Essay on the Elements of Poetry*—it would be in reality a disguised system of morals and politics.' Writing again to Davy four months later (3 February 1801) he complained that illness was preventing him from writing the treatise, which was now to be called *Concerning Poetry, and the Nature of the Pleasures Derived from it* and was to deal with 'the affinities of the feelings with words and ideas.' The more he thought about the Preface the less he agreed with it, and talking to Wordsworth only made matters worse: 'We have had lately some little controversy on this subject, and we begin to suspect that there is somewhere or other a radical difference (in our) opinions.'[3]

'Somewhere or other'—at the age of thirty Coleridge is very certain he wants to write a treatise on aesthetics but still uncertain what to put into it. A fortnight later he decided on a pragmatic approach, a study of contemporary poetry, 'one volume essays, the second selections. . . . The object is not to examine what is good in each writer, but what has *ipso facto* pleased and to what faculties, or passions, or habits of the mind they may be supposed to have given pleasure.'[4] The final object, in fact, an aesthetic theory, is kept in view, but a new approach has been found to it. More importantly the Preface has already become 'Wordsworth's' and Coleridge is now talking of impartial mediation between the old and the new schools of poetry. He goes on: 'Of course Darwin[5] and Wordsworth having given each a defence of their mode of poetry and a disquisition on the nature and essence of poetry in general, I shall necessarily be led rather deeper, and these I shall treat of either first or last.' As for his disagreement with Wordsworth, 'this I shall endeavour to go to the bottom of, and acting the arbiter between the old school and the new school hope to lay down some plain and perspicuous, tho' not superficial, canons of criticism respecting poetry.' He had high hopes of writing the book quickly; he wrote to Tom Wedgwood (20 October 1802) promising that 'very shortly .... I shall present you from the press with my opinions in full on the subject of style both in prose and verse,' about which he claimed to have 'thought much and patiently.' By now he has moved so far from the Preface that he feels poetic diction to 'require a certain aloofness from [the] language of real life, which I think deadly to poetry.' But still the treatise was not written.

By the summer of 1803 he had come to a fresh and utterly surprising decision on the form the book was to take: it was to be contained in an autobiographical frame and his views were to be stated in the context of the events that had made them. In September he wrote in his notebook: 'Seem to have made up my mind to write my metaphysical works as *my Life*, and in my Life—intermixed with all the other events or history of the mind and fortunes of S. T. Coleridge.'[6] This decision, at least, was irrevocable, but why he took it we shall never know. Perhaps it was an acknowledgement of failure, of some private incapacity ever to write a work of formal logical design however often he aspired to do so. Or it may have been a recognition of a distinctive talent, of an intense personalism that haunts everything he wrote down to the most crabbed and back-broken of his paragraphs, an inescapable I AM. No one can deny that the form of the *Biographia*, eccentric (indeed unique) as it is, is perfectly suited to what Coleridge has to offer, however easy it is to object that he has offered too much or too little. He had found a plan flexible enough to admit of the fragmentary and the inconclusive as the difficulties of his theme might demand. It was a good choice, in the circumstances. Not knowing all the answers he was in a position fairly and frankly to say why.

By the end of 1803 the distinction between imagination and fancy was already formulated,[7] an incisive restatement of an ancient value-judgment, and only health and leisure seemed wanting to write the book. But for twelve years little or nothing was done towards it. Instead ill health drove him to Malta and Italy (1804–6), indecision and money troubles diverted his energies, while his views on aesthetics were dissipated in public lectures which were never published in his lifetime. By March 1815, still without a permanent home, he had settled for a year with his friends the Morgans at Calne in Wiltshire. A group of friends, one of them J. M. Gutch, the Bristol printer, now advanced him money on the security of his manuscripts with the prospect of a collection of his verse, published and unpublished, to be issued later in the year. After fifteen years of hesitation and delay the *Biographia* was begun.

II. 1815

By September 1815 the manuscript was complete and in the hands of Gutch at Bristol[8] after six months or less of crowded work; but the story of its composition is confused and doubtful. The traditional story we may dismiss at the outset. On 20 August, Mary Lamb, writing to Sarah Hutchinson, spoke of a letter she had recently received from Mrs Morgan, Coleridge's hostess at Calne: 'Your old friend Coleridge is very hard at work on a preface to a new edition which he is going to publish in the same form as Mr Wordsworth's—at first the preface was not to exceed five or six pages, it has however grown into a work of great importance. I believe Morgan has already written nearly two hundred pages [i.e. as Coleridge's amanuensis]. The title is *Autobiographia Literaria*: to which are added *Sybilline Leaves* [*sic*], a collection of poems by the same author.'[9]

Mary Lamb's understanding of Mrs Morgan's understanding of what Coleridge or her husband told her was, in fact, that Coleridge was collecting his verse for publication as Wordsworth had done for his two-volume collection of *Poems* of March 1815, set out to write a brief preface to it and was carried away into writing a work of hundreds of pages. This would be an astonishing story on any evidence, but as it happens there is no evidence for it beyond this letter of Mary Lamb's, and that is at second hand. It is one woman's report to another of what a third has told her of her husband's (or lodger's) conversation: evidence of a sort that is daily dismissed in courts of law. What did happen (and it is easy to see how the misunderstanding arose) is explained by Coleridge himself in a letter probably written within a few days of the events it describes and addressed to his friend Dr Brabant (29 July 1815): 'The necessity of extending what I first intended as a preface to an *Autobiographia Literaria, or Sketches of my Literary Life and Opinions* as far as poetry and poetical criticism is concerned, has confined me to my study from eleven to four and from six till ten since I last left you. I have just finished it, having only the correction of the MSS. to go thro'. I have given a full account (*raisonné*) of the controversy concerning Wordsworth's poems and theory, in which my name has been so constantly included. I have no doubt that Wordsworth will be displeased, but I have done my duty to myself and to the public in (as I believe) compleatly subverting the theory and in proving that the poet himself has never acted on it except in particular stanzas which are the blots of his compositions.'

The statement seems perfectly explicit and gives rise to two conclusions:

(i) That by July 1815 Coleridge had already written a work which he called *Autobiographia Literaria* which did *not* include the 'critique of Wordsworth.' This must have consisted, approximately, of vol. i of the first edition, or chapters 1–13, a work primarily philosophical and remarkably similar to his project of the years 1800–3 quoted above—'my metaphysical works as *my Life*, and *in* my Life.'

(ii) That in July, believing this work to be more or less complete, he sat down to write a preface to it which outgrew his intentions by developing into a long discussion of the theories of the 1800 Preface, i.e. vol. ii of the first edition, or chapters 14–22 at least. It must have been this 'preface' which Mary Lamb, or Mrs Morgan, confused with the preface to his poems, *Sibylline Leaves*, which in the event appeared in August 1817 with nothing but a factual three-page preface. The confusion is the more understandable if we remember that Coleridge seems from the beginning to have regarded the *Biographia* as a whole, if not as a preface in the conventional sense, at least as a companion volume to his collection of verse.[10] In fact the sheets of *Sibylline Leaves*, printed for Gutch by John Evans of Bristol in 1815, appeared two years later with the then meaningless register 'Vol. ii' in their signatures.

Apparently this volume was meant to follow upon a one-volume *Biographia*, the two to represent the author's literary achievement—a splendid reply to the repeated and deeply resented charge of idleness.

But a book, as the evidence proves, the *Biographia* was always intended to be, a prose work in its own right to be published alone between separate boards. It is important that the legend put about by Mary Lamb's letter should be silenced. It is not simply that it is untrue; it has also made it altogether too easy for those who have criticized the design of the book, the first of whom was Coleridge himself in the course of it, to dismiss it as nothing better than a series of digressions, 'Biographical Sketches' indeed, as the concessive sub-title has it. But this will not do. The design of the work may be unorthodox and was certainly obscured by adventures in the press, but it does exist and demands to be understood.

We must approach with caution, however, since the most important decision of all has left no record. Coleridge now had a philosophical work of some dozen chapters; he had an unpremeditated essay embodying his ideas of fifteen years past concerning the theories of the 1800 Preface which was growing longer every day and which promised to become nearly as long as the work itself. It had been begun as a preface, but it must soon have seemed natural to stand the book on its feet and put philosophy before criticism, the two parts pivoted on the imagination theory. Philosophy could explain and establish this theory: a discussion of the language and subject of poetry could then apply it. It may well be that it was a lost note from Coleridge, written to his printer Gulch in the high summer of 1815 warning him to expect twice the prose he had bargained for, that led to a fateful miscalculation.

But for Coleridge the old plan stood, and material intended for two volumes, one of prose and one of verse, was delivered to Crutch in Bristol in September 1815. Coleridge was elated. In six months he had achieved more than in a dozen years and unexpectedly fulfilled an old ambition. He could hardly wait for the *Biographia* to see the light. Of the form of the book he felt uncertain, since it followed a plan neither narrative nor logical but a disconcerting combination of the two. So 'immethodical a miscellany,' he called it disparagingly, and 'this semi-narrative.'[11] But about its substance he had no reservations. It was definitive. In a letter to Sotheby (31 January 1816) he expressed impatience to see the book out, both because it would help his financial position by setting out plainly the achievements of his career and because it 'settled the controversy concerning the nature of poetic diction, as far as reasoning can settle it.' He had recorded his old achievements and added another.

III. 1815–1817

An unusual disappointment was in store for him. Early in 1816 Gulch told him he had miscalculated the size of the manuscript, paginated for two volumes of some three hundred pages each and exhausted the manuscript half-way through the second volume. The sheets were printed, and the cost of remaking would be prohibitive. It was not only a crippling disappointment but an apparently insoluble dilemma as well. The only solution seemed to be to add a further set of chapters at the end to make up the second volume. But the book was already bigger than Coleridge had originally intended; he had said his say and he had other urgent tasks to hand. By April he had left Calne for his final home with Dr Gillman at Highgate and Gutch's sheets had been bought by the London firm of Gale & Fenner. In the circumstances the quickest solution was to use some of his published writings as a make-weight. He seems to have considered his rejected tragedy *Zapolya* for the purpose and bought back the copyright from Murray, but sensibly decided it would be out of place. By September 1816 the task was urgent and had to be dismissed. On 22nd he wrote to Fenner that he planned to 'commence the next week with the matter which I have been forced by the blunder and false assurance of the printer to add to the *Literary Life* in order to render the volumes of something like the same size. I not only shall not, but I cannot think of or do anything till the three volumes complete [i.e. two of the *Biographia* and one of *Sibylline Leaves*] are in Mr Gale's house.' The problem was pressing, but it was complex.

To begin with the printed sheets as they stood represented a completed work and presumably had a conclusion of their own. If he had to incorporate new material this last would have to be scrapped and the final chapter that remained (ch. 22) would have to be rewritten, at least at the latter end, so that the work could be extended without a premature conclusion. This surely explains why Fenner's printing begins in mid-chapter, at p. 145 of volume ii[12] and not at the beginning of 'Satyrane's Letters.' The old conclusion had to be replaced with connective tissue. There is no certain evidence that Coleridge rewrote the latter part of chapter 22 (ii. 145–82) and padded out his examination of Wordsworth's characteristic defects and excellences, but there is a natural presumption that he did so. He needed more material, he avails himself here even more liberally than usual of long quotations, and the Fenner section of the chapter is nearly three times as long as the Gutch, which surely suggests it more than replaces the original ending. The final note to the chapter was obviously added at this time and has misled Coleridge scholars ever since, though to interpret it as literally as they have done is to suggest a bibliographical impossibility: 'For more than eighteen months have . . . . *Sibylline Leaves* and the present volumes, up to this page, been printed and ready for publication.' Something corresponding to 'this page' may well have been printed in Bristol, but for Coleridge to be able to add a note at this point proves that this page (ii. 182) must have been printed in London.[13]

Coleridge rewrote and probably expanded the latter part of chapter 22, the end of his critical section, adding to it an explanatory note to justify the insertion of three letters written home from Germany during his youthful visit there (1798–9) and already printed in *The Friend*. He revised them and entitled them 'Satyrane's Letters.' But he still had space to fill, and he needed more material in some sense autobiographical. He chose the review he had written with Morgan for the *Courier* damning Maturin's tragedy *Bertram*, which had been preferred by Drury Lane to his own *Zapolya*. And still his vexations were not quite over. The book needed a conclusion and he still had the old one to hand; it may well have been the last pages of the book we now have, an impassioned defence of his religious orthodoxy. We cannot be certain. But it is clear that Coleridge was in a hurry, that the conclusion would have followed strangely upon a most unchristian attack upon a successful rival and that some bridge-passage was necessary if it were to be used at all. There is an undated and uncollected letter to his printer Curtis which may belong to this moment of distraction: 'The introductory pages wanting for the *Life and Opinions* I am now employed on, and if I can finish it before I go to bed I will. The remainder, should there be any, I will endeavour to finish in town to-morrow after eleven o'clock; for from seven to eleven I shall be engaged in going to and having an interview with Mr Southey.' The only recorded visit of Southey to London from his Keswick home which would fit the terms of this letter was a visit made towards the end of April 1817, three months before the *Biographia* appeared and probably at the very time when the additions were going to press. Now the middle of the existing Conclusion, a complaint against Hazlitt for two reviews of the *Statesman's Manual* which had appeared in December 1816, can only have been written early in 1817. This is probably the 'introductory pages' referred to in this letter, introductory to the religious apologia. And this apologia was probably the conclusion of the *Biographia* of the 1815 manuscript, printed by Gutch, scrapped by Fenner, and reinstated now at the end of the extended work, its first pages rewritten to include the complaint against Hazlitt.

There were then four additions made to the original *Biographia* at the behest of the printer, three certain and one likely. The three certain additions are 'Satyrane's Letters,' the critique of *Bertram* ('Chapter XXIII'), and part of the Conclusion. The likely addition is the latter part of chapter 22, which may well have been padded. Only the last two additions are organic. The attack upon Hazlitt at the beginning of the Conclusion merely resumes the subject of Coleridge's mistreatment at the hands of reviewers, a recurring theme throughout the book. And the latter part of chapter 22, whether padded or not, cannot run beyond Coleridge's original intention in substance, since the argument at the head of the chapter was printed in Bristol and is observed throughout. But no defence can be made for 'Satyrane's Letters' or the critique of *Bertram*. They were no part of Coleridge's original intention; he added them when desperately in search of make-weights and they add nothing to the substance of the book. For these reasons they are excluded from this edition, which is therefore the first to present the *Biographia* as nearly as possible according to the author's intentions.

IV. 1817 and After

In July 1817, after a delay of nearly two years, a desperate scramble and real financial injury to Coleridge himself, the *Biographia* appeared in two ill-printed demy octavo volumes from the house of Fenner. It must have been a dreary enough occasion. The delay had robbed Coleridge of his first joyful anticipation of the success of the book, the irrelevant additions had obscured his intentions, and there were many misprints. To end all the book was damned by *Blackwood's*, while the *Quarterly Review* ignored it altogether. It was never reprinted in Coleridge's lifetime. Even Wordsworth, the reader he most ardently respected, refused to do more than skim the book and found 'the praise extravagant and the censure inconsiderate.'[14] Failure must have seemed complete. But the leaves were being turned by two young men who were both strangers to Coleridge. In November 1817 John Keats wrote to Dilke for a copy of *Sibylline Leaves*, and a close echo of Coleridge's language in his famous letter concerning 'negative capability' (21 December 1817) suggests that he read the *Biographia* at the same time.[15] And Shelley, established at Marlow, read the book as soon as it appeared and retained a key phrase which four years later he appropriated for his *Defence of Poetry*.[16] These small beginnings were characteristic. The book has always been 'seminal' and has always been recognized as such, a proper object for respect and for plunder. But its very existence as a book, with one notable exception,[17] has been doubted and denied by those best qualified to speak. By the strangest of oversights no editor has so far sought to rescue it from the undignified legend set about by Mary Lamb's letter that the book is an extended afterthought, an exercise in garrulity; or even from the extraneous matter that Coleridge was forced by circumstances to insert. Design and purpose have been denied it, and yet its greatest originality is its design.

Not that Coleridge's original plan for the book demands our praise or even our attention. Coleridge had such a plan, but he broke it. He set out to write a work of metaphysics to which he hoped the events of his life would give a continuity: he ended by producing a work of aesthetics to which such narrative as there is has failed to give continuity. But there is another unity, and it is peculiarly Coleridgean. He succeeds for the first and (so far) for the last time in English criticism in marrying the twin studies of philosophy and literature, not simply by writing about both within the boards of a single book or by insisting that such a marriage should be, but in discovering a causal link between the two in the century-old preoccupation of English critics with the theory of the poet's imagination. Here at chapters 12 and 13, mid-point in the *Biographia*, the theory finds its proper setting and fulfils its just service, the link is forged. The operation is effected without modesty, with more than enough appeals to authority and much heralding and hesitation, none of which is defensible by strict standards. Chapters 10 and 11, in particular, are a lamentable exhibition of cold feet. But Coleridge was right to appreciate the difficulty and importance of what he was trying to do. He was trying to solve with superior and up-to-date intellectual tools a problem which his predecessors in their detached and dilettante way had been considering ever since Hobbes and Dryden had stated the difficulty in the 1650's and 1660's. Aesthetics, after all, were a well-established parlour-game in eighteenth-century England. When Edmund Burke, in defiance of the real bent of his genius, produced in his twenty-eighth year a treatise called *A Philosophical Enquiry into the Origin of our Ideas of the Sublime and Beautiful* (1757) he was doing what many young authors had done to attract attention to themselves. But all these early attempts to justify literary criticism by philosophic methods fail to impress. Hobbes was too much of a professional philosopher to indulge his literary interests except as a hobby; Dryden too much of a professional man of letters to offer more than a brilliant aside on the subject and the eighteenth-century aestheticians (Addison, Burke Kames, Reynolds, Beattie and many others) were dilettanti in criticism, coiners of theories that never found currency. Johnson managed to write the critical masterpiece of the age, the *Lives of the Poets*, without once referring to the theories of any of them. Vulgar and abrupt as it must have seemed, the Preface of 1800 had put them all to flight by asking two questions of practical interest to poets and readers alike, and Coleridge made one of the most important decisions of his life in deciding to follow up this *succès de scandale* by abandoning poetry and writing an elaborate treatise on the new aesthetic. His delay was unfortunate, the delay of his printers doubly frustrating. But all this need not prevent us now from understanding his intention. He was not writing an autobiography, not even an account of his literary life, and any sort of biographical approach to the book is certain to be disappointed.[18] Nor was he writing an essay in the history of ideas, a task for which he was peculiarly unfitted for two reasons: his memory, though capacious, was inaccurate and inventive, and he had no more than an occasional curiosity to know the provenance of ideas. 'I regard truth as a divine ventriloquist: I care not from whose mouth the sounds are supposed to proceed.'[19] A queer fish among English critics, his curiosity was all for ideas. He did not even care about being entertaining, and shrugged off the charge of obscurity with the retort that 'my severest critics have not pretended to have found in my compositions triviality, or traces of a mind that shrunk from the toil of thinking.'[20] There was a task to be done, and it is still undone: to convince that criticism as evaluation is never much better than an arbitrary rule-of-thumb, however stimulating a game it may be, and that 'the ultimate end of criticism is much more to establish the principles of writing than to furnish rules how to pass judgement on what has been written by others.'[21] He wrote in the infancy of psychology, but he could see that the claims of poetry to respect all depended upon a study of those mental faculties common in their operation to poet and reader. To isolate and define these faculties would give the study of literature a security it had never had. His object, as he told Byron a few weeks after sending the *Biographia* to the press, was 'to reduce criticism to a system by the deduction of causes from principles involved in our faculties.'[22] Of course his success is debatable. The imagination-concept may be the wrong place to start; or, even if it is the right place, Coleridge's definitions and distinctions might be exposed as imprecise or question-begging. So much remains to be done, even as a beginning. To set out from the *Biographia* and go straight on in the same inquiring spirit could give the criticism of to-morrow a profundity and a certainty we lack to-day.

Notes

1. Letter to Robert Southey, 29 July 1802.
2. Letter to William Sotheby, 13 July 1802. But the letter is torn and the reading conjectural. *Cf. Notebooks*, 187n.
3. Letter to Sotheby, op. cit.
4. Letter to Southey, op. cit.
5. Erasmus Darwin (1731–1802), who included a brief 'Apology' and 'Philosophical Notes' in his *Botanic Garden* (1789–91).
6. Quoted by George Whalley, *The Integrity of 'Biographia Literaria,' Essays and Studies*, new series VI (1953). *Cf. Notebooks*, 1515.
7. Letter to Richard Sharp, 15 January 1804: 'Imagination, or the modifying power in the highest sense of the word, in which I have ventured to oppose it to Fancy, or the *aggregating* power.'

8. Letter to John May, 27 September 1815.

9. *Letters of Charles Lamb, etc.*, ed. E. V. Lucas (1935), II. 172.

10. On 30 March 1815 Coleridge had written to Byron: 'A general Preface will be pre-fixed [to the volume of verse], on the principles of Philosophic and general criticism relatively to the fine arts in general; but especially to poetry'—i.e. vol. i of the first edition of the *Biographia*.

11. pp. 52–3, 93 below.

12. p. 254 below. For this discovery I am indebted to Mr Herbert Davis's examination of the copy in the Bodleian Library.

13. Dykes Campbell in his *Narrative* (1894), and following him T. J. Wise in his *Bibliography* (1913), state that the Bristol printing ends at ii. 128. There is no evidence for this. They have apparently accepted Coleridge's figure of ii. 182 literally and then suffered a misprint.

14. Crabb Robinson, *Diary*, December 1817.

15. p. 256 below.

16. p. 169 below.

17. George Whalley. *The Integrity of 'Biographia Literaria,'* op. cit.

18. p. 281n. below.

19. p. 89 below.

20. p. 124 below.

21. p. 217 below.

22. Letter to Byron 17 October 1815.

—George Watson, "Introduction," From
*Biographia Literaria or Biographical Sketches of
My Literary Life and Opinions,* edited by George
Watson, Dutton: New York, 1906, pp. ix–xxi.

Chronology

1772   Samuel Taylor Coleridge is born in the vicarage at Ottery, St. Mary, Devonshire, on October 21.

1775   Begins formal schooling at Dame Key's Reading School.

1778   Attends Henry VIII Free Grammar School.

1781   His father, John Coleridge, dies.

1782   Admitted to Christ's Hospital School in July.

1791   Enters Jesus College, Cambridge University, in July.

1793   Enlists in the King's Regiment, 15th Light Dragoons, under the pseudonym Silas Tomkyn Comberback.

1794   Obtains a discharge from the King's Regiment and returns to Cambridge. Meets Robert Southey at Oxford. *The Fall of Robespierre* published (with Southey) under Coleridge's name. Meets Godwin. Leaves Cambridge in December, without a degree, in order to pursue the scheme of Pantisocracy.

1795   Moves to Bristol in January and meets William Wordsworth. Marries Sara Fricker of Bristol; they settle in Clevedon, Somerset. Lectures in Bristol through November on politics and history.

1796   Hartley Coleridge born. Publishes *Poems on Various Subjects* and edits the March through May issues of *The Watchman*. Moves with his family to Nether Stowey.

1797   The Wordsworths move to Alfoxden to be near Coleridge. Composes *The Rime of the Ancient Mariner* and publishes *Poems* composed by him, Charles Lamb, and Charles Lloyd.

1798   A second son, Berkeley, is born; he later dies. Josiah and Thomas Wedgwood settle a lifetime annuity of 150 pounds on Coleridge. Writes "Frost at Midnight," "France: An Ode," "Fears in Solitude,"

Kubla Khan, and part one of *Christabel.* In September, the first edition of *Lyrical Ballads* is published anonymously with Wordsworth, while they are traveling through Germany with Dorothy Wordsworth and John Chester.

1799   Enters the University of Göttingen in February. Returns to England in July and contributes to the *Morning Post.* Meets Sara Hutchinson.

1800   Settles with family at Greta Hall, Keswick, where Derwent is born. Finishes translation of Schiller's *Wallenstein* in late spring. Second edition of *Lyrical Ballads* published with a preface by Wordsworth.

1802   The Southeys move to Greta Hall. Sara Coleridge is born. Writes "Dejection: An Ode." The third edition of *Lyrical Ballads* is released.

1803   Abandons a tour of Scotland with William and Dorothy Wordsworth.

1804   In May leaves for Rome and Malta, having decided to separate from his wife and with the hope that the climate will improve his health, which had been weakened by rheumatism and opium addiction.

1806   Returns to England by way of Italy. Separates from his wife.

1807   De Quincey meets Coleridge in Somerset.

1808   From January to June, gives his first series of lectures, on "Principles of Poetry" at the Royal Institution in London. Later is guest, along with De Quincey, at the Wordsworth home in Grasmere.

1809   Begins *The Friend.* Contributes to *The Courier,* continuing to do so through 1817.

1810   *The Friend* is completed. Leaves the lake district for London and has a falling out with Wordsworth.

1811   Lectures on the English poets in London. Josiah Wedgwood withdraws his half of the legacy.

1812   Lectures in London and Bristol. Reestablishes his friendship with Wordsworth.

1813   Early play *Osario,* revised as *Remorse,* performed at Drury Lane Theatre in London.

1814   Stays with his friend John Morgan in London and Calne, Wiltshire.

1815   Begins dictating *Biographia Literaria* in Calne. Health is declining.

1816   Stays at Highgate, London, as patient of James Gillman. In June, publishes a volume of poetry containing *Christabel, Kubla Khan,* and "The Pains of Sleep." Also publishes *The Statesman's Manual; or The Bible the Best Guide to Political Skill and Foresight.*

1817   Publishes *Biographia Literaria, Sibylline Leaves,* and his two lay sermons.

1818 Lectures on English poetry and the history of philosophy. Publishes a selection from *The Friend* and *On Method*, a preliminary treatise to the *Encyclopedia Metropolitana*.

1819 Ends lectures on the history of philosophy.

1825 Publishes *Aids to Reflection in the Formation of a Manly Character*.

1828 *Poetical Works* published. Tours Germany with Wordsworth.

1830 *On the Constitution of Church and State* is published.

1834 Dies on July 25 at the Gillman residence in Highgate.

1836 Four volumes of Coleridge's *Literary Remains* are published, edited by Henry Nelson Coleridge.

1840 *Confessions of an Enquiring Spirit* is published.

Index